KU-652-791

Contents

Welfare Economics

ROBIN BOADWAY
NEIL BRUCE

Basil Blackwell

© Robin Boadway and Neil Bruce 1984

First published 1984
Basil Blackwell Publisher Limited
108 Cowley Road, Oxford OX4 1JF, England

Basil Blackwell Inc.
432 Park Avenue South, Suite 1505
New York, NY 10016, USA

British Library Cataloguing in Publication Data

Boadway, Robin W.
    Welfare economics.
    1. Welfare economics
    I. Title   II. Bruce, Neil
    330.15'5   HB99.3

    ISBN 0-631-13326-7
    ISBN 0-631-13327-5 Pbk

Typeset by Unicus Graphics Ltd, Horsham, West Sussex
Printed in Great Britain by Bell & Bain Ltd, Glasgow

878671
6000814964

To Bernie and Janis

Preface

Most economists are prepared, even eager, to make prescriptions and recommendations about economic matters based on their specialized knowledge. This practice is so widespread that a catalogue of examples would easily fill this volume. It is a source of concern to many people that economists who are so eager to prescribe policies often disagree among themselves as to which policies should be followed, and even advocate conflicting policies. This is a legitimate concern, especially since the basis for their differing views is often obscure, not only to the interested listener, but even to the economists themselves.

In all cases where economists make policy prescriptions they are transcending the scientific territory of positive economics, which is predictive and descriptive, and are practising normative or welfare economics. Positive economics is an important element in welfare economics because it describes what is feasible and predicts the observable implications of particular policies. However, positive economics is not the only element in welfare economics. In order to conclude that a situation is 'good' or 'bad', or that policy x is more desirable than policy y, it is necessary to accept certain ethical premises. These premises may be strong or weak. They also may represent the peculiar ethics of the economist making policy statements or, more usefully, may represent the economist's view of an ethical consensus.

Inevitably, many economists practise welfare economics without distinguishing the ethical premises and the positive economics on which their conclusions rest. When they differ about positive economics there is hope that such differences can be resolved by careful empirical research. When they differ on ethical premises it is necessary to make one's premises explicit and champion them with an appeal to persuasion and consensus.

In this book we systematically develop the foundations of modern welfare economics. We particularly stress the twin pillars of positive economics and ethical premises, and examine both the weaker ethical premises underlying economic efficiency and the stronger premises underlying social welfare maximization. We believe a good understanding of welfare economics is an important ingredient in the constructive use of economics in policy-making. It also adds interest and zest to the study of economics itself.

In Part I of this book we present the pure theory of welfare economics and construct a coherent, if abstract, framework for the practice of welfare economics. In Part II we focus on the technical problems encountered in putting the pure theory to work. In particular, we address the problem of finding a criterion for measuring welfare change which synthesizes the positive and ethical components of welfare economics. While particular applications of welfare economics lie beyond the scope of this book, we do conclude with a chapter on cost–benefit analysis where many of the principles developed are put into practice.

We have tried to make our discussion as comprehensive as possible and have included both mainstream material and material not normally covered in treatises on the subject. Thus, we discuss the notion of efficiency as well as the measurement of welfare change under uncertainty, and in an intertemporal framework. A detailed account is made of the sources of market failure and of the measurement of welfare change in distorted economies. We have tried to present a comprehensible account of the vast, and often daunting, literature on social welfare functions. And, we have discussed in detail the notion of a compensation test and its implementation as a measure for ordering Pareto non-comparable states. The overriding theme of the entire book is the notion of welfare economics as the study of ordering social states, and the relevance of the concepts of ecnmic efficiency, the compensation principle, and the conventional measures of welfare change to that.

We have attempted to present the material in a reasonably non-technical manner. We do presume, however, that the reader has a good understanding of undergraduate microeconomics, but we review the more advanced theoretical concepts utilized in the presentation. We also expect that the reader is familiar with basic multivariate calculus. We hope the level of presentation will make the material accessible to advanced undergraduate students in addition to graduate students and professional economists.

In preparing this book we have benefited from comments and discussion on various chapters by several people including Chuck Blackorby, Richard Harris, Jack Mintz, Tony Shorrocks, Dan Usher, John Weymark and David Wildasin. We also were assisted in the preparation of the manuscript by Simon Anderson, Steve Clark and Helen Gaglia, all graduate students at Queen's. We are grateful to all of these people. We also owe a great intellectual debt to the many authors who have contributed to the body of knowledge we present and synthesize in this book. We hope we have done them justice. Finally, we would like to express our appreciatin to Dorothy MacKenzie who spent many weeks on the word processor preparing the manuscript.

CHAPTER 1

The Study of Welfare Economics

1 The Scope and Purpose of Welfare Economics

Welfare economics is the framework within which the normative significance of economic events is evaluated. In order to make statements
about the consequences for economic welfare of an event we must go
beyond the study of *positive* economics, which is concerned with the
effects of an event on objectively measurable economic variables such as
price and quantity. That is, the welfare economist wishes to determine
the desirability of a particular policy – not in terms of his or her own
values, but in terms of some explicitly stated ethical criteria.

This book presents the modern theory of welfare economics, and the
techniques of its application, as a unified whole. At the outset it is useful
to outline precisely our view of the nature of welfare economics (or,
more generally, normative economics) and of its scope and limitations.
In this introductory chapter we shall attempt to summarize the contents
of the subsequent chapters and to indicate how each is related to the
underlying theme of welfare economics.

Welfare economics can be viewed as an investigation of methods of
obtaining a *social ordering* over alternative possible *states of the world*.
A social ordering permits one to compare all states of the world and rank
each one as 'better than', 'worse than', or 'equally as good as' every other.
Ideally, we would like the ordering to be complete (so that all states could
be ranked or ordered) and transitive (so that if state A is at least as good
as state B, and state B is at least as good as state C, then state A must be
at least as good as state C in the ranking). The term 'state of the world'
can be interpreted as a complete description of a possible state of an
economy including economic characteristics, political conditions such as
freedom of speech and non-discrimination, physical characteristics such as
the weather, and so on. We are primarily interested in ranking states which
differ in economic characteristics, such as outputs of commodities,
supplies of factors to different uses, and distributions of commodities over
households. That is, we are interested in ranking different *allocations of
resources*, where this is used in its broadest sense to refer to the combinations of commodities produced and consumed by each decision-maker in

the economy and the combinations of factors used in the production of each commodity. When we refer to a state of the world, or a *social state*, we are usually referring to a particular allocation of resources. We abstract from all other possible characteristics of the state of the world by assuming them to remain the same over the states under comparison. This convention ought to be construed as meaning not that non-economic characteristics are irrelevant in ranking social states, but only that most (though not all) of the tools we are going to develop and use are designed specifically to rank states differing only in economic characteristics.

The ranking of social states is inevitably a normative procedure; that is, it involves making *value judgments*. For each set of value judgments adopted, a different social ordering results. Therefore there is no objective or unique way to order social states. This does not imply that nothing useful can be said. On the contrary, some value judgments might, in fact, command widespread support, and rankings based on them might therefore legitimately form the basis for actual policy prescriptions. The use of welfare economics for policy purposes is, we would argue, based on this premise. Much of the welfare economic analysis underlying policy prescriptions is based on a certain set of value judgments which are widely accepted among economists, including ourselves.

A good deal of welfare economics is based on the concept of *economic efficiency*. This concept is used to order social states on the basis of some minimal value judgments. Two main value judgments are involved. The first is that the social ordering ought to be based on individual orderings of alternative social states, that is, on individual preferences, where it is implicitly assumed that each individual is the best judge of his or her own preferences. This assumption is called *individualism*. There are obviously a number of problems with it, the main one being that some individuals may be judged incompetent to formulate their own preferences, for example because of insanity or youth. This is partly overcome by our practice of referring interchangeably to the basic decision-maker as an individual and a household, thereby allowing for the fact that parents may determine preferences on behalf of their children. A second problem concerns the treatment of preferences of persons not alive at the time (e.g. the deceased and the unborn). The households upon whose preferences the social ordering is based are assumed to have preferences that are complete and transitive and, more generally, satisfy the axioms of rational consumer behaviour usually posited in microeconomics and discussed in chapter 2. It is important to note that we do not preclude the possibility that an individual's ordering of social states depends upon the commodities consumed by others as well as the commodities consumed by himself or herself; that is, individuals can have sympathetic or antipathetic preferences. In this way individuals can rank entire resource allocations or states of the world.

The second widely accepted value judgment is the *Pareto principle*, which says, in its strongest form, that if state A is ranked higher than state B for one person, and all other persons rank A at least as high as B, then A should be ranked higher than B in the social ordering. Although one can imagine certain circumstances in which the Pareto principle may conflict with other fundamental value judgments (such as freedom of speech), much of both theoretical and applied welfare economics is based upon it. In our analysis we assume it to be a desired property of the social ordering.

In order to make use of these two ethical principles, it is necessary to have a theory of how an individual's level of welfare or utility is determined by the state of the world. This theoretical basis is provided by the utility maximizing theory of consumer choice. This theory posits that consumers will rank alternative states according to a set of *preference orderings*. We can then attempt to 'aggregate' the preferences of different households using the 'dominance' notions contained in the Pareto principle. Unfortunately, this procedure permits only a *partial* ordering of social states. In particular, we cannot compare two states where one is preferred by one or more households and the other is preferred by one or more other households. Such states are said to be *Pareto non-comparable* and can only be ranked if additional value judgments are made. Since many states are Pareto non-comparable, this is an important limitation. For example, we are precluded from making judgments about policies which have income redistributive effects (unless individuals are sufficiently altruistic that everybody feels better off after the redistribution).

Despite this discouraging fact, the normative analysis of economic efficiency proceeds with only individualism and the Pareto principle as value judgments. Since individualism and the Pareto principle represent rather weak value judgments, to be able to rank two states according to these criteria has strong appeal. There is an important relationship between resource allocations generated by the market economy and those ranked highly by the Pareto criterion. This relationship is summarized in what are referred to as the *two basic theorems of welfare economics*. First, under certain assumptions concerning the convexity of individual preferences and technology, any allocation of resources generated as a general equilibrium of a perfectly competitive economy is *Pareto optimal*; that is, there is no other feasible allocation which ranks above it according to the Pareto principle. Secondly, the converse is also true: any Pareto optimal allocation of resources can be achieved by the solution to a general equilibrium in a competitive economy.

Certain assumptions must be satisfied to ensure that these two basic theorems hold. If any of these assumptions are not satisfied, then the market allocation of resources may not necessarily be Pareto optimal – that is, there may be some other allocation of resources which dominates those actually attained – and there is said to be *market failure*. The existence of market failure implies that there are some opportunities for mutual gains that are not being exploited (since there are other feasible allocations not attained in which everyone can be better off). Such situations are described as 'inefficient'. The study of welfare economics is useful in identifying such inefficiencies and in recommending and evaluating 'corrective' policies.

Even in the absence of market failure, the fact that competitive economies are Pareto optimal is of limited use. There are, in general, a large number of Pareto optimal allocations of resources in the economy, each associated with different combinations of levels of well-being of the various households in the economy. For example, in a competitive market economy, the equilibrium actually achieved depends upon the pattern of ownership of society's primary factors of production (e.g. land, labour, capital) among the households of the economy. Unfortunately, the many Pareto optimal outcomes themselves are Pareto non-comparable. Furthermore, even a particular Pareto optimal allocation does not dominate all non-Pareto optimal allocations on Pareto grounds; that is, certain non-Pareto allocations will be Pareto non-comparable with respect to Pareto optimal ones. This reflects the fact that rankings based solely upon the Pareto principle are incomplete.

One attempt to deal with this incompleteness is to extend the Pareto principle by means of a *hypothetical compensation test.* By this is meant the following. Even if two resource allocations are Pareto non-comparable, it may still be the case that if it is possible for those who are better off in state A than in state B to compensate those who are worse off such that, if the compensation actually were paid, all persons would be better off than in state B. In this case the hypothetical compensation test would be satisfied and state A would be ranked higher than state B according to this criterion. This criterion is used extensively in applied welfare economics in order to separate the efficiency issues, discussed above, from the equity issues to be discussed below.

There are some difficulties with relying upon the Pareto criterion, augmented by the compensation test, as a method of ordering social states. First, the acceptance of the criterion requires that one adhere to the strong value judgment inherent in the hypothetical compensation test. If some persons are worse off in state A than is state B, the fact that they could *hypothetically* be made better off by a transfer of some sort may be small consolation. Secondly, it transpires that there are different notions of compensation which depend upon the nature of transfers that are assumed to be hypothetically possible. For example, the compensation may be viewed as taking the form of lump-sum distributions of either a bundle of goods or purchasing power, or the compensation may be carried out by distorting taxes and transfers. Finally, even if one did accept the compensation test, a complete ordering of social states is still not possible. Some states, such as the Pareto optimal ones, cannot be ranked by the compensation test.

For these reasons, a complete study of welfare economics attempts to go beyond the concepts of economic efficiency based on the Pareto principle. This involves devising some means of weighting the utilities of different households, and this, in turn, requires that stronger value judgments be made. The value judgments can be codified into a *social welfare function* (SWF) or ordering. The SWF is an important conceptual tool in welfare economics, since it is the means by which a complete social ordering is obtained.

The choice of an SWF is constrained by the ethical assumptions to be incorporated and the information about individual utilities assumed to be available. The latter depends on the extent to which individual utilities are measurable and the extent to which the utility measures can be compared among households. The least restrictive informational assumptions are that the individual utilities are only *ordinally* measurable and *non-comparable* among households. The types of social welfare functions available under such assumptions are extremely limited and violate some reasonable equity assumptions. A necessary condition to obtain a wider choice set of social welfare functions is that household utilities be comparable with each other in some way. It is also useful if household utility is measurable on a scale that is more informative than an ordinal scale. In general, as the comparability and measurability assumptions are strengthened, the choice set of social welfare functions expands.

As mentioned, an SWF will incorporate both informational assumptions and ethical ones. A fairly weak set of ethical judgments will lead to an SWF which is said to be *welfaristic*, where the term 'welfaristic' means that the SWF depends only on the utilities achieved by the individuals in the economy and not on any other information. The ethical principles underlying a welfaristic SWF include the Pareto principle as well as some slightly more technical ones known as the independence of irrelevant alternatives and unrestricted domain. These will be introduced in more detail in section 4.

Given sufficiently strong measurability and comparability assumptions, the welfare economist can choose among many welfaristic social welfare functions. There are several considerations relevant to the choice of an SWF, of which some involve a further ethical judgment and others are purely for analytical convenience. The economist may argue, for example, that it is reasonable to include an 'egalitarian ethic' in the social welfare function because such an ethic would be widely agreed upon. But how egalitarian should the social welfare function be? One can choose an extremely egalitarian SWF or a weakly egalitarian SWF. For this reason it is often useful to choose social welfare functions which embody important variable properties, such as the degree of egalitarianism, into a parameter which can itself be varied. More generally, social welfare functions may be chosen for their tractability and flexibility as well as for the ethical norms they represent.

Despite this rather arbitrary procedure, the use of an SWF is an important element in modern welfare economics. With such a device, the framework of welfare economics is complete and well structured in principle. The remaining problems concern the application of this framework, or the study of *applied welfare economics*, to which we now turn.

In applying welfare economics, we immediately face a conundrum. Much of the theory of welfare economics was designed to produce an ordering or ranking of social states, either at the individual level or for society as a whole. This ordering can be represented by an ordinal function, either an ordinal utility function for the individual or an ordinal social welfare function. In applied welfare economics we are often asking for something much more; we would like to have a measure of welfare which enables us to measure the *welfare change* in going from one allocation to another. It is important to realize that the yardsticks of measurement used in practice are to some extent arbitrary. Since all we know is a ranking of social states, there are an indefinitely large number of measuring or numbering schemes which can be applied to the ordering and which preserve the ordering intact. In technical terms, if a particular welfare function faithfully ranks alternatives according to an ordering of social states, then any 'composite' welfare function derived from an increasing function of the first welfare function will do just as well. The particular representation or transform that we choose is purely for convenience. Thus we often find it useful to obtain a monetary representation of household utility functions, defined as the amount of money required to attain various utility levels at a set of reference prices. This monetary representation is referred to as a *money metric*, and its value is obtained from a very important technical tool, the *expenditure function*. To repeat, this money metric is simply one of many ways of representing the household's ranking of social states. No significance ought to be attached to the numbers other than as reflections of an ordering. Applied welfare economics makes use of this money metric of household utility to investigate the measurement of welfare change in a variety of circumstances.

The use of this money metric to measure welfare change for an individual is generally restricted to the case in which the individual cares only about his own consumption bundle and not about those of others. Indeed, much of welfare economics is devoted to measuring welfare change in an economy of 'selfish' individuals. This is done partly for simplicity and partly to reflect the prevailing view that most economic decisions are made by a narrowly defined 'caring' unit. It also has the important advantage that our welfare change measures can, in principle, be measured on the basis of observed market prices and quantities. That is because the price of a good measures its marginal benefit to a consumer in terms of the money metric. The tools of applied welfare economics developed under these assumptions would not generally be applicable in an economy consisting of non-selfish individuals.

Welfare change measures for an individual involve obtaining an estimate of the change in value of the money metric resulting from either a change in the bundle of commodities consumed by the individual or, because the commodity bundle chosen by the individual depends upon prices and income, from a change in the prices and income facing the individual. There are a number of alternative money metrics we could use. The two most commonly used are the *compensation variation* (CV) and the *equivalent variation* (EV). For the most part our exposition uses CV.

From the measure of CV for an individual facing exogenous changes in prices and income, it is a simple step to measure the CV for changes in resource allocation in a single-person economy. Now the prices and income facing the individual are no longer exogenous, but are determined by the interaction of the demand and supply sides of the economy. To analyse the supply side requires that we introduce the production possibilities of the economy. Changes in resource allocation can come about through changes in the primary factor supplies or the technology of production on the supply side. Alternatively, they can come about through changes in the actions of government, in the form of either tax changes or the introduction of public projects.

Obviously the single-person economy is an analytical myth. However, because it is much more difficult to observe individual commodity bundles than aggregate commodity bundles, it is worth while to determine the conditions under which we can treat the many-person economy as if it were a single-person economy, and treat the aggregate money metric (CV) as if it were a single person's CV. Unfortunately, the conditions are quite stringent. For this reason, applied welfare economics must confront the problems of measuring welfare change in a many-consumer economy in a manner which is consistent with some underlying social ordering or (ordinal) social welfare function. Although this task is difficult, it is not impossible, and simplifying assumptions must inevitably be made. The culmination of this effort lies in the field of cost–benefit analysis or project evaluation, in which the tools of theoretical and applied welfare economics, and in particular the measuring rod of a money metric, are brought to bear on the social evaluation of public projects. Although much cost–benefit analysis is concerned with specific problems encountered in evaluating investment, the general methodological issues are those addressed in welfare economics.

In this book we expound the methodology and techniques of welfare economics as outlined above. We approach the various issues in roughly the same order in which they were presented above; that is, chapters 2–6 deal with the theory of deriving a social ordering over states of the world, and chapters 7–10 deal with the uses to which the social ordering is put. We focus on the theoretical underpinnings of welfare economics and on the general methodological problems encountered in its application. We also survey its application in the form of cost–benefit analysis. Space precludes us from considering all the applications of welfare economics, since they are found in virtually all areas of economics including international trade, industrial organization, public finance and macro-economic policy-making.

The analysis found in the subsequent chapters is meant to be reasonably thorough and carefully argued. In places it may be fairly subtle as well. It might therefore be helpful at this point to provide a precis of the main currents of arguments and results found in the book. This should prove helpful as an overview of each chapter which the reader can use to navigate through the detailed analysis. Also, it will enable readers (or teachers in welfare economics courses) to skip sections or entire chapters without losing the chain of argument or the knowledge of how the different sections fit together as a whole. Without suggesting that he or she may wish to do so, the reader could even, we think, read either chapters 2–6 or 7–10 independently. What follows, then, is a survey of the contents of the subsequent chapters.

2 The Welfare of the Household

In this book we take the view that society's welfare ultimately depends upon the welfare of its constituent households. Furthermore, we follow much of the literature on welfare economics in assuming that social welfare depends *only* on the welfare of households. This has been referred to as the assumption of *welfarism* by Sen (1979) and can be deduced on the basis of some rather weak value judgments as discussed in chapter 5. The welfare of the household therefore provides the fundamental information upon which social orderings are based, and we begin by establishing exactly what is meant by the welfare of the household.

One further important value judgment required is that the welfare of the household must either correspond with the household's own view of its welfare, or at least be consistent with the household's preferences. The assumption that social welfare must respect household preferences is called *non-paternalism*. This assumption is rather important for many of the results of theoretical and applied welfare economics, since household preference orderings are reflected in the choices the household makes when faced with alternative situations. We can therefore deduce information concerning the household's preference orderings on the basis of choices actually taken. In principle, we could obtain the entire preference ordering if enough choice situations were presented to the household. The bulk of chapter 2 is devoted to reviewing the standard theory of consumer choice. Most of this is done in the context of a selfish household, that is, one that cares only about its own consumption. There is, however, no reason why it cannot be extended to cases in which household preference orderings over social states depend also upon the consumption of other households.

According to the basic theory of household choice, the household has a preference ordering over all alternative bundles of commodities which satisfies certain assumed properties. These properties ensure that the preference ordering can be represented by an ordinal utility function. The consumer is confronted with a social state which is represented by a budget set from which the consumer can choose a bundle of commodities. The budget set will be determined by the set of prices and income facing the household. The household then chooses the most preferred bundle in the budget set, or the one which maximizes its utility function. Since the budget set depends upon prices and income, the bundle chosen does also. As prices and income change, so does the bundle demanded. We characterize the choice by the household as a set of *demand functions*, one for each commodity, and each depending on prices and income. These demand functions reflect what we know about household preferences. Several properties of demand functions are discussed at length in chapter 2.

The demand functions can be thought of as the solution to the household's utility maximization problem. Given the prices and income facing the consumer, the demand functions determine the bundle of goods which yields the highest value of the utility function. If those demand functions are substituted for the commodities as arguments in the utility function, the result is the *indirect utility function*, which shows the maximum utility that can be achieved for any set of prices and income.

The household choice problem can be stated in an equivalent way, known as the *dual* to the utility maximization problem. Given the prices of commodities, the utility maximizing choice can be characterized as the bundle of commodities which minimizes the expenditure required to attain the given level of utility. The solution to this problem will be a set of demand functions showing the quantities of each commodity demanded for various combinations of prices and utility levels. These are the *compensated demand functions*. If the compensated demand functions are substituted into the expression for expenditure which is being minimized, the *expenditure function* is obtained. This determines expenditure as a function of prices and utility; that is, it shows the level of expenditure required to attain a given utility level at a given set of prices. Just as the expenditure minimizing problem is equivalent to the utility maximizing problem, the expenditure function is the inverse of the indirect utility function.

The expenditure function is an invaluable device in welfare economics since, given the set of prices, it associates with each utility level a dollar value. It is therefore a way of 'measuring' utility. It is what we refer to as a *money metric* of utility. Since the value of the expenditure function depends upon the set of prices used, there will be many different money metrics that can be used to represent individual preferences. Two common ones correspond to the compensating variation and the equivalent variation measures of welfare change, the measures used in chapters 7–10.

The theory of choice is initially developed in the context of a static economy, in which the household is free to choose the bundle of goods that enters its preference ordering subject to its budget constraint. It can, however, be extended to other settings. Three of these are considered in chapter 2. The first concerns the case in which the household is unable to increase beyond a certain level the quantity consumed of one or more of the commodities which enter its preference ordering, despite the fact that it would be willing to do so. The household is said to face a *quantity constraint*. There are several circumstances in which this may be relevant. The most common cases concern public goods and externalities. Public goods are those goods which are jointly consumed by many households at the same time. No one household can vary the quantity it consumes independently from other households. Externalities exist when a household's preference ordering includes goods consumed by other households. In this case the quantity of the good is determined by the consuming households. If some goods are quantity constrained in this manner, the planner cannot obtain full information about household preferences from observed choices. The marginal value which the household attaches to the quantity constrained good cannot be observed from market data since it does not bear the same one-to-one relationship with prices as do the marginal values of other goods. The planner cannot rely on observed market behaviour to induce the household's preference ordering.

The second extension of consumer choice theory is to an intertemporal setting. The theory of household choice in the static setting applies directly in this case by treating as different commodities the same physical commodity consumed in different time periods. Provided the consumer is unconstrained in his ability to buy and sell all dated commodities subject to his budget or wealth constraint, all of the previous analysis applies, including the derivation and properties of the compensated and uncompensated demand functions, the indirect utility function and the expenditure function. One must only be careful to measure prices of future commodities in terms of a common *numéraire*, chosen to be one of the goods consumed.

The third extension of the theory of choice is to the case of uncertainty. The analysis of decision-making under uncertainty is still in a process of development: we restrict ourselves to one widely accepted branch of the theory, the so-called *expected utility hypothesis*. It is postulated that the future will consist of one of several possible states of nature. Since one and only one state of nature will occur, the possible states of nature are exhaustive and mutually exclusive. The household is assumed to be able to attach a subjective probability to each state of nature and to know the exogenous prices and income it will face (i.e. its budget constraint) in each possible state. The household must make purchasing commitments before knowing exactly what state of nature will occur. Thus the consumer must choose among alternative risky prospects or lotteries.

The household is assumed to have a preference ordering over these alternative prospects and to choose the one which is most preferred. It turns out that if we impose certain other relatively weak axioms, known as the von Neumann–Morgenstern axioms, on consumer preferences, the preference ordering of the household can be represented by an expected utility function – that is, by a probability-weighted sum of utilities achieved in each state of nature. A noteworthy feature of the expected utility hypothesis is that the utility functions that are aggregated into the expected utility function must be cardinal utility functions. That means they must 'measure' utility in the same way as, say, ounces and pounds measure weight.

The theory of choice under uncertainty is again a straightforward extension of the static theory. In this case, we treat as different commodities the same commodity obtained in different states of nature. These are referred to as *contingent commodities*. With a full set of markets, the household should be able to purchase any combination of contingent commodities it wishes, subject to its budget constraint. In practice, perfect contingency markets do not exist. Stock markets fulfil an equivalent role, but stock markets involve the purchase of claims to individual firms' profits which are uncertain, rather than direct purchases of income claims contingent on states of the world. Stock markets will not be equivalent to perfect securities markets unless certain conditions hold and if they do not, the household will not be able to purchase the desired bundle of contingent commodities. In this case, the household would again be quantity constrained.

With perfect markets for contingent commodities, or perfect securities markets, the planner could infer the household's preference orderings over alternative risky choices. If in addition the von Neumann–Morgenstern axioms were satisfied, the planner could infer experimentally an underlying cardinal utility function for the household which is aggregated to give the expected utility preference ordering. We shall use these revealed preference orderings in our discussion of welfare change measurement under uncertainty in chapters 7–10. In the absence of perfect markets, we could not proceed in this manner.

As the preceding discussion indicates, the planner can infer the preference orderings of the household from the behaviour of the household provided the household is fully able to choose among bundles of commodities within its budget constraint. These household preference orderings or ordinal utility functions form the basic information set available to the planner to obtain social orderings. Although, as we shall see in chapter 5, it is possible to aggregate household orderings into a social ordering, the forms of social welfare functions that this allows are fairly limited. This should not be surprising, since the information available to the planner is rather limited. For example, although it is known that an individual prefers state one to state two, it is not known by how much. The consideration of the welfare of the household concludes with a discussion of the other sorts of infomation on individual utility functions that might be useful to the planner. With an ordinal utility function, the household only compares and orders alternative commodity bundles. If, in addition, the household can compare and rank changes in commodity bundles, a cardinal utility function can be deduced. Adding to this the possibility of comparing and ranking proportionate changes in utility, we obtain ratio scale utility functions. At the extreme, full information yields fully measurable and specified utility functions. The addition of more and more information on individual utility functions will permit more and more types of social welfare functions, as noted in chapter 5. Of course, the additional information on individual utility functions must come from somewhere other than the revealed market behaviour of the household.

3 Pareto Optimality and Market Equilibrium

In generating social orderings, it would seem preferable to make as few value judgments as possible, and to make ones which are reasonably widely acceptable. One value judgment which seems to fulfil this property is the Pareto principle. As discussed earlier, it says that society should prefer state A to state B if at least one household prefers state A to state B and none prefers state B to state A. Chapter 3 analyses the properties of social orderings which are obtained when one augments individual preference orderings with the Pareto principle.

Of special interest are social states which are Pareto optimal. These are states which are not Pareto preferred by any other; that is, there will be no other feasible state which has the property that at least one person is better off in it (i.e. prefers it) and no one is worse off. Pareto optimality is interesting both because Pareto optimal states represent the best states in the social ordering obtained from the Pareto principle, and because under certain circumstances decentralized markets will render Pareto optimal allocations of resources. Chapter 3 discusses this in detail.

A Pareto optimal resource allocation can be characterized by a series of 'conditions', referred to as the Pareto optimality or efficiency conditions. They are the *exchange efficiency*, *production efficiency* and *overall efficiency* conditions. The exchange efficiency conditions characterize the allocation of a given aggregate bundle of commodities among the households of the economy, such that it would not be possible by reallocating the commodities to make one household better off without making another worse off. This will be the case when the marginal rate of substitution between any pair of commodities is the same for all consumers. In a competitive economy in which all households face the same prices and are interested only in their own consumption, this condition will be satisfied since each household in maximizing its utility will set its marginal rate of substitution equal to the price ratio. For a given aggregate bundle of goods, there will be a large number of exchange efficient allocations of resources, each corresponding to a different distribution of utility levels among households. These alternative exchange efficient allocations cannot be socially ranked using only the Pareto principle, since none is Pareto preferred to any other. Herein lies the limitation of the Pareto principle as a sole criterion for obtaining social orderings.

The production efficiency conditions characterize the efficient allocation of the economy's factors of production in producing output. The economy will be producing efficiently if factors of production are allocated in such a way that it is not possible to reallocate factors so as to produce more of one good without producing less of another. This will be the case when the marginal rate of technical substitution between any pair of factors is the same in the production of all goods using those factors. In a competitive economy in which all firms face the same factor prices and have production functions which depend only on their own inputs, the production efficiency conditions will be satisfied. This is because each firm will minimize costs by choosing a factor input combination such that the factor price ratio is equal to the marginal rate of technical substitution between all pairs of factors employed. Once again, there will be a large number of ways of allocating the factors so as to satisfy the production efficiency conditions; that is, there will be numerous combinations of goods produced which are productively efficient. These combinations will represent points on the economy's production possibility frontier. Points within the frontier will be inefficient.

For each of the many points on the production possibility frontier satisfying the production efficiency conditions, there will be a large number of ways of allocating the bundle produced among consumers so as to satisfy the exchange efficiency conditions. There are thus a very large number of allocations which satisfy both the production efficiency and exchange efficiency conditions. These can be reduced somewhat by invoking the overall efficiency conditions. An allocation will be Pareto optimal overall if it is not possible to reallocate production *and* distribution so as to make one person better off while making no one else worse off. As will be shown in chapter 3, this will be the case if the marginal rate of substitution between each pair of commodities equals the marginal rate of transformation. In a competitive economy in which all firms are price-takers and face the same prices as consumers, this condition will be satisfied. Firms will all produce at the point where price equals marginal cost. Since the ratio of prices equals the marginal rate of substitution of households and the ratio of marginal costs equals the marginal rate of transformation, the overall efficiency condition is satisfied. This presumes that the exchange efficiency and production efficiency conditions are simultaneously satisfied.

Not all points which are exchange and production efficient will be overall efficient. However, a good many will be. They will represent combinations of household utility levels which are non-comparable using only the Pareto principle. These combinations are usually summarized in society's *utility possibilities frontier*, which depicts the various utility levels that can be achieved when resources are allocated efficiently in the economy. Some additional value judgments are required to choose the most preferred point on the utility possibilities frontier.

Allocations which are not Pareto optimal are not using the resources of the economy efficiently, as it will always be possible to find another allocation of resources which makes everyone better off. To put this in different terms, there are some 'gains from trade' which are not being fully exploited if the economy is operating non-optimally. In the above discussion, the competitive price system was the device through which gains from trade were being exploited. Chapter 4 investigates the circumstances in which the market mechanism fails to achieve a Pareto optimum. Some insight can be gained into the problem by noting that if resources are allocated inefficiently, mutual gains from trade ought to be possible. The question of market failure can be viewed as an investigation of what prevents these mutual gains from being exploited.

It is useful to think of market failure as arising from three fundamental causes, although these ought not to be thought of as exhaustive or mutually exclusive. The first is when one household has monopoly (or monopsony) power over others in the economy. As is well known in the case of a monopoly seller, the price will not be set at marginal cost so the overall efficiency conditions will be violated. In this case, if the seller and buyers could negotiate, they could strike a bargain and make everyone better off. What prevents this from occurring is that there are a large number of buyers. The gains from trade take the form of consumers' and producers' surpluses, and these must be divided by a bargaining process. The bargain would entail each buyer contributing part of his consumer surplus; the contribution may differ from buyer to buyer. This is not possible when there are large numbers of buyers for, more generally, the same reasons that price discrimination is not possible. The possibility of resale means that the seller cannot enforce on consumers a price above the going market price. If it were not for the fact that a large number of buyers existed, the problem of inefficiency might not exist. For example, with one buyer and one seller (bilateral monopoly), the market outcome may be efficient if the two parties can negotiate with full information on each side. The bargaining process determines how the gains are divided.

The second source of market failure is the presence of externalities and public goods. If one household's consumption bundle enters the preference ordering of one or more other households, market prices do not fully reflect the marginal benefit of the consumption to society, and the bundle chosen by the household will be inefficient. If other households obtain a positive marginal benefit (an *external economy*), the choosing household will be induced to consume too little of the good since no weight is given to the external benefit provided to others. (The opposite holds for a negative marginal benefit to others, or an *external cost*.) Once again, an unexploited gain from trade exists. In principle, the households ought to be able to strike a mutually beneficial bargain; for example, by those who benefit from an external economy bribing those who generate it to increase consumption. If there were only a small number of households involved, such a bargain might be feasible and the externality would be 'internalized'. However, if a large number of persons are affected, such a bargain would be unenforceable. There would be no incentive for any one individual to contribute to the bribe, since his contribution would be an insignificant part of the entire bribe and he would benefit from the increased consumption of the externality even if he did not contribute; that is, he could not be excluded. This is known as the *free rider problem*, and it arises from the inability to exclude households from the consumption of a jointly consumed commodity, in this case the externality.

The phenomenon of public goods is an extreme form of an externality. A public good is a good which is jointly consumed, but which is typically provided publicly since the externality is so large compared with the own benefit that no one household would consume any if there were no public provision. An example might be defence. Here the free rider problem consists of inducing households to pay the government voluntarily for the benefits received from the public good. Since the incentive for them to do so is very small, the public sector resorts to some coercive method of financing public goods, such as taxation.

The third source of market failure arises from *informational asymmetries*, and is most commonly found in the context of uncertainty. If some household has information that others do not have, the former may be able to exploit it much like a monopoly firm exploits its market power. One case of this is known as *moral hazard* and is found most obviously in insurance markets. Suppose a household wishes to purchase insurance against the risk of loss arising from an accident. The price at which the insurance can be offered depends upon the probability of the loss occurring. If the insured household can influence the probability of loss, say by varying expenditures on preventative activity, it can exert some influence over the price the market is able to charge. In this case, the household can exploit its influence over price to its own advantage and prevent resources from being allocated efficiently in insurance markets.

Another instance of informational asymmetries is known as *adverse selection*. In this case a number of persons are seeking to buy insurance but their risk characteristics differ. For some households (high risk households) the probability of an accident is higher than for others (low risk households). The difficulty arises if the households themselves know their own risk characteristics but the insuring firms do not. The insurance companies are unable to tailor a specific insurance policy for each type of person. The consequence, as discussed in chapter 4, is that the insurance market may not even have an equilibrium, and if it does it may be inefficient.

The existence of market failure provides a rationale for having the planner interfere with the market mechanism. Of course, market failure is a necessary but not a sufficient condition for intervention since the planner may not be able to do any better than the market. The analysis of appropriate corrective actions in the face of market failure would take us too far afield, and is not considered in this book. The reader may instead consult a book on public finance (e.g. Atkinson and Stiglitz, 1980; Boadway, 1979; Musgrave and Musgrave, 1976).

As mentioned above, the Pareto criterion by itself cannot provide a complete social ordering. There will be many allocations which are Pareto non-comparable, including all the various Pareto optimal allocations themselves. Chapters 5 and 6 consider the additional information or value judgments that are required in order to generate complete social orderings, or social welfare functions. Before summarizing these chapters, we review the attempt that was made in the literature of the 1930s to increase the power of the Pareto principle by the use of the compensation test, discussed in chapter 3.

The argument is as follows. If some persons are better off in state A than in state B and some are worse off, so that the states cannot be ranked using the Pareto criterion alone, it may be the case that the gainers in a move from B to A could have compensated the losers for their losses and still have been better off. If so, the compensation test is satisfied in going from B to A. If we accepted the compensation test as a way of comparing states, state A would rank superior to state B. The intuitive appeal of this criterion is that in a sense there are potential gains from trade for all households in going from B to A, so that if the compensation was actually paid all households would be better off. In this sense, the compensation test is like an extension of the Pareto principle.

There is some ambiguity as to exactly what form the compensation takes. In the 'strong' form of the test, it takes the form of a redistribution of a fixed bundle of goods. It could, however, be imagined to take the form of a lump-sum redistribution of purchasing power. In this case, the redistribution would be accompanied by a change in the production mix of the economy, unlike the strong case. Between these two extremes, the compensation could take the form of distortionary transfers as with the tax-transfer system of the government.

Whatever form it takes, the compensation is not actually paid, and this is the source of the difficulties with the compensation test as a means of ordering social states. Since the compensation is not actually paid, state A is not Pareto preferred to state B. Furthermore, there will be many social welfare functions for which B ranks higher than A despite the fact that the compensation test ranks them the other way. The compensation test may give contradictory rankings as well; that is, the move from B to A may satisfy the compensation test but so may the move from A to B. Even in the absence of this problem, the compensation test may give intransitive rankings. Finally, there will be some alternatives which the compensation test will be unable to rank. For example, Pareto optimal allocations cannot be ranked. This means that the compensation test cannot provide a complete ordering of social states. The reason is that, like the Pareto principle, it avoids making interpersonal comparisons of welfare. The next two chapters investigate the sorts of interpersonal utility comparisons which can be used to generate particular social welfare functions.

4 Social Welfare Functions

In chapters 3 and 4 it is established that if the planner knows individual preference orderings and invokes individualism and the Pareto principle, the best that can be achieved is a partial ordering of social states. In order to achieve a complete ordering we need either to have more information or to invoke more value judgments or both. Chapters 5 and 6 are devoted to investigating the consequences of adding more information on individual utilities as well as invoking somewhat stronger value judgments. The starting point for the analysis is the justly famous result by Arrow (1951a) known as the *Arrow possibility theorem*. Much of the literature on social welfare functions can be viewed as extensions of Arrow's result: in particular, as investigating the consequences of relaxing some of the stringent requirements imposed by Arrow.

The Arrow theorem is concerned with investigating the ways of constructing a social ordering or social welfare function when the only information available is the preference orderings of the individual households and when the planner is precluded from making interpersonal comparisons of welfare. The social ordering is assumed to be required to satisfy three properties. The first is the Pareto principle (or at least a weak version of it, as discussed in chapter 5). The second is that the procedure for aggregating individual utilities must apply whatever the preference orderings of each household happen to be. This is called the *unrestricted domain* assumption. The third is called *independence of irrelevant alternatives*. It implies that the ranking of two social states ought to depend only on the households' rankings of those two states and not on the ranking of any other states. Arrow proved that if the social ordering is to depend on individual orderings and is to satisfy these three properties, then the social ordering must be dictatorial; that is, the social ordering must coincide with some arbitrary person's preference ordering. This is obviously not a very satisfactory outcome, and the subsequent literature has concerned itself with weakening the requirements of Arrow's theorem in order to broaden the set of social orderings available.

Much of the literature has been concerned with increasing the planner's information. In Arrow's set-up, the planner is allowed to know only the preference orderings of households. As discussed in chapter 5, this information base can be broadened in two ways. Firstly, individual utilities can be made more measurable. In Arrow's analysis, utility functions are ordinal. Conceivably, utility could be measured on a cardinal scale or on a ratio scale or could be fully measurable. Secondly, utilities could be comparable between households. The degree of comparability could vary as well. Utility levels may be comparable between persons, so that one could make statements like, 'Household one is better off than household two in state A'. Level comparability is possible even under ordinal utility functions. Changes in utility may be comparable between persons as well, or both levels and changes may be comparable. This would be possible with cardinal measurability but not ordinal. In the extreme, household utilities would be fully measurable and fully comparable: that is, the planner would have full information.

In general, the more measurable and comparable are household utilities, the more information will the planner have as a basis for aggregating utilities into a social ordering, and the wider will be the scope of possible social welfare functions. With the limited information used by Arrow, only dictatorship is possible, whereas with full information, any form for the social welfare function is possible. The latter case corresponds to what is known as the Bergson–Samuelson social welfare function, which denotes social welfare as a general function of individual utilities. When the possibilities are wide ranging, some further value judgments are needed to select a specific form.

To see the sorts of possibilities that arise with additional information, let us outline some of the consequences of expanding the measurability and comparability information. If measurability is increased, but there remains no comparability, the force of the Arrow theorem still applies – only a dictatorship is possible. Some interpersonal comparability is required to obtain interesting social orderings. The least information case is that which retains ordinality but allows levels of utility to be compared across persons. In this case, all households can be ranked in each social state according to their level of utility attained, and this information is available to the planner. Any social ordering which requires only information on the rankings of households by utility level is now possible. Two commonly cited forms of this are the *maximin* and the *leximin*. The maximin social ordering ranks social states according to the level of utility attained by the worst-off household (which may vary from state to state). The leximin case is similar to maximin except that it stipulates that in the event that the worst-off person is indifferent between two states, the ranking of the states is determined by the least-well-off household that is not indifferent. These social welfare functions, though still not very appealing, would probably command wider support than would the arbitrary dictatorship of Arrow.

If changes in utility can be compared, but not levels, those social orderings which rely only on changes in household utility are permissible. Notice that for changes in utility to have any meaning to begin with, utility must be at least cardinally measurable. One social ordering which uses information on changes in utility only is the *classical utilitarian* social welfare function. According to this, if the sum of changes in utility of households is positive when going from state A to state B, state A is preferred to state B. Of course, if both levels and changes in utility are comparable over households, both utilitarian and leximin or maximin forms are permissible, as well as some others as discussed in chapter 5.

As one goes on to ratio scale comparability, where proportionate changes in utility can be measured and compared, any homothetic social welfare function is permitted, such as the Bernoulli–Nash, or Cobb–Douglas, form. Finally, with full measurability and comparability, any social welfare function is possible provided that it is increasing in each household's utility (so the Pareto principle will be satisfied). As mentioned above, one can interpret the full information case as the Bergson–Samuelson social welfare function.

It is clear, then, that adding information to the Arrow framework will expand the set of possible social welfare functions. Although this is helpful, it does not solve the problem as to which social welfare function is the appropriate one to use. For that one needs further value judgments. To put matters differently, the fact that utilities are fully measurable and comparable does not imply that we know how to aggregate them. The form of the social welfare function depends very much on the ultimate value judgments we choose to make. There is some literature in which authors attempt to deduce the form of the social welfare function from first principles, and this is reviewed in chapter 6.

Ethical postulates are an essential ingredient in all welfare economics even if it is restricted to questions of economic efficiency. In chapter 6 we examine the ethical foundations of redistributive economics, in which we wish to rank states that yield higher utility levels for some households and lower levels for others. Not surprisingly, ethical assumptions that are stronger and more controversial than the Pareto principle must be made.

A distributive criterion that does not require interpersonal comparisons defines an allocation as 'fair' if no household derives more utility from the consumption bundle of another than it does from its own bundle. Fair allocations which are also Pareto optimal always exist in exchange economies but they do not necessarily exist in production economies when households differ in their tastes and endowments.

A related criterion, egalitarian equivalence, requires that a utility distribution be capable of being generated by an equal (and therefore, envy free) division of some aggregate, but not necessarily feasible, bundle of goods. Pareto optimal and egalitarian equivalent allocations always exist. Unfortunately, such equity concepts do not lead to a complete social ordering.

A complete and non-dictatorial social welfare ordering requires some form of interpersonal utility comparisons: that is, each household's utility in a social state must be weighed against the utility of other households. In chapter 6 we consider some ethical arguments for such social welfare orderings. An important idea is that of a household's *moral preferences*. A household has a moral preference for some social state if it prefers it in ignorance of how it will fare in that social state; that is, a household is shielded from morally irrelevant information concerning vested interests. Properties of social welfare orderings can be derived by considering a household's choice under such uncertainty. If a household chooses under uncertainty in a manner consistent with the axioms of the expected utility hypothesis, then its moral preferences can be represented by an additively separable social welfare ordering. Alternatively, if a household chooses according to the maximin criterion, its social welfare ordering will place all weight on the utility of the worst-off households. The relative merits of these two 'theories of justice' are considered in chapter 6. That chapter also examines closely the question of interpersonal utility comparisons and the concept of horizontal equity.

5 Welfare Change for a Single Household

Chapters 7–10 are concerned with the principles of applied welfare economics, or the measurement of welfare change. Chapters 2–6, as we have seen, are devoted to the theory of obtaining social orderings of resource allocations. These orderings form the basis for the measurement of welfare change. In chapters 7 and 8, the principles of welfare change measurement for a single household are considered. In this case, only the preferences of the single household are relevant, as revealed through its behaviour in markets. Chapter 9 then extends the analysis to a multi-household economy in which social orderings are relevant. Here, more information will be required than that obtained from individual market behaviour. Some aggregation principle will be required. The final chapter applies the analysis to to the evaluation of public projects, or cost–benefit analysis.

It is important to emphasize at the outset that, in measuring welfare change for the household, the only information that is assumed to be available is the preference orderings of the household. That is, we are assuming that the utility of the household is measurable only ordinally and not, say, cardinally. As we have discussed, this is implied by the assumption that welfare change measures will be based solely upon the observed behaviour of the household. This immediately raises the difficulty that we would like to measure welfare change by some cardinal scale, such as pounds sterling. Since the scale is only required to represent the ordering of alternative states by the household, the choice of scale is essentially arbitrary. Any scale can be chosen provided it is consistent with the underlying preference ordering of the household. The particular scale chosen will simply be one possible way of numbering the house-hold's indifference levels in an increasing way. For technical (and historical) reasons, we select a particular way of numbering the indifference levels using the pound as the unit of measurement. However, the reader ought always to be aware of the fact that this is essentially arbitrary. In particular, it does not really mean much to say that the household's utility has, for example, increased by x pounds in moving from situation 1 to 2 and y pounds in moving from 2 to 3.

The scale we use for 'measuring' utility levels is the amount of income or expenditure required to reach a utility level at a set of reference prices. In technical terms, it is the value of the expenditure function in terms of some *numéraire* or measure of purchasing power (e.g. pounds). We refer to this as our money metric of utility; it is a particular cardinalization of the household's preference ordering. The value of the money metric depends upon the set of reference prices chosen. In principle, any set of reference prices could be chosen, but some are more convenient than others because of their geometric properties.

Suppose we wish to measure the welfare change in going from situation 1 to situation 2, where prices and income could be different in the two situations. The welfare change involves measuring the difference in income required to achieve the utility levels of situations 1 and 2 at a given set of prices. In the two-good case, this is just the distance between two parallel budget lines which are tangent to the two indifference curves reached and which have a slope whose absolute value is equal to the relative reference prices. If the actual prices of situation 2 are used as the reference prices, the welfare change measure is the compensating variation (CV), a well-known measure of welfare change. If the original prices are used, the measure is the equivalent variation (EV). These two measures are frequently used since their magnitude can be given a precise interpretation in terms of areas to the left of compensated demand curves. For example, CV is the sum of consumer-surplus-type areas to the left of compensated demand curves for all goods whose price has changed, plus the change in income. The compensated demand curves used are those corresponding to the original utility level. Similarly, EV is the sum of comparable areas to the left of the compensated demand curves corresponding to the new situation. In our exposition we arbitrarily use CV as the measure of welfare change between two situations, although we could equally have used EV or any other measure corresponding to another set of reference prices.

Chapters 7 and 8 are concerned with measuring the welfare change between two situations for a single household facing alternative budget constraints and for a single-consumer economy, respectively. Ultimately, whatever the source of the change, the two situations can be characterized as a different set of prices and income facing the consumer. The welfare change measures simply convert those changes in prices and income into changes in the money metric, or CV. A number of illustrative examples are presented to indicate the nature of the analysis, though they are by no means exhaustive. In chapter 7, welfare change measures are derived for various tax changes facing the consumer, including substituting an excise tax for a lump-sum tax, introducing a new tax into an already tax-distorted situation, and taxing labour income.

In all cases the welfare change measures can be given an exact geometric interpretation as areas beneath compensated demand curves. In many cases, full information on compensated demand functions may not be directly available, so one must rely on approximate measures of welfare change. A general discussion of the ways of approximating welfare change measures is presented. If only prices, incomes and quantities in the two situations are available, approximate measures such as quantity indices can be used. It is shown that the *Laspeyres* and *Paasche quantity indices* are first-order approximations to EV and CV, and are generally unreliable as representations of preference orderings for the household. Second-order approximations are more frequently used in the literature, but they require some information on the magnitude of substitution effects at the initial or final point, depending on whether one is approximating CV or EV. It may be the case that one has direct estimates available for ordinary or uncompensated demand functions but not compensated ones. In that case, the appropriate consumer surplus areas beneath the compensated demand curves may be approximated by the corresponding areas beneath ordinary demand curves, the so-called Marshallian consumer surpluses. The circumstances are discussed in which this is a reasonably close approximation.

Finally, the discussion of welfare change of the individual in chapter 7 is extended to the measurement of welfare change in intertemporal and uncertain environments. The extension is reasonably staightforward given, as we have seen in chapter 2, that the theory of household choice can be readily extended to these settings by the appropriate redefinition of a commodity to include the period in which it is consumed as well as the state of nature in which it is consumed. In the intertemporal case, the CV measure is analogous to that of the static case except that now the set of prices includes both present period prices and prices in each future period. Assuming perfect capital markets, this CV measure can be further expressed as the discounted present value of the CV change within each period. The CV in each period, however, depends on the prices in all periods.

Similarly, in the uncertainty case, CV can be expressed as a probability-weighted sum of the measure of utility change in each state of nature. Here we have to be a bit careful since, under the expected utility hypothesis, the utility representation in each state of nature is cardinal, and will not generally correspond with our money metric of utility. Therefore, the money metric has to be transformed to be compatible with the cardinal representation of utility in the expected utility expression. Having done that, we can then measure the change in expected utility for any change in prices or income in the various states. As an example, an analysis is given of the effect on the welfare of a consumer from an increase in the variability of prices and from price stabilization schemes.

Chapter 8 extends our perspective from a single household facing a given budget constraint to a single-household economy. Now, instead of a budget constraint, the economy's production possibilities frontier constrains the consumer. Single-consumer economies are naturally mythical, but they are useful analytical devices. The circumstances in which single-consumer economies can be used to represent actual economies is taken up in the next section.

The introduction of the production possibilities constraint means that we have to account for the supply side of the economy as well as the demand side. We are now in the realm of general equilibrium. Even so, the CV measure from changes in resource allocation still ultimately depends upon the changes in prices and income facing the household. However, the prices and incomes are now endogenously determined by the workings of the market economy rather than being exogenously given. Income will include payments for primary factors of production owned as well as any pure profits from production.

A number of simple examples of resource allocation changes are used to illustrate the principles of measuring welfare change in single-consumer economies. These include introducing tax distortions as well as imposing further tax distortions on already distorted economies. In each case the measure of welfare change is derived using CV as the basis, and geometric interpretations are given. Now the geometry can involve both consumer surplus areas beneath demand curves as well as producer surplus areas beneath supply curves.

Another set of examples concerns the evaluation of public sector expenditure projects. The criteria are analysed evaluating such projects based on CV. If the financing of such projects is by distorting taxes, the analysis enables us to derive an expression for the *social cost of public funds*. Basically, this concept refers to the fact that when one additional pound of funds is raised by distortionary taxation, the opportunity cost is more than one pound owing to the fact that some additional deadweight loss is created by the tax distortion. This additional loss must be included as a cost of public projects financed by distortionary taxation.

The final task of chapter 8 is to introduce the methodology of optimal policy analysis in a distorted economy. The problem to be considered here is the following. Suppose the planner has control over a certain number of policy instruments, such as taxes, but that he is precluded from being able to eliminate all distortions from the economy either because there are some distortions he cannot control directly or because he has to raise some tax revenue and must do so using distorting taxes. The problem for the planner is to choose the set of policy instruments (taxes) which minimizes the cost of the distortions or, equivalently, takes the economy to the most preferred social state that is feasible given the inevitability of distortions. This sort of analysis is generally called the *theory of second best*. An outline of the nature of the problem is presented, and it is applied to the special case of finding the least distorting way of raising a given amount of tax revenues when lump-sum taxation is not available. This is called the *optimal tax problem*.

6 Welfare Change in a Many-Household Economy

The economy, of course, consists of many households, and welfare change measures should correspond with the social orderings obtained by aggregating household preferences appropriately. Since the social ordering requires more information and value judgments than do household orderings, it will in general be impossible to obtain welfare change measures solely on the basis of the household orderings of social states inferred from their market behaviour individually or collectively. None the less, much policy analysis is performed using aggregate measures of welfare change (e.g. the aggregate CV), implicitly assuming that aggregate market behaviour can be treated as if it were generated by a single (representative) household whose preferences coincide with the social ordering. Chapter 9 begins with a discussion of the interpretation of the aggregate CV (that is, CV inferred from aggregate market data) and with a discussion of the circumstances in which it can be used as a proper money metric for the social ordering.

There are two fundamental problems with using the aggregate CV as a welfare measure. The first is that, except in special circumstances, one cannot obtain a set of well-behaved preferences that would yield the observed aggregate demands. For one thing, aggregate demand functions which show aggregate demand as a function of prices and aggregate inome will not exist if aggregate demand depends upon the distribution of income as well as the aggregate amount of income. This is a well-known result in the theory of demand. For another thing, the aggregate CV, or the value of the money metric (expenditure function) for the economy as a whole, will correspond with incomes required by the economy to achieve particular community indifference curves. Since community indifference curves generally intersect, a transitive social ordering cannot be based upon aggregate CVs.

The second problem is that, even apart from the above difficulty, it is not clear what welfare interpretation one should put on the aggregate CV. To take one suggestion, suppose that we avoid the above problem and assume that there exists a set of well-defined community indifference curves which underly aggregate CV observations. This would come about if all individuals had identical and homothetic preferences (an unlikely eventuality). In this case, as chapter 9 shows, the sign of the aggregate CV is equivalent to the satisfaction of the compensation test, so if one adhered to this test, aggregate CV would be a useful measure of social welfare change. There are difficulties with this interpretation, however. For one thing, the ordering obtained will be incomplete in the following sense. The aggregate CV would not pick up purely redistributive changes in this world since aggregate demands would not change if preferences are identical and homothetic. This is just a reflection of the incompleteness of the social ordering obtained under the compensation test. Another difficulty is that, if community indifference curves did intersect, as one would normally expect, the sign of the aggregate CV would not necessarily coincide with the satisfaction of the compensation test. This is demonstrated in chapter 9.

There is one circumstance discussed in chapter 8 in which it is perfectly justitifiable to use the aggregate CV as an index of the social ordering. If the planner is continually redistributing income in a lump-sum fashion so that the marginal social utility of income is always equated for all households, the aggregate CV would correspond to an underlying social preference ordering and would be a proper measure of social welfare. It seems obvious that this ideal redistribution is not being done in practice, so this justification for the aggregate CV is rather weak.

As we have stated, the social ordering will generally require more than simply household preference orderings as its information base. It will require some degree of household welfare comparability and probably some measurability as well. In addition it will require a method for aggregating individual welfare. The measurability and aggregation techniques implicit in the aggregate CV are rather special. The aggregate CV 'measures' utilities by our arbitrary money metric and simply adds the utilities together. This cardinalization of individual utilities has a property which not all would find satisfactory for measuring utilities – constancy of the marginal utility of income. The aggregate CV is like a classical utilitarian social welfare function applied to individuals with constant marginal utilities of income. That is why purely redistributive changes do not affect it.

In order to obtain a measure of social welfare change which corresponds with more general social welfare functions, our metric for measuring household utilities and the method of aggregating it must be made to reflect the available information on measurability and comparability, as well as the form of the social welfare function to be used for purposes of aggregation. Chapter 9 discusses how the money metric must be transformed and aggregated to correspond with various social orderings. Basically, the problems are as follows. The money metric we use attaches particular numbers to various levels of indifference. The number is the income required to achieve that level of utility at a given set of reference prices. Since this measurement scale may not correspond with that used by the planner as the appropriate utility measure for the household, the money metric must be transformed to correspond with that of the planner. For example, taking the logarithm of the money metric would transform it from a metric which has constant marginal utility to one with diminishing marginal utility. In any case some transform must be applied to the money metric.

It may be the case that the same transform can be applied to the money metric of all households. This will be true if it is the case that all households obtain the same utility from a given level of real income. If so, all households can be transformed by the same function, and then the transformed money metric can be appropriately aggregated into a social welfare function. Thus, the social welfare function can be viewed as being some function of household money metric utilities, with the money metric of each household entering symmetrically.

If households have different abilities to convert money metric income into utility, a different transform ought to be applied to each household's money metric income. This would complicate matters considerably, since then all households' money metric income would not enter the social welfare function symmetrically. This problem could be avoided if we could amend household money metric incomes or real incomes for systematic differences in the ability to convert income into utility. The vehicle for doing this is a set of *equivalence scales*, which convert an individual's actual real income into that required by a representative person to achieve the same utility level. The equivalent income for each household thus obtained can then be aggregated into a social welfare function with the equivalent incomes entering symmetrically.

The social ordering can then be written as some symmetric function of household real incomes or equivalent incomes as the case may be. We are often interested in measuring the change in social welfare from a change in resource allocation (and thus real incomes). Using the social welfare function, we show in chapter 9 how the change in social welfare can be viewed as a weighted sum of the changes in real incomes of all households, where the weights reflect the marginal social utility of real income of the households. This is the procedure that would be used in measuring social welfare change for the economy. This procedure can be somewhat cumbersome for the following reason. The marginal social utility of real income of a particular household will in general depend upon the levels of real income of all households in the economy (i.e. upon the distribution of real incomes). This implies that if one is evaluating a change in which only a small number of households experience changes in their real income, this change cannot be evaluated without full knowledge of the real income distribution of all households.

That problem can be avoided if the social ordering fulfils one property – *strong* or *additive separability*. As is discussed in chapter 9, if this property is satisfied the marginal social utility of real income of a household can be written as a function of the real income of that household alone and not of other households. This means that when evaluating social welfare changes, the planner need only have information on the real incomes of those households that have been affected by the change. Strong separability is not an unreasonable property for the social welfare function to possess. It means essentially that the marginal rate of substitution of real income between two households in the social ordering (i.e. the increase in real income of one household that would just compensate for a fall in real income of another) is independent of the level of utility of any other household in the economy.

The final section of chapter 9 explores the relationship between conventional income distribution measures and inequality statistics on the one hand, and social welfare functions on the other. For example, the Lorenz curve is often used to characterize an income distribution. It can be shown that if the Lorenz curve for one distribution lies everywhere outside that for another, and if the social welfare function is quasi-concave, then social welfare will be higher under the latter distribution. In addition, the social welfare functions that would give the same social orderings as various inequality statistics (e.g. Gini coefficient) are discussed.

7 Cost–Benefit Analysis

The final chapter of the book deals with the application of the tools of the measurement of welfare change to a particular sort of problem – the evaluation of investment projects. There is a large and well-developed literature on cost–benefit analysis, and the purpose here is to survey some of the strands of that literature and relate it to the underlying principles of welfare change measurement developed in the preceding chapters. In keeping with much of the literature, the discussion is restricted for the most part to single-person or identical-person economies. That is, CV or aggregate CV is used as the measure of welfare change. Equity or redistributive considerations that would arise if one used a social welfare function are ignored. Also, most of the discussion is restricted to the case of small projects; that is, projects which have no perceptible influence on prices in the economy.

The need for cost–benefit analysis arises when private profitability does not rank projects according to the social ordering. This might be for several reasons. Prices of inputs and outputs may not reflect their true marginal costs or benefits if the inputs are purchased or the outputs are sold on distorted markets. The social values of inputs and outputs purchased and sold may not capture all the costs and benefits of a project. For one thing, there may be externalities arising from the project which ought to be accounted for. For another, some of the project inputs or outputs may be non-marketed items which none the less have to be evaluated. Also, if markets are distorted elsewhere, there will be indirect welfare effects arising from induced changes in resource allocations on these markets. Finally, the discount rate used to determine private profitability may differ from the social discount rate if there are capital market distortions of one sort or another.

Cost–benefit analysis is an attempt to arrive at a measure of welfare change which incorporates all these items missed by the private profitability criterion. The procedure is as follows. The costs and benefits within each period are summed. In the case of inputs and outputs of the project, *shadow prices* are determined which account for distortions on the markets themselves or for the fact that the items are non-marketed. The non-marketed items may include time saved, risk-taking, health improvements etc. In chapter 10, the principles involved in deriving shadow prices are discussed in detail for three special cases. One involves the shadow pricing of labour when there are distortions in labour markets (including unemployment). Another is the evaluation of tradeable commodities when tariffs are levied on international trade. The third is the cost of financing public projects through debt or taxes when distortions exist in capital markets. In addition, there is an analysis of the evaluation of some non-marketed costs and benefits, especially the cost of risk-taking.

In addition to the evaluation of inputs and outputs themselves, indirect effects in each period must be evaluated. These indirect effects may include externalities emitted elsewhere in the economy (such as pollution). The evaluation of externalities is problematic since no market price exists from which social values can be deduced. The other sort of indirect effect is the change in net benefits resulting from changes in resource allocation on distorted markets elsewhere. Thus, if price exceeds marginal cost elsewhere in the economy, the marginal social benefit will exceed the marginal social cost if output is increased. Any induced increases in output on such markets will contribute a positive net benefit to society which ought to be attributed to the project itself.

Finally, the benefits and costs within each period must be aggregated into a single measure of welfare change. This is done by converting all current benefits and costs into an equivalent value in terms of present period consumption; that is, by aggregating the present value of all benefits and costs. The appropriate discount rate for determining the present value is the rate at which society would just be willing to substitute present for future consumption at the margin – the *social discount rate*. In chapter 10 we discuss the circumstances in which the market interest rate is the social discount rate. This basically requires both perfect capital markets and and an absence of intergenerational externalities in savings. If these conditions do not hold, the social discount rate will differ from the market interest rate. We discuss what, in principle, the social discount rate ought to be in these circumstances.

Chapter 10 concludes the analysis of the book. Space has precluded us from considering actual empirical applications of welfare economics. Instead, we have concentrated on developing the analytical underpinnings of, and the tools for, applied welfare economics. We hope thereby to equip the reader to apply welfare economics to any problem that might arise.

PART I

THE PURE THEORY OF
WELFARE ECONOMICS

CHAPTER 2

The Welfare of the Household

1 Introduction

The theory of consumer or household behaviour plays two roles in welfare economics. Firstly, it is a positive theory of how a household alters its behaviour in response to a change in the economic environment. Secondly, it is a normative theory of household welfare based on the assumption that the household selects the utility maximizing consumption bundle from the menu of alternatives available to it. Both of these roles are important elements of modern welfare economics. For this reason we shall briefly survey those aspects of consumer theory relevant to the study of welfare economics.

The importance of the utility of the individual household to welfare economics is derived from a basic value judgment that the welfare of a society should depend on the welfare of its members. In fact it is commonly assumed in the study of welfare economics that society's welfare depends *only* on the welfare (utility) attained by its members. Following Sen (1977), this assumption is known as *welfarism*. Welfarism, although in accord with the humanistic view that society should function for the benefit of its members, is not innocuous. Some important convictions, by no means irrelevant for welfare, may be excluded by welfarism. For example, the existence of inviolable rights and basic equity norms (such as 'equals should be treated as equals') may be desirable for reasons above and beyond their utility consequences.

In any event, even if some persons reject the view that household utilities *only* should matter, the view that household utilities *at least* should matter is commonly accepted. For this reason it is necessary to consider what is meant by household utility and how household utility can be evaluated or revealed. The important assumption in this chapter is that the household's welfare is identified with its own perception of its utility. We shall call this postulate *non-paternalism*. Although it is commonly invoked in welfare economics, it is not absolute. We shall encounter a number of cases where household sovereignty over what is good for it is (or should be) compromised. For the vast majority of concerns, however, *non-paternalism* is a desirable posture by policy-makers. If this were not so, welfare economics would not be very interesting.

2 Household Choice in a Static, Certain Environment

Households make many decisions, including the obviously economic ones such as which commodities to consume, how to earn the income to pay for them, how much to save, what assets to hold, whether to purchase insurance etc. They also make many apparently non-economic decisions such as whether to get married, whether to go to church, whether to complain to the neighbour about his dog etc. The economic theory of household decision-making is defined not by the subject matter of the choice variables but by the method of analysis. According to the economic theory, a household's actions depend on the variables that determine the set of opportunities open to it, and on the preferences of the household. Conformity, habit, childhood trauma and the like may determine a household's specific preferences. However, such motivations are ignored in order to concentrate on the more general properties of preferences that are unlikely to be peculiar to a particular household and are therefore more likely to be relevant in analysing the behaviour of groups of households or of a 'representative' household. The economic theory makes testable predictions about how the decisions of a household (or, more correctly, a group of households) are altered by changes in its set of opportunities (for example, changes in prices and/or incomes). It also permits inferences about how such changes alter the utility of the household.

The simplest economic model of household decision-making concerns a household that must choose how to spend an exogenous income on different goods. The framework is static, in order to abstract from intertemporal choice considerations such as saving for future consumption, and certain, in order to abstract from issues relating to differences between the actions of the household and the uncertain utility consequences of these actions.

2.1 *The budget set*

The budget set defines the consumption opportunities available to the household. A household with exogenous money income m and facing a vector of fixed and non-negative money prices $p = [p_1, \ldots, p_N]$ for N different goods can purchase any bundle (vector) of goods that has a value which is less than its exogenous income. That is, if $x = [x_1, x_2, \ldots, x_N]$ is a vector of goods (where it is assumed that the quantity x_i of each good i satisfies $x_i \geq 0$) then $\Sigma_i p_i x_i \leq m$ means that x is within the household's budget. In the case where there are only two goods, the *budget set* is represented by the triangular area OAB in figure 2.1. The *budget line* is the negatively sloped line AB. The absolute value of this slope is equal to the relative price of the two commodities (p_1/p_2 when good 1 is on the horizontal axis). The budget line can be shifted towards or away from the origin by income changes (or equiproportionate changes in money prices) and pivoted by changes in relative prices. The heart of the economic

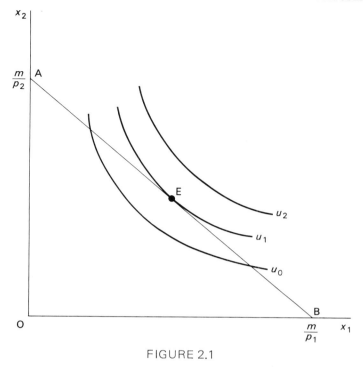

FIGURE 2.1

theory of the household is to explain how such events alter the household's consumption bundle, given a general form of its preferences.

The budget set notion can be extended in many ways. The menu of choice can be extended so that income, rather than being exogenous, is the product of the wage rate and the hours of labour chosen by the household. Again, it may be assumed that the prices facing the household depend on its choice of x, so that the budget line is non-linear. In addition, the budget set concept can be extended by generalizing the notion of a commodity. For example, commodities can be distinguished by the date of consumption, with the budget set constraining the household's intertemporal choice between consuming now or later. Uncertainty can be introduced by distinguishing the commodity by the presently unknown state of the world in which it is consumed. In this case, the budget line constrains household's choice among state-contingent commodities.

2.2 *Preferences and utility*

In most cases the budget set permits the household to consume any of a large number of commodity bundles. The household chooses among available bundles on the basis of its preferences. The conventional meaning of 'preference' connotes characteristics that are peculiar to the individual such as a person's 'preference' for classical music. But since economic theory is concerned with the behaviour of a representative rather than a specific household, preferences include only the most general characteristics; that is, those that are likely to be shared by most, if not all, households.

Primarily it is assumed that the household can compare any two commodity bundles and declare that one is at least as good as the other. In short form, when x is at least as good as y, then xRy. If xRy and yRx, then the household is said to be *indifferent* between x and y. It is assumed that the household is rational in the sense that its preference ordering is *reflexive* (xRx or x is at least as good as itself), *transitive* (if xRy and yRz then xRz) and *complete* (xRy or yRx or both for any two commodity bundles x and y). If a further assumption about *continuity* of preferences is made, then the household's preferences can be represented by a real valued utility function $u(x)$. A utility function $u(x)$ will be a suitable representation of household preferences if $u(x) \geqslant u(y)$ whenever xRy for any pair of commodity bundles x and y. This utility function can be represented by a set of indifference curves of the familiar shape exhibited in figure 2.1, providing two further assumptions are made. The first is *non-satiation*, which states that utility is non-decreasing in any commodity and is increasing in at least one. This implies that the indifference curves have negative (or at least non-positive) slopes. The second is *strict quasi-concavity* which, in the two-good case, means decreasing marginal rates of substitution. In general, strict quasi-concavity implies a preference for diversity in consumption rather than specialization.

It should be emphasized that nothing is implied about how these indifference curves are numbered, except that indifference curves further from the origin correspond to higher levels of household utility and receive higher utility numbers. In other words it is assumed that the household's utility level is just *ordinally measurable*. That is, if some function $u(x)$ is a suitable representation of the household's preferences, so is $v(x) = f(u(x))$, where $f(\ )$ is any increasing function.

One restriction on preferences that is sometimes useful is that of *strong* or *additive separability*. In this case commodities can be partitioned into groups indexed $g = 1, \ldots, G$ and the utility function can be represented by

$$u = \sum_{g=1}^{G} \beta^g u^g(x_g) \tag{2.1}$$

where (β^g), $g = 1, \ldots, G$, are positive constants. That is, utility is the weighted sum of the utilities obtained from each commodity group x_g. The property of consumer preferences which gives rise to the additively separable form for the utility function is that the marginal rate of substitution between pairs of commodities in separate groups is independent of the level of consumption of any other commodity in any group other than the two considered. As Goldman and Uzawa (1964) have shown, this is a necessary and sufficient condition for additive separability.

Another restriction on preferences that is sometimes encountered in welfare economics is *homotheticity*. A utility function is homothetic if there exists an increasing monotone transformation $f(u)$ which is linear homogeneous. That is, u satisfies

$$\lambda f(u) = u(\lambda x); \quad \lambda > 0$$

for some $f(u)$ with $f'(u) > 0$. The empirical implication of homotheticity is that all *income expansion paths* (the locus of utility maximizing consumption bundles traced out as income changes) are linear and pass through the origin. This implies that every good has an income elasticity of one.

A slightly weaker restriction on preferences is *quasi-homotheticity* which requires that

$$\lambda f(u) = u(\lambda(x - \gamma)); \quad \lambda > 0$$

for some $f(u)$ with $f'(u) > 0$ where γ is an n vector of constants sometimes interpreted as 'subsistence' quantities of the goods. The empirical implication of quasi-homotheticity is that all income expansion paths are linear and pass through point γ. The income elasticity of any good need not equal 1 but approaches 1 as x becomes large relative to γ.

The importance of homotheticity (or quasi-homotheticity) in welfare economics is two-fold. Firstly, it is useful in obtaining a money measure of utility as we shall see in this chapter. Secondly, it is useful when we wish to 'aggregate' many consumers into a single 'representative' consumer as done in later chapters.

Given a certain income and a certain set of prices, the household makes a choice, shown as point E in figure 2.1, where it achieves its highest utility subject to the constraints of its budget. Technically, point E is the solution to the problem

$$\max_{[x_1, \ldots, x_N]} u(x_1, \ldots, x_N) \qquad (2.2)$$

subject to

$$\sum_{i=1}^{N} p_i x_i = m$$

The solution to this problem, for each set of income and prices facing the household, defines the household's vector demand function:

$$
\begin{aligned}
x_1 &= x_1(p_1, \ldots, p_N, m) \\
&\ \vdots \qquad\qquad\ \vdots \\
x_N &= x_N(p_1, \ldots, p_N, m)
\end{aligned}
\qquad (2.3)
$$

These demand functions have well-known properties including the *adding-up* property,

$$\sum_{i=1}^{N} p_i x_i = m$$

and the *zero-degree homogeneity* property, which states that multiplying all prices and income by a constant leaves the quantity demanded of each good unchanged. (See Deaton and Muellbauer, 1980; Green, 1976; and Phlips, 1974, for further discussion of demand function properties.) These demand functions are known as *Marshallian* or *uncompensated* demand functions. By substituting the demand functions into the utility function we obtain the *indirect utility function*

$$v(p, m) = u(x_1(p, m), \ldots, x_N(p, m))$$

which expresses household utility as a function of its income and the prices it faces. Note that $v(\ )$ is an ordinal function since u itself is ordinal. $v(\ )$ is obviously homogeneous of degree zero in prices and income. In addition, it is increasing in m and p and quasi-convex in p.[1] Also, its derivatives yield the uncompensated demand functions according to *Roy's theorem*, sometimes referred to as Roy's identity. That is,

$$-\frac{\partial v/\partial p_i}{\partial v/\partial m} = x_i(p, m) \tag{2.4}$$

assuming that the derivatives on the left-hand side are well defined.[2]

The problem (2.2) of maximizing household utility subject to the household budget constraint is commonly referred to as the *primal* consumer maximization problem. There also exists an equivalent *dual* minimization problem, where the household must minimize the expenditure required to obtain a given level of utility at given prices. That is,

$$\min_{[x_1, \ldots, x_N]} \sum_{i=1}^{N} p_i x_i \tag{2.5}$$

---

[1] Quasi-convexity implies that for any two price vectors p^1 and p^2 such that $v(p^1, m) \geqslant v(p^2, m)$, $v(\lambda p^1 + (1 - \lambda) p^2, m) \leqslant v(p^1, m)$ where $0 < \lambda < 1$. That is, if we draw a diagram with the price of good 2 measured on the vertical axis and 1 on the horizontal axis, the indirect indifference curves will have the same shape as those of the direct indifference curves shown in figure 2.1. However, in contrast to the direct utility function, higher levels of utility correspond to indirect indifference curves that are closer to the origin.

[2] This is proved as follows. The indirect utility function is $v(p, m) = u[x(p, m)]$. Differentiating by p_i yields $\partial v/\partial p_i = \Sigma_j u_j \, \partial x_j/\partial p_i = \lambda \Sigma_j p_j \, \partial x_j/\partial p_i$, where $u_j = \partial u/\partial x_j = \lambda p_j$ by the first-order conditions of the consumer's maximization problem. From the consumer's budget constraint, $x_i + \Sigma_j p_j \, \partial x_j/\partial p_i = 0$. Therefore $\partial v/\partial p_i = -\lambda x_i$. Since λ is the marginal utility of income, we have Roy's identity.

subject to

$$u(x_1, \ldots, x_N) = u$$

where u is given.

Although the household is not likely to be required to solve this optimization problem in practice, we consider it here because it introduces some useful concepts in welfare economics. The commodity demand functions that solve (2.5) for each feasible set of prices and level of utility are known as the *compensated* or *Hicksian* demand functions:

$$
\begin{aligned}
x_1 &= x_1^c(p_1, \ldots, p_N, u) \\
&\vdots \qquad\qquad\qquad\qquad\qquad (2.6)\\
x_N &= x_N^c(p_1, \ldots, p_N, u)
\end{aligned}
$$

These compensated demand functions have several well-known properties, including *symmetry*, which requires that $\partial x_i^c/\partial p_j = \partial x_j^c/\partial p_i$, and *negativity*, which requires that $\partial x_i^c/\partial p_i \leqslant 0$. They are homogeneous of degree 0 in p and satisfy the *adding-up* property, so

$$\sum_{i=1}^{N} p_i x_i^c(\ ) = e(p, u)$$

where $e(\ )$ is the minimized expenditure, the value of (2.5) when x_i are given by (2.6). The function $e(\ )$ is known as the *expenditure function*. It is concave in p, homogeneous of degree one in p, and increasing in p and u. The vector of partial derivatives of $e(\ )$, $[\partial e/\partial p_i]_{i=1,\ldots,N}$ yields the vector of compensated demand functions $[x_i^c(\ )]_{i=1,\ldots,N}$. This is referred to as *Hotelling's lemma*. Note finally that the expenditure function $e(p, u)$ is the inverse of the indirect utility function $v(p, m)$; that is, $m = e(p, u)$ can be derived by inverting $u = v(p, m)$, and vice versa. These properties of the expenditure function are discussed more fully in Deaton and Muellbauer (1980). These dual concepts of the compensated demand function and the expenditure function play an important role in modern welfare economics. (A good discussion of duality and consumer theory also may be found in Deaton and Muellbauer, 1980.) The connection between the compensated demand function and the ordinary (Marshallian or uncompensated) demand function is given by *Slutsky's equation*. It states:

$$\frac{\partial x_i}{\partial p_j} = S_{ij} - x_j \frac{\partial x_i}{\partial m}$$

where the derivatives are evaluated at the same prices and income and where $S_{ij} = \partial x_i^c / \partial p_j$ is the compensated Slutsky substitution term.[3] The Slutsky matrix $[S_{ij}]_{i=1, \ldots, N; j=1, \ldots, N}$ is an $N \times N$ square matrix of compensated substitution terms which has the well-known properties of the compensated demand curves. In addition to symmetry and negativity, the zero-degree homogeneity property implies that

$$\sum_{i=1}^{N} p_i S_{ij} = 0$$

for any column j of the Slutsky matrix.

A useful application of the expenditure function is as follows. For a set of reference prices p^R, $e(p^R, u)$ expresses the minimum expenditure needed by a household to attain the indifference curve, labelled u. We can now substitute the indirect utility function $v(p, m)$ into the expenditure function to obtain the *equivalent income function* $e(p^R, p, m)$ where

$$e(p^R, p, m) = e(p^R, v(p, m))$$

$$= \sum_{i=1}^{N} p_i^R x_i^c(p^R, v(p, m)) \tag{2.7}$$

The equivalent income function allows us to find the level of income needed at some vector of reference prices $[p^R]$ in order for the household to attain the same utility level it enjoys from income m when faced with price vector p. Equivalent income is sometimes referred to as *money metric utility* and is important for measuring household welfare in a meaningful sense. (The term 'money metric utility' is derived from Samuelson, 1974. King, 1981, uses the equivalent income function.)

If we assume preferences are quasi-homothetic we can express the money metric utility in a simple form. The expenditure function for a quasi-homothetic utility function can be expressed (see Deaton and Muellbauer, 1980).

$$e = a(p) + u \cdot b(p)$$

where we have numbered our indifference curves so u is quasilinear homogeneous and $a(p)$, $b(p)$ are linear homogeneous. This can be inverted to obtain the indirect utility function. Combining the two functions yields money metric utility

$$e(p^R, p, m) = a(p^R) + \frac{b(p^R)}{b(p)} (m - a(p))$$

---

[3] A simple derivation of Slutsky's equation is as follows. Write the ordinary demand for good i as $x_i(p, m) = x_i(p, e(p, u))$. At the consumer's equilibrium, this must equal the compensated demand $x_i(p, u)$. Differentiate the equation $x_i(p, u) = x_i(p, e(p, u))$ by p_j to obtain $(\partial x_i / \partial p_j)_u = \partial x_i / \partial p_j + (\partial x_i / \partial m)(\partial m / \partial p_j)$, or rearranging and using Hotelling's lemma $\partial x_i / \partial p_j = S_{ij} - x_j \partial x_i / \partial m$, the Slutsky equation.

Note that the functions $a(\ )$ and $b(\ )$ can be estimated from consumer demand data since, with quasi-homothetic preferences, the uncompensated demand function for good i is given by:

$$x_i = a_i(p) + \frac{b_i(p)}{b(p)}(m - a(p)).$$

3 Household Welfare in a Static, Certain Environment

In section 2 it was argued that the household chooses among commodity bundles available to it so as to maximize utility. This implies certain testable hypotheses about how the household will respond to changes in its budget set. It also permits certain inferences about what happens to household welfare when the prices and income it faces change. For this reason the theory of consumer choice is very useful to the welfare economist. But before proceeding there are at least two non-trivial, but usually implicit, assumptions that must be made. The first is the identification of the household's welfare with its own perceived satisfaction or utility. As stated earlier, this non-paternalistic assumption that a household has 'sovereignty' over how its welfare is to be measured is not an absolute rule. As a matter of practice, the consumption of some commodities such as heroin is proscribed by society. Even though the household may feel that access to less expensive heroin would raise its utility, such utility gains are unlikely to be considered to augment social welfare. On the other hand some goods, such as good nutrition and education for children, may be deemed to raise the household's welfare even if the household decides otherwise. Such demerit and merit goods violate notions of *non-paternalism*. In most instances they are obvious enough that they can be dealt with as special cases, and so we can proceed with the assumption that household welfare is identical to household utility.

The second implicit but important assumption underlying the inference of household welfare is that the preference structure of the household does not change. If a household receives an extra bundle of flowers this year over last, *ceteris paribus* it is probably valid to assume its utility has risen or at least not fallen. If, however, the household has become allergic to flowers in the meantime, this inference would be wrong. On an economy-wide scale it would be difficult, if not impossible, to determine if preferences have changed and how. Consequently one must proceed on the assumption that the household's preferences are unchanging or, at least, that changes in preferences are independent from the policy changes being evaluated.

Even with the above assumptions, the welfare economist is faced with a serious problem. Utility is the subjective satisfaction of the household and cannot be observed directly. It must be inferred from observable attributes of household consumption behaviour and the hypothesis of utility maximization. This problem is an old one and has attracted considerable attention, much of it being concerned with defining cost-of-living indexes. Fundamentally, cost-of-living indexes attempt to ascertain how a household's *real* income is changed when its money income and the money prices it faces are changed. When real income is defined in terms of a household's ability to achieve a given level of utility (instead of its ability to consume a given bundle of goods, as in the familiar Laspeyres and Paasche cases discussed in chapter 7) the corresponding 'true' price and quantity indexes can be derived from the expenditure function. Welfare economists are often concerned with evaluating the effects on household utility of events other than changes in prices and income (such as changes in the amount of public goods), but we will restrict our attention to changes in prices and income in this section.

When some event (such as a change in government policy) alters the household's (maximum) utility level, it is useful to express such an effect in the same units in which we measure income or expenditure. There are two methods, identified by Hicks (1939), that are valuable because they are always fully consistent with the underlying change in utility of a single household. The first is to find the change in expenditure that would just compensate the household for the policy change (that is, would hold the household at its initial utility level) if the household were to face a new set of prices. The second is to find the change in expenditure that would have an effect on household utility equivalent to that of the policy change itself if the consumer were to face the original set of prices. In fact, as we shall show, these two procedures for measuring utility are methodologically the same. Both can be expressed as the first differences of the expenditure function, and differ only in terms of the reference prices or utility levels which are held constant.

Recall that the expenditure function $e(p, u)$ gives the minimum expenditure required by the household to achieve utility level u when facing prices p. Let the superscript 0 denote the initial situation and the superscript 1 denote the terminal (i.e. post policy change) situation. Assume that the policy change affects the household only by changing the prices it faces and the income it has from $[p^0, m^0]$ to $[p^1, m^1]$, which alters the consumption bundle chosen from x^0 to x^1 and the utility level from u^0 to u^1 in figure 2.2. For concreteness, we assume the policy change increases the utility of the household $(u^1 > u^0)$ and we will define the Hicksian measures so that they will be positive (negative) if utility rises (falls).

The Hicksian *compensating variation* is

$$CV = m^1 - e(p^1, u^0) \tag{2.8}$$

After the policy change the household has money income m^1 and faces prices p^1. If it had money income $e(p^1, u^0)$ and faced prices p^1 it could just achieve the utility level u^0. Thus CV is the change in the household's income that would restore to the household its initial utility level (i.e. just compensate for the policy change). In figure 2.2, the compensating variation is shown for the case where the money price of good x_1 falls,

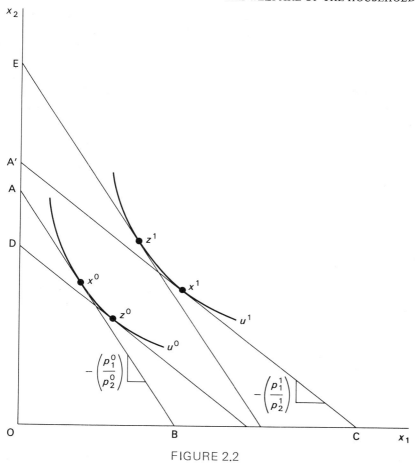

FIGURE 2.2

shifting the household's budget line from AB to A′C and changing the household's chosen consumption bundle from x^0 to x^1 and its maximum utility from u^0 to u^1. The compensating variation is equal to A′D units of the *numéraire* good x_2.

The Hicksian *equivalent variation* is:

$$EV = e(p^0, u^1) - m^0 \tag{2.9}$$

By the definition of the expenditure function, adding EV to the household's initial income will result in the same change in utility as (i.e. is equivalent to) the policy change. In figure 2.2, EV is shown as AE units of the *numéraire* good x_2.

It is apparent from (2.8) and (2.9) and also from figure 2.2 that when $e(p^i, u^i)$ is substituted for m^i, the compensating and equivalent variations differ only in the set of reference prices the household is assumed to face when its income is changed. Nevertheless, in general, the actual values of CV and EV will not be the same. It is useful to express CV and EV in a slightly different way. If we add m^0 to and subtract m^0 from (2.8), do the same with m^1 in (2.9), and recall that $m^i = e(p^i, u^i)$, we have:

$$CV = e(p^0, u^0) - e(p^1, u^0) + \Delta m \tag{2.8'}$$

$$EV = e(p^0, u^1) - e(p^1, u^1) + \Delta m \tag{2.9'}$$

where $\Delta m = m^1 - m^0$. That is, CV and EV can be expressed as the difference in the expenditure function between initial and terminal prices plus the change in the household's money income. The difference between CV and EV is that the change in the expenditure function is evaluated for initial utility level held constant for CV and terminal utility level held constant for EV. Expressions (2.8') and (2.9') can be used to clarify the relationship between these exact Hicksian variations and consumer's surplus values calculated as areas under uncompensated or Marshallian demand curves. Since the partial derivative of the expenditure function with respect to the price of commodity i is just the compensated demand function $x_i^c(p, u)$ we can use the fundamental theorem of calculus to express CV as the integral

$$CV = -\sum_{i=1}^{N} \int_{p_i^0}^{p_i^1} x_i^c(p, u^0)\, dp_i + \Delta m \tag{2.8''}$$

It can be expressed in this form because the symmetry property of the compensated demand function implies that the value of CV is independent of the path followed along the indifference surface between $x^c(p^0, u^0)$ and $x^c(p^1, u^0)$; therefore we can choose the path of integration to be one where each price is changed holding others constant. This yields (2.8''). By the same reasoning, the EV can be expressed as

$$EV = -\sum_{i=1}^{N} \int_{p_i^0}^{p_i^1} x_i^c(p, u^1)\, dp_i + \Delta m \tag{2.9''}$$

The case where the price of a single good x_1 changes from p_1^0 to p_1^1 holding all other prices and income constant is expressed diagrammatically in figure 2.3. Assuming $\Delta m = 0$, CV as expressed by (2.8'') is equal to the area $p_1^0abp_1^1$ bounded by the compensated demand curve where the household is held at its initial utility level. The equivalent variation of (2.9'') is given by the area $p_1^0cdp_1^1$ bounded by the compensated demand curve corresponding to the terminal utility level. We have assumed x_1 is normal, so $x^c(p, u^2)$ lies to the right of $x^c(p, u^0)$ since $u^1 > u^0$. Therefore, EV is greater than CV.

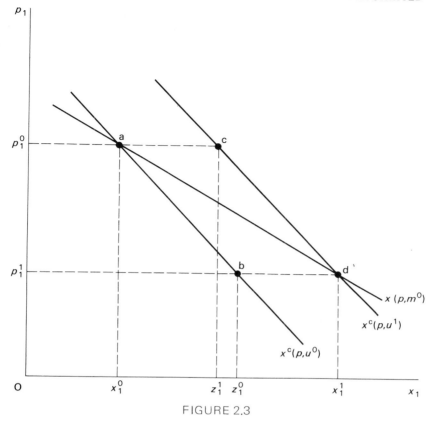

FIGURE 2.3

Note that the Marshallian consumer surplus $p_1^0 a d p_1^1$ lies between CV and EV and is also unique. But this is true only for the case where the price of a single good is changed. If there are many goods and more than one commodity price change, the Marshallian consumer surplus value is not independent of the order in which the prices are changed (see Mohring, 1971) and therefore is not an exact utility indicator. It must be emphasized that the compensating and equivalent variations are not subject to this difficulty and are unambiguous indicators of changes in utility. For this reason, Hicksian measures are preferable to Marshallian measures of welfare change. Their use will be taken up in more detail later in the book.

4 Household Welfare with Quantity Constraints

In the previous section we assumed that the household could vary the arguments of its utility function subject only to price and income constraints. In many cases the consumption levels cannot be varied by the household. For example, the quantity of a public good such as the level of national defence or a publicly provided good such as the frequency of refuse collection cannot be varied by the individual household. In some cases households cannot change the quantity of leisure they enjoy because their hours of employment are fixed by institutional considerations. Also, the services of durables owned by the household, such as shelter, cannot be varied on a day-to-day basis in response to changes in their implicit rental rates because of the large adjustment costs involved in doing so. Incomplete or imperfect markets also impose similar forms of quantity constraints. For example, a household may not be able to increase its overall level of current consumption if it cannot borrow against future labour income. In an uncertainty context, the consequences of a given household action may depend on events beyond the household's knowledge or control, and in general the household is limited in its ability to make contracts that depend on these external events. Thus, in a sense, the actual state-dependent levels of consumption in the utility function may be quantity constrained.

The canonical case of a quantity constraint, which we will use to develop the main ideas in this section, is a binding quantity ration that may arise under wartime coupon rationing, for example. If such a quantity ration is binding the household is unable to alter the levels of consumption of different goods up to the point where the marginal rate of substitution between them is equated to the ratio of their market prices. For example, in figure 2.4 the household maximizes its utility at point R when faced with the binding quantity constraint $\bar{x}_1$. At R the slope of u^0 is different from the ratio of prices as given by the slope of budget line AB.

The problem with measuring household welfare when there are quantity constraints arises from the absence of an observable set of prices with which to value changes in the consumption bundle. If we consider only a change in the quantity ration of a single good there is obviously no problem. But what if there are a number of rationed goods and the quantity constraints are altered in different directions? Or what if a quantity constraint is relaxed simultaneously with a rise in the price of the rationed or some other good?

We can make use of the expenditure function to develop the conceptual issues involved. Assume there is a binding quantity constraint $\bar{x}_1$ on the first commodity and that all the other commodities are unrationed. The household also must pay p_1 for each unit of $\bar{x}_1$. Then we can define the *constrained expenditure function* $e(p, \bar{x}_1, u)$ as:

$$e(p, \bar{x}_1, u) = p_1 \bar{x}_1 + \min_{x_2, \ldots, x_N} \sum_{i=2}^{N} p_i x_i$$

subject to

$$u(\bar{x}_1, \ldots, x_N) = u$$

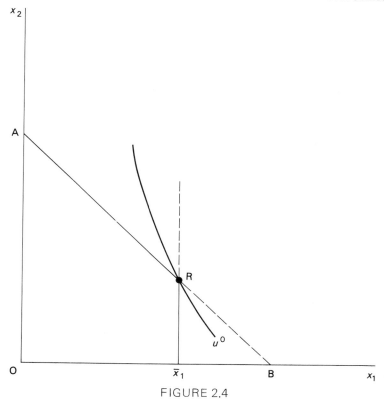

FIGURE 2.4

This constrained expenditure function bears the same envelope-type relation to the unconstrained expenditure function as does the short-run cost function to the long-run cost function in the theory of the firm.[4] The derivative of the constrained expenditure function with respect to the price of a non-rationed good i yields the constrained compensated demand function $x_i^c(p, \bar{x}_1, u)$. Other than the fact that the quantity constraint of the rationed good enters the demand function, these constrained compensated demand functions have the same negativity and symmetry properties as the unconstrained (or 'notional') functions for the non-rationed case and can be used to extract compensating and equivalent income measures for price changes. The derivative of the expenditure function with respect to the ration constraint $\bar{x}_1$ is given by:

$$\frac{\partial e}{\partial \bar{x}_1} = \frac{\partial e}{\partial u}\frac{\partial u}{\partial \bar{x}_1} = p_1 - p_1^*$$

[4] In particular, the constrained expenditure function lies everywhere above the unconstrained expenditure function except at a point of tangency. This tangency occurs at a price p^* at which the household would choose an amount of the rationed good just equal to the maximum amount permitted under the quantity ration.

where p_1^* is the virtual or 'shadow' price of the rationed good. Because $\partial e/\partial u = (\partial u/\partial m)^{-1} = 1/\lambda$ evaluated at the same point, we have $\partial u/\partial \bar{x}_1 = \lambda p_1^*$ or $(\partial u/\partial \bar{x}_1)/(\partial u/\partial x_i) = p_1^*/p_i$ using $\partial u/\partial x_i = \lambda p_i$.

In terms of figure 2.4, the absolute value of the slope of the indifference curve u^0 at point R is equal to p_1^*/p_2. In essence, p_1^* is the price at which $\bar{x}_1$ would be voluntarily chosen when the household is faced with the same prices of the non-rationed goods and when the household is given just enough income to enjoy u^0. This shadow price can be found by solving the notional or unconstrained compensated demand function $x_1^c(p_1, \ldots, p_N, u)$ for the value of p_1 that yields $x_1^c(\ ) = \bar{x}_1$.[5]

Using shadow prices, income equivalent measures can be assigned to various policies that change the prices and quantity constraints faced by the household. For example, if there are changes in M quantity constraints $(dx_1, \ldots, dx_M)$, then differentiating the conditional expenditure function we get:

$$de = \sum_{i=1}^{M} (p_i - p_i^*)\, d\bar{x}_i$$

This represents the change in expenditure that compensates the household for the utility effect of the change in the quantity rations. If this is accompanied by price changes then the term

$$\sum_{i=1}^{N} x_i\, dp_i$$

must be added. If discrete (non-differential) changes in quantity rations are to be evaluated, then integral expressions must be evaluated.

The difficulty in evaluating the welfare effects of quantity rations is that the required shadow prices are not directly observed. They are implicit valuations placed on an extra unit of rationed goods by a household and, therefore, may be specific to a household. A recurrent problem in welfare economics is the imputation of shadow prices in cases where market prices do not exist, or where market prices do not reflect the marginal valuation of an extra unit of the commodity because of the existence of non-pecuniary constraints.

5 Household Welfare in an Intertemporal Setting

In the previous section, household welfare was identified with its utility in a given period which, in turn, was constrained by its fixed level of expenditure in that period. In practice the household is not constrained

---

[5] A good discussion of household behaviour under rationing is found in Neary and Roberts (1980).

by a fixed level of expenditure in any given period because it can reallocate its expenditure among periods by saving and dissaving. In a framework which includes such intertemporal substitution in consumption, one generally cannot identify a household's welfare with its current utility or measure household welfare in terms of some current income equivalent.

The analysis of household choice can be extended to include inter-temporal issues by generalizing the definition of a commodity. The consumption of a commodity is distinguished not only by type (denoted by subscript $i = 1, \ldots, N$) but also by date (denoted by subscript $t = 1, \ldots, T$) at which it is consumed. For example, $x_{i,t}$ is the consumption of commodity type i at date t and is different from $x_{i, t+1}$, although they may be very close substitutes. Let $x_t = (x_{1t}, \ldots, x_{Nt})$ denote the vector of goods consumed by the household at time t. There are T such vectors, one for each period, so let $x = (x_1, \ldots, x_T)$ be the $N \times T$ vector of goods consumed over the household's lifetime of T periods. We assume that the household can completely and transitively order all such lifetime consumption bundles. Thus, with continuity, we can define a household's lifetime utility as:

$$u = u(x_{11}, \ldots, x_{N1}; \ldots; x_{1T}, \ldots, x_{NT}; b_T)$$

where b_T is a bequest left to descendent households. This lifetime utility function is assumed to have the same general properties of the atemporal, one-period utility function including non-satiation and quasi-concavity. Sometimes an additional property called strong temporal separability is assumed for the lifetime utility function. In this case it can be expressed as:

$$u = \sum_{t=1}^{T} \delta^t v(x_t) + h(b_T)$$

where $\delta < 1$ is the one-period pure rate of time preference which is assumed to be the same for all periods, and where all within-period utility functions $v(x)$ are the same. In the case where $T = 2$ and $N = 1$, we can represent this lifetime utility function in figure 2.5. On the vertical and horizontal axes we measure period two and period one consumption of the single good, respectively. The slope of every indifference curve is $-1/\delta$ where it intersects the 45° line. The strict quasi-concavity of the utility function implies that the household will not want to concentrate its consumption in one period but spread consumption over its lifetime.

The analogue to the one-period budget constraint is the household's lifetime wealth constraint. Let i_t denote the one-period interest rate between period t and period $t+1$ at which the household can freely borrow and lend, and let

$$m_t = \sum_{i=1}^{N} p_{it} x_{it}$$

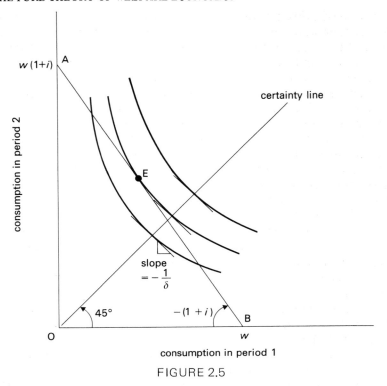

FIGURE 2.5

denote the household's expenditure at time t. The household's lifetime budget constraint is:

$$\sum_{i=1}^{T} D_t m_t + D_T \theta_T = w$$

where

$$D_t = \prod_{s=1}^{t} (1 + i_s)^{-1}$$

is the discount rate applied to a dollar accruing in period t, and w is the present value of the household's earnings discounted to the first period plus the present value of any inheritance it receives. The two-period case, where there are no bequests or inheritances and the household receives all of its income in the first period, is shown in figure 2.5. The household's lifetime budget set is given by the set OAB. If it is assumed that the money price of the commodity is constant, the budget line AB has a slope of $-(1+i)$ and intersects the horizontal axis at household wealth w. The household is assumed to maximize its lifetime utility. Thus, it equates the marginal rate of substitution between any two commodities (distinguished by type and/or date) to their relative price. In figure 2.5 the maximum lifetime utility point occurs at E, where the marginal rate of substitution between present and future consumption is equal to $1 + i$.

The extended notion of household choice and utility poses a dilemma for the welfare economist of choosing between current and lifetime utility as an indicator of household welfare. Current utility is not the objective function maximized by the household but is, indirectly, a choice variable. If the policy objective is equal to something that the household can vary then an incentive is created for the household to alter its behaviour. On the other hand, taking the lifetime utility of the household as its level of welfare raises equity issues.

For example, consider a household that once earned a very high real income but spent it all and is now destitute in retirement. Policies that utilize current utility rather than lifetime utility as a welfare indicator may give rise to *ex ante* incentives which encourage other households to squander their income and not provide for old age. But using high lifetime utility as a measure of welfare means that little should be done to help this household, which seems unjust *ex post*.

These considerations, and a parallel set of considerations arising from uncertainty (discussed in more detail in the next section), also raises the question of whether the household should be assumed to spend its income in its own best interest. Spending too much and saving too little in the intertemporal context is similar to spending too much on liquor and too little on education in the static context. In general, it is assumed that paternalistic policies concerning how and when a household should spend its income are resorted to only in special cases. Thus, paternalistic considerations may play a role in some policies (e.g. forced saving for retirement through public pensions) but in most cases lifetime utility constitutes the appropriate indicator of household welfare.

Adopting lifetime utility as the indicator of household welfare raises some problems concerning the assignment of an income equivalent measure. Although the temporal separability assumption permits us to recover period expenditure functions $e_t(p_t, u_t)$, these period expenditure functions are of limited use if maximizing u_t is not the objective of the household. The reason is quite easy to understand. Suppose an exogenous event changes p_t *ceteris paribus*. This will alter not only the household's current utility but also its utility in other periods even if the event occurs only in period t. This is because the household will readjust its saving to allocate the gain or loss in utility across its lifetime, thus 'smoothing' its lifetime utility profile. Finding the change in current expenditure which restores current utility to its original level (or has equivalent effects on its current utility) will not be the appropriate indicator of the change in household welfare because such current compensating and equivalent variations ignore the spillover effects of the event in period t into other periods. To be correct, the appropriate income compensations or equivalents must be derived from an expenditure function which holds lifetime rather than current utility constant. Finding such measures may require more information than just the current behavioural parameters of the household.

6 Household Welfare under Uncertainty

In the previous sections it was assumed that the household operates in an environment of perfect certainty where known and certain consequences follow from the household's decisions or actions. In many circumstances, particularly those where current actions give rise to future consequences, the household takes actions for which the consequences depend on an event that is beyond its control and is unknown to it at the time it makes its decision. It is conventional to call the unknown event 'the state of the world' which may be the state of tomorrow's weather or the advent of World War III. If there are S different states of the world we can denote them by the index s, where $s = 1, 2, \ldots, S$. We can again generalize our notion of a commodity by identifying it not only by type (subscript i) and by date (subscript t), but also by the prevailing state of the world (subscript s). We will ignore intertemporal considerations for simplicity.

Let x_i denote the 'action' of the household which, for concreteness, could be the act of putting money in a coffee machine, and x_{is} denote the 'consequence' in state s, where the state is determined by whether the machine works or not. The household chooses a vector of actions $x = (x_1, \ldots, x_N)$ and, after the state of the world is revealed (say) to be s, it enjoys consequences $(x_{1s}, \ldots, x_{Ns})$. More generally we can consider the $N \times S$ vector $x = (x_{11}, \ldots, x_{1S}; \ldots; x_{N1}, \ldots, x_{NS})$, which denotes the consequences of any actions in every state of the world. Making the same assumptions about the household's preferences as were made in the previous sections, we can write utility as a function of the consequences which depend on its actions (which the household controls) and the state of the world (which it does not). That is,

$$u(x) = u(x_{11}, \ldots, x_{1S}; \ldots; x_{N1}, \ldots, x_{NS})$$

We have assumed that the household utility does not depend on the state of the world *per se* but only on the consequences.

So far the analysis of household behaviour and welfare need not differ materially from the certainty analysis of the previous sections. Consider now the possibility that a household can undertake *state-contingent contracts*. These contracts specify a price p_{is} per unit of commodity type i that must be paid in all states of the world for a commodity which is delivered only in the sth state of the world. In this case the household's choice problem is mathematically and economically similar to the certainty case. It chooses a set of consequences

$$[x_{is}]_{i=1, \ldots, N; s=1, \ldots, S}$$

so as to find

$$\max u(x_{11}, \ldots, x_{1S}; \ldots; x_{N1}, \ldots, x_{NS})$$

subject to

$$\sum_{i=1}^{N} \sum_{s=1}^{S} p_{is} x_{is} = m$$

Household welfare can be identified with the constrained maximum utility level and the analysis of household utility can proceed along the lines described in previous sections. Relative prices, to which the household equates its marginal rate of substitution between commodities (defined by type and state), are observable, and expenditure functions of the usual type can be specified. Note that the above analysis does not imply that the household chooses the full insurance or certainty solution (i.e. consumption vectors that are independent of the state of the world) except in special cases. Rather the main conclusion is that, with state-contingent prices, one can once again identify household actions with ultimate utility consequences.

In reality the household does not face a complete set of state-contingent prices and the uncertainty analysis does differ materially from the certainty case. Suppose the household can make no state-contingent contracts at all; that is, it must choose a vector of actions $(x_1, \ldots, x_N)$ at known prices $(p_1, \ldots, p_N)$ subject to its budget constraint and then accept the consequences as dictated by the future state of the world. For any N vector of actions there will be an $N \times S$ vector of possible outcomes $[(x_{11}, \ldots, x_{N1}), \ldots, (x_{1S}, \ldots, x_{NS})]$. If the household's preferences satisfy certain postulates then we can analyse household behaviour in terms of its *expected utility*.

In order for the expected utility hypothesis to explain choice under uncertainty, the household's preferences must satisfy the usual postulates of completeness, consistency and continuity and satisfy two more postulates which we will call *probabilistic equivalence* and *probabilistic independence*. The former requires the individual to be indifferent between two actions offering the same outcomes with the same probabilities. In other words, the household does not care about the processes generating the underlying uncertainty except in terms of the probabilities and outcomes generated. The latter means that a household's preference between two actions which offer the same outcome in some states of the world must be independent of those outcomes. For example, whether two lotteries both offer one pound if the state of the world s occurs, or one million pounds if the state s occurs, does not affect the household's preference between those two lotteries. This is the same additive separability assumption with respect to preferences that we discussed under certainty, but it is more plausible in this context because the states are mutually exclusive. Unlike the case of preferences between two goods, both of which are consumed, the household either gets outcome x_s or it does not.

Thus these postulates, known as the von Neumann and Morgenstern (1947) postulates, imply that the household's utility function is additively separable. This means that there exists a vector of numbers $[\pi_1, \ldots, \pi_s]$ that can be chosen to add up to one, so that the household chooses among actions $(x_1, \ldots, x_N)$ so as to maximize:

$$E(u) = \sum_{s=1}^{S} \pi_s u(x_{1s}, \ldots, x_{Ns}) \qquad (2.10)$$

subject to

$$\sum_{i=1}^{N} p_i x_i = m$$

where u is a suitably defined utility index and x_{is} is the outcome of action i in state s. The π_s $(s = 1, \ldots, S)$ can be interpreted as subjective probabilities assigned by the household to each state of the world. Note that the household's objects of choice are its actions and not the ultimate objects of its utility (the consequences).

The expected utility expression (2.10) represents the consumer's preference ordering over the uncertain outcomes implied by various actions. Since $\phi[E(u)]$ is an equally good representation, where $\phi[\ ]$ is a monotonic increasing transformation, expected utility is an ordinal concept. However, one of the important properties of the von Neumann–Morgenstern expected utility hypothesis is that the subutility indices $u(\ )$, which are weighted and added to measure expected utility, are cardinally measurable. That is, for $E(u)$ to be a consistent preference ordering over uncertain prospects, the utility index u must be unique up to a (i.e. is as good as any) positive affine transformation.

To see the reason for this, consider the simple case of two states of the world with associated probabilities π_1 and π_2, where $\pi_1 + \pi_2 = 1$. Consider three possible outcomes (or vectors of outcomes) denoted x, y and z chosen such that the consumer is indifferent between the certain outcome x and an uncertain outcome comprising y with probability π_1 and z with probability π_2. Then, assuming the person's preferences satisfy the axioms of the expected utility hypothesis, a suitable utility index $u(\ )$ will have the property:

$$u(x) = \pi_1 u(y) + \pi_2 u(z)$$
$$= \pi_1 u(y) + (1 - \pi_1) u(z) \qquad (2.11)$$

Furthermore, any other utility index, say $v(\ )$, representing this person's preferences must also satisfy an expression such as (2.11). Solving (2.11) for π_1 and doing the same for the alternative index $v(\ )$, we obtain the relation that must hold between the indices $u(\ )$ and $v(\ )$:

$$\frac{u(x)-u(z)}{u(y)-u(z)} = \frac{v(x)-v(z)}{v(y)-v(z)} \qquad (2.12)$$

In the case in which more than two states of the world exist, the relationship becomes somewhat more complicated. It can readily be shown that the relation (2.12) will only be satisfied if $u(\ )$ and $v(\ )$ are positive affine transforms of one another; that is, if they are related as follows:

$$v(\ ) = a + bu(\ ), \ b > 0$$

This means that once a suitable utility index is found to represent preferences, any other positive affine transformation of the index will do just as well. Thus $u(\ )$ is a *cardinal index* of utility.

The above discussion also suggests how, in principle, a suitable cardinal index for use in the expected utility hypothesis can be obtained experimentally. Suppose the outcomes $x, y, z, \ldots$ are scalars. Since the utility index is cardinal we are free, as with temperature and weight scales, to choose arbitrarily an origin and units of measurement. This will be implicitly done by assigning utility numbers to any two outcomes, say x and y. Thus we could set $u(y) = 100$ and $u(x) = 200$, assuming x is preferred to y. The following experiment could be performed. The individual whose preferences are to be obtained could be asked to select a value of π_1 such that he or she is indifferent between the certain outcome x and the uncertain prospect y and z with probabilities π_1 and $1 - \pi_1$. Once a value of π_1 is stated, (2.11) would be used to deduce what value of $u(z)$ would be consistent with the revealed indifference. In a similar manner, the utility value for any other outcome could be obtained and a cardinal index of utility constructed.

This discussion can be clarified by considering the case in which there is a single commodity x and two states of the world. On the horizontal and vertical axes of figure 2.6 are units of consumption of the good in states 1 and 2 (x_1, x_2), respectively. The preference ordering over uncertain outcomes (x_1, x_2) with given probabilities π_1 and π_2 is represented by a set of indifference curves. Along each indifference curve, expected utility $E(u) = \pi_1 u(x_1) + \pi_2 u(x_2)$ is constant, so by total differentiation:

$$d[E(u)] = 0 = \pi_1 u'(x_1)\,dx_1 + \pi_2 u'(x_2)\,dx_2$$

From this we can deduce the slope of the consumer's indifference curve to be:

$$\frac{dx_2}{dx_1} = -\frac{\pi_1 u'(x_1)}{\pi_2 u'(x_2)}$$

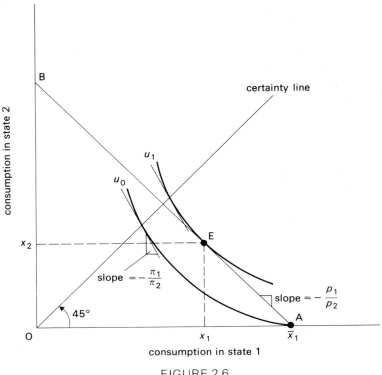

FIGURE 2.6

Two properties of the indifference curves might be noted. First, since $x_1 = x_2$ along the 45° line it is called the *certainty line* and the slope of the indifference curve at the intersection with this line is $-\pi_1/\pi_2$. Secondly, if $u''(\ ) < 0$, the absolute value of the slope of an indifference curve will increase as we move down it, implying that the indifference curve will be strictly convex.[6] In this case the household is a *risk-averter*. If $u'' = 0$, indifference curves are straight lines with a slope of $-\pi_1/\pi_2$ and the household is *risk neutral*. If $u'' > 0$, indifference curves are strictly concave and the household is a *risk-lover*.

In the absence of state-contingent prices, the household has little to do but spend all its income on the single type of commodity which can be thought of as a joint good which provides fixed quantities of the state-dependent goods in each state. (If there were many types of commodities it would have to decide on how to allocate its income in each state, of course.) Suppose in state 1 the household gets $\bar{x}_1$ units of the good and zero units in state 2 (so state 2 is the 'bad' state). The household then acquires the utility level labelled u_0 in figure 2.6. If we now introduce

---

[6]   Because $u(\ )$ is cardinally measurable, the sign of $u''(\ )$ is not arbitrary as would be the case if $u(\ )$ were only ordinally measurable.

state-contingent markets in which the household is a price-taker, it will face a budget line AB with the slope $-p_1/p_2$ and will choose some utility maximizing combination consumption in each state given by the point E. In this case it agrees to give up $\bar{x}_1 - x_1$ if state 1 should occur in exchange for receiving x_2 if state 2 should occur. Household utility is increased to u_1.

If state-contingent prices exist, the demand functions can be expressed in terms of the prices of the state-contingent goods (the consequences) and household income. Therefore if some event alters the actions available to the household, or the consequences of a given action, or the state-contingent prices and income facing the household, we can evaluate the effect on household welfare by procedures analogous to those carried out under the certainty case.

When there are no state-contingent prices the problem is more complicated because welfare must be measured in terms of actions and the prices of actions. The demand functions for actions depend on the action prices, household income and the riskiness of the actions (i.e. the relationship between the actions and their consequences). If we are willing to hold the elements determining riskiness constant, we can measure the welfare of the household in terms of its action demand functions. In this case the action can be thought of as a joint good over the possible states of the world, and the action price is the price of the joint good. We can specify expenditure functions $e(p_1, \ldots, p_N, u)$, where u is a specified level of expected utility which has the property that the derivative of e with respect to p_i is the compensated demand function for action x_i. If actions and action prices can be observed, equivalent or compensating income measures can be assigned.

There is still the problem of evaluating the welfare effects of policies that alter the 'riskiness' of actions by altering the relationship between an action and its consequences. For example, a requirement that food products be dated for freshness may alter the relationship between the action of purchasing an edible product and the consequence of consuming it. Any such change in the riskiness of actions cannot be evaluated on the basis of observed household actions and action prices. In principle it can be evaluated using the state-contingent 'shadow' prices p_{is}^* that the consumer implicitly attaches to commodity type i in state s, but these prices must be imputed and cannot be observed. Moreover, they will be household specific.

One possible method for evaluating the effects of changes in riskiness on household welfare is outlined as follows. Suppose a household undertakes N actions so as to maximize expected utility derived from a budget determined by given income and action prices. The *ex post* utility achieved then depends on the state of the world. We can use the expenditure function defined on action prices to find the income needed to achieve the *ex post* utility that occurs in each state to get a distribution of income equivalents $(m_1, \ldots, m_s)$ for each state of the world. Now using equivalent income as the uncertain parameter we can expand the indirect utility function $v(p, m)$ around the mean equivalent income m. As is well known, utility then depends positively on m and negatively on the variance of m, and depends also on higher moments. Risk can be defined as some function of the moments of the distribution of $(m_1, \ldots, m_s)$ (often only the second moment) and a price for risk can be inferred from observations of rates of return on risky assets. Changes in risk resulting from any policy can then be valued. The difficult step (theoretically) in all this is to go from a multivariate distribution of the consequences of actions to a univariate distribution of income equivalents.

A final comment about uncertainty raises an issue analogous to that discussed under intertemporal welfare. Should the policy-maker choose *ex ante* (expected) utility or *ex post* utility as the welfare of the household? The non-paternalistic answer is *ex ante* utility, but in many cases *ex post* utility will be considered. Indeed, much of the popular discussion about the government's role as a 'safety net' makes sense only if *ex post* rather than *ex ante* utility is chosen as the indicator of household welfare. However, as mentioned earlier, if the objective of the planner is *ex post* utility, which is not the objective of the household, unwanted incentive effects may be induced.

7 The Measurement of Household Utility

As far as the individual household is concerned, all that is required in order to be able to choose rationally among alternatives is an ordering or ranking of the alternatives. That is, for the purposes of household choice or household welfare maximization, an ordinal utility function defined over all alternatives will suffice. (In the case of uncertainty, we have seen that the ordering of risky alternatives can further be expressed as a probability-weighted sum of cardinal subutility functions of the underlying uncertain outcomes.) Furthermore, in principle the planner can infer the household orderings by observing the choices the household makes in alternative situations. We can think of the household orderings as *information* that the planner might have available for making social orderings.

As we shall see in chapter 5, there are ways of aggregating household utilities into an aggregate social ordering or social welfare function even if household utilities are only ordinally measurable. However, the types of social welfare functions that are possible are quite limited if only ordinal utility functions are available to the planner. This is not surprising since if utility functions are ordinal the planner will know, for example, that the utility of person A is higher in state one than in state two, but he will not know by how much it is higher. It would, therefore, be more useful to the planner if household utility functions were 'more measurable' so that there would be information about intensity of preference on which to aggregate the household utilities into a social welfare ordering.

There are several senses in which the household's utility function can be 'more measurable'. Some of the more common ones will be outlined here, in particular those that will be used in our later discussion on social welfare functions. Four different degrees of measurability will be discussed – ordinal, cardinal, ratio scale and full.

7.1 Ordinal measurability

In the preceding discussion of this chapter, utility functions have been assumed to be ordinal. This implies that any utility function can be used to represent the household's preference provided only that the utility numbers associated with alternative states give the same rankings of those states as do the household's preferences. As mentioned above, a utility function $u(x)$ will be a satisfactory representation of preferences if

$$u(x) \geqslant u(y) \quad \text{whenever } x \mathrm{R} y$$

where x and y are any two alternative states (or bundles of goods). There will, of course, be a large number of utility functions which satisfy this property. Such utility functions are related to one another in the following way. Suppose $v(x)$ is another suitable utility function. Then

$$v(x) \geqslant v(y) \quad \text{whenever } u(x) \geqslant u(y)$$

for any x and y. This is equivalent to saying that $u(x)$ and $v(x)$ are increasing functions of each other. Thus, if a function $u(x)$ is a suitable representation of a household's preference orderings, any other increasing function (or monotonic transformation) of $u(x)$ will be as well, such as $v(x) = \phi(u(x))$, where $\phi' > 0$.

An ordinal utility function is said to be unique up to a monotonic transform. It can readily be shown that, no matter what the particular transform taken, the signs of first derivatives are unchanged by a monotonic transform, but signs of higher order derivatives can change. In addition, monotonic transforms leave the marginal rates of substitution between all pairs of goods unchanged; that is, they leave the indifference curve map unchanged.

7.2 Cardinal measurability

Cardinal utility functions, already encountered earlier, give more information to the planner than do ordinal utility functions. In addition, simply by ranking alternative commodity bundles, cardinal utility functions give some information on the magnitude of change in utility levels in going from one bundle to another. To see exactly what is implied, we need a more formal characterization of the concept of cardinal measurability. As with temperature scales or weight measures, cardinal measurement allows one the freedom to choose both the origin (e.g. the freezing point) and the units of measurement (degrees Fahrenheit or Celsius). This implies that if a particular utility function has been found which adequately

c

represents the utility for a particular choice of origin and units of measurement, any positive affine transform of that utility function will provide the same information. For example, if $u(x)$ is a measuring scale for utility in the same sense that the Fahrenheit scale is a measuring scale for temperature, then the utility function $v(x)$ will be a suitable function if $v(x) = a + bu(x)$, $b > 0$. Thus it is said that if utility is cardinally measurable, the utility function is unique up to a positive affine transformation.

To see exactly what information cardinal measurability gives to the planner, we can stipulate exactly what remains unchanged when utility functions are subjected to a positive affine transform. For one thing, the signs of the first and second derivatives of the utility function (and higher order ones as well) are unchanged. If the marginal utility of consuming a particular good is positive and diminishing, it will always remain so under any positive affine transformation. In addition, as with temperature scales, if the change in utility in going from one bundle x to another bundle y exceeds the change in going from w to z under utility function $u(x)$, then the same will remain true for any positive affine transform of $u(x)$. That is,

$$\text{if} \quad u(y) - u(x) \geqslant u(z) - u(w)$$

$$\text{then} \quad v(y) - v(x) \geqslant v(z) - v(w)$$

for $v = a + bu$, $b > 0$. Naturally, as with ordinal functions, relative levels of utility from different bundles are unchanged as well.

Although cardinal measurability provides more information than ordinal measurability, it is not obvious how that additional information is to be readily obtained. The information available to construct ordinal utility functions is just the revealed choice of households when faced with various budget sets. This reveals the household's ordering of alternative commodity bundles but not the scale of utility measurement.

7.3 *Ratio scale measurement*

This type of measurability is similar to cardinal measurability in that it leaves open the choice of units of measurement, but differs from it in that it leaves the origin unchanged. Thus it provides somewhat more information than cardinal measurement. The characterization of ratio scale measurability is as follows. Suppose that the units of measurement of utility have been chosen and that, for that set of units, the function $u(x)$ correctly represents the utility attained by the household for any bundle of goods x. Then, any other utility function which is a positive multiple of $u(x)$ will serve just as well, such as $v(x) = bu(x)$, $b > 0$. The ratio scale transformation changes the units of measurement without changing the origin of the measuring scale.

The implications of ratio scale measurability for the information available to the planner are as follows. First of all, ratio scale measurability has all the information of cardinal measurability. In addition, any ratio scale transformation will leave unchanged the ranking of proportionate changes in utility between pairs of alternatives. That is,

if $\quad \dfrac{u(y) - u(x)}{u(x)} \geqslant \dfrac{u(z) - u(w)}{u(w)}$

then $\dfrac{v(y) - v(x)}{v(x)} \geqslant \dfrac{v(z) - v(w)}{v(w)}$

for $v = bu$, $b > 0$.

7.4 *Full measurability*

Ordinal measurability allows only the ordering of levels of utility; cardinal utility allows the ordering of changes in utility as well; and ratio scale measurability allows the ordering of proportionate changes in utility on top of that. If complete information is available on the household utility, we say that the household utility is fully measurable. In this case, there will be a unique utility function associated with the household's preferences.

These concepts of measurability, and the information that they imply, will be used extensively in chapter 5 when we discuss the aggregation of individual utilities into a social welfare function. In the meantime, we shall be considering exactly how far we can get in ordering states if we are restricted to ordinal utility functions for households.

8 Summary

In this chapter we have surveyed the highlights of consumer choice theory as it relates to the welfare of the household. A value judgment known as non-paternalism is commonly invoked in order to identify the household's utility with its welfare. In some cases this value judgment is relaxed, such as in the case of merit goods. Paternalistic considerations also arise in the context of intertemporal choice and choice under uncertainty.

The ordinal property of a household's preferences (that is, its indifference curve map) is all that is revealed by its demand function. This does permit inferences to be made about whether a household's utility has risen or fallen. A sufficient indicator is given by calculating the compensating and equivalent variation measures associated with the change. In principle, one problem with doing this is that households may face non-price (quantity) constraints because of market imperfections or lack of markets. Such constraints may arise in the context of uncertainty or for institutional reasons. In order to determine whether a household's utility has risen or fallen on the basis of its observed behaviour, shadow prices for quantity rationed goods must be imputed.

An additional assumption that may be made about a household's utility function is additive separability. This means that the utility from consuming some commodities or groups of commodities is independent of the consumption of other commodities. This assumption is often made when dealing with the household's intertemporal preferences or its preferences under uncertainty. In these contexts it is plausible that partitions of goods by date or by state of the world can be treated as independent in the household's preferences.

Finally we distinguish clearly what is meant by the measurability of utility. Ordinally measurable utility means that a household's indifference curves can be numbered in any increasing manner, whereas fully measurable utility means that indifference curves can be numbered in only one way. In between these two extremes lie cardinally measurable and ratio scale measurable utility. Measurability will be very important when the problem of aggregating utilities of different households is addressed.

CHAPTER 3

Welfare in a Many-Household Economy: The Pareto Criterion

1 Introduction

In chapter 2 we were concerned only with measuring the welfare of an individual household. Unless we are dealing with the economy of Robinson Crusoe or an economy where decisions are made by an egotistical dictator, we cannot stop there. In practice, most economies are populated with millions of households, most of whom have different tastes and different consumption opportunities. If we accept the postulate of welfarism, we are faced with an enormous problem. Somehow we must distil welfare statements about an event from its effects on millions of different households. This problem of aggregating the preferences of a pluralistic society into meaningful and operational welfare criteria for the society as a whole will be the focus of our attention for the next few chapters, and will also be important in the later chapters on applied welfare analysis.

In the nineteenth century, economists solved the problem of aggregating household welfare in a rather direct manner. The utility of every household was assumed to be cardinally measurable in principle, as are temperature and mass. Classical economists, following the precepts of Jeremy Bentham, simply added these cardinal utilities together, and the welfare effects of public policy were evaluated in terms of whether the 'sum of satisfaction' was raised or lowered. We now know this *utilitarian* aggregation of individual welfare rests on strong and restrictive ethical assumptions. It not only requires cardinal utility but also requires comparability among household utilities. Without a comparability assumption, adding household utilities would be like adding apples and oranges and therefore meaningless.

At the turn of the century, Vilfredo Pareto, a great Italian economist, was the first to define concepts of society's welfare that do not rest on such cardinality and comparability assumptions. Pareto is regarded as the father of ordinal utility theory because he recognized that the laws of consumer demand do not require declining marginal utility of income and the implied cardinality of utility measurement. For this reason he rejected the utilitarian sum of cardinal utilities approach and defined a criterion for changes in society's welfare that rested on far weaker assumptions. Today we refer to his criterion as the *Pareto criterion*.

In defining the Pareto criterion we shall refer to any allocation of goods and services across the many households in the economy as a *state* of the economy. Associated with each state is an H element *utility vector* $(u_1, \ldots, u_H)$ that gives the level of utility for every household where H is the number of households in the economy. The Pareto criterion allows us to compare the social welfare of two states by determining whether the associated utility vector of one state dominates that of the other state. That is, are the utilities of some households higher in state x than in state y, and is the utility of no household lower in x than in y? If so, state x is deemed to yield a higher level of society's welfare than state y according to the *strong* Pareto criterion. If the utility of every household is higher in state x, then x is preferred according to the *weak* Pareto criterion.

It is important to recognize that only very weak assumptions about household utility measures are needed for the Pareto criterion. We only need to ascertain whether any household is better off in one state as compared with another; that is, only the ordinal property of the utility function is needed. Moreover, we do not have to make comparisons of the utilities of different households, so that units and levels of utility need not be comparable among households. The price of this generality is high, however. Any two states for which some households are made better off and others are made worse off in one state as compared with the other cannot be ranked according to the Pareto criterion; that is, the Pareto ranking of states is *incomplete*. Unfortunately, in many applications it will be the case that some households gain and others lose, and the Pareto criterion cannot help us there. Nevertheless, the Pareto criterion does play an important role in welfare economics. In fact, welfare statements based on the Pareto criterion are central to notions of economic efficiency.

It should be mentioned that although most economists find the value judgment implicit in the Pareto criterion fairly weak, it has been criticized as being too strong. One criticism is that a state may be ranked as having higher social welfare according to the Pareto criterion even though *relative* disparities have been increased. For example, a state in which the rich are made richer and the poor are made no worse off may be ranked above a state in which the poor are made less impoverished *relative* to the rich. This statement is true providing the household utility functions are *selfish* (that is, a household derives utility only from its own consumption). If, in fact, the poor (or the rich) find their utility reduced when the rich get richer, *ceteris paribus*, the Pareto criterion will not rank a state of relative impoverishment as superior. Thus this criticism misses the mark, but it does raise a basic issue; apart from such external utility effects, the Pareto criterion is, of necessity, neutral to the distribution of utility. A state of extreme utility disparity can be superior to one of utility equality providing somebody is better off and nobody is worse off in utility terms.

Another criticism of the Pareto criterion is that made by Sen (1970). He shows that the criterion can conflict with liberal values. He defines liberalism as a belief that every household should be decisive in the choice between at least one pair of states. For example, a household should be allowed full discretion over whether or not it chooses to read a particular book. He then shows that when externalities in utility exist (that is, one household's choice alters the utility of another) the goal of liberalism can conflict with the Pareto criterion.[1] In other words, a state that is preferred according to the Pareto criterion may be illiberal. Since Sen's example requires a particular type of consumption externally, it is not clear how significant the conflict between the Pareto principle and liberalism is in practice.

2 Economic Efficiency in an Exchange Economy

If state x allows a welfare improvement over state y according to the Pareto criterion, then state x is said to be *Pareto superior* to state y and state y is *Pareto inferior* to state x. If all households enjoy the same level of utility in states x and y, then x and y are *Pareto indifferent*. If state x is neither Pareto superior, nor inferior nor indifferent to y then states x and y are *Pareto non-comparable*. Pareto non-comparable states are ones for which some households are made better off but others are made worse off in moving from one state to the other.

A *feasible state* is one that can be achieved given the economy's resource constraint. Any feasible state for which no feasible Pareto superior state exists (i.e. there is no scope for a Pareto improvement) is said to be *Pareto optimal*. If a state is Pareto optimal it means there is no change that can be made in the economy, given the constraints determining feasibility, that can make any household better off without making another household worse off. There are many Pareto optimal states; in fact, if goods are perfectly divisible and households' utility functions are continuous, there will be an infinite number of them. The set of Pareto optimal states may include a state where a single household gets all of the national income while the rest starve, and a state where all households get equal incomes. Moreover, all Pareto optimal states are non-comparable (lumping Pareto indifferent states together), and therefore the Pareto criterion cannot be used to choose among them.

The most important and useful aspect of the Pareto criterion is the relationship between Pareto optimality and the equilibrium of an economy in which resources are allocated by an ideal market mechanism.

---

[1] Sen's example is one where household A prefers that neither household reads a certain book but, if a household is to read the book, that it be itself and not B. Household B prefers that both households read the book but, if only one household is to read the book, that it be A. Thus a state where reading the book is prescribed for A and proscribed for B is Pareto optimal, and conflicts with the liberal requirement that A and B should choose whether or not they wish to read the book.

In a system of *competitive* markets, all market participants make decisions to supply and demand commodities and factors on the assumption that their actions will not alter the market prices they face; that is, all participants are *price-takers*. A competitive *general equilibrium* is a situation where a set of relative commodity and factor prices is established such that all the markets clear (i.e. the supply of every commodity and factor is equal to its demand). Note that this definition precludes (or ignores) the existence of 'free' goods for which supply exceeds demand. Given some assumptions about the objectives of the firms and households, plus some conditions on household preferences and the technology of production (these assumptions and conditions will be made more precise later), three important theorems can be proved. The first is simply that a competitive general equilibrium exists under the conditions stated. The next two theorems are referred to as the *fundamental theorems of welfare economics* and are welfare statements about a competitive general equilibrium based on the Pareto criterion.

First fundamental theorem of welfare economics (the direct theorem)
Under certain assumptions, a state (allocation of goods and factors) resulting from a competitive general equilibrium is Pareto optimal.

Second fundamental theorem of welfare economics (the converse theorem)
Under certain assumptions, every Pareto optimum state (allocation of goods and factors) can be realized as the outcome of a competitive equilibrium given the distribution of claims on income.

These theorems are quite general. For simplicity we shall assume a differentiable economy and consider interior allocations only. We shall also concentrate on the two-dimensional (two goods, factors, households etc.) economy so that the main ideas can be given a geometric interpretation. The reader is referred to Varian (1978, chapter 5) and Arrow (1951b) for general proofs of both theorems. To begin with we shall consider a pure exchange economy in which two consumers, Alice (*a*) and Bob (*b*), are given endowments of two commodities, good 1 and good 2. In the next section we shall extend our analysis to the case where the commodities are produced and Alice and Bob have endowments of two productive factors, labour *L* and materials *M*.

Suppose for simplicity that Alice has an endowment consisting only of good 1 shown as $O^a \bar{x}_1$ in figure 3.1. If she cannot engage in exchange she will have to consume her endowment, which gives her utility level u_0^a. If Alice can trade and faces a relative price of good 1 in terms of good 2 as given by the absolute value of the slope of the budget line passing through $\bar{x}_1$, she will choose to sell $\bar{x}_1 - x_1^a$ units of good 1 in exchange for $O^a x_2^a$ units of good 2 and achieve utility level u_1^a. By facing Alice with different positive relative prices of good 1 we can trace out her *offer curve*, labelled OC^a. This offer curve tells us the amount of good 1 Alice is willing to exchange for a given amount of good 2 at any relative price. The absolute value of the slope of a budget line from point $\bar{x}_1$ to a point on the offer

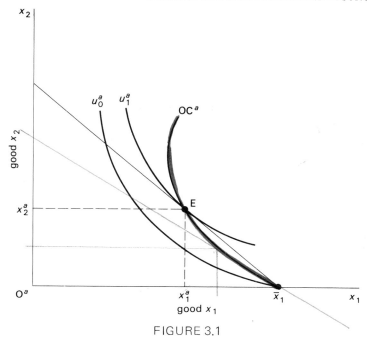

FIGURE 3.1

curve is the relative price of x_1 for x_2 or the terms of trade. The highest indifference curve available to Alice at each relative price is tangent to the budget line at its intersection point with the offer curve. More generally, Alice's endowment could consist of some of both goods; that is, any point on figure 3.1. Given the relative price, her budget line must pass through the endowment point. The offer curve is obtained by rotating the budget line through the endowment point and drawing the locus of equilibrium points chosen.

We can draw a similar diagram for Bob and suppose for simplicity that he receives an endowment consisting only of good 2. By constructing the *Edgeworth box* diagram of figure 3.2 we can examine the general equilibrium in this simple model of two-person and two-commodity exchange. The dimensions of the Edgeworth box are equal to the endowments of good 1 (horizontal) and good 2 (vertical). The origins for Alice's and Bob's consumer diagrams are O^a and O^b, respectively. Assuming that Alice has claims on the entire endowment of good 1 and Bob has claims on the entire endowment of good 2, we can identify the initial endowment point at the lower right-hand corner. More generally, the endowment point can be any point in the Edgeworth box.

Of special interest is the *contract curve* $O^a E O^b$. It is the locus of all allocations of the two goods such that the indifference curves of Alice are tangent to those of Bob (note that Bob's indifference curves are inverted in this diagram since they are drawn with respect to O^b). Thus,

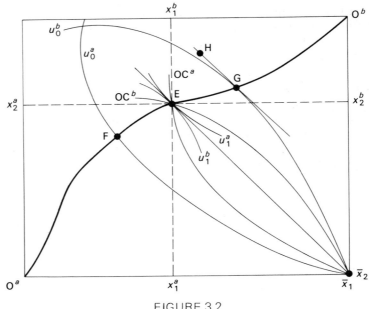

FIGURE 3.2

at each point on the contract locus the marginal rate of substitution between good 1 and 2 (i.e. the slope of the indifference curve) for Alice is equal to that for Bob. At any point that is not on the contract curve, including our initial endowment point, the marginal rates of substitution of Bob and Alice will be different. This opens the possibility of mutually beneficial trade. For example, the indifference curves reached by Alice and Bob when they consume their endowments (u_0^a and u_0^b) form a lens-shaped area within which lie points that are Pareto superior to the initial endowment and which can be reached by Alice and Bob if they trade claims on the commodities. At any point that is within this lens-shaped area but which is not on the contract curve segment FG, there exists the possibility of still further Pareto improving trades. Once Alice and Bob are on the contract curve no further Pareto improvements are possible, so one household can gain utility only at the expense of the other. Thus any point on the contract curve is a Pareto optimal allocation of the endowments.

In an exchange economy, a competitive general equilibrium can be established by assuming that an 'auctioneer' calls out the relative price of goods 1 and 2. In response, Alice (Bob) supplies good 1 (good 2) and demands good 2 (good 1). These offers are given by the offer curves OC^a and OC^b for Alice and Bob, respectively. If the goods demanded and supplied are not equal, the auctioneer calls out another relative price. The competitive general equilibrium is established at the point of inter-section of the offer curves labelled E, where Alice offers $\bar{x}_1 - x_1^a$ in exchange for x_2^a, and Bob exactly reciprocates. Trade takes place and Alice and Bob enjoy the higher levels of utility u_1^a and u_1^b, respectively.

At every point on a household's offer curve, the marginal rate of substitution between the goods is equal to the relative price called out by the auctioneer, so it follows that E must lie on the contract curve. From the shapes of the indifference curves at the endowment point it should be clear from geometric reasoning that a price line must exist so that Alice and Bob trade to a point such as E on the contract curve within the segment FG. Thus a competitive general equilibrium exists and the resulting allocation of goods is Pareto optimal. We have now 'proved' the direct or first theorem of welfare economics.

As stated, all points on the contract curve O^aEO^b are Pareto optimal allocations of the endowment $\bar{x}_1$ and $\bar{x}_2$. Corresponding to each point on the contract curve is a utility level for Alice and Bob. An alternative representation of these points along the contract curve is shown in figure 3.3, where the utility of Alice is measured on the vertical axis and that of Bob on the horizontal axis. The *utility possibilities curve*, labelled UPC, is a representation of the contract curve in this space. It bounds a set which contains all of the utility distributions (that is, points denoting utility

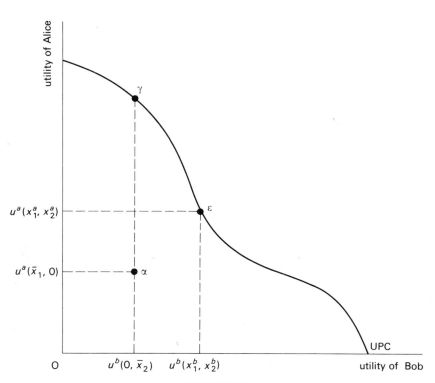

FIGURE 3.3

levels of Alice and Bob) that can be attained given the fixed endowment of goods. Without making a cardinality assumption about utility it is not possible to assign the property of convexity to this set, so we have drawn the utility possibilities curve as neither convex nor concave. However, the utility possibilities curve must have a negative slope, if it is assumed that there are no externalities in consumption.

The slope of the UPC can be derived as follows. By totally differentiating the utility function of household h we get

$$\frac{du^h}{u^h_2} = MRS^h_{12}\, dx^h_1 + dx^h_2 \quad \text{for } h = a, b$$

where MRS is marginal rate of substitution and u^h_2 is the marginal utility of good 2. Since $MRS^a_{12} = MRS^b_{12}$ for Pareto optimal allocations and $dx^a_i = -dx^b_i$, we have

$$\frac{du^a/u^a_2}{du^b/u^b_2} = -1$$

Cross-multiplying and using $u^h_i = \lambda^h p_i$, where λ^h is the marginal utility of income for household h, we get

$$du^a/du^b\,|_{UPC} = -(\lambda^a/\lambda^b)$$

This is, the absolute slope of the UPC in figure 3.3 is equal to the ratio of the marginal utilities of income of Alice to Bob evaluated at the representative allocations.

The competitive equilibrium allocation of point E in figure 3.2 corresponds to a point ϵ on the utility possibilities curve in figure 3.3. It is apparent that ϵ is just one among an infinite number of Pareto optimal distributions on the utility possibilities curve. However, it is also apparent that ϵ is superior to the suboptimal utility distribution α that would have occurred had the two parties not been able to engage in exchange at all.

The converse or second theorem of welfare economics states that any Pareto optimal utility distribution (i.e. a point on the utility possibilities curve UPC) can be attained by a competitive market system for some distributions of claims on the commodities. Claims on commodities in this exchange economy result from the ownership of commodity endowments. We now show that any point on the contract/utility possibilities curve such as γ can be reached by engaging in exchange in a competitive market from some endowment point not on the contract curve. Through any interior point (e.g. point G corresponding to γ) on the contract curve in figure 3.2 we can draw a price line. The absolute value of the slope of this line is the relative price of the two goods and is equal to the common marginal rate of substitution at point G. Any endowment point (e.g. point H) along this budget line corresponds to a distribution of claims on the goods such that a competitive general equilibrium exists at G. This 'proves' the second or converse theorem. ⏐

A Pareto optimal allocation satisfies certain conditions. In the two-person, two-commodity exchange economy, ⏐the *Pareto optimal conditions* can be simply stated: the marginal rates of substitution for Alice and Bob must be equal and their individual consumption bundles must add up to the endowment bundle. More generally, with H consumers and N goods, we have the conditions:

$$MRS^h_{1,N} = \phi_1 \qquad \text{for all } h = 1, \ldots, H$$
$$\vdots \qquad\qquad\qquad \vdots$$
$$MRS^h_{N-1,N} = \phi_{N-1} \qquad \text{for all } h = 1, \ldots, H \qquad (3.1)$$
$$\sum_{h=1}^{H} x_i^h = x_i \qquad \text{for all } i = 1, \ldots, N$$

These conditions are referred to as *exchange efficiency conditions*, and constitute the first-order necessary conditions obtained from an explicit maximization problem. Namely,

$$\max_{x_1^a, x_2^a} u^a(x_1^a, x_2^a)$$

subject to

$$x_1^a + x_1^b = \bar{x}_1$$
$$x_2^a + x_2^b = \bar{x}_2$$

and

$$u^b(x_1^b, x_2^b) = \bar{u}^b$$

where $\bar{u}^b$ is a feasible utility point.⏐

A useful analytic device can now be introduced. Consider a state of the economy such as the competitive equilibrium point E in figure 3.2 and the associated utility distribution given by point ϵ in figure 3.3⏐We can now find the set of all *aggregate* endowments of the commodities which can be allocated across households so as to achieve that distribution of utilities or any Pareto superior distribution of utilities. This set is called the *Scitovsky set* ⏐and is labelled $A(x^e)$ in figure 3.4.⏐The Scitovsky set ⏐is drawn for a particular allocation of goods across the households. In general, let x^e denote an $N \times H$ vector whose element x_i^h is the consumption of good i by household h. Thus, in the two-person two-good case, $x^e = [x_1^a, x_2^a, x_1^b, x_2^b]$.⏐

⏐The boundary of a Scitovsky set is labelled CIC in figure 3.4 and is usually called a *community indifference curve* or *Scitovsky indifference*

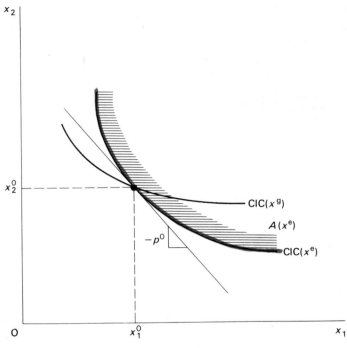

FIGURE 3.4

curve. The community indifference curve labelled CIC(x^e) in figure 3.4 represents all the commodity endowments that can be distributed so as to just achieve the utility distribution associated with a particular allocation x^e of bundle [x_1^0, x_2^0]. Aggregate bundles corresponding to points in the interior of the Scitovsky set can also be allocated in a manner which yields the stated distribution of utilities but, in addition, such interior points can be allocated so as to achieve a Pareto superior distribution of utilities.

The CIC can be derived diagrammatically from the Edgeworth box diagram of figure 3.2 by moving Bob's indifference curve along that of Alice's, starting at point E so as to keep them tangent. The origin O^b then traces out the CIC. Given that Bob and Alice have strictly convex indifference curves, the Scitovsky set will be strictly convex.

Three points about the CIC and the associated Scitovsky set should be stressed, all of which are valid in the general case with N goods and H consumers. First, all points on the CIC represent exchange efficient allocations of the specified aggregate endowment bundles. Secondly, the slope of the CIC equals the common MRS of the households at a Pareto optimal allocation. If we let p^0 denote the relative price of good 1 faced by both consumers in general equilibrium, then

$$p^0 x_1^0 + x_2^0 < p^0 x_1 + x_2$$

for any other (x_1, x_2) in the Scitovsky set. That is, the aggregate expenditure needed to obtain the utility distribution resulting from a given allocation is minimized at the equilibrium relative price. Finally, and importantly, there can be many (under divisibility and continuity assumptions there can be infinitely many) CICs passing through a given point in output space. Each CIC represents a different allocation of the given endowment along the contract curve. For example, we can draw the CIC through (x_2, x_1) corresponding to an allocation other than x^e (e.g. x^g) on the contract curve of figure 3.2. This CIC, denoted CIC(x^g) in figure 3.4, will have a slope equal to the common MRS at point G in figure 3.2. Only under quite restrictive assumptions will a single CIC pass through each aggregate output point. These conditions correspond to the 'aggregation' conditions for aggregate household demand functions.[2]

3 Economic Efficiency in a Production Economy

We now consider an economy where the households are endowed with primary resources (called inputs or factors) rather than final products. These factors can be transformed into final goods according to a production technology. In general, a production technology permits a large number of different possible output combinations to be produced from a given endowment of factors. The conditions (3.1) considered in section 2 are only conditions for a Pareto optimal allocation of a *particular* aggregate output point. With production there are many such points! For this reason we shall no longer call these conditions the Pareto optimal conditions (we shall reserve this term for a broader set of conditions) and shall now refer to them as conditions for *efficient exchange.*

For simplicity, we shall assume that the households own the factors of production directly. Suppose there are two factors, labour L and materials M, and assume that Alice owns an endowment (L^a, M^a) while Bob owns (L^b, M^b). In order to consume commodities they hire out factors to the productive entities (the firms) which produce goods 1 and 2 according to neoclassical production functions $F_1(L_1, M_1)$ and $F_2(L_2, M_2)$ respectively, where L_i is the amount of labour's services and M_i is materials used in producing good i. The production function of a good can be represented by an *isoquant map* as shown in figure 3.5, where the quantity of labour services used in producing good i is measured on the vertical axis and the quantity of materials used in producing good i is measured on the horizontal axis. Each isoquant represents the quantities of labour services and materials needed to produce a given number of units of the output. The absolute value of the slope of an isoquant at any point is called the marginal rate of technical substitution (MRTS$_i$) between the factors used in producing the commodity i. The marginal product of factor f in

---

[2] The aggregation conditions are that all households face the same prices, have linear Engel's curves for all goods and that the Engel's curves of all households are parallel.

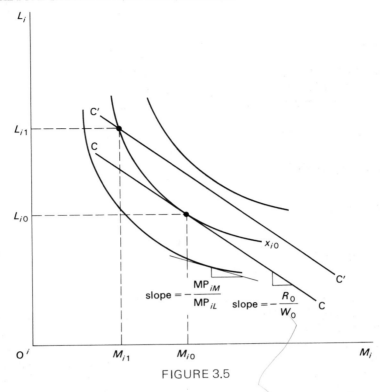

FIGURE 3.5

producing good i, which is denoted MP_{if}, is equal to the partial derivative of the production function $F_i(\ )$ with respect to factor f. That is,

$$MP_{iM} = \partial F_i / \partial M_i$$

$MRTS_i$ is equal to the ratio MP_{iM}/MP_{iL}.[3] As shown in figure 3.5, it is assumed that this ratio decreases as M_i increases so that the isoquants are convex.

The firm is assumed to maximize its economic profits, given the factor and output prices that it faces in the market, and given its production technology. That is, the representative firm i (we assume the representative firm can be named by the output it produces) maximizes profit π where

$$\pi_i = p_i x_i - WL_i - RM_i$$

[3] The definition of an isoquant is given by $F_i(L_i, M_i) = x_i$, where x_i is a fixed level of output. Totally differentiating yields $MP_{iL}\ dL_i + MP_{iM}\ dM_i = 0$, which can be rearranged to obtain:

$$\frac{dL_i}{dM_i}\bigg|_{dx_i=0} = -\frac{MP_{iM}}{MP_{iL}} = -MRTS_i$$

and

$$x_i = F_i(L_i, M_i)$$

W is the price of a unit of labour services and R is the price of a unit of materials. By substitution we can eliminate x_i from the definition of profits and the firm's problem can be expressed as:

$$\max_{L_i, M_i} p_i F_i(L_i, M_i) - WL_i - RM_i$$

The first-order conditions are:[4]

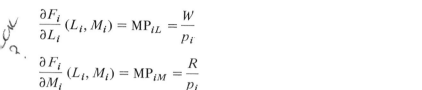

$$\frac{\partial F_i}{\partial L_i}(L_i, M_i) = \mathrm{MP}_{iL} = \frac{W}{p_i} \qquad (3.2a)$$

$$\frac{\partial F_i}{\partial M_i}(L_i, M_i) = \mathrm{MP}_{iM} = \frac{R}{p_i} \qquad (3.2b)$$

These conditions can be solved for the factor demand functions $L_i(p_i, W, R)$ and $M_i(p_i, W, R)$ by firm i. Substituting these demands into the production function $F_i(\ )$ yields the *output supply function* $x_i(p_i, W, R)$. These functions are homogeneous of degree zero in prices, so we can divide through by a *numéraire* price or price index and express the functions in terms of relative prices. Finally we can substitute the optimal values of x_i, L_i and M_i into the definition of profits to get the *profit function*. The derivatives of the profit function with respect to p_i, W and R yield the output supply and factor demand functions by *Hotelling's lemma*. (See a more complete discussion of this in Diewert, 1974.)

Of particular importance is the combination of factors chosen by a profit maximizing firm to produce a given level of output. A profit maximizing firm will seek to produce its output by methods that minimize its costs of production. That is, the profit maximization problem is analytically separable into two subproblems: first, find the cost minimizing combination of factors for producing any given output level, and secondly, produce the output level that maximizes profit. The cost minimizing factor combination is chosen by the firm if the marginal cost of increasing its output by a unit is the same for all factors. For example, the marginal cost of producing an extra unit of output by adding a unit of labour is W/MP_{iL}. $1/\mathrm{MP}_{iL}$ is the amount of labour that must be added to an extra unit of output and W is the cost of an extra unit of labour. The firm is cost minimizing only if

$$W/\mathrm{MP}_{iL} = R/\mathrm{MP}_{iM} \qquad (3.3)$$

otherwise the firm could reduce its total costs by adding more of the

[4] The second-order conditions require the strict concavity (i.e. diminishing returns to scale) of the production function.

factor that permits production at the (relatively) low marginal cost and simultaneously reducing its use of the factor with high marginal cost.

In figure 3.5, the cost minimizing factor combination for a firm facing factor prices W_0 and R_0 is shown. The firm produces x_{i0} units of output using L_{i0} units of labour and M_{i0} units of materials. This occurs at the point where the x_{i0} isoquant is tangent to the lowest possible isocost line (labelled CC) which has a slope with absolute value R_0/W_0. At any other factor combination (e.g. L_{i1} and M_{i1}) the costs of producing the output level x_{i0} are higher, as indicated by the isocost line $C'C'$. Thus the necessary condition for cost minimization is that the absolute value of the slope of the isoquant equals the input price ratio, or

$$\text{MRTS}_i = \frac{\text{MP}_{iM}}{\text{MP}_{iL}} = \frac{R}{W} \qquad (3.3')$$

Clearly (3.3') is just a rearrangement of condition (3.3).

The second stage of the firm's profit maximization problem is to choose an output level where the (common) marginal cost is equal to the output price. That is, $p_i = \text{MC}_i = W/\text{MP}_{iL} = R/\text{MP}_{iM}$. The conditions (3.2a) and (3.2b) incorporate both of the conditions that price equals marginal cost and that MRTS_i equals relative factor prices.

We can now analyse the general equilibrium conditions for efficient production in the two-household, two-factor and two-good case. In figure 3.6 we have constructed an Edgeworth box diagram by inverting the production diagram for the representative firm producing good 2. The dimensions of the box are equal to the total factor endowments owned by the households, with the endowment of materials $M = M^a + M^b$ measured on the horizontal axis and the endowment of labour's services $L = L^a + L^b$ measured on the vertical axis. We have assumed that the entire endowments of the households are made available to the firms and are fully employed. Variable factor supplies could be introduced without materially changing our results, as could the existence of produced factors such as intermediate goods and the services of durable capital. We exclude these complications to simplify the exposition.

Any point in the Edgeworth box represents an allocation of the factors to the production of the two commodities. Efficient factor allocations are those for which it is not possible to increase the output of one commodity without reducing the output of another. Point F in the box is not a point of production efficiency because production of both commodities can be increased by choosing a point in the lens-shaped area formed by the two isoquants x_1^0 and x_2^0. The allocations which are efficient in this sense are those on the contract curve O^1EO^2. At any point such as E on this locus, the isoquants for the two goods are tangent. This implies that

$$\frac{\text{MP}_{1M}}{\text{MP}_{1L}} = \frac{\text{MP}_{2M}}{\text{MP}_{2L}} \qquad (3.4)$$

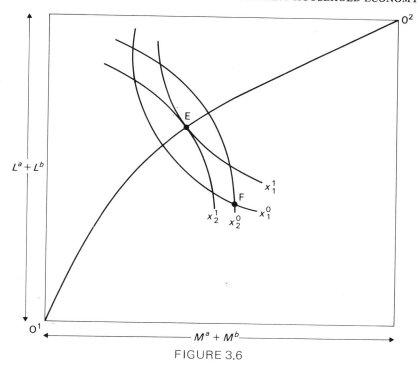

FIGURE 3.6

As stated earlier, and as can be seen from the contract locus, a given endowment of factors makes possible, in general, a large number of (in this case, infinite) possible output combinations. It it useful to express this relationship explicitly in output space. In figure 3.7 we measure the output of good 1 on the horizontal axis and good 2 on the vertical axis. Reading off the output levels from the isoquants in figure 3.6, we can translate the contract curve into the *production possibilities curve* (PPC) labelled PP in figure 3.7. The PPC, also known as the transformation curve, bounds the set of all feasible output combinations that can be produced from the given factor endowments. The points on the PPC are points of efficient (and full employment) production and dominate interior points because more of some commodity and no less of others can be obtained by producing on the PPC.

Unlike the analogous utility possibilities set we have assumed that the production possibilities set is convex (strictly so in figure 3.7). This is because we can make plausible and verifiable assumptions about the production functions, namely non-increasing returns to scale and different factor intensities in each production sector, that will ensure this property. The slope of the PPC has an important interpretation. Suppose we imagine increasing the production of good 2 along the PPC by transferring a unit of labour services out of good 1 production and into good 2 production. Good 2 production rises by $dx_2 = MP_{2L} \, dL_2$, and good 1 produc-

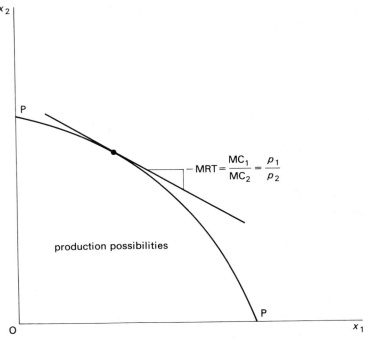

FIGURE 3.7

tion falls by $dx_1 = -MP_{1L}\,dL_2$ since $dL_1 = -dL_2$. The absolute value of the term

$$\left.\frac{dx_2}{dx_1}\right|_{dL_1 = -dL_2} = -MP_{1L}/MP_{2L}$$

can be called the *marginal rate of transformation* (MRT) for labour services (MRT_L). It represents the marginal rate at which one good can be transformed into another by reallocating the supply of labour in production. We also have the MRT_M of materials equal to MP_{2M}/MP_{1M} and similarly for any other factors that may exist. From the conditions (3.4) it is easily seen that for movements between efficient production points along the contract locus, MRT_L equals MRT_M and this common MRT is the absolute slope of the PPC.

By multiplying and dividing MP_{2L}/MP_{1L} by W we see that the MRT is also equal to the ratio of marginal costs MC_1/MC_2. Moreover, because profit maximizing firms set price equal to marginal cost, we obtain $MRT = p_1/p_2$; that is, the absolute value of the slope of the PPC at any point is equal to the relative output prices faced by the producers. Finally, note that the value of output is maximized on the boundary. Let p^*

denote the relative price of x_1 and x_2 faced by firms. Then at the point (x_1^*, x_2^*) where $MRT(x_1^*, x_2^*) = p^*$, the following condition is met:

$$p^* x_1^* + x_2^* > p^* x_1 + x_2$$

for any other (x_1, x_2) in the production possibilities set. Thus, profit maximizing firms maximize national product at the prices they face.

✕ The conditions for efficient production and efficient exchange do not complete the Pareto optimal conditions, as shown in figure 3.8. Point F is on the PPC and therefore corresponds to an efficient allocation of factors. It is also on the frontier of the Scitovsky set (the CIC), implying efficient exchange. It is not a Pareto optimal point because the MRT (the slope of the PPC) is not equal to the MRS (the slope of the CIC). This inequality would occur if producers and consumers faced different relative prices (perhaps due to excise taxes or some other type of output market distortion). It is easy to see why point F is not Pareto optimal. By definition an output point such as G on the CIC through F can be found that can be allocated so that all households are indifferent between G and F. But G lies in the interior of the PPC. Thus there exist points such as E that are feasible and in the interior of the Scitovsky set. At point E there is more of every good than at point G. Therefore there exist allocations of E that are Pareto superior to G and, consequently, to F. ▮

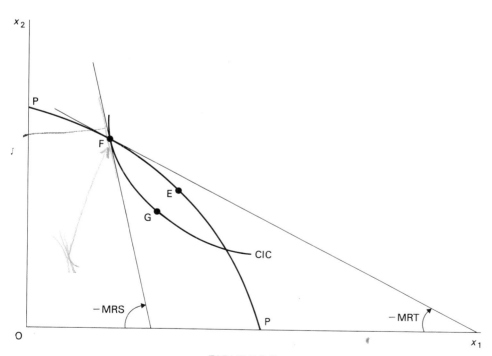

FIGURE 3.8

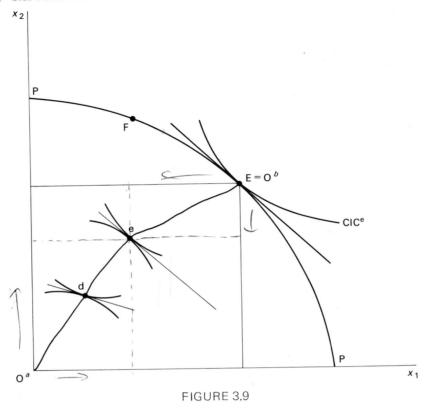

FIGURE 3.9

Figures 3.9 and 3.10 are used to illustrate Pareto optimality in a production economy. Point E in figure 3.9 is a point of efficient production
and exchange and is also a competitive general equilibrium. We can
construct the exchange Edgeworth box with origin O^b at E as shown. The
equilibrium factor prices, along with the distribution of factor ownership and some arbitrary means of distributing pure profits, if any,
determine a distribution of income across households. Output prices and
the income distribution determine the allocation of the output bundle
between Alice and Bob as allocation labelled e, where the common MRS
of the households is equal to the common MRT of the factors in production. For this allocation of goods we can construct the CIC^e bounding the
Scitovsky set. It is tangent to the PPC at E. Note that we can draw a line
tangent to the PPC and the CIC^e which separates the two sets. This line,
which is called a *separating line* (or, with N commodities, a separating
hyperplane) has a slope with an absolute value that is equal to the relative
price of good 1 to good 2. The fact that all production points lie below
the separating line means that competitive firms cannot increase profit
beyond that at output E. The fact that all points in the interior of the
Scitovsky set lie above the separating line means that no utility increasing

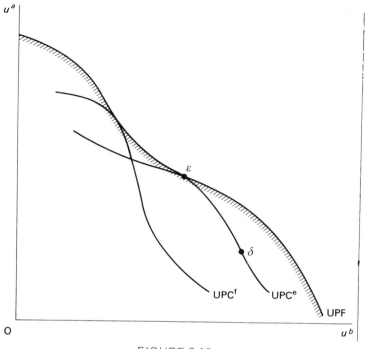

FIGURE 3.10

Pareto improvements are possible for consumers. Thus E is a Pareto optimal equilibrium. Note that a separating line cannot be drawn at point F in figure 3.8.

Corresponding to the contract curve in figure 3.9 is a utility possibilities curve labelled UPC^e in figure 3.10. In fact, for every production point on the PPC we can construct a contract curve and a corresponding UPC. The envelope of the UPC forms the *utility possibilities frontier* (UPF) (sometimes referred to as the grand UPC). The UPF consists of points such as ϵ in figure 3.10. An allocation such as d in figure 3.9 would map to a point such as δ in figure 3.10 on the interior of the set bounded by the UPF. The absolute slope of the UPF is equal to the ratio of the marginal utility of income of household a to that of household b, since it is everywhere tangent to a UPC.

In brief, the UPF bounds all of the utility distributions that can be achieved for the given endowment of factors. Points on the UPF itself correspond to Pareto optimal states. For a state to be Pareto optimal the following three sets of conditions must be set:

Efficient exchange

$$\frac{\partial u^h/\partial x_i^h}{\partial u^h/\partial x_j^h} = \frac{\partial u^g/\partial x_i^g}{\partial u^g/\partial x_j^g} = \text{MRS}_{ij}$$

for all households h and g and all goods i and j;

$$\sum_{h=1}^{H} x_i^h = x_i$$

for all goods i.

Efficient allocation of factors

$$\frac{\partial F_i/\partial M_i}{\partial F_j/\partial M_j} = \frac{\partial F_i/\partial L_i}{\partial F_j/\partial L_j} = \mathrm{MRT}_{ij}$$

for all factors M and L and all goods i and j;

$$x_i = F_i(L_i, M_i, \ldots)$$

for all goods i and

$$\sum_{i=1}^{N} L_i = \sum_{h=1}^{H} L^h$$

for all inputs L.

Efficient output choice

$$\mathrm{MRS}_{ij} = \mathrm{MRT}_{ij}$$

for all goods i and j.

It should be stressed that these conditions are *necessary* conditions for an interior Pareto optimal allocation only. With the further assumption that the Scitovsky and the production possibility sets are convex (as shown in figure 3.9) these conditions are also sufficient for Pareto optimality.

Although we cannot prove rigorously the two basic theorems of welfare economics within this diagrammatic framework, we can illustrate them. The first theorem states that any competitive general equilibrium will be Pareto optimal – that is, it will yield a distribution of utilities on the UPF. At a competitive general equilibrium, there will be an input/output price vector that clears the factor and output markets. All households face the same relative prices of the goods they consume and, in maximizing utility, they equate their MRS to the common relative prices. Thus, the conditions of efficient exchange are met. Profit maximizing firms hire factors so as to minimize production costs by equating MRTS_i to the relative factor prices as in (3.3'). By rearrangement this yields the conditions for the efficient allocation of factors. Finally, by facing households and firms with the same price vector, the condition for efficient output choice is met, since firms choose output so as to equate price to marginal cost.

Although allocation (E, e, ϵ) is Pareto optimal, it is one among many on the UPF. The second theorem states that every Pareto optimal point on the UPF can be reached by a competitive general equilibrium for some distribution of factor ownership and pure profits. That is, for any point on the UPF we can construct a Scitovsky set that will be tangent to the production possibilities set. The tangency point corresponds to a competitive general equilibrium conditional on a distribution of factor ownership that yields the particular utility distribution on the UPF.

Finally, note that if households have parallel and linear income expansion curves the contract curve coincides with the diagonal of the Edgeworth box. Then there will be a unique CIC independent of the distribution of factor ownership and a unique output point corresponding to every point on the UPF (which is itself coincident with a UPC). This case is illustrated in figure 3.11. This case is useful in welfare economics since general equilibrium can be illustrated with a PPC and a map of nonintersecting CICs (referred to as a community preference field). Moreover, in the algebraic formulation of the problem, Pareto optimality corresponds to maximizing the utility of a *representative household* subject to feasibility constraints. The same procedure can be used if HHs are identical in all respects.

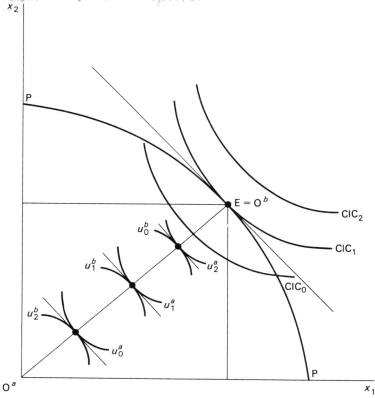

FIGURE 3.11

bility constraints. The same procedure can be used if households are identical in all respects.

4 The Relevance of Pareto Optimality in Welfare Economics

The Pareto criterion allows us to rank many states of the economy (a state now corresponds to both an allocation of inputs into production and an allocation of outputs among consumers) as inferior on social welfare grounds because other states dominate them in utility terms by allowing some or all households to be better off while making none worse off. The criterion can be used to identify the Pareto optimal set of states as the proper subset of the set of all feasible states which cannot be dominated by other feasible states. Necessary and sufficient conditions for a state to be Pareto optimal can be found. Finally, the two basic theorems provide a two-way link between the set of Pareto optimal states and the set of resource allocations outcomes of perfect competition. Although this sounds impressive, some economists such as Sen (1975) argue that these results do not warrant the emphasis they have been given in welfare economics. In this section we briefly assess the relevance (or irrelevance) of Pareto optimality and the basic theorems to welfare economics.

The primary relevance of the basic theorems relates to the social welfare consequences of the market mechanism. The idea that a market system, utilized by households and firms who pursue their own objectives, provides a decentralized method of resource allocation with desirable consequences for social welfare, predates the Paretian notions of social welfare and the modern concepts of general equilibrium. It is, in fact, the central theme in Adam Smith's *Wealth of Nations* (1776). But the modern basic theorems go far beyond the 'invisible hand' aphorism of Adam smith by defining precisely the sense in which the market outcome is desirable, the conditions that the market outcome must satisfy, and the circumstances under which the market will satisfy them. Our discussion will focus on these conditions and circumstances.

First of all we must emphasize that the two basic theorems are very different in terms of their welfare implications. Moreover, the conditions under which they hold are also different. The first (or direct) theorem is *descriptive* in that it describes the welfare consequences of a well-defined market system in accordance with a well-defined welfare criterion. It is the modern counterpart to Adam Smith's invisible hand theorem. Its main conclusion is that, within an ideal market institution, a set of relative price signals can lead a multitude of agents, all pursuing their own selfish interest without regard to the 'social good', to make decisions that lead to an allocation of resources which is socially desirable according to the Pareto criterion.

The relevance of this conclusion lies in the relevance of Pareto optimality and in the likelihood that any real world market mechanism does or can be made to satisfy the assumptions required for the theorem to hold. We have not yet made all of the assumptions underlying the direct theorem explicit. In addition to the assumption of price-taking behaviour by all market agents who face the same prices, it is assumed that households maximize utility and firms maximize economic profit. It is also assumed that no household is satiated within a small neighbourhood of its consumption point for the allocation in question. Most importantly, it is assumed that there are no externalities or non-market dependencies among the decisions of the households and firms of the types discussed in chapter 4. This rules out empathy and envy among the households and technological externalities in production among firms and between firms and households. The first theorem does not depend on convexity in production or preferences because the question of the existence of a general equilibrium is begged. To be sure that a competitive general equilibrium exists, however, convexity assumptions are needed.

The limitations of the first theorem are obvious. Even if we grant the assumptions about the market mechanism necessary for it to hold, the Pareto optimal state attained is just one among many. If we go beyond the Pareto criterion and exclude states with extreme disparity in utility, we cannot be sure that the competitive general equilibrium will correspond to a state within the desirable subset of Pareto optimal states. Moreover, for numerous reasons any actual market mechanism is unlikely to conform to the idealized market mechanism enshrined in the perfectly competitive model. Deviations of actual markets from ideal markets are sometimes referred to as 'market failures' and will be dealt with in chapter 4. In some cases the markets will actually fail to exist such as in the case of public goods or state-contingent commodities. In other cases, the markets will exist but they will be 'imperfect' because of distortions such as taxes, monopoly rents, externalities etc.

The second theorem of welfare economics is sometimes described as being of 'deeper significance' to the study of welfare economics. It states that any Pareto optimal state can be supported by a perfectly competitive general equilibrium for some distribution of factor ownership or lump-sum redistribution of factor income. The second theorem is *prescriptive* in that it states that a desired distribution of utility can be, but is not necessarily, achieved by an institutional mechanism which satisfies a precise set of conditions. For this reason, the second theorem permits the Pareto optimal conditions to be utilized as a 'reform programme', and it can be used as such by socialists as well as free marketeers, as evident in the work of Lange (1938) and Lerner (1944). It does, however, have special significance for the efficacy of the decentralized market system. It implies that, ideally, the government can be limited to a redistributive rather than a planning or allocative role in the economy. Allocative decisions by the government need only be made when there are bona fide cases of market failure.

Unlike the direct theorem, the converse theorem requires that the production set and the Scitovsky set be strictly and globally convex. If not, a separating line may not exist. This is discussed in chapter 4.

The relevance of the second theorem lies in the hope, first, that the market economy is sufficiently close to the ideal competitive institution described; secondly, that lump-sum (i.e. costless) redistribution of claims on commodities is possible; and thirdly, that the convexity assumptions are satisfied around desired Pareto optimal allocations. In this case, the role of the government can be relegated to a redistribution function and the myriad of allocative decisions can be left to the market place.

As we shall see in the next chapter, there are good reasons for doubting that any of these hopes will be completely realized. The market economy is imperfect, redistribution imposes social costs by distorting incentives, and non-convexities are likely to be present in some production processes. In this case, the relevance of the converse theorem is largely a matter of belief and ideology ranging from the Chicago view that, for most purposes, the real world institutions approximate the ideal structure in terms of outcome (see Reder, 1982), to the Sen (1975) view that the converse theorem implies nothing whatsoever about the efficacy of the market system as compared to a Lange (1938) and Lerner (1944) type market socialism.

We shall return to the relevance of Pareto optimality and the fundamental theorems in chapter 4.

5 Extending the Fundamental Theorems

The two fundamental theorems of welfare economics were illustrated above in a very special setting. The setting was a simple one consisting of two households, two goods and two factors; the equilibria were strictly interior, with production of each good using both factors and households consuming both goods; the setting was static, excluding durability of goods and factors and intertemporal tradeoffs by the households; and the setting was one of certainty, with all prices and the consequences of the households' and firms' actions known. The question we wish to address in this section is, 'Do the fundamental theorems still hold when we generalize the setting?'.

The setting can be generalized to include as many goods, factors and households as desired provided that the number of households is finite. The number of efficiency conditions increases but the meaning of them is the same as that derived from the geometric intuition of the two-factor, two-good and two-household setting. Also, the assumption of interior equilibria, and the assumption of differentiability required by such equilibria, can be dispensed with. Arrow (1951b) has proved the two fundamental theorems with arbitrary numbers of commodities and economic agents using only the properties of point sets, such as the production and Scitovsky sets, in linear space. Such a proof allows for 'corner solutions' which would occur if, as is likely, some household does not consume every commodity or if the production or Scitovsky set contains 'kinks'. When corner solutions are permitted, the conditions for Pareto optimality cannot be expressed solely in terms of equalities but, rather, require that certain inequalities hold at the corners. We have considered the equalities implied by interior solutions because such solutions are 'cleaner' and more easily explained. Nothing of substance is lost by this assumption.

Generalizing the fundamental theorems to an intertemporal and uncertain setting does raise some additional issues, so we consider each in turn.

5.1 *The fundamental theorems in an intertemporal setting*

The extension of the fundamental theorems to an intertemporal setting where agents (i.e. firms and households) make decisions within a finite time decision horizon is relatively straightforward. One simply 'dates' commodities and factors and treats a commodity (factor) at different times as a different commodity (factor). Provided that the decision horizon and the number of agents is finite, this simply increases the (finite) dimensions of the setting but leaves the analysis essentially unchanged.

It is useful to consider a simple intertemporal setting in order to understand the implications of the fundamental theorems when applied to such a setting. Assume that a single good is consumed by two households during two periods. Let x_t^h denote consumption of the single good by household h in period t. Intertemporal exchange efficiency is illustrated in figure 3.12, where the dimensions of the Edgeworth box represent the total endowment of the good available in the first period (horizontal) and in the second period (vertical). The contract curve, along which the MRS between first- and second-period consumption of Alice equals that of Bob, consists of all allocations of the given endowment which are exchange efficient. Along this curve it is not possible to raise the consumption of any household in any period without the consumption of some household in some period being reduced.

Given the initial allocation, a competitive general equilibrium and an associated relative price of period one and period two consumption exists such that Alice and Bob trade to reach an allocation on the contract curve. In the two-period context, the relative price is equal to one plus the one-period real interest rate. A real interest rate is one expressed in terms of a *numéraire* good (rather than in money terms). In the diagram, Alice 'lends' some of her claims on first-period consumption to Bob who repays her $1 + r$ units of goods in the second period for each unit received.

As in the static case, the contract curve can be represented alternatively by a utility possibilities curve which bounds the feasible utility distributions made possible by the existing endowment. Note that a utility point describes a distribution of lifetime utility levels of Alice and Bob and not their utilities in a particular time period. Also, as in the static case, any point on the UPC can be mapped into a community indifference

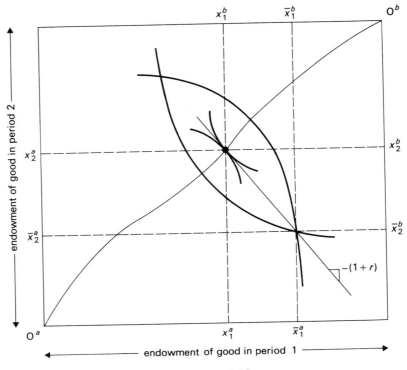

FIGURE 3.12

curve drawn with aggregate first-period consumption on one axis and aggregate second-period consumption on the other.

We can extend the analogy further and identify conditions of inter-temporal production efficiency. Non-perishable factors may be used up in producing first-period consumption or saved and used in producing second-period consumption. Production efficiency requires that any two factors be allocated between first- and second-period production so that their MRTS in each period be equal. An issue that arises in the inter-temporal setting concerns the fact that capital factors are not only durable but are, themselves, produced by a production process in the manner that intermediate products are in the static setting. As a result, it is possible to use productive capacity in the first period to produce investment goods which augment or replace existing capital for production in the second period.

Suppose, in our simple case, that the single good is produced using capital and labour, and that the output in period t, denoted q_t, can be consumed in the first period or added to the capital stock ('invested') and used for producing output in the next period. Assuming labour is non-durable and the endowment of labour in each period is fixed, we can

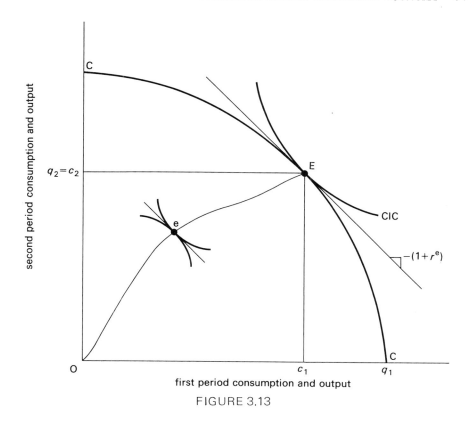

FIGURE 3.13

subsume the labour input into the form of the production function and express the production technology by:

$$q_1 = F_1(k_1) \tag{3.5}$$
$$q_2 = c_2 = F_2(k_2 + q_1 - c_1) \tag{3.6}$$

Here k_t is the endowment of capital at time t, q_t is output produced, c_t is output consumed at time t, and $F_t(\ )$ is the production function at time t.[5] Because of diminishing returns, $F_t''(\ ) < 0$. Substituting (3.5) into (3.6) yields the consumption possibilities curve (CPC) labelled CC in figure 3.13, which can be expressed as:

$$c_2 = F_2(k_2 + F_1(k_1) - c_1)$$

Since $F_2'' < 0$, the CPC is concave as shown in figure 3.13.

The absolute value of the slope of the CPC is the MRT. Assuming capital is productive, MRT > 1 somewhere along the CPC. Firms faced

---

[5] Generally, k_2 is equal to the undepreciated stock of capital remaining from the first period.

with a given real interest rate r will maximize the present value of their real profits by choosing a level of output such that $MRT = 1 + r$. In this case the present value of the discounted national expenditure $c_1 + (1/1 + r) c_2$ is maximized over the (c_1, c_2) combinations available along the CPC. Output produced but not consumed in the first period is retained within the community of firms as investment.

A competitive general equilibrium is illustrated in figure 3.13. As in the static case, the interior of the Scitovsky set (the set of potentially Pareto preferred consumption vectors) is separated from the consumption possibilities set by a tangent line which has a slope with an absolute value equal to the relative price of the two activities; in this case, the relative price is one plus the equilibrium real interest rate r^e. At this price, the desired saving by the utility maximizing households (who have claims on the entire product) is just sufficient to finance the desired borrowing for investment by the profit maximizing firms. In addition, households borrow and lend among themselves so as to equate their MRS between period one and two consumption to $1 + r^e$. The equilibrium allocation of period one and two consumption between Alice and Bob lies on the contract curve inside the exchange Edgeworth box constructed at the equilibrium values of aggregate first- and second-period consumption. A lifetime–utility distribution on the utility possibilities frontier is reached, so the equilibrium is Pareto optimal. Finally, because of the convexity of the consumption possibilities and Scitovsky sets, any point on the utility possibilities frontier can be reached by a competitive market general equilibrium.

The intertemporal efficiency of the competitive market mechanism can be extended to the case of many time periods, goods, factors and households. Two problems arise in generalizing it to the multidimensional case. The first concerns the informational requirements of the fundamental theorems. Because agents must equate various marginal rates of substitution/transformation by means of relative prices observed in a market, they must be able to undertake contracts allowing them to exchange, at a known price, a haircut now for x litres of ice cream next summer. This can be accomplished by assuming that there exists a complete set of spot and forward markets in all commodities. Alternatively it can be assumed that only spot markets exist (at least for most commodities) and that agents know prices in all spot markets plus the (term structure of) real interest rates on assets that act as stores of value. In this case the relative price of a haircut in terms of ice cream next summer is equal to the spot price of a haircut now multiplied by one plus the real interest rate on an asset held between now and next summer, divided by the spot price of a litre of ice cream next summer. This obviates the need for forward markets but requires that the agents have knowledge of prices in all spot markets.

The second problem is encountered in generalizing the fundamental theorems to many periods. Provided that the time dimension of the setting is finite there is no problem. In this case, economic decisions do not have to extend beyond some finite time horizon T. Since there is no natural interpretation that can be given to T for an economy (even though the decision-makers may have a finite life), it is useful to consider whether the finite horizon assumption can be relaxed. It turns out that the assumption that the world ends at some finite time T is usually necessary for the fundamental theorems to hold. It is instructive to consider the reasons for this requirement.

Suppose the economy does end at some known and finite time T. Then agents who will be alive the instant before will arrange to have used up any durable goods and factors by that time so that nothing is wasted. Let k_t be the stock of durable capital at time t that can be held for future production or 'eaten', and let p_t be its relative value (say, in units of leisure). If the world ends at time T then efficiency requires that $D_T p_T k_T = 0$, where D_t is a discount factor. In other words, $k_T = 0$ (all durable capital is eaten) or $p_T = 0$ (all durable capital is worthless) at Doomsday, otherwise some household could consume more in some period with no household consuming less in any period. The condition $D_T p_T k_T = 0$ is known technically as a *transversality condition*. It means Doomsday will be efficient if nothing else. We can imagine pushing time T further and further into the future, and nothing is changed providing T is finite. But if T is unbounded, the correspondence between competitive equilibria and Pareto optimality is broken.

Two related 'market inefficiencies' that occur when $T = \infty$ have been identified. In a classic paper, Malinvaud (1953) argued that producers may overaccumulate durable capital in the infinite time horizon setting. Specifically, the so-called transversality condition requires that the discounted value of the capital stock vanish at infinity either because the capital stock is used up or because the price of capital goods rises more slowly than the discount factor D_t vanishes as $t \to \infty$. That is, $D_T p_T k_T$ must go to zero as T becomes indefinitely large. If not, the firm can arrange to 'sell off' a unit of capital at infinity (i.e. never) and profit (and the consumption of some household) can be raised in some (or every) period. This violates the definition of intertemporal economic efficiency.

As Malinvaud pointed out, nowhere do market prices induce producers with finite life to make decisions that ensure that the condition will be satisfied. If $T = \infty$, there is an infinite number of producers and each one can 'pass the buck' to another. Unlike the finite time horizon setting there does not exist a latter-day generation of households and firms whose market decisions bring about efficiency at the end. Consequently, private decision-makers may accumulate a stock of durable capital such that the economy has more capital per head than would be needed on the 'golden rule' path.[6] Although every generation could consume more goods (which

---

[6] The 'golden rule' refers to an accumulation rule for which consumption per caput is maximized. This occurs when the marginal product of capital equals the natural rate of growth (the sum of the growth rate of the labour force plus the rate of technical progress). Although it need not be efficient for an economy to follow the golden rule path, it is never efficient to accumulate capital in excess of that accumulated on the golden rule path. For a discussion of this issue, see Burmeister (1980).

D

would be a Pareto improvement) the decentralized decision-making never allows this gain to be realized.

In a celebrated article, Samuelson (1958) demonstrated a related point – that competitive markets do not lead to exchange efficiency in an economy of infinite life populated by individuals of finite life. But, unlike Malinvaud, Samuelson does not require a stock of durable capital for efficiency to be violated. Samuelson considers mortal households who wish to smooth consumption over the earning and non-earning (say, retirement) periods of their lives. To do so, middle-aged households in their peak earning years offer goods to younger households at the present time which are to be repaid when the older households retire. But the outcome of such an exchange process need not be, and in general is not, efficient. To see this consider the case where each household lives for two periods, is endowed with one unit of a single good in each period, and is indifferent between consuming both units in one period or consuming one unit per period. No intertemporal trade will occur and each household consumes its endowment. Nevertheless, the first generation can be made better off without making any other generation worse off if the earning generation in every subsequent period agrees to transfer consumption goods to the retired generation in exchange for a reciprocal transfer when it is retired. With immortal economic institutions, this sort of 'chain letter' or 'Ponzi game' will work because there is never a terminal generation that must pay for the increased consumption of the first generation.

In both the Malinvaud and Samuelson scenarios some household in the economy can increase its consumption in some period(s) without anyone decreasing consumption in any other period. This makes possible a once and for all improvement in the welfare of some generation at the expense of a generation infinitely removed into the future. There is nothing in the decentralized market process which ensures that such an opportunity will be exploited by myopic (finite life) agents. This result has aroused considerable controversy and research which is far too extensive to survey here. However, two points are noteworthy.

Firstly, the inefficiency may not occur if it is assumed that the economy is populated with decision-makers of infinite life who peer into the indefinite future and make decisions which ensure that the market prices satisfy the transversality conditions. This assumption is unrealistic when applied to mortal households but is plausible when applied to 'immortal' firms or to 'dynastic' households who care about their immediate heirs, who in turn care about their immediate heirs, and so on.

Secondly, under certain circumstances, the exchange inefficiency of the Samuelson overlapping generations model can be eliminated by introducing a fiat asset. In this case, the young generation acquires socially costless pieces of paper that have value only because the next generation is willing to surrender goods and services for them as an asset to hold for its own retirement. As long as every generation plays this game, as everybody does in an economy with fiat money or government debt, the link between optimality and competitive markets may be restored.

5.2 *The fundamental theorems in an uncertain setting*

The fundamental theorems can be extended to an economy that is subject to event (or 'technological') uncertainty. As discussed in chapter 2, section 6, this occurs when the objective of the decision-maker (the consequences) depends not only on its actions but also on external events, which can be described by the 'state of the world' parameter s. In this case a commodity can be identified not only by type and date but also by the unknown environmental conditions under which it is consumed. Thus, x_{its} denotes the consumption of a commodity of type i at time t in state of the world s.

The conditions of exchange efficiency will be satisfied if utility maximizing households can engage in trade in a competitive market in *state-contingent claims* on the commodities. That is, a relative price exists for every commodity distinguished not only by type and date but also by the state of the world. Such a contract would involve the payment of the price by the household in every state of the world for the delivery of the commodity which takes place only in the specified state of the world.

To simplify matters, suppose there is a single commodity, a single time period, two states of the world and two households. Exchange efficiency can be illustrated in figure 3.14 using the Edgeworth box with

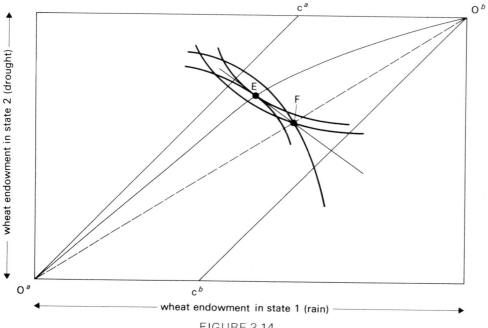

FIGURE 3.14

dimensions equal to the state-contingent endowment of the good (say wheat). The amount of wheat available in state 1 (say rain) is measured on the horizontal axis and the amount in state 2 (say drought) is measured on the vertical axis. Risk-averse households, Alice and Bob, have indifference curves of the usual shape which yield a contract curve $O^a EO^b$. $O^a C^a$ and $O^b C^b$ are the certainty ($45°$) lines of Alice and Bob, respectively.

Given some initial claims on wheat in each state (for example, the crop-sharing point F on the diagonal where both households get fixed shares of the total amount of wheat produced regardless of the state of the world), there exists a relative price of wheat in state 1 to wheat in state 2, given by the absolute value of the slope of the line FE, such that Alice and Bob exchange claims on the commodity in each state to reach the equilibrium allocation E. This point lies on the contract curve, indicating that there is a Pareto efficient sharing of the risk. Note that if there were no social risk, and thus the endowment was certain (i.e. the Edgeworth box is square in figure 3.14), then Alice and Bob could always arrange, through competitive markets, to consume a certain consumption bundle even if their initial endowment is uncertain. More generally, the 'full' insurance equilibrium will not be chosen, even with complete markets, but existing risk will be shared in a manner such that no household can be made better off without some other being made worse off.

As in previous cases, we can represent the contract curve in utility space by a utility possibilities curve. Also, each point on the UPC can be used to derive a CIC between state 1 and state 2 consumption.

This analysis can be generalized to many types of goods, states of the world and households provided that there exists a price for the delivery of each type of good contingent on each state of the world. This market for contingent claims on commodities can be duplicated by a market in certainty claims (i.e. non-contingent) on commodities plus a market in state-contingent securities. Security s, which pays the holder a unit of the *numéraire* good in state s and nothing otherwise, can be thought of as an 'insurance policy' against state s. Let p_s denote the price of security s and let $p_i(s)$ be the price of a certainty claim on the commodity which will depend on the state of the world that actually occurs. Then we can always find p_s and $p_i(s)$ so that $p_s p_i(s) = p_{is}$, where p_{is} is the s-contingent claim on a unit of commodity type i. An equilibrium state-contingent price vector $[p_{is}]_{i=1,\ldots,N,\ s=1,\ldots,s}$ can be duplicated by equilibrium price vectors $[p_i(s)]$, $i = 1,\ldots,N$ and $[p_s]$, $s = 1,\ldots,S$ if there exist perfect insurance markets; that is, an insurance policy can be purchased for every contingency.

We can now introduce production considerations. Firms may be able to alter the total amounts of the commodities available in each state. For example, by planting a 'costlier' drought-resistant strain of wheat, firms may alter production so as to achieve a greater wheat output in the drought state at the expense of a smaller wheat output in the rain state. A simplifying assumption we shall make is that of multiplicative uncertainty of production as assumed by Diamond (1967a). In this case we can think of there being a number of 'firms' (production processes actually) that produce according to:

$$q_f = \phi_f(s)\, g_f(k_f)$$

Here q_f is the output of some commodity type by firm f, k_f is a vector of inputs used by firm f, $g_f(\ )$ is a concave production function and $\phi_f(\ ) > 0$ is a multiplicative factor that depends on the state of the world. For a given vector of inputs, the firm produces a 'joint product' with a particular output value for each state of the world realized.

For simplicity, let us assume that there are two firms e and f, two states 1 (rain) and 2 (drought), two inputs m and n and a single commodity type. Firm e plants drought-resistant (rain-intolerant) wheat and firm f plants rain-resistant (drought-intolerant) wheat so $\phi_e(2) > \phi_f(2) \geqslant 0$ and $\phi_f(1) > \phi_e(1) \geqslant 0$. The two inputs are endowed in fixed amounts, so

$$k_{je} + k_{jf} = k_j \qquad j = m, n$$

The two inputs are allocated between the two firms efficiently when the MRTS of inputs m and n are equal for both firms. Note that these are the standard production efficiency conditions which will be satisfied when the firms minimize the factor cost of producing a given state-dependent level of output; that is, the firms need not care about the uncertainty factor in choosing the most efficient combination of inputs. This result is only true in the case of multiplicative uncertainty.

The efficient production conditions determine the convex production possibilities set shown in figure 3.15. If all inputs are used by firm e (firm f), output is $\bar{q}^e$ ($\bar{q}^f$). If the input proportions differ in the two firms and/or there are diminishing returns to scale, the production set will be strictly convex.

Two cases can be considered. The first is one in which there exist state-contingent markets for wheat. Firms maximize profits, defined for firm f as

$$\sum_{s=1}^{S} p_s \phi_f(s)\, g_f(k_f) - w k_f$$

where p_s is the price of a unit of wheat delivered in state s and w is the vector of input prices. Households sell inputs and purchase state-contingent claims on wheat. There exists an equilibrium price vector and a resulting allocation which is Pareto optimal. This is illustrated in figure 3.15. As in the certain economy, there exists a separating line which has a slope with an absolute value equal to the relative price of a claim on wheat in state 1 to a claim in state 2. Assuming convexity in the production and preference sets (the latter requires risk aversion) any such Pareto optimal allocation can be realized by an equilibrium price vector.

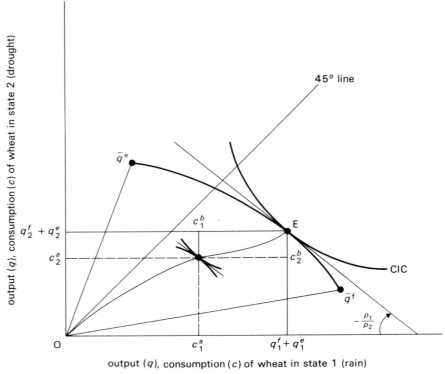

FIGURE 3.15

Alternatively, Diamond (1967a) has shown that the fundamental theorems will also be satisfied in a 'stock market' economy if certain conditions are met. In his model, firms issue shares in *ex post* residual profits (e.g. $\pi_f(s) = \phi_f(s) g_f(k_f) - wk_f$ for firm f in state s). Households are endowed with the ownership of factors and some initial endowment of firms' shares, which are then traded in competitive markets. Factor prices are determined in the usual way. The relative price of a share in firm e to one in firm f is equal to the ratio of the expected utility of a profit share in firm e to the expected utility of a share in firm f by the marginal shareholder. If the number of firms with independent production processes is equal to the number of states (the so-called *spanning* condition) the state-contingent commodity market result is duplicated by the stock market economy.

For example, consider the equilibrium of a household facing a given relative price of shares. In figure 3.16, point G is the certainty claim on wheat resulting from the household's sales of inputs and point E (F) is the claim on wheat in each state if the household holds it endowment of shares solely in firm e (f). By trading shares the household can (assuming

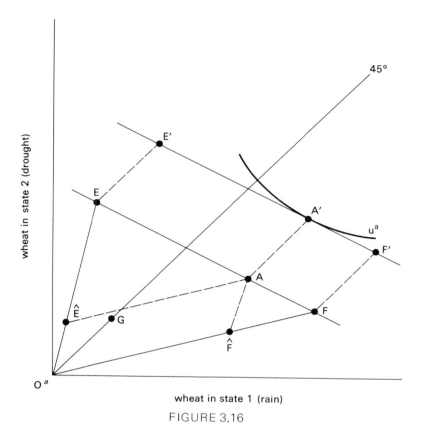

wheat in state 2 (drought)

wheat in state 1 (rain)

FIGURE 3.16

that short sales of shares are possible) reach any point on budget line E'F' which has a slope with an absolute value equal to the relative price of the shares. The household then maximizes utility at point A'. Using the parallelogram rule, the equilibrium shareholdings of the household E and F can be found.

Clearly, the relative price of the shares of the two firms plays the same role as does the relative price of wheat in the two states in the complete contingent markets case. Thus, the general equilibrium in figure 3.15 is duplicated. Diamond also shows that if the spanning condition is not met, so that the stock market economy does not duplicate the contingent market economy, the stock market economy still achieves a restricted Pareto optimum. The restriction is that feasible reallocations of goods across households must take place only in terms of the same composite groups of commodities that are possible through trading shares of the firms. Of course, if Pareto optimality is defined in terms of un-restricted reallocations of goods, the stock market economy would not be Pareto optimal without the spanning condition.

6 The Compensation Principle and the Efficiency Criterion

The strength of the Pareto criterion lies in the fact that it does not require the utilities of different households to be compared or 'weighed'. Its weakness lies in the fact that it yields an incomplete ordering. The severity of this weakness is illustrated in figure 3.17, where a Pareto optimal allocation giving rise to utility point E on the utility possibility frontier UPF is compared with an 'inefficient' allocation corresponding to utility point I within the UPF. Since one household is made worse off in moving to the efficient allocation E, the Pareto criterion cannot rank E relative to I. In other words, the Pareto criterion *per se* does not rank every Pareto optimal allocation superior to a non-optimal allocation.

An attempt to overcome this deficiency is generally known as the *compensation principle*, first enunciated by Hicks (1939) and Kaldor (1939). According to this principle, state *a* is preferable to another state if, in state *a*, it is *hypothetically* possible to undertake costless ('lump-sum') redistribution and achieve an allocation that is superior to the other state according to the Pareto criterion. This is the criterion proposed

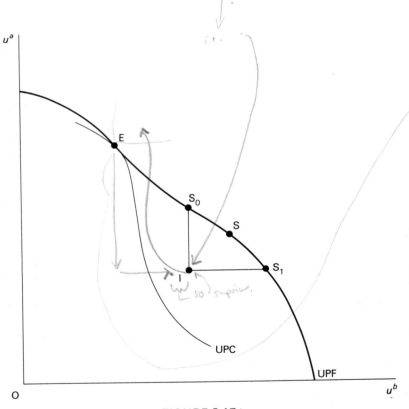

FIGURE 3.17

by Kaldor (1939). Hicks (1939) offered a slightly different criterion – state *a* is preferable to another state if, in the *other* state, it is *not* possible, hypothetically, to carry out lump-sum redistribution so that everyone could be made as well off as in state *a*. For now we shall concentrate on the Kaldor criterion.

There are two versions of the compensation principle itself. The *strong* compensation principle limits the hypothetical redistribution to a re-allocation of the aggregate bundle produced in state *a*. The *weak* compensation principle allows the aggregate bundle of goods produced to change as redistribution occurs in a manner consistent with the production possibilities available in state *a*. In essence, the weak principle conceives of the redistribution being carried out in terms of purchasing power over goods rather than in the goods themselves.

It is apparent from figure 3.17 that the weak compensation principle will always rank a Pareto optimal allocation such as E superior to any allocation that is not Pareto optimal, such as I. Lump-sum redistribution of purchasing power, with the production point varying as needed, would allow any utility point on the UPF to be reached including any points in the range $S_0 S_1$. All such points are preferable to I by the Pareto principle. Note that the strong compensation principle need not rank E above I since the compensation involves redistributing the fixed bundle produced at E along the utility possibility curve (UPC) corresponding to that bundle. The UPC through point E may not lie above I. This case is illustrated in figure 3.17.

From this discussion it is apparent that the weak version of the compensation principle ranks any Pareto optimal allocation above any allocation which is not Pareto optimal, whereas the strong version does not. Moreover, the weak version will rank all pairs of alternatives that the strong test does, but not vice versa; that is, the weak test provides a more complete ranking of social states. For this reason we shall focus the remainder of our discussion on the weak version. At this level the only controversial aspect of the compensation principle is the *hypothetical* and *lump-sum* nature of the redistribution. If the redistribution were actually realized, the entire exercise would be a direct application of the Pareto principle itself. The purpose of considering hypothetical redistribution is to try and separate the *efficiency* and *equity* aspects of the policy change under consideration. It is argued that whether or not the redistribution is actually carried out is an important but *separate* decision. The mere fact that it is possible to create potential Pareto improving redistribution possibilities is enough to rank one state above another on efficiency grounds.

A number of economists have criticized this presumption. Little (1957) has argued that an equity assumption is needed to make the hypothetical compensation principle legitimate. Not only is it necessary to make a Pareto improvement possible (by moving from I to any point S between S_0 and S_1 in figure 3.17), it is also necessary that the implicit redistribution from S to E be equitable. Other economists have attacked the

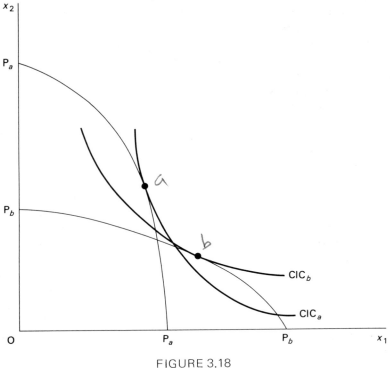

FIGURE 3.18

assumption that the hypothetical redistribution is costless or lump sum. If actual redistribution is costly, then the fact that Pareto improvements can be achieved with lump-sum redistribution seems particularly irrelevant.

Although the weak compensation principle consistently ranks any Pareto optimal allocation above any allocation that is not Pareto optimal, problems arise when the compensation principle is used as a criterion for evaluating any other types of change. Consider the problem of national income measurement. In figure 3.18, some event alters the production possibilities set in the economy from OP_aP_a to OP_bP_b. According to the weak compensation principle, OP_bP_b is superior because it intersects the interior of the initial Scitovsky set CIC_a. This means that it is possible to hypothetically redistribute goods and production so that a Pareto improvement occurs.[7]

Now, however, suppose that the actual distribution of utilities in state b corresponds to a Scitovsky set bounded by CIC_b. Recall that, in

---

[7] Aggregate bundles of goods lying on the interior of the Scitovsky set can be distributed so as to achieve a Pareto improvement over any point on the CIC. All points on the CIC yield the same distribution of utilities as the actual state. A point on the interior contains more of all goods than some points on the CIC and therefore can be allocated to achieve a Pareto improvement over the actual allocation.

general, CIC can intersect each other. Consequently, it is possible that the initial production possibilities set OP_aP_a can intersect CIC_b as shown in figure 3.18. This raises a paradox pointed out by Scitovsky (1941). It is possible to hypothetically redistribute purchasing power (i.e. goods and production) in state b so that a Pareto improvement is achieved over the actual distribution in state a, yet it is *also* possible to hypothetically redistribute purchasing power in state a so as to achieve a Pareto improvement over the actual distribution in state b!

By inspection of figure 3.18, it should be clear to the reader that this 'reversal' paradox is only possible if CIC_a and CIC_b intersect. Under certain circumstances the CIC will form a 'community preference field' and will not intersect (see Gorman, 1961). These circumstances require households to have linear and parallel Engel's curves or income expansion lines. Unfortunately this is a very restrictive requirement; therefore it would be useful to overcome the reversals problem in some other way.

Scitovsky (1941) suggested a possible solution. Note that the reversal occurs because the Kaldor criterion is met in going from a to b and also in going from b to a. Equivalently, the Kaldor criterion is met but the Hicks criterion is not met in going from a to b. Scitovsky suggested a 'double' criterion – both the Kaldor and Hicks criteria must be met. That is, state b is preferable to state a if and only if it is possible to undertake a hypothetical lump-sum redistribution in state b and achieve a Pareto improvement over state a *and* it is not possible to undertake hypothetical lump-sum redistribution in state a and achieve a Pareto improvement (or even an equivalence) over state b.

Figure 3.19 illustrates the case where the double criterion is met. The production possibilities set OP_bP_b intersects the interior of the Scitovsky set for state a (bounded by CIC_a) and OP_aP_a does not intersect the interior of the Scitovsky set bounded by CIC_b. However, figure 3.19 also illustrates a problem, pointed out by Gorman (1955), with the double criterion. Although it rules out reversals, it does not rule our intransitivities.

Consider a third state c with production possibilities set OP_cP_c and corresponding Scitovsky set bounded by CIC_c. Clearly state b is preferable to a and state c is preferable to b by the double criterion. One might expect that c must therefore be preferable to a by the double criterion to ensure transitivity. Yet, as shown in figure 3.19, this need not be the case.[8]

Another compensation criterion, suggested by Samuelson (1950), precludes reversals and intransitivities. This criterion ranks state b above state a if and only if hypothetical lump-sum redistribution in state b can achieve any distribution of utilities that is feasible in state a *and* result in a Pareto improvement over some distributions of utilities in state a. In

---

[8] While c may not be shown to be preferable to a by the double criterion, a can never be shown preferable to c. Thus, cyclical preferences cannot arise.

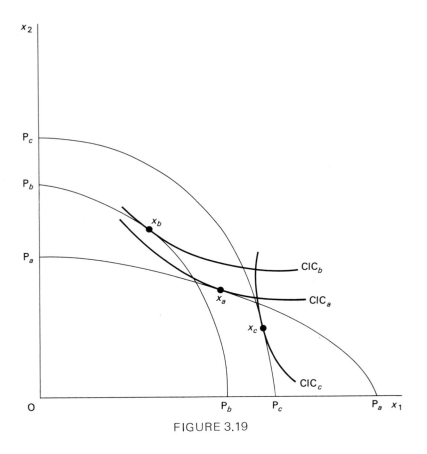

FIGURE 3.19

other words, the utility possibilities frontier corresponding to state b lies outside that of state a somewhere and inside that of state a nowhere.

The Samuelson criterion is illustrated in figure 3.20, where CIC_a bounds the Scitovsky set corresponding to the actual distribution of utilities in state a and CIC'_a bounds the Scitovsky set for another feasible distribution of utilities in state a. The Samuelson criterion requires that the production possibilities set OP_bP_b intersects the interior of CIC_a and every CIC'_a. This is obviously far more restrictive than the Kaldor, Hicks or double criteria. Indeed, if tastes are sufficiently dissimilar across consumers, the Samuelson criteria could require that OP_aP_a lie entirely within OP_bP_b.

To summarize, the Samuelson criterion rids the compensation principle of the difficulties posed by reversals and intransitivities but is very restrictive. It would also require a great deal of information to establish that the Samuelson criterion is met, since Scitovsky sets for hypothetical distributions of utility must be known. As we shall see in chapter 9, it is difficult enough to establish that a simple Hicks or Kaldor criterion is met, let alone the Samuelson criterion. Finally, and furthermore, even with the

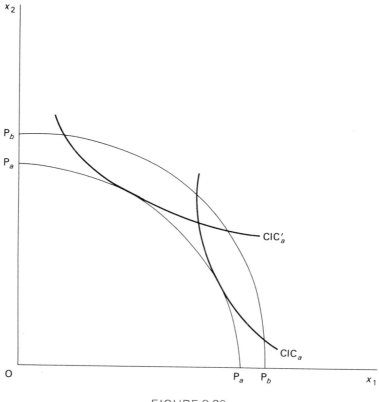

FIGURE 3.20

Samuelson criterion, the compensation principle cannot completely order social states. Many social states will remain non-comparable. To overcome this problem it will be necessary to make stronger assumptions than those implicit in the Pareto principle and the compensation principle. These assumptions will be examined in chapters 5 and 6.

7 Summary

The (strong) Pareto criterion of social welfare states that an event leads to a social improvement if some or all of the households in the economy are made better off and none is made worse off. A state in which no Pareto improvement is feasible is said to be Pareto optimal.

The Pareto criterion is interesting for two reasons. First, it does not require utility comparisons among different households and requires only that any household's utility be ordinally, rather than cardinally, measureable. Secondly, there is a two-way correspondence between Pareto optimality and allocations which are equilibria of an ideal competitive market mechanism. The implication is that there exists a vector of prices at which independent utility and profit maximizing agents make decisions that lead to an allocation of resources which is desirable in terms of the Pareto criterion. These fundamental theorems can be extended to intertemporal and uncertainty contexts.

The compensation principle is invoked to extend the power of the Pareto principle by ranking states on the basis of their *potential* for Pareto improvements through lump-sum redistribution. The weak compensation principle, which considers hypothetical lump-sum redistribution of purchasing power, allows any Pareto optimal allocation to be ranked above any allocation that is not Pareto optimal. The compensation principle is subject to a number of difficulties even if one is willing to accept its presumptions. These difficulties, the possibilities of reversals and intransitivities, can only be removed by means of a stringent compensation criterion. Even then, the compensation principle does not permit a complete ranking of social states.

There are two obvious shortcomings to a welfare economics based on the fundamental theorems. Firstly, the Pareto criterion tells us nothing about the desirability of different redistributive policies, since such policies generally make some households better off and others worse off. Secondly, in practice it is unlikely that an ideal market mechanism exists or even can be designed. Therefore, desirable economic policies will extend beyond any redistributive policies that may be needed in a Pareto optimal economy. We discuss the tools of welfare economics that are needed to solve the first problem in chapters 5 and 6. But first, in chapter 4, we examine the use of the Pareto criterion in an economy where the existing market institutions are unlikely to lead to a Pareto optimal allocation of resources.

CHAPTER 4

Market Failure and the Theory of the Second Best

1 Introduction

In chapter 3 it was shown that under certain conditions a competitive market equilibrium exists such that the many households and firms in the economy, faced with the equilibrium relative prices, make economic decisions which exhaust the mutually beneficial advantages made possible through the processes of production and exchange. This result relegates the role of the public sector to that of providing the institutional and legal framework under which the market operates and, possibly, to redistributing income. In this chapter we shall consider the circumstances under which this 'decentralized efficiency' fails to hold and whether there are non-market mechanisms that permit the exploitation of existing Pareto improvements.

As mentioned, different economists view the fundamental theorems differently in terms of their relevance and importance. It is fairly obvious that, as a description of actual markets, the competitive market assumptions of chapter 3 are unrealistic. Whether this diminishes the relevance of the fundamental theorems is less clear. Rather than engage in this rather futile debate we shall organize our discussion of market failure around the following questions: Why do markets fail? That is, why should mutual utility gains not be exploited by decentralized decision-makers? And what are the implications of market failures for welfare economics based on the Pareto principle?

In section 2 we try to identify the fundamental sources of market failure and consider some specific examples. We also consider, in section 3, the question of whether such market failures provide a *prima facie* case for 'allocative' public sector policies. In section 4 we discuss the theory of the second best. This theory is concerned with welfare criteria where it is the case that, for some reason, at least one of the Pareto optimal conditions cannot be satisfied.

2 Market Failure: Causes and Cases

Actual markets differ from ideal markets in numerous ways – at least descriptively. We are concerned with reasons why actual markets may fail to have the optimality properties ascribed by the fundamental theorems. We try to reduce the many descriptive imperfections to a small number of fundamental market failures. These market failures include (1) non-convexities (2) non-competitive behaviour (3) externalities resulting from a lack of property rights (4) externalities resulting from jointness in consumption and production including public goods (5) informational externalities. We shall discuss each source of market failure and consider specific examples.

2.1 Non-convexities

In chapter 3 we indicated that a convexity assumption is necessary for the second theorem of welfare economics (that any Pareto optimal allocation can be achieved by a competitive market equilibrium for some lump-sum redistribution of factor ownership or claims on commodities) to hold. Both the Scitovsky set and the production possibility set must be convex. If not, there may exist allocations which are Pareto optimal, but which cannot be achieved by a decentralized market process. Such cases are called market failures resulting from non-convexities.

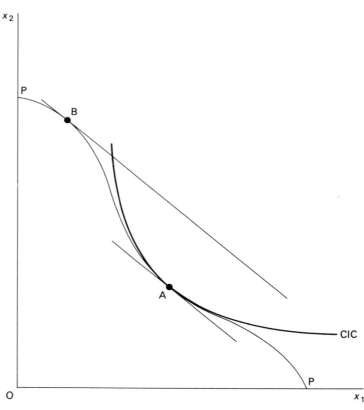

FIGURE 4.1

The case of non-convexities in production is illustrated in figure 4.1. The allocation corresponding to aggregate bundle A is Pareto optimal since point A is on the frontier of the production possibilities set (PP) and on the frontier of the Scitovsky set (CIC). Nevertheless, this allocation cannot be achieved by a competitive market for any distribution of claims on commodities.   Consider the line tangent to PP and CIC at A. The absolute value of the slope of this line corresponds to the relative price of the two goods and is equal to both the MRT and the common MRS of x_1 for x_2. But this relative price will not result in a market-clearing equilibrium at point A. Profit maximizing firms faced with this relative price would produce at point B where the value of the aggregate production bundle is greatest. Thus the Pareto optimal point A cannot be achieved by decentralized markets and the second theorem fails to hold.

Non-convexities in preferences for goods by the households also lead to a failure of the second theorem. This is illustrated in figure 4.2 where the Scitovsky set (bounded by CIC) is non-convex. Again, the Pareto optimal allocation associated with point A cannot be the equilibrium of a competitive market. At the relative price given by the absolute value of the slope of the tangent line at A, the households would demand the aggregate consumption bundle B.

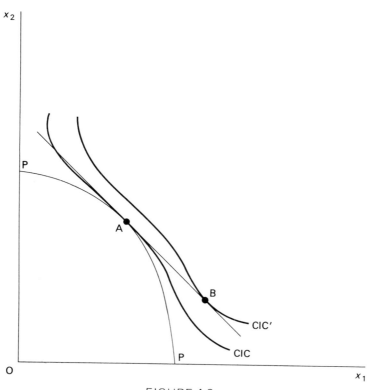

FIGURE 4.2

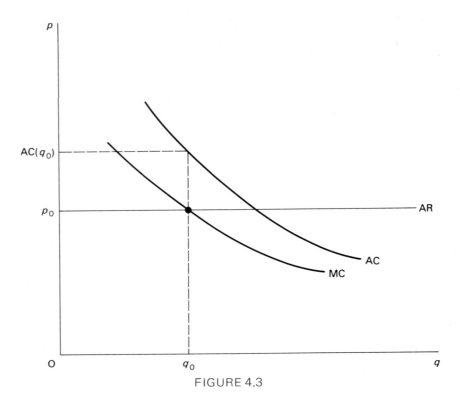

FIGURE 4.3

In both of the above cases, the tangent line at the Pareto optimal output and allocation A is not a separating line. Because of a non-convexity, it intersects either the production possibilities set, or the preferred set of the households (the interior of the Scitovsky set) or both. Therefore the relative price given by the slope of the tangent line is not an equilibrium relative price for any distribution of claims on the commodities. Firms, households or both are inclined to supply and/or demand an aggregate commodity bundle other than the bundle labelled A at this relative price.

A partial equilibrium example of the production non-convexity is the case of the decreasing cost industry illustrated in figure 4.3. In such an industry average cost declines, and thus marginal cost lies below average cost everywhere in the relevant range of output. A competitive equilibrium cannot exist because a price-taking firm facing the price p_0 would not produce q_0, where $p = MC$, but would want to increase its output without bound. Note that at q_0 the firm would earn negative economic profits since average cost exceeds average revenue. Thus the Pareto optimal output q_0 requires that the production of q_0 be financed, at least in part, through some means other than sales revenue.[1]

---

[1] Actually, if the producer can engage in multipart pricing (i.e. charging more for inframarginal units of output) it may be able to produce q_0 and be self-financing.

This is not to say that the private sector would not produce a good that is subject to decreasing costs, but that the private market equilibrium could not be Pareto optimal. Because average cost is declining, mergers permit reduced costs until a single firm produces the entire industry output. This outcome, known as a 'natural monopoly', is typical for many utilities. If the single firm were unregulated, it would not produce q_0 but would attempt to exercise its monopoly power. Even if the firm is regulated, it may be impossible to design regulations such that the firm produces q_0 and breaks even. In many cases, the only possible Pareto optimal solution is for the good to be produced by the public sector.

2.2 Non-competitive behaviour

An important assumption underlying the fundamental theorems is that all of the participants in the market are 'price-takers'; that is, they make their allocative decisions on the assumption that their actions do not influence market prices. This seems reasonable only when the market is populated with numerous buyers and sellers. In many cases and for different reasons, there are sufficiently few agents on one side of the market that they are aware that their actions alter market prices. The polar case is that of a single seller (monopoly) or single buyer (monopsony) faced by price-taking agents on the other side of the market.

We shall illustrate the case of market power in the pure exchange economy. Suppose there is a single seller of good x_1 (Alice) facing many price-taking buyers of x_1 (Bobs) who sell x_2. In an exchange economy, each agent is a buyer and seller so Alice has monopoly power in selling x_1 and monopsony power in purchasing x_2. That is, she realizes that by altering the amount of x_1 sold she can alter the relative price of x_1 and x_2 (her 'terms of trade') in her favour. She can then choose a market equilibrium which gives her a higher level of utility than she received at the competitive equilibrium. This equilibrium will not, in general, be Pareto optimal.

The consequences of monopoly in an exchange economy are illustrated in figure 4.4. Suppose that initially Alice is endowed with $\bar{x}_1$ units of good one and none of good two, and the Bobs have $\bar{x}_2$ units of good two and none of good one. At the initial endowment point F, Alice gets utility u_0^a and the Bobs, who are all assumed identical, get an aggregate utility of u_0^b. Under the hypothetical competitive equilibrium at E, Alice would reach utility u_1^a and the Bobs would reach u_2^b. This would be a Pareto optimum. With monopoly/monopsony power Alice recognizes that by altering the amount of x_1 sold she can attain any point on Bobs' offer curve of OC^b. She chooses the point M on OC^b that is just tangent to her highest indifference curve u_2^a. In equilibrium she sells $\bar{x}_1 - x_1^a$ units of x_1 at the relative price given by the absolute value of the slope of line FM. The monopoly relative price of x_1 is higher than the competitive equilibrium price, and whereas Alice is better off, the Bobs are worse off.

Point M is not on the contract curve and therefore is not Pareto optimal. Note that all of the points in the shaded area bounded by u_2^a and u_1^b repre-

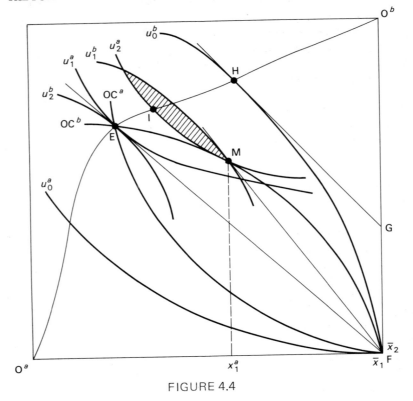

FIGURE 4.4

sent Pareto improvements (through trade) over M. The relative price lines tangent to both sets of indifference along that portion of the contract curve do not go through the initial endowment point. So, unless side payments can be negotiated or price discrimination can be practised by Alice, there is no means of reaching the contract curve.[2]

It might seem curious that Alice would settle for the point M when it appears that she could exploit her monopoly bargaining strength to further advantage. Clearly she would prefer any point between I and H along the contract curve to the monopoly equilibrium point M, and presumably the Bobs would consent to trades that reach such points since they would be no worse off than without trade. The difficulty in attaining such points in a decentralized market is that no set of uniform prices exists which, if faced by the Bobs, would induce them to choose a point along the contract curve between I and H. Such points could be attained

---

[2] Perfect price discrimination is possible if Alice can charge a different price for each unit of x_1 sold. In this case she could appropriate all of the gains from exchange and reach point H. The Bobs are no better off than they were without exchange; nevertheless, H is Pareto optimal. However, price discrimination requires that Alice be able to prevent resale among the buyers and have the information necessary to determine the right price for each unit of x_1 sold.

by charging the Bobs a lump-sum payment and letting them purchase x_1 at a price lower than the monopoly price. For example, Alice could attain point H by imposing a lump-sum payment FG and charging a price given by the absolute value of the slope of GH. This price may even be lower than the competitive price.

The problem is: How does Alice get the Bobs to pay the lump-sum fee FG? It appears that the Bobs would be willing to do so collectively but each Bob will have an incentive to be a 'free rider'; that is, to avoid the lump-sum payment and enjoy the lower price. Unless Alice can practise price discrimination, this cannot be prevented[3] and the lump sum payment FG cannot be acquired voluntarily from the Bobs. The monopoly equilibrium M is the best Alice can do if she is restricted to setting a uniform price, and can neither practise price discrimination nor collect a lump-sum payment.

One might wonder whether this market inefficiency could be eliminated by removing the asymmetry in market power. Suppose the Bobs were able to form a union (coalition) and prevent free riders by some legal means such as a compulsory check-off. Would Alice and the union of Bobs not negotiate to reach a point on the contract curve? This idea, that countervailing power would be efficient, was espoused by Galbraith (1953).

In fact, such 'bilateral monopolies' may not negotiate to a point on the contract curve if communication between the parties is imperfect and/or no legal means exists to ensure that the other party will not renege on the contract negotiated. This is illustrated by the famous 'prisoner's dilemma'. Suppose two parties, A and B, can take two possible actions I and II. This gives four possible outcomes as shown in the 'pay-off matrix' of figure 4.5. For each outcome, the first number shows the pay-off (say units of a *numéraire* good) to party A and the second to party B.

It is Pareto optimal for A and B both to undertake action I, in which case they each receive 10 units of goods. But if either party chooses I and the other 'cheats' and chooses II, then the party choosing I gets nothing. If the parties adopt a *maximin* strategy – that is, each chooses an action which gives the best pay-off given that the other party does the best it can given that action – then both households will choose action II and get a sure outcome of 5. The Pareto outcome is not realized. Of course, if the parties can communicate and negotiate a firm agreement that each party undertake action I then Pareto optimality can be achieved.

All of this discussion of non-competitive behaviour has been in terms of a highly simplified exchange economy, but the results all apply to production economies and to more sophisticated instances of market power. In all cases, an agent with market power can increase its utility by setting terms which are not Pareto optimal. Even though mutual gains exist in monopolistic equilibrium, they cannot be realized through the workings

---

[3] If Alice asks for a single lump-sum fee, the Bobs would have to pool their funds, thus raising the 'free rider' problem. If Alice asks for a per caput lump-sum fee (FG/B where B is the number of buyers), her monopoly will be eroded since a single buyer could pay the fee and then earn monopoly profits by reselling x_1 to others.

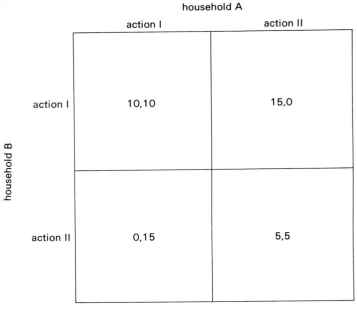

FIGURE 4.5

of the price mechanism once some agent recognizes that those prices can be influenced by its actions. How serious such inefficiencies are is a matter of controversy.

2.3 *Externalities arising from a lack of property rights*

In order for the decentralized market mechanism to work, firms and households must be able to exchange claims on the right to use a factor or consume a good. This requires a well-defined system of property rights that excludes agents from using a good or factor for which they have not paid. It also allows agents to exclude themselves from consuming an unwanted commodity or factor without compensation.

For many goods and factors, it is prohibitively costly or otherwise infeasible to assign and/or enforce property rights. Such items are then 'common property'. With common property, some agents may be unable to appropriate all of the returns to a productive activity in which they engage or, alternatively, other agents can 'free ride' and enjoy the fruits of another's labour and expense. There are numerous examples of externalities resulting from the existence of common property. They may be trivial, such as a household's inability to charge a price to a passer-by who stops to gaze at its beautiful garden, or they may be substantive, such as the case of firms and households dumping waste products into the air or on unowned land.

Gordon (1954) identified a classic case of a common property externality in the fishery. When a fisherman increases his catch, he reduces the equilibrium stock of fish and raises the cost of 'finding' a fish to other fishermen. Because this cost is external to the fisherman, he ignores it when making his decision of how many fish to catch. The common property here is the 'inventory' of fish in the sea; once a fish is caught, property rights on it are established. The result of this common property externality is over-fishing, which leaves a stock of fish in the sea that is too small. In most cases, property rights on the stock of fish are partly restored by imposing fishing quotas, but this is a very rough corrective policy which does not work at all if the fish can travel outside national boundaries.

Inventive activity is analogous to the fishing activity. In this case property rights on an invention cannot be established until it is discovered. The common property is the stock of undiscovered inventions. 'Over-fishing' corresponds to duplicative and otherwise excessive inventive activities. Similarly, the commonly owned roadway leads to a misallocation of resources. A person's use of the roadway slows traffic marginally, thus imposing costs on fellow travellers, but the costs are not considered by the person when making a decision to use the roadway.

The inefficiency resulting from the common property resource can be illustrated geometrically using figure 4.6. This diagram depicts the cost

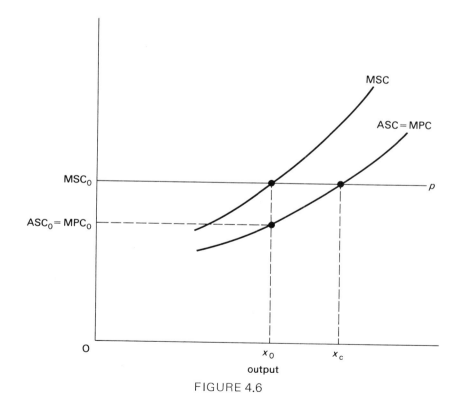

FIGURE 4.6

curves for an output produced using a common property resource. For example, it can be thought of as a fishing ground, or a congested roadway. Using the fishing analogy, additional output x is produced by using more and more variable factors such as labour and fishing boats, where the average and marginal costs eventually rise since the fishing ground itself is of a fixed size. Since the fishing ground is commonly owned, fishermen treat it as if it were free despite the fact that it is a scarce resource of a given size. Free entry into the fishing ground combined with the free use of the fishing ground implies that the output of the fishing ground will expand to the point at which price equals marginal private cost (MPC), which equals average social cost (ASC) and includes only the costs incurred by the fishermen and not the opportunity cost of the fixed factor, the fishing ground.

The marginal social costs of the industry are shown by the curve MSC, which is the curve that is marginal to the ASC = MPC curve. It shows, for the fishing ground as a whole, the marginal cost of additional output. The optimal output of the fishing ground is x_0, where price equals marginal social cost. At this output the difference $MSC_0 - ASC_0$ represents the marginal scarcity rent of the fishing ground or, equivalently, the marginal external cost imposed on other fishermen when one fisherman produces an extra unit of output. Owing to the common property nature of the resource, fishermen do not take this into account.

Figure 4.6 could also be interpreted as illustrating the overuse of a congested roadway (Walter, 1961). If the output x is interpreted as trips on the roadway, and the cost curve ASC shows the average social (marginal private) cost per trip, including the implicit cost of the time used in travelling, the analogy is straightforward. Since the capacity of the road is fixed, the time per trip rises as the quantity of trips rises. Individual users, however, ignore the impact of their marginal trip on slowing down other drivers. Therefore, x_c trips are taken rather than the optimal amount x_0. Here the difference $MSC_0 - ASC_0$ can be interpreted as the marginal externality or congestion cost.

A common property resource exists because property rights are not assigned. One obvious solution to it, as recognized by Knight (1924), is to assign property rights. If the fishing ground of figure 4.6 were owned by a firm or the government, and users of the fishing ground were charged a price equal to the scarcity value of it, the common property resource problem would disappear, and the fishing ground would be used optimally.

2.4 *Externalities arising from jointness in production and consumption*

Whenever an activity by some agent influences the output or utility of another, and this effect is not priced by the market, an externality is said to exist. We saw that externalities can result from a lack of property rights. They can also arise from jointness in consumption and production. By jointness of consumption we mean that a consumption activity undertaken by one household affects the utility of one or more other households. Jointness of production occurs when one firm's activity affects the production possibilities of one or more other firms. The externality may be negative (e.g. pollution) or positive (e.g. literacy), unilateral (e.g. the noise from a highway impinging on a residential neighbourhood) or reciprocal (e.g. Meade's (1952) classic case of the pollination of an apple orchard by a honey producer's bees). The externality may occur among households, among producers or between producers and households.

The first theorem of welfare economics will generally fail in the presence of jointness of consumption or production externalities. This is because decentralized households and firms in a competitive economy will not take account of the external benefits or costs of their actions when making their decisions. Put another way, the Pareto optimality conditions will differ in the presence of externalities from those discussed in chapter 3. For example, suppose that the consumption of x_1 by household A also affects the utility of household B, so B's utility function may be written $u^b(x^b, x_1^a)$ where x^b is the vector of B's own consumption. It can be readily shown that the exchange efficiency condition in this case becomes

$$\frac{u_1^b}{u_i^b} = \frac{u_1^a}{u_i^a} + \frac{\partial u^b/\partial x_1^a}{u_i^b}$$

or

$$MRS_{x_1^b, x_i^b}^b = \frac{p_1}{p_i} = MRS_{x_1^a, x_i^a}^a + MRS_{x_1^a, x_i^b}^b$$

Since, under competitive conditions, household A chooses the commodity bundle which makes $p_1/p_i = MRS_{x_1^a x_i^a}^a$, the exchange efficiency conditions are not satisfied. In particular, household A neglects the influence of its consumption of x_1 on B. That influence may be positive or negative according to whether the effect is an external economy or diseconomy.

Joint production externalities lead to an analogous problem. For example, if the use of an input L by firm x influences the production of firm y, the production efficiency conditions become:

$$\frac{f_L^y}{f_K^y} = \frac{w}{r} = \frac{f_L^x}{f_K^x} + \frac{\partial f^y/\partial L_x}{\partial f^y/\partial K_x}$$

Firm x, by equating f_L^x/f_K^x with w/r, behaves inefficiently.

The inefficiencies arising from externalities can be readily illustrated geometrically. Consider the simple case in which an agent A, which could be a household or a firm, undertakes an activity which is jointly consumed by agents A and B. Suppose the activity is a 'good' from the point of view of agent B, so we have a case of an external economy. Figure 4.7 shows the marginal benefit from the activity, labelled x, for A and B (MB^a, MB^b) and the marginal cost MC. In the case of joint consumption externalities, MB^a would be A's marginal rate of substitution of the

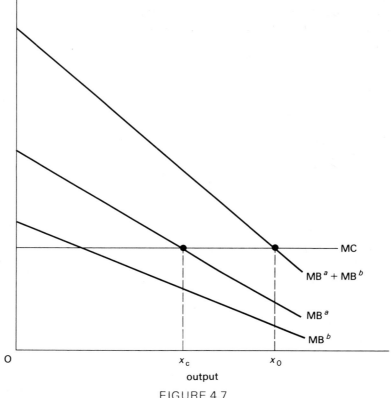

FIGURE 4.7

activity x to A in terms of some *numéraire*, and MB^b is that for B. MC would be the relative price of x in terms of the *numéraire*. Agent A acting independently would choose activity level x_c, at which point $MB^a = MC$, but a Pareto optimum requires that activity x be carried on at level x_0 where $MB^a + MB^b = MC$. This would only be attained if A were somehow induced to take account of the joint consumption benefits of its activity x. We return to this question below.

A similar sort of analysis applies when the externality is a diseconomy, except that then MB^b would be negative. In that case, as the reader can verify, the optimal output x_0 would be below the decentralized output.

As mentioned before, externalities can be reciprocal in the sense that the activities of two or more agents affect each other. An interesting case to consider is that of reciprocal consumption externalities, sometimes referred to as the problem of *interdependent utility functions*. Following Schall (1972), suppose the utility functions of Alice and Bob are given by

$$u^a = u^a(x_1^a, x_2^a, x_1^b, x_2^b) \tag{4.1a}$$

$$u^b = u^b(x_1^b, x_2^b, x_1^a, x_2^a) \tag{4.1b}$$

Each household's utility depends on the consumption bundle of the other household as well as on its own. The externality could enter positively (the case of altruism) or negatively (the case of envy). Let us consider the altruistic case.

Pareto efficiency in exchange requires that

$$\frac{u_{1a}^a + u_{1b}^a}{u_{2a}^a + u_{2b}^a} = \frac{u_{1b}^b + u_{1a}^b}{u_{2b}^b + u_{2a}^b} \tag{4.2}$$

where $u_{ij}^h = \partial u^h / \partial x_i^j$ is the marginal utility of household h from a unit of good x_i consumed by household j.[4] However, households choosing their own consumption bundles at given market prices will equate u_{1a}^a / u_{2a}^a to u_{1b}^b / u_{2b}^b. Thus, in general, the competitive equilibrium will not be Pareto efficient in the presence of interdependent utilities. Each household will select a non-optimal bundle of commodities.

There is, however, one special case in which the first-order conditions will be satisfied. Suppose that $u_{1b}^a / u_{2b}^a = u_{1b}^b / u_{2b}^b$. That is, the marginal rate of substitution of B's consumption of good one for good two in A's utility function is the same as that in B's utility function. That is, A's altruism respects B's preference ordering and A's preferences are said to be *non-paternalistic* (see Archibald and Donaldson, 1976). Similarly, for B, $u_{1a}^b / u_{2a}^b = u_{1a}^a / u_{2a}^a$. If these conditions are satisfied, the Pareto efficiency condition (4.2) will hold in a competitive equilibrium, that is, when $u_{1a}^a / u_{2a}^a = u_{1b}^b / u_{2b}^b$.

However, the Pareto efficiency conditions are only necessary, not sufficient, conditions for a Pareto optimum. In this case, it is quite possible that even with the exchange efficiency conditions satisfied, resources may not be allocated efficiently. This is the case in which Pareto improving redistribution may be possible, and is illustrated in figure 4.8, adopted from Schall (1972). Figure 4.8(a) shows an Edgeworth box diagram for a two-person exchange economy constructed for the case in which interdependent utilities exist. Alice's indifference curves are drawn from the origin O^a. As one moves northeast along the contract curve from O^a, Alice gets more and Bob less of the goods available. Since Alice is altruistic there may well come a point beyond which further redistribution from Bob to Alice would make Alice worse off. The point Q is such a point.

---

[4] Condition (4.2) is derived from the maximization problem:

$$\max_{x^a, x^b} u^a (x_1^a, x_2^a, x_1^b, x_2^b)$$

subject to

$$u^b (x_1^b, x_2^b, x_1^a, x_2^a) = u^b$$

and

$$x_i^a + x_i^b = x_i \quad \text{for } i = 1, 2$$

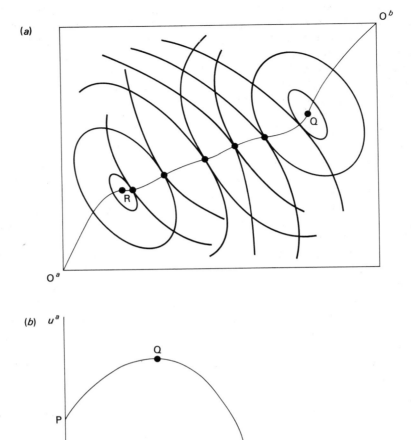

FIGURE 4.8

It is the point of maximum utility for Alice, or Alice's *bliss point*. North-east of Q, Alice becomes worse off. Similarly, for Bob, his bliss point is R. Points southwest of R make him worse off. The contract curve drawn shows all points satisfying the Pareto efficiency condition (4.2). The lower panel translates the points along the contract curve joining O^a and O^b into the utility possibility curve PQRS. All points along PQRS satisfy (4.2).

If the altruistic preferences of Alice and Bob are non-paternalistic, the competitive market economy will take us to a point along the contract curve in figure 4.8(*a*) or, equivalently, along the utility possibility curve of figure 4.8(*b*). However, inspection of (*b*) indicates that not all points along PQRS are Pareto optimal; only those points along the portion QR will be. For points along PQ, redistribution of purchasing power from Alice to Bob will make both better off. Similarly, along RS, redistribution from Bob to Alice will make both better off. This redistribution is referred to as Pareto optimal redistribution, following Hochman and Rodgers (1969).[5] If Alice were to voluntarily make transfers to Bob, or vice versa as the case may be, the inefficiency would be avoided.

Whenever an externality exists, there is a potential gain from trade by internalizing it. One way this might be done is through a system of side payments from one party (the one affected by the externality) to another (the one emitting it) as suggested by Coase (1960) and Buchanan and Stubblebine (1962). The potential role for side payments raises the question of why externalities do not voluntarily get internalized apart from the lack of an assignment of property rights. In other words, if a firm's activity influences the output or utility of another, why is a Pareto optimal equilibrium not established with this external influence priced in the same way as other inputs and outputs are?[6] That is, why are property rights not enforced in this case? There are two reasons. The first is that externalities can lead to a non-convexity of the type discussed in section 2.1. Secondly, pricing of externalities resulting from jointness in consumption and production is possible only if a small number of parties are involved.[7] More generally, if external effects are widespread they produce a free rider problem similar to that of the public goods case considered in section 2.5.

Let us examine the possibility of a non-convexity for a production externality where the production of x is negatively affected by the output of y. That is, $x = f(L_x, y)$ where $f(\ )$ is a production function with $f_y = \partial f/\partial y < 0$ and L_x is the amount of input L used in producing x. Assuming the externality is unilateral, we have $y = g(L - L_x)$ where L is the endowment of the input.

The production possibility curve is shown in figure 4.9. As more y is produced, x output falls both because less input is used in x and because of the negative externality. As a result, the output of x can reach zero even when $L_x > 0$ at $\hat{P}$. As more L_x leaves x production, y output increases without further losses in x output; that is the production possibilities set P'$\hat{P}$P is non-convex. Consequently, even if the externality is 'priced', an equilibrium such as A in figure 4.9 cannot be achieved by a market equilibrium since producers would want to shift production to point P'.

---

[5] There is an interesting literature on Pareto optimal redistribution. For example, see Hochman and Rodgers (1969).

[6] Cheung (1973) found that side payments do occur in the classic case of a reciprocal externality – the orchard owner and the honey producers.

[7] In such circumstances, strategic behaviour is likely.

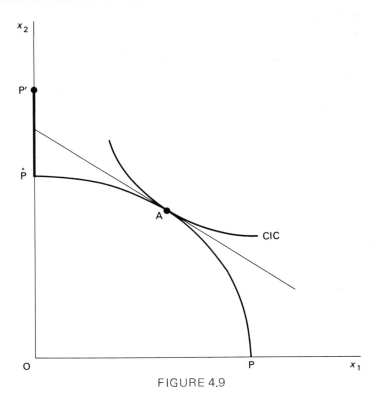

FIGURE 4.9

2.5 Jointness in production and consumption: public goods

Pure public goods   In the competitive market economy of the fundamental theorems, all goods and factors are purely 'rival'; that is, the use of
a unit of a good or factor by any agent precludes its use entirely by anyone else. A pure 'public' good or factor is one for which the use by any
agent has no effect on the amount available for use by others. Examples
of public goods include a television or radio signal and nuclear deterrent.
There are also public factors such as knowledge and publicly unwanted
goods such as pollution – my consumption of dirty air does not diminish
the amount left for you.

For a public good, exclusion may be feasible – for example, a TV signal
may be 'scrambled' so that only a paying subscriber can tune to it – or
infeasible, as in the case of national defence. In any case, exclusion cannot
play the same role as it does for private (rival) goods. Since the marginal
social cost of an extra user is zero, it is never Pareto optimal to set prices
that will exclude anyone who derives positive marginal utility from the
public good.

Samuelson (1951) derived the Pareto optimal conditions for the provision
of pure public goods. Suppose for simplicity that there are H households

who are identical in all respects, and let x be the per caput consumption of the private good and y be the total output of the public good. Suppose also that private and public goods are produced by simple one-input production functions $f(L_x)$ and $g(L_y)$, respectively. Because housholds are identical, we can find the Pareto optimal provision of the public good by maximizing the utility of the representative household subject to the production constraint. That is:

$$\max_{x,y,L_x} u(x,y)$$

subject to

$$Hx = f(L_x)$$

$$y = g(L - L_x)$$

where $L = L_x + L_y$ is the given amount of labour input available to the economy, and H is the population. Substituting the constraints into the utility function and maximizing with respect to L_x, the first-order condition is:

$$H\frac{u_y}{u_x} = \frac{f_L}{g_L} \tag{4.3}$$

The left-hand side is the social marginal benefit and is equal to the number of households times the marginal rate of substitution (MRS) between public and private goods. The right-hand side is the ratio of the marginal products of the inputs or the marginal rate of transformation (MRT). If households are not identical they will not have the same MRS between public and private goods. In this case, the first-order condition is:

$$\sum_{h=1}^{H} MRS^h = MRT \tag{4.3'}$$

The important attribute of public goods that leads to market failure is that exclusion, whether or not feasible, is economically inefficient. Any pricing scheme that excludes a household that will not pay is inefficient. But if exclusion is not possible, the free rider problem is present. Households will want to conceal their preferences in order to enjoy the public good without paying for it. As a result, too little of the public good, if any, will be produced privately.

In general, this provides a strong argument in favour of producing such goods through the public sector and financing them by involuntary taxation rather than by user fees. There is still the problem of preference revelation. If exclusion cannot be used to extract private valuations of public goods, how does the public sector determine the right amount to produce (i.e. that satisfying (4.3) or (4.3'))?

This problem is unresolved. There do exist various means of inducing individuals to reveal their preferences, but these *preference revelation mechanisms* are too complex to put into practice; moreover, they are not immune to manipulation by coalitions.[8] In practice, policy-makers must find other means of imputing shadow prices for public goods in order to determine the optimal amounts to produce.

Mixed public goods   Many goods are neither purely rival nor purely public. 'Mixed public goods' are those subject to congestion costs as the number of users increases. These include goods conventionally provided by the public sector, such as parks and roads, and also goods provided by the private sector, such as concerts, motion pictures, golf course facilities etc.

In all cases, at some point the addition of another user reduces the enjoyment of others. In most cases, congestion alters the 'quality' of the good rather than the amount but it is also useful to think of congestion as altering the 'amount' of the good per user. In this way, mixed public goods can be thought of as an intermediate case between the polar cases of pure private goods and pure public goods.

The Pareto optimal conditions for the optimal amount of a mixed public good are found by maximizing the utility of the representative household

$$u(x, y(z, n))$$

subject to

$$Hx = f(L_x)$$

$$z = g\left(\frac{(L - L_x) n}{H}\right)$$

where z is the output of the mixed public good produced by a representative producer, n is the number of households jointly consuming the mixed public good output of a producer, and H/n is the number of producers of the mixed public good. Note that the representative household derives utility from its consumption of the private good (x) and its consumption of the mixed public good $y(z, n)$, which depends positively on the producer output and negatively on the number of households

[8] Further details on preference revelation in particular and public goods in general can be found in Boadway (1979, chapters 4 and 6) and in Green and Laffont (1979).

sharing it.[9] The first-order (Pareto optimal) conditions are:[10]

$$n \frac{u_y(\ )\, y_z(\ )}{u_x(\ )} = \frac{f_L(\ )}{g_L(\ )} \tag{4.3''}$$

$$-y_n(\ ) = y_z(\ )\, g_L(\ )\, \frac{L - L_x}{H} \tag{4.4}$$

These two equations, together with the constraints, can be solved for the Pareto optimal values of private output Hx, output of the mixed public good per producer z and the number of producers of the mixed public good H/n. Equation (4.3'') is just a Samuelson-type condition. The left-hand side of (4.4) represents the congestion cost of raising the club size by a small amount. The right-hand side equals the increase in club output made possible by the reduction in the number of clubs. Labour used per club equals $(L - L_x)/(H/n)$, so $(L - L_x)/H$ is the increase in labour input per club upon increasing n by one unit.

An interesting question concerns the possibility of providing the Pareto optimal allocation of mixed public goods through a decentralized decision-making process. Tiebout (1956) analyses the case where mixed public goods such as police protection, fire protection and local parks are provided by local governments. He argues that if the communities are geographically isolated so that households who are not citizens (and taxpayers) of the locality can be excluded from the benefits of the local public goods, and if households are mobile and can choose a community solely on the basis of the local public good and lump-sum tax package offered them, then given a sufficiently large number of households with similar tastes and a sufficiently large number of producers, there will be an optimal allocation of the local public goods achieved. That is, (4.3'') and (4.4) will be satisfied by a competitive market in private goods and by 'voting with one's feet' in choosing local public goods.

A homologous case, analysed by Buchanan (1965), is that of a privately produced 'club' good such as a swimming pool or a golf course in which a private producer makes available a good which is consumed jointly by members. Clearly such club goods are just examples of mixed public goods. But in this context it is obvious that many goods including concerts, motion pictures etc. fall into this category. For this reason it is useful to

---

[9] Utility could initially rise as the number of users rises (playing on an empty tennis court without a partner is not much fun) but this would be a 'non-economic' region of production. We restrict our analysis to the relevant range of production where congestion costs are positive.

[10] Substituting the constraints into the utility function yields

$$u\left(\frac{F(L_x)}{H}, \ y\left(g\left(\frac{(L - L_x)\, n}{H} \right), n \right) \right)$$

Maximizing over L_x and n gives (4.3'') and (4.4) after manipulation.

know whether decentralized market decision-making will lead to a Pareto optimal allocation.

It is straightforward to show that the decentralized market solution will be Pareto optimal in the economy of a single representative consumer. The budget constraint of the consumer is

$$m = x + pz \tag{4.5}$$

where p is the 'membership fee' of a club offering 1 unit of z measured in units of the *numéraire* private good, x is consumption of the private good and m is the income of the representative household. By the zero-profit condition, $p = c(z)/nz$ where $c(z)$ is the total costs of a club offering z units of the club good. Using (4.5) we can solve for x to give

$$x = m - \frac{c(z)}{n}$$

and substitute this value into the utility function of the household to get

$$u\left(m - \frac{c(z)}{n}, y(z, n)\right)$$

Maximizing over z and n yields

$$n\frac{u_y(\ )y_z(\ )}{u_x(\ )} = c'(z) \tag{4.6}$$

$$c'(z) = -\frac{c(z)y_z(\ )}{ny_n(\ )} \tag{4.7}$$

where $c'(z)$ is the marginal cost of z in terms of x. Noting that $c'(z) = f_L/g_L$, and $c(z) = w(L - L_x)/(H/n)$ and $w = f_L$, we get the Pareto optimal equations (4.3'') and (4.4) directly from (4.6) and (4.7).

This result, that mixed public goods can be optimally provided by a decentralized mechanism, is very important. It means that jointness *per se* does not lead to market failure. The remarkable thing is that the result is quite general. It can be extended to economies with consumers having different tastes providing there exist a large enough number of consumers having similar tastes, and it holds even if mixed public goods are produced with increasing returns to scale. The important assumptions are that exclusion is possible and that costs rise eventually because of congestion, so that the optimal number of consumers sharing the good is finite and small relative to the total population.[11]

---

[11] For more details see Berglas (1976, 1981).

2.6 Asymmetric information and market failure

The efficiency of a competitive market equilibrium depends on all of the decentralized decision-makers having 'full' information. The market mechanism itself plays an informational role by conveying information in the form of relative prices to decision-makers about the relative costs and benefits of different actions. It was explained in chapter 3, section 5.2, that this price mechanism would result in Pareto optimality even if decision-makers do not know the consequences of their actions with certainty, providing state-contingent markets, or their equivalent, exist.

It is obvious that 'perfect insurance' markets of the type required for Pareto optimality do not exist in practice.[12] It is useful to consider the reasons why insurance markets may fail to exist and why those that do exist may not exploit all of the mutual benefits to risk-sharing. Two types of informational externalities impede the functioning of insurance markets, generally referred to as *adverse selection* and *moral hazard*. We consider each in turn.[13]

Adverse selection   This occurs when one party to the transaction does not have full information about the nature of the exchange being made. Akerlof (1970) illustrated the phenomenon in a used-car market where buyers of used cars, unlike the sellers, know only the 'average' quality of the cars being traded and not the quality of the specific car being purchased. Rothschild and Stiglitz (1976) examine the same phenomenon in an insurance market, where insurers are able to observe only the average probability that the policy holders will make a claim and not the probability of a particular policy holder doing so. In both cases, the only possible equilibrium is one where the markets are dominated by one quality (risk class) of goods (policy holders). In the used-car market, the owners of good used cars will find the market price offered by ignorant buyers insufficient to induce them to sell their cars, whereas owners of poor cars will accept such offers readily. In insurance markets, insurers will be induced to 'tailor' contracts towards certain risk classes of policy holder.

We will briefly analyse adverse selection in the context of insurance for physical disability. In figure 4.10 there are two classes of policy holder who have the same endowment point F of state 1 (policy holder able) and state 2 (policy holder disabled) goods. With no insurance, the high (low) risk policy holder is on the indifference curve labelled u_0^h (u_0^ℓ). The absolute value of the slope of the indifference curve at the 45° (certainty) line is equal to $(1 - \pi^h)/\pi^h$ for the high risk policy holder, whereas for the low risk policy holder it is $(1 - \pi^\ell)/\pi^\ell$, where π^h (π^ℓ) is the probability of state 2 for the high (low) risk policy holder and $\pi^h > \pi^\ell$.

---

[12] Recall that even if markets are not 'complete' in this sense, it is still possible that Pareto optimality of a constrained type may exist in a 'stock market' economy.

[13] A good discussion of information and uncertainty including adverse selection and moral hazard is found in Hirshleifer and Riley (1979).

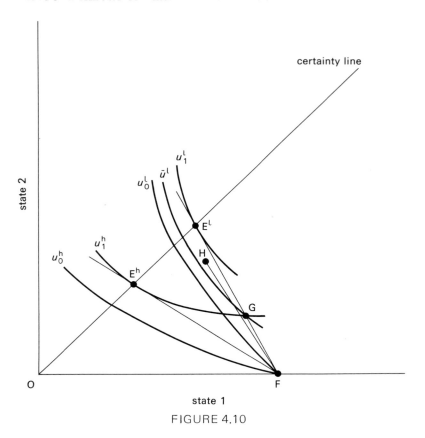

FIGURE 4.10

Consider an insurance contract with price p that pays one dollar in the event that state 2 occurs. Suppose such contracts are sold by risk-neutral and competitive firms so that the actuarial value of the contract must be zero;[14] that is, $\pi(1-p)-(1-\pi)p = 0$ or $p = \pi$ where π is the probability that the insurer will have to pay an indemnity.

If the insurers can observe the probability for each class of policy holder and set a price to each accordingly, then a Pareto optimal allocation of risk is achieved in a 'separating' equilibrium of insurance markets where $p^h = \pi^h$ and $p^\ell = \pi^\ell$. In figure 4.10, h-class (ℓ-class) policy holders face the budget line FE^h (FE^ℓ) extended and choose point E^h (E^ℓ). Both risk classes choose full insurance and enjoy an increase in utility to u_1^h and u_1^ℓ, respectively.

Now suppose the insurer can observe only the average probability of a policy holder becoming disabled. The insurer can no longer distinguish the

[14] This is the zero-profit condition. If insurers as a group are risk averse and risk is not independent then the zero-profit condition would require the actuarial value of the contract to be positive in order to compensate the insurers for bearing risk.

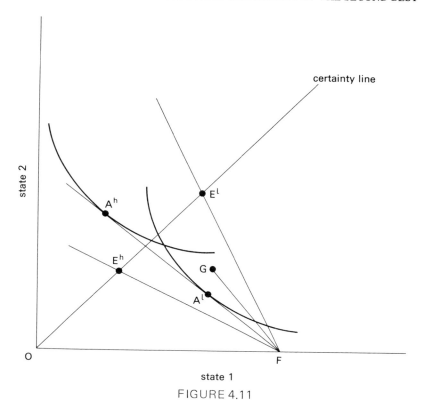

FIGURE 4.11

high risk from the low risk policy holder and must offer the same terms to all. The insurers' zero profit condition requires that they set price $p = \bar{\pi}$, where $\bar{\pi}$ is the average probability of the policy holder becoming disabled and where $\pi^{\ell} < \bar{\pi} < \pi^{h}$. A potential 'pooling' equilibrium is shown in figure 4.11, where all policy holders face budget line $FA^{\ell}A^{h}$ extended, with high risk policy holders choosing point A^{h} and low-risk policy holders choosing point A^{ℓ}. Note that the high risk policy holders 'overinsure' by choosing a larger consumption in the bad state than in the good, whereas the low risk policy holder 'underinsures'. This is because, in a pooling equilibrium, the low risk policy holders effectively subsidize the high risk group.

Rothschild and Stiglitz (1976) argue cogently that even this ineffi-cient equilibrium will not exist. Their reasoning is as follows. We have assumed that insurers must make offers in terms of prices only. Actually, nothing stops insurers from offering terms which specify both price and the maximum quantity of insurance that can be purchased.[15] In this case,

---

[15] It is assumed in all of this that the insurers can monitor the total quantity of insurance pur-chased by a policy holder. Rothschild and Stiglitz (1976) consider this an 'accurate' assumption.

the pooling equilibrium shown cannot exist. An entrant firm can offer a lower price for a policy but with a maximum insurance level (given by point G in figure 4.11) and earn positive economic profits. Note that offer G would be attractive to the low risk but not the high risk policy holders. This possibility occurs whenever there is a pre-existing pooling arrangement; therefore such an arrangement cannot be an equilibrium.

The above describes market 'signalling'. Low risk policy holders signal that they are such by their willingness to accept contract G. One might expect that this would lead to a separating equilibrium such as that illustrated in figure 4.10, where policy holders can either purchase unrestricted insurance at the price given by the absolute value of the slope of FE^h or purchase the contract FG offering a limited amount of insurance at a lower price. As shown, the low risk policy holders purchase the restricted contract whereas the high risk policy holders purchase the unrestricted contract. In some cases this outcome is realized. But Rothschild and Stiglitz proceed to demonstrate that even a signalling equilibrium may not exist. Depending on the number of policy holders in each class purchasing insurance, it may be possible to offer a contract such as FH in figure 4.10 which is attractive to both types of policy holder but earns non-negative profits. This would imply that no equilibrium exists when the probabilities of each policy holder cannot be observed even though 'signalling' is possible. Thus signalling does not, in general, substitute for full information.

Moral hazard   We have assumed that policy holders can trade but not modify risk. In practice, policy holders can undertake risk *reduction* actions which decrease the size of the loss associated with risk, and risk *prevention* actions that decrease the probability of the loss. The ability to purchase insurance will diminish a policy holder's incentive to expend its own resources on risk reduction and prevention. For example, a homeowner who is fully insured against burglary could be inclined to increase the size of the potential loss, by holding more valuables in the home, and the probability of the loss, by spending less on locks and other burglary prevention devices.

It should be stressed that such actions may be perfectly consistent with Pareto optimality. In figure 4.12, a household has a certain level of wealth OF which is kept in state 1 but lost in state 2. Without insurance or expenditure on loss reduction the state-contingent consumption point is F. By expending wealth or effort the household can reduce the size of the loss. Suppose risk reduction actions make available the points on FF'.

The uninsured household will be in equilibrium at point E and expend FG of its wealth on loss reduction. If it is now offered actuarially fair insurance it will face a budget line with a slope equal to the slope of an indifference curve where it crosses the certainty line. Given the opportunity to purchase such insurance, the best policy for the policy holder is to devote FH of its own resources to loss reduction (or 'self-insurance') and purchase insurance policies that take it to the certainty line at E'.

Although the policy holder's expenditures on loss reduction are reduced to FH, this does not imply a market inefficiency. Since the insurance

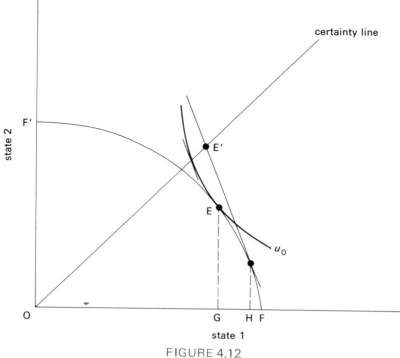

FIGURE 4.12

policies are actuarially fair, the risk-neutral insurers are equally well off, so the utility gain of the policy holder is a Pareto improvement. The implication is that, with fixed probabilities of loss, the insurers can ignore (and should ignore) any economizing on loss reduction expenditures by policy holders.[16]

When, however, the policy holders can alter the probability of loss and insurers cannot monitor and/or write contracts contingent on such actions, a market failure occurs. To see this, consider figure 4.13 where an uninsured household, with wealth F and undertaking no risk reduction expenditures, achieves the utility level u_F. Letting π_F equal the probability of the loss (state 2) with no risk reduction, the absolute value of the slope of u_F at the certainty line is $(1 - \pi_F)/\pi_F$. Suppose the household can reduce the probability of state 2 to $\pi_G < \pi_F$ by undertaking risk reduction expenditures FG. It can then achieve a utility level u_G at G without insurance. The corresponding indifference curve will be steeper than u_F at the point where it crosses the certainty line (because $(1 - \pi_G)/\pi_G > (1 - \pi_F)/\pi_F$). As drawn, indifference curve u_G intersects the certainty line further from the origin than u_F, implying that the utility level u_G at G exceeds that at F, u_F; therefore the household will undertake the risk reduction expendi-

[16] For more details, see Marshall (1976).

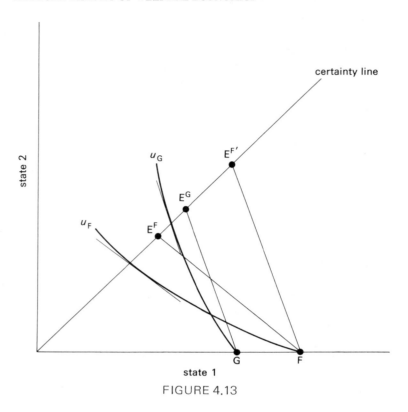

FIGURE 4.13

ture.[17, 18] As long as such gains are possible the household will continue to make risk reduction expenditures until it reaches the indifference curve which intersects the certainty line furthest from the origin.

Now assume that the household can purchase insurance at actuarially fair prices based on the probabilities determined by its risk reduction expenditures. In this case, the household (policy holder) would undertake an extra dollar of risk reduction expenditures provided that the fair price line intersects the certainty line at a point further from the origin. For example, the policy holder would spend FG on risk reduction if E^G is farther from the origin than E^F. The optimal amount of risk reduction expenditures occurs when the fair price line intersects the certainty line at the point furthest from the origin. Let us assume that the point is E^G and FG is the Pareto optimal amount of expenditure on risk reduction. In

[17]   At the certainty line the probabilities are irrelevant, so we can compare the utility levels at F and G even though the probabilities at F and G differ. Note that u_G could intersect the certainty line closer to the origin, in which case the household would not undertake the risk reduction expenditures.

[18]   As always, there is a possibility of non-convexity. The first dollar of risk reduction may not increase utility (i.e. u_G intersects the certainty line below u_F) but larger risk reduction expenditures will increase utility.

this case, the competitive market equilibrium with full information is efficient.[19]

Market failure from moral hazard occurs when insurers cannot monitor risk reduction expenditures and/or write insurance contracts conditional on such expenditures. In this case, policy holders assume that the price they face is independent of their expenditures on risk reduction. When facing price $p_G = \pi_G$, the policy holders would perceive that they can increase their utility by spending nothing on risk reduction, thereby reaching point $E^{F'}$. Of course, if nothing is spent on risk reduction, insurance contracts priced at p_G would have negative actuarial value to insurers. They would alter prices to $p^F = \pi^F$ and a competitive equilibrium would then occur at E^F. This is an equilibrium because policy holders will have no incentive to undertake risk reduction expenditures despite the fact that it is Pareto optimal for them to do so.

We see that with moral hazard regarding risk prevention the resulting market equilibrium will not be Pareto optimal. Obviously, one should wonder whether this 'inefficiency' can be avoided by any other means; after all, the public sector would also be unable to observe risk prevention activities. If so, one could argue that the market equilibrium yields a constrained Pareto optimum – that is, one limited by the informational constraints. However, Arnott and Stiglitz (1981) have recently shown that, in market equilibrium, Pareto improvements could be achieved through 'corrective' taxes and subsidies on risk prevention activities. For example, lump-sum tax-financed subsidies on locks, burglar and smoke alarms etc. could yield a Pareto improvement by encouraging the risk prevention activities on which too little private expenditures are made. Similarly, taxes on alcohol, cigarettes etc. would encourage health risk prevention.

3 Market Failure and the Role of the Public Sector

We have discussed the important reasons why a Pareto optimal allocation of resources may not be achieved through a decentralized market system. Of primary importance is the inability of every market participant to exclude, at the appropriate shadow price, those who benefit from its actions. Likewise, a household or firm must have some means of extracting compensation from others who impose costs upon it.

Exclusion may not be feasible for technological reasons, as in the case of national defence, or for institutional reasons, as in the case where property rights cannot be assigned. In other cases, exclusion would only yield a Pareto optimal outcome if the appropriate 'personalized' prices can be ascertained and enforced (for example, public goods and insurance).

---

[19] This result was shown by Spence and Zeckhauser (1971). It only holds if the insurers are risk neutral. If insurers are risk averse, insurance prices contain a variable loading factor. If such prices depend on the actions of the policy holders, they can exploit monopsony power (Marshall, 1976, pp. 885–7).

When exclusion is impossible, the free rider problem and the associated prisoner's dilemma arise, leading market participants to undertake actions on the basis of their own private interest which are not Pareto optimal.

In all cases of market failure, the marginal social benefit of devoting an extra unit of resources to a particular activity will differ from the marginal social cost. Market participants, motivated by private marginal benefits and costs, will not be induced to devote the optimal amount of resources to the activity. In some cases, such as waste disposal, there will be too few resources used; in other cases, such as erecting barriers to entry, there will be too many resources used.

In the face of market failure, there may exist a role for the public sector above and beyond that of redistributing income and providing the legal institutions necessary for the operation of a market economy. The government may have to involve itself in the actual allocation of resources.

Why should the government be able to undertake mutually beneficial allocative actions which private agents cannot? The answer lies in the government's monopoly on the legal use of coercive power. To put it bluntly, the government can extract involuntary payments and/or prohibit activities with the threat of force. This permits it to finance public goods (or factors) which private agents value in excess of cost but would not voluntarily pay for, without exclusion, because of the free rider problem. Similarly, the government can levy 'corrective' taxes and subsidies, set quotas, regulate prices and profits etc. in order to direct private allocative activities. A corrective tax/subsidy can eliminate any divergence between private and social marginal cost or benefit.

It is worth emphasizing that this view of the benefits of governmental allocative functions is quite different from the superficial view that the government 'knows better', and provides a co-ordinated and planned approach to resource allocation in contrast to what are thought to be the unco-ordinated and unplanned actions of private decision-makers. The central conclusion of the fundamental theorems is that a supervisory or planning role for the government is not necessary for efficient resource allocation. Private decision-makers need not 'see beyond their noses' or care about anything but their own selfish ends to achieve a Pareto optimal allocation of resources in a perfectly competitive market. Prices will convey the necessary information.

This is not meant to imply that informational considerations are not important in defining the scope and rationale for government intervention in the allocative process. As mentioned earlier, markets may fail because private decision-makers do not have complete information. It is also the case that private agents may devote too few resources towards obtaining some types of information and too many resources towards obtaining other types of information. It is relatively easy to make economic arguments favouring a governmental role in gathering information. However, such arguments usually designate a role for the government in disseminating information to market participants rather than becoming directly involved in the allocative process.

It should be stressed that although the government sector may pursue 'corrective' policies in an economy which is not Pareto optimal, it could also be a cause rather than a cure of market failure. Government tax and transfer policies may lead to a non-optimal allocation of resources in an economy that would otherwise be Pareto optimal. This is because the existence of non-lump-sum taxes and subsidies alters the relative prices perceived by different agents, causing the Pareto optimal conditions not to be satisfied.

We shall refer to a market economy where Pareto optimality is not obtained as a *distorted* market economy. We now turn to an examination of the relevance of the Pareto criteria in such economies.

4 The Theory of the Second Best

In this chapter we have examined a number of reasons why decentralized decision-making may not yield a Pareto optimal allocation of resources, and have argued that such 'market failures' imply a potential role for allocative policies by governments (centralized decision-makers with coercive power) in addition to their redistributive policies. By an appropriate set of tax/subsidies, regulations, and/or public production decisions, the government could achieve *potential* Pareto improvements in social welfare which, in turn, can be realized with the appropriate redistributive policies.

In this section we discuss a basic problem encountered in designing and evaluating allocative policies. Unless these policies correct for all of the distortions and market failures so as to bring about a 'first-best' Pareto optimal allocation, the remaining conditions for a Pareto optimum provide, in general, no guidance. In other words, although it may be desirable to set price equal to marginal cost in (say) a public utility if all of the other Pareto optimal conditions are satisfied, it may or may not be desirable if any one of the other conditions is not satisfied.

The goal of efficiency (potential or actual Pareto improvements) in a context that precludes the attainment of Pareto optimality is generally referred to as the 'second-best' criterion. The term 'second-best' is credited to Meade (1955), but a number of second-best type problems were analysed earlier in the post-war period, including customs unions (Viner, 1950) and the excess burden of taxation (Corlett and Hague, 1953). Ramsey's (1927) remarkable paper on taxation came much earlier but is clearly the solution to a problem that we would now label 'second best'.[20]

Lipsey and Lancaster (1956) cast the problem in a general framework of policy optimization. They considered the policy of maximizing an objective function $F(x_1, \ldots, x_n)$ subject to a feasibility constraint $G(x_1, \ldots, x_n)$ and a 'second-best constraint'

$$F_1(\ )/F_n(\ ) = k\,G_1(\ )/G_n(\ )$$

---

[20] The literature on the second best is vast. For an excellent survey and a further discussion of the issues raised in this section, the reader is directed to Harris (1981).

where $k \neq 1$, that precludes at least one of the Pareto equalities.[21] The first-order conditions to such an optimization problem are quite complicated and involve second-order cross-derivatives of the objective function and the feasibility constraint.

Lipsey and Lancaster then proclaim a 'general theorem for the second-best optimum' which states that, in general, if one of the Pareto equalities is unattainable, the others, although still attainable, are undesirable. From this theorem, it follows that there is no *a priori* way to rank different states of the world on the basis of the remaining Pareto optimum conditions.

> Specifically, it is not true that a situation in which more, but not all, of the optimum conditions are fulfilled is necessarily, or is even likely, to be superior to a situation in which fewer are fulfilled. (Lipsey and Lancaster, 1956, p. 12)

Furthermore, removing one of a number of 'second-best constraints' may raise or lower welfare.

There is no doubt that the second-best theorem has very negative implications for welfare economics. It means that the intuitively simple ideas captured in the Pareto optimum conditions cannot be relied on without reservations and that rules for second-best optimality are, in general, much more difficult than the simple Pareto rules.

4.1 *The interpretation of the second-best constraint*

The most controversial aspect of second-best theory, and the reason why Lipsey and Lancaster do not really provide a 'general theory', lies in the nature and the interpretation of the second-best constraint. For example, Lipsey and Lancaster's second-best constraint is clearly interpreted by them to correspond to an output market distortion in the market for good 1 that forbids the equality between the price and marginal cost in that industry, both being measured in units of the *numéraire* good n.

McManus (1958) points out the inadequacy of this interpretation and concludes that good n cannot be interpreted as a *numéraire* good but, rather, the Lipsey and Lancaster second-best constraint forbids the equality of the marginal rate of substitution between good 1 and good n and the marginal rate of transformation between the same two goods.

The actual source of the second-best constraint, and why it should be considered a constraint at all, are important issues. In many analyses, the constraint represents the behaviour of a 'deviant' agent such as a monopoly or a third country in a customs union problem. In other analyses, for example taxation, the constraint arises because the taxation of non-market activities (and hence lump-sum taxation) is deemed infeasible. In

---

[21] The objective functions can be the utility of the representative consumer, in which case we remain within the Pareto criterion framework.

still other cases, the constraint represents a 'sacred cow' distortion that cannot be removed for (say) political or historical reasons.

Perhaps the most reasonable interpretation of the second-best constraint is that it reflects the reality of public sector decision-making. No co-ordinated and comprehensive policy-making apparatus is likely to exist. Rather, public works projects are evaluated independently of competition policy, which is evaluated independently of tax policy etc. Each policy-making group takes the conditions in those sectors of the economy outside of its mandate as 'given'. These 'givens' may include conditions that do not correspond to Pareto optimality.

This interpretation leads naturally to a question on which the theory of the second best has direct bearing: When is it appropriate to satisfy the Pareto optimal condition in one sector of the economy independently of whether conditions of Pareto optimality are met elsewhere? This is the question of whether *piecemeal* policies are appropriate. Unfortunately, the theory of the second best is quite negative in this regard – the conditions under which piecemeal policies are appropriate are quite stringent.

The most optimistic view on the possibility of piecemeal policy is that of Davis and Whinston (1965) who divide the economy into 'deviant' (i.e. non-competitive) and 'non-deviant' (i.e. competitive) decision-making agents. They show that if the planner is given certain tools, and the deviant agents follow a rule which is, in essence, independent of the planner's actions, there exists a set of prices for which the decentralized decision-making agents undertake decisions which bring about a second-best optimum. Deviant and non-deviant agents do not necessarily face the same prices in this scheme (i.e. there is a set of optimal taxes implicitly required). McFadden (1969) showed that, in some special cases, the deviant and non-deviant agents are faced with the same set of prices.

Since the Davis–Whinston result holds only for a particular model of the second-best constraint, it is of limited significance. In fact, conditions under which piecemeal policy prescription are appropriate are quite stringent and depend on the model or problem being considered in general. The sufficient condition is that the cross-price elasticities of uncompensated demand and supply between the distorted sector and any undistorted sector are equal to zero. One such case is analysed by Boadway and Harris (1977).

4.2 *Evaluating efficiency gains from 'small' changes*

Although the foregoing discussion implies that second-best welfare economies will be difficult to treat in many cases, the task is not impossible. One approach that eliminates many of the difficulties associated with the second-best approach is the 'second-better' or 'nth-best' approach where only small policy changes in a distorted economy are evaluated (Meade, 1955, 1976). This approach considers only a small (differential) change in, say, some set of distortions. The benefits of adopting this approach are threefold. Firstly, only local rather than global information about the objective and constraint functions is needed. Secondly, there is no need to derive necessary 'rules' for optimization which, in the case of second-best problems, may be very complex and difficult to explain. Thirdly, because incremental changes are being considered, a necessary and sufficient criterion is derived. As Harris (1976) and others have noted, the second-order (sufficiency) conditions for a second-best optimization problem depend on third-order derivatives of the objective and feasibility constraint functions. Specifically, the standard convexity assumptions which (along with the first-order conditions) are sufficient for a Pareto optimum are not sufficient for a second-best optimum.

The shortcomings of this approach are substantial nevertheless. The problem of separating the efficiency and equity effects of a given partial policy change is unsatisfactorily resolved. The use of the compensation principle to accomplish this end raises the problem of consistently ranking different distorted states of the world. Even if these difficulties are overcome, there is still no guarantee that a 'hill-climbing' procedure will converge on a global optimum, second-best or otherwise.

In figure 4.14, the curve labelled FF can be called a *utility feasibility curve* (after Samuelson, 1950). It is the locus of utility distributions that are attainable with lump-sum income redistribution, assuming that the existing market distortions are held constant in some sense. The UFC lies

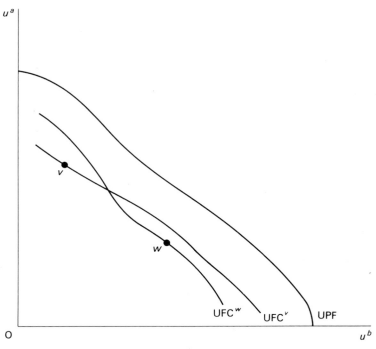

FIGURE 4.14

everywhere inside the utility possibilities frontier, labelled UPF in figure 4.14; this is the locus of Pareto optimal utility distributions.

To begin with, the UFC could be positively sloped in some range; that is, in the mere presence of distortions, the redistribution of income in a lump-sum manner can yield Pareto improvements.[22] It seems necessary to preclude this possibility before examining the efficiency effects of a policy that alters the distortions in the economy. Accordingly, we have only drawn the negatively sloped region of the UFC in figure 4.14.

A policy change shifts the UFC. Potential improvements are possible under state v (say, a particular set of distortions) if UFC^v lies outside UFC^w. As before, reversal and intransitivity problems arise if the UFCs cross. As shown in figure 4.14, the policy change (say altering a set of distortions from w to v) allows the Kaldor test to be passed in moving from w to v and in moving from v to w. For sufficiently small changes in policy, such reversals cannot occur, but this is still a problem in principle. As discussed in chapter 3, section 6, we can define more general compensation criteria that are not subject to this difficulty, but the information requirements for putting them into practice are great.

5 Conclusions

Although the concept of Pareto optimality and the fundamental theorems of welfare economics provide considerable insight into the relative desirability of different allocations of resources, they are subject to two limitations. Firstly, they are of limited use in providing guidance about economies where Pareto optimality is unlikely to be achieved because some sort of institutional constraints limit the states of the world that can be achieved above and beyond the resource constraints. Secondly, the Pareto ranking leaves many states, including all Pareto optimal states, non-comparable. The first difficulty has been discussed in this chapter and the second difficulty will be addressed in chapters 5 and 6.

In this chapter we have identified the main causes of market failure which occur when decentralized decision-making through a market mechanism does not lead to a Pareto optimal allocation of resources. Market failure can occur if (1) the preferences of the households or the production technologies of the firms are non-convex (2) some economic agents are not competitive price-takers (3) unpriced externalities exist because of a lack of property rights or because there is jointness in production and/or consumption (including the special case of public goods), (4) markets fail to exist at all. In every case, a private agent making an economic decision on the basis of market prices does not reap the full marginal social benefit or bear the full marginal social cost of its actions.

---

[22] This is a generalization of a point made by Foster and Sonnenschein (1970). For more on this, see Bruce and Harris (1982, pp. 768–70).

Public sector allocative policies can yield Pareto improvements in the presence of market failure because of the government's power to extract involuntary payments from private agents. This permits the government to finance productive activities which would not break even at Pareto optimal prices and/or to levy corrective taxes and subsidies. The government can also regulate economic activities directly.

A major problem for the study of welfare economics is posed by 'the theory of the second best'. The main thrust of this theory is to undermine the usefulness of the Pareto optimal conditions as a guide to economic efficiency. If any one of a number of Pareto optimal conditions cannot be met, then satisfying the remaining conditions is not necessarily desirable (i.e. Pareto improvements can be achieved by violating the remaining conditions). Although the second-best framework does not yield intuitively appealing results like the conditions of Pareto optimality it is, nevertheless, essential for treating welfare economics in the imperfect, but eventful, real world.

CHAPTER 5

Social Welfare Orderings: Requirements and Possibilities

1 Introduction

The central objective of the study of welfare economics is to provide a framework which permits meaningful statements to be made about whether some economic situations are socially preferable to others. Ultimately we would like to rank all economic situations (social states) so we would like this ranking to be *complete* (so that every social state can be compared and ranked to another) and *consistent* (so that the ranking is reflexive and transitive). We shall call such a complete and consistent ranking of social states a *social welfare ordering* (SWO). Just as with household orderings, if a continuity assumption is made the SWO can be represented by a *social welfare function* (SWF) that assigns a number to each social state.

States cannot be socially ordered without someone making prior value judgments, although sometimes such value judgments are implicit. Value judgments are statements of ethics which cannot be found to be true or false on the basis of factual evidence. The value judgments contained in a SWO may be weak (i.e. broadly accepted) or strong (i.e. controversial). An example of a relatively strong value judgment is Rawls's (1971) difference principle, which states that inequalities are 'just' if and only if they work to the advantage of the least-well-off household. A far weaker value judgment is the weak Pareto principle, which states that a social state x is socially preferred to y if x is unanimously preferred to y by all households in the economy.

Another weak value judgment that is called *individualism* requires that the preferences of the individual households should matter when determining the SWO. This value judgment, commonly made throughout welfare economics, imposes certain informational requirements on the choice of an SWO. Specifically, information about each household's preference over social states and about how a given level of utility for any household compares with that of another household may be required. These requirements are called the *measurability* and *comparability* requirements, respectively. In this chapter we shall examine how value

requirements and informational requirements limit the set of SWO possibilities from which the planner can choose.

In order to be concrete, we shall identify a social state with an allocation of N goods over the H households;[1] that is, an allocation $[x]$ is an
$N \times H$ vector where element x_i^h is the amount of good i consumed by
household h. In chapter 3 we saw that allocations can be partially ordered
in terms of efficiency criteria. This partial SWO is based on two weak
value judgments – the Pareto principle and individualism. The Pareto
partial ordering is also informationally undemanding. Household utility
need only be ordinally measurable and utility comparisons across households are unnecessary.

The most serious drawback of the Pareto partial ordering is that it is
not a complete ordering. The usefulness of the partial ordering may be
enhanced by allowing the definition of a social state to include hypothetical lump-sum transfers of goods (or generalized purchasing power) among
households, as discussed in chapter 3. Nevertheless it remains a partial
ordering. Only those situations where all households are made better or
worse off (the strong Pareto principle does allow some households to be
indifferent) can be ranked. If some households are made better off and
others worse off in moving from x to y, even when lump-sum redistribution is assumed to be possible, the Pareto principle cannot tell us anything.
Thus, whenever there is a utility conflict among the households, such as
created by a move along a utility possibilities frontier, we need more than
the Pareto principle. Ideally we should have an SWO. Although such an
SWO need not incorporate the Pareto principle, most SWOs commonly
used do incorporate it, since it is not the Pareto principle *per se* that is the
problem but rather the fact that orderings based on it alone are
incomplete.

In reality, utility conflict among the households in the economy is
resolved by some means or other, whether it involves property rights and
market prices, collective bargaining or the redistributive powers of the
government. In this chapter we are not concerned with such 'positive'
distribution theory. Rather we are concerned with the ethical problem
of resolving the conflict inherent in finding the normative solution to the
distribution problem. Specifically, some households in the economy may
prefer state x to y whereas others prefer y to x. Given that the household
preferences should be taken into account, how should the policy-maker
aggregate such conflicting preferences into a single SWO? This is the
central question of normative social choice theory.

Before considering the determination of SWO possibilities, it is useful
to describe the broad framework of normative social choice theory and
introduce some commonly encountered terminology. Unfortunately, the
nomenclature in this realm is as extensive as it is distressing. We shall
try to avoid introducing unnecessary terminology and explain, in intuitive
language, those terms that we do introduce.

---

[1]   Supplies of factors could be introduced as negative elements in the allocation vector.

2 The Framework of Normative Social Choice Theory

The objective is to derive an SWO over social states from the households' orderings of the social states. The means of aggregating the household orderings into the SWO is called the *social choice rule* (SCR) (following Sen, 1970).[2] If the household orderings are continuous they can be represented by household utility functions, and if the SWO is continuous it can be represented by an SWF. In this case, the SCR is a social welfare *functional* (SWFL) which is defined over the set of possible household utility functions.

The most general form of the SWF (over social states) is the so-called *Bergson–Samuelson* (B–S) SWF, expressed as

$$W(x) = F((u^1(x), u^2(x), \ldots, u^H(x))$$

The function $W(x)$ may take any form, although it is usually assumed to satisfy at least three properties. Firstly, it is assumed that it can be defined over utility space; that is, $W(x)$ can be evaluated from an H vector of utility values. In this case, the SWF can be written as $W(u)$ and represented by a social welfare indifference curve map as in figure 5.1. If the social welfare depends only on the utility outcomes of the social state in this way, it is said to satisfy *welfarism* (Sen, 1977). This will be discussed further in the next section. Secondly, the B–S SWF is usually assumed to incorporate a version of the *Pareto principle* known as the strong Pareto principle. This means the SWF is increasing in each household's utility *ceteris paribus*. Thus, the social welfare indifference curves are negatively sloped and those further from the origin correspond to higher levels of social welfare, so $W_3 > W_2 > W_1$ in figure 5.1. Finally, the B–S SWF is often assumed to be strictly quasi-concave so that social welfare indifference curves have the shape shown in figure 5.1. This assumption reflects the egalitarian ethic that inequality in utilities among households, *per se*, is socially undesirable.

In figure 5.1, the B–S SWF is combined with the utility possibilities frontier (UPF) discussed in chapter 3 and labelled UPF. The social welfare maximum occurs at point E which corresponds to the particular allocation of goods and resources that is Pareto optimal and maximizes social welfare. The social welfare optimum could be attained in principle by a combination of perfectly competitive markets combined with lump-sum redistribution, although neither are likely to exist in practice. At the social welfare optimum the slope of the UPF is equal to the slope of an SWF indifference curve. As discussed in chapter 3, the absolute value of the slope of the UPF is given by $\lambda^h(\ )/\lambda^g(\ )$ where $\lambda^h(\ )$ is the marginal utility of income of household h. The absolute value of the slope of the SWF

---

[2] Arrow (1963) called the means of aggregating household preferences a social welfare function. In order to avoid confusion with the conventional Bergson–Samuelson definition of a social welfare function, we adopt Sen's terminology.

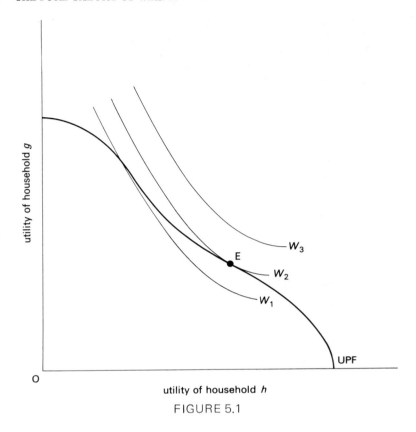

FIGURE 5.1

indifference curve is known as the *marginal rate of social substitution* (MRSS) in utility and is given by W_h/W_g, where $W_h = \partial W(\ )/\partial u^h$. Thus, at the social welfare optimum,

$$\frac{W_h}{W_g} = \frac{\lambda^h}{\lambda^g} \qquad \text{for all } h, g$$

or

$$\frac{W_h}{\lambda^h} = \frac{W_g}{\lambda^g} = \ldots = \phi \tag{5.1}$$

where ϕ is the common social marginal utility of income for every household.

Analytically this is all well and good, but how can such a framework be utilized in the practice of welfare economics? And under what circumstances does a general B–S SWF exist? The first question is addressed in the second part of this book. The second question will be answered in this chapter. It will be found that the general B–S SWF, although flexible in form, is demanding in terms of informational requirements. Other 'popular' SWFs are found to be less informationally demanding but far more specific in functional form. Perhaps the oldest and best-known form is the simple *utilitarian* (or 'Benthamite') SWF, where

$$W = \sum_{h=1}^{H} u^h \tag{5.2}$$

In this case, social welfare is the unweighted sum of household utilities. Slightly less restrictive is the *generalized utilitarian* or weighted sum SWF, where

$$W = \sum_{h=1}^{H} a_h u^h \tag{5.2'}$$

and a_h, $h = 1, \ldots, H$, are positive constants. Other specific forms are the *Bernoulli–Nash* (B–N) SWF, where

$$W = \prod_{h=1}^{H} u^h \tag{5.3}$$

and the *generalized* B–N SWF, where

$$W = \prod_{h=1}^{H} (u^h)^{a_h} \tag{5.3'}$$

In this case, social welfare is the product (weighted or unweighted) of the household utilities. Note that the B–N SWF is utilitarian in the logarithms of utility. Also there is the *Rawlsian* or *maximin* SWF

$$W = \min[u^1, \ldots, u^H] \tag{5.4}$$

where social welfare is identified with the utility of the worst-off household.[3] The social welfare indifference contours for these three SWF forms (utilitarian, B–N and maximin) are shown in figures 5.2(a), (b) and (c), respectively.

All of the five SWF forms described above are special cases of a more general SWF known as the *isoelastic* form or

$$W = \frac{\sum\limits_{h=1}^{H} a_h (u^h)^{1-\rho}}{1 - \rho} \tag{5.5}$$

---

[3] This SWF is termed 'maximin' because it involves maximizing the minimum value of the utility vector and is related to the maximin strategy encountered in game theory.

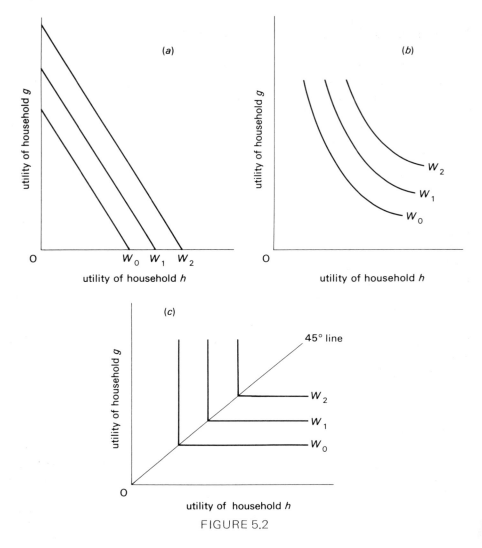

FIGURE 5.2

where $1/\rho$ is the (constant) elasticity of substitution of an SWF in-difference contour. If $\rho = 0$ and $a_h = 1$ for all h, (5.5) reduces to the utilitarian case. As $\rho \to 1$ and $a_h = 1$ the limiting expression for (5.5) is the B–N SWF. As $\rho \to \infty$, (5.5) reduces to the maximin form.[4] It should be noted that since the SWO is an ordering, the SWF representing it will be an ordinal function. Therefore, an SWF formed by taking an increasing function of any one of the above functional forms is also a legitimate representation.

---

[4] Multiplying (5.5) by $1-\rho$ and taking the $(1-\rho)$th root yields the CES functional form. Since this is just a monotonic transformation of W it is permitted by the ordinality of W. We can now use the well-known limiting cases of the CES function to obtain the results in the text. A good proof of the limiting case of the CES function is found in Varian (1978, p. 18).

3 Informational Restrictions and the Social Welfare Ordering

We have said that a *social welfare ordering* (SWO) that completely and transitively orders all social states (say, allocations of goods across households) is a desirable objective in the study of welfare economics. In this section we begin an examination of SWO possibilities, a topic that will concern us for much of this chapter. An important point here is that we wish to restrict the choice of an SWO to those that satisfy certain requirements. If we are able to choose any SWO, out of the air so to speak, then the SWO possibilities are unlimited. With such liberty, however, the SWO concept may not be very interesting. For this reason we constrain the SWO to satisfy certain requirements. Surprisingly, imposing particular combinations of requirements, each of which seems reasonable in other contexts, is found to restrict the SWO possibilities rather drastically.

We shall examine the SWO possibilities under two sorts of restriction. Both sorts of restriction pertain to the information that policy-makers are permitted to utilize when deriving a social ordering. The first set of restrictions implies a property that Sen (1977) has called *welfarism* (W) or *strong neutrality*. Basically this restricts the information that can be utilized in ranking social states to utility information corresponding to those social states. The second set of restrictions, which are called *invariance requirements*, are informational requirements pertaining to the measurability and interpersonal comparability of the individual utilities.

3.1 *Welfarism*

An SWO has the property of welfarism if the ranking of social states depends only on the utility levels of the households. Specifically, information about how the utility levels are obtained is irrelevant for determining how the social states should be ordered. That is, states having the same welfare consequences are indistinguishable for social welfare purposes. This is a strong requirement for it implies that social welfare depends solely upon the numerical value of utility attained by each individual regardless of the measurement conventions by which numerical utility levels are arrived at.

Three conditions are sufficient for welfarism. We will state (nonformally) each in turn.

Universality or unrestricted domain (condition U) This condition requires that any logically possible H vector of individual utility functions is admissible in determining the social ranking. That is, the same SWO must be used to aggregate individual utilities regardless of what the individual utility functions happen to be. The only thing asked of the households' preferences is that each household be able to order consistently (i.e. reflexively and transitively) all social states. It seems reasonable to require the SWO to be universally applicable in this sense.

Pareto indifference (condition PI)   If all households are indifferent between two social states, the SWO must rank the two states equivalently.

Independence of irrelevant alternatives (condition I)   This condition requires that the social ranking of any two social states x and y be the same whenever the utility levels attached to x and y by the individual households are the same. This implies that the social ranking must be unchanged if any or all households' indifference curves are renumbered in a way that leaves the indifference curve numbers associated with states x and y unchanged. This also means that the social ranking of x and y must be independent of the availability of other social states and of the households' preferences over social states other than those being ranked.

A proof that conditions U, PI and I imply welfarism is given by Sen (1979). Intuitively it can be seen how welfarism is implied for states which are socially equivalent through the PI condition. This condition requires that x and y be ranked as equivalent if all households are indifferent between them. In other words, all other information about x and y is irrelevant, and this is the heart of welfarism. Conditions U and I generalize this informational parsimony to strict rankings of x and y.

3.2 *Invariance requirements*

These requirements limit the measurability and comparability of household utility functions. *Measurability* refers to the sense in which the real numbers attached to a given household's utility levels are meaningful (i.e. convey information). *Comparability* refers to the sense in which the real numbers attached to different households' utility levels can be meaningfully compared. Comparability in this sense is a statement about utility information that is commensurable among households, and should not be confused with the welfare judgment of how (or whether) to trade off one household's utility against another.

Assumptions about measurability and comparability can be formalized by considering the set of transformations that can be applied to an H household utility vector without changing the SWO. Following Sen, we let $\psi(\ ) = [\psi^1(\ ), \ldots, \psi^H(\ )]$ be a vector of transformation functions with one element for each household's utility function.

Measurability concerns the transformations applicable to the individual household's utility function. The most restrictive measurability assumption is that the household's utility function is fully measurable or measurable with an absolute scale (AS). In this case a unique real number is attached to each indifference curve of a household. Alternatively, the only admissible transformation of scale is the identity transformation. That is, $v^h(\ ) = u^h(\ )$ where $u^h(\ )$ is a utility representation of the preferences of household h (i.e. a numbering of its indifference curves) and $v^h(\ )$ is the admitted transformation of that utility representation.

The least restrictive measurability assumption is that utility is measurable only with an *ordinal scale* (OS).[5] In this case indifference curves can be numbered in any arbitrary manner, but higher indifference curves must be given higher numbers in order that the numerical scale preserves the ranking of the indifference curves. Formally, this permits the utility function of a household h to be rescaled by taking any monotonic increasing transformation of it. That is, a transform of u^h, $v^h( ) = \psi^h(u^h)$ for any $\psi^h(u^h)$ with $\partial\psi^h/\partial u^h > 0$, conveys the same information as u^h, and therefore the SWO should be the same if u^h is replaced with v^h.

Lying between AS and OS measurability is a *ratio scale* (RS) and a *cardinal scale* (CS) measurability. RS measurability means that any positive linear transformation of u^h, $v^h( ) = b^h u^h( )$ where b^h is a positive constant, conveys the same information as u^h. CS measurability means any positive affine transformation of u^h, $v^h( ) = a^h + b^h u^h( )$ where $b^h > 0$, conveys the same information as u^h. An example of a cardinally measurable entity is temperature. Fahrenheit, Celsius and kelvin scales all convey the same information and are positive affine transformations of each other.

Comparability means the extent to which utility information measured for the individual household can be meaningfully compared across households. The assumption of *non-comparability* (NC) means that none of the information measured for individual utility can be used when making across-household comparisons. *Full comparability* (FC) means that all of the information available for the individual household is available for comparisons across-households. *Partial comparability* (PC) means that only some of the household information is available for comparisons across households.

It should be realized that the assumption about comparability is not necessarily independent from the assumption about measurability. If, for example, utility for a household is measurable only with an ordinal scale, then increments in utility cannot be compared across households since they cannot be compared for a single household. On the other hand, when utility is measurable to an absolute scale for the single household there must be full comparability across households because the utility level of every household is associated with a unique real number, and real numbers are comparable. Another way of looking at this is that the only admissible transformation under AS is the identity transformation which is, trivially, the same for every household.

In the following sections we shall consider the SWO possibilities under different assumptions about measurability and comparability. In general we shall see that, without comparability, SWO possibilities are extremely limited regardless of the degree of measurability of utility. Under full comparability, however, the SWO possibilities are increased as the measurability of individual utility is increased. SWO possibilities are narrowed,

---

[5] This is the least restrictive case apart from the trivial case of measurability with a *nominal* scale, which allows an arbitrary numbering of the indifference curves.

often to a single case, if only partial comparability is possible or if additional restrictions are imposed.

The additional restrictions we shall consider are drawn from the following. The *weak Pareto principle* (PW) states that social state x must be preferred to y in the SWO if every household strictly prefers x to y. The *strong Pareto principle* (PS) requires x to be socially preferred to y even if some households are indifferent, provided that at least one household strictly prefers x to y and none prefers y to x. *Anonymity* (A) requires that only the utility levels, and not which households get which utilities, should matter in socially ranking the states. In other words, if u' is a vector of utilities associated with state x and u'' is a permutation of the elements of u', then the utility vector of u' and u'' must be ranked the same by the SWO *vis-à-vis* other utility vectors. *Separability* (SE) requires that the social ranking of x and y depends only on the preferences of households that have a strict preference between x and y, and not on the levels of utility of the households which are indifferent between x and y. *Minimal equity* (EM) requires that if all households, except the one in the best-off position, prefer x to y then x is preferred to y in the social ordering. *Strong equity* (ES) requires that the set of utility distributions which are as least as good as the reference utility distribution u_0 be strictly convex, as shown in figure 5.3. This means that if the SWO is a SWF, it is strictly quasi-concave. Finally, *continuity* (CO) requires the 'at least as

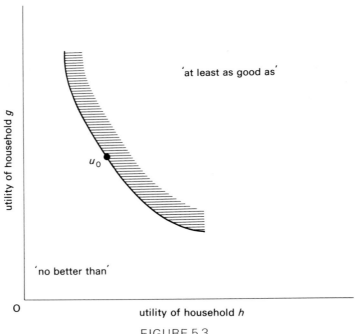

FIGURE 5.3

good as' set be closed so the SWO can be represented by an ordinal social welfare function (SWF).[6] Some SWOs, such as lexicographic orderings, do not satisfy this property and therefore are precluded by the requirement of continuity.

4 Non-comparability and Dictatorship Possibilities

In this section we consider the question addressed by Arrow (1951a) in his celebrated monograph *Social Choice and Individual Values*. In particular, if utility functions are ordinal and non-comparable so that the informational assumptions are OS and NC (which are all that are required to define Pareto optimality), then what SWO possibilities are permitted if one also restricts the SWO to incorporate the weak Pareto principle and welfarism?[7, 8] The answer is somewhat surprising: OS–NC, W and PW imply that the only possible SWO is a dictatorship. That is, social orderings must coincide with the preferences of some individual in the economy regardless of the preferences of the others.[9]

Arrow proved this remarkable theorem by contradiction. In such proofs, one uses the requirements of U, I, PW and the transitivity of the SWO to 'uncover' a dictator. However, with the full welfarism assumptions of this chapter, it is possible to show diagrammatically why the SWO possibility must be a dictatorship in a two-household economy and to give some intuitive meaning to the proof.[10]

To begin with, the welfarism assumption permits us to examine the SWO in terms of the rankings of the two-household utility levels as in figure 5.4, where the utility of household g is measured on the vertical axis and that of household h is measured on the horizontal axis. Consider any utility point, for example $u_0 = [u_0^g, u_0^h]$, as a reference point. We wish to rank all other utility points relative to u_0. We can use u_0 as an origin and divide the utility space into quadrants. Ignoring the boundaries for now, we can immediately rank points in quadrants I and III relative to

---

[6]   Technically, continuity means that the 'at least as good as' set and the 'no better than' set of utility points are closed and contain their own boundaries. Intuitively, this means that, assuming welfarism, for any utility point in the utility space of figure 5.2 and for any ray from the origin there must exist a point on the ray indifferent (in terms of social welfare) to the closer point. In other words, we have social welfare indifference curves. This cannot be the case with a lexicographic SWO. In this case, the only possibility of social welfare indifference occurs if all households are indifferent.

[7]   Relaxing the weak Pareto principle simply permits reverse dictatorships, where the SWO is the exact opposite of the 'dictator's' preferences.

[8]   Arrow actually used a weaker form of welfarism that applied only to strict rankings. In terms of our definitions, he used U, I and PW. That is, non-welfare desiderata were permitted in the event that all households were indifferent. This subtlety is not important in what follows.

[9]   This result is sometimes presented in the form of an impossibilities theorem. In this case, dictatorship is precluded by assumption directly, or indirectly by a stronger assumption such as anonymity.

[10]   The following discussion is adapted from a fine paper by Charles Blackorby, David Donaldson and John Weymark (1983) which introduced this diagrammatic framework for analysing social choice questions.

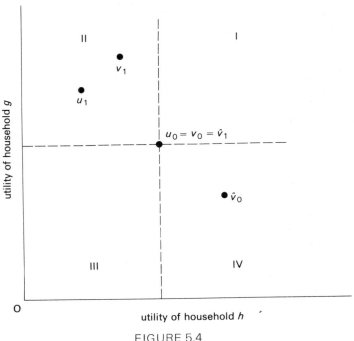

FIGURE 5.4

u_0. By the weak Pareto principle, all points in I must be ranked higher than u_0, whereas u_0 must be ranked higher than all points in quadrant III. The problem is to rank points in quadrants II and IV relative to u_0.

Consider now the informational invariance requirement OS–NC used by Arrow. Formally this assumption means that the social ordering of social states (and by welfarism, the social ordering of utility points) must remain unchanged when the H vector of utility representations is transformed by $\psi = [\psi^1(\ ), \ldots, \psi^H(\ )]$. OS implies that each household transformation $\psi^h(\ )$ is monotonically increasing and NC implies that a different transformation can apply to each household's utility function. This means that any household's indifference curves can be renumbered in any manner which preserves the rankings of its indifference curves, and that different renumberings can be applied to the indifference curve maps of different households.

With the OS–NC assumption we can now show that all points in quadrant II must be ranked against u_0 in the same way. Consider point u_1 in quadrant II, where $u_1^h < u_0^h$ and $u_1^g > u_0^g$. By completeness of the SWO, either u_1 must be ranked above u_0, or u_0 ranked above u_1, or u_1 and u_0 ranked as equivalent. Suppose, without loss of generality, that u_1 is ranked above u_0 according to an SWO. This ranking must be preserved when we apply increasing monotonic transformations to u^g and u^h where, by NC, we can apply different transformations u^g and u^h. Consider applying the transformation $v^g = \psi^g(u^g)$, $v^h = \psi^h(u^h)$ such that $v_0^g = u_0^g$ and $v_0^h = u_0^h$; that is, point u_0 is mapped back to itself. But, by the choice of $\psi(\ )$, point $[\psi^g(u_1^g), \psi^h(u_1^h)]$ can be mapped anywhere into quadrant II. All that must be retained is $v_1^g > v_0^g$ and $v_1^h < v_0^h$. Thus all points in II must be ranked the same with respect to u_0.

We can now rule out the case that all points in II are ranked equivalent to u_0. Suppose this to be the case, and consider a transformation that maps u_0 back to u_0 and u_1 to v_1, where $v_1^g > u_1^g$, $v_1^h > u_1^h$. By PW, v_1 must be ranked above u_1. However, we have already supposed that v_1 and u_1 are both indifferent to u_0. This violates transitivity. Thus either all points in II are ranked above u_0 or u_0 is ranked above all points in II. They all cannot be equivalent with u_0.

By the same line of reasoning we can prove that all points in quadrant IV must be ranked above u_0 or u_0 ranked above all points in IV. It can be further established that if u_0 is ranked above all points in II (or vice versa), all points in IV must be ranked above u_0 (or vice versa). This follows because the relationship of u_0 to points in II is the same as that of points in IV to u_0. That is, if u_1 is preferred to u_0 then we can transform the utility scales so that $\hat{v}_1 = \psi(u_1) = u_0$ and $\hat{v}_0 = \psi(u_0)$ lies in quadrant IV. Thus if u_1 is ranked above u_0 then $\hat{v}_1$ ($= u_0$) is ranked above $\hat{v}_0$.

Finally, it is obvious that if two quadrants are ranked the same way with respect to u_0 then points on the boundary between the two quadrants are ranked in the same way. Therefore, what we have established so far is that either quadrants I and II (and their common boundary) are preferred to u_0 and u_0 is preferred to III and IV, or quadrants I and IV are preferred to u_0 and u_0 is preferred to II and III. In the former case, we still have not ranked the points along the horizontal line through u_0, whereas in the latter we have not ranked the points along the vertical line through u_0. For illustration, let us concentrate on the former case. There are two possibilities here:

Strong dictator   The first possibility is that all points along the horizontal line through u_0 are socially indifferent. In other words, this line is a social welfare indifference curve. This implies that household g is a strong dictator, since if it is indifferent between two states, the states are ranked indifferent socially. The entire preference map would consist of a series of horizontal lines and the SWF would correspond with household h's own ordinal utility function. Of course, if h were the dictator, the SWO would be represented by a set of vertical lines. This result generalizes readily to the case of more than two persons. The SWF would simply be represented by the dictator's utility function.

Lexicographic dictatorship   The assumptions we have made do not require that all points along the horizontal line through u_0 be socially indifferent as they would be under the strong dictator. It is also possible that u_0 is preferred to any point to its left but not preferred to any point to its right. Since u_0 was arbitrarily chosen, any point on the horizontal line is preferred to any point to its left. In other words, the ranking of points on the horizontal line increases as one moves right. Such a social ordering corresponds to a *lexicographic dictatorship*, analogous to the lexicographical ordering of bundles by a household familiar from consumer theory.[11] In this case, there is some arbitrary ordering such that if, as in this example, household g is the prior dictator but is indifferent between two social states, then the mantle of dictatorship falls on household h providing h strictly prefers one state to the other. If not, the next household becomes the dictator, and so on. As with household preferences, when the social ordering is lexicographic over utilities it is not continuous; that is, there is no possibility of indifference between social states. The SWO cannot, in this case, be represented by a SWF.[12]

So far we have talked about possibility results. We will obtain an *impossibility result* (i.e. the set of SWO possibilities is empty) by imposing a non-dictatorship requirement directly (in addition to welfarism and weak Pareto), or by imposing a requirement such as anonymity which rules out dictatorship by implication. This is why the Arrow result is often referred to as the *Arrow impossibility theorem*.

Suppose we substitute the strong Pareto principle (PS) for the weak one. This is sufficient to rule out the strong dictator as a possibility, since now no one person can dictate social indifference. The strong Pareto principle states that if someone is made better off and no one is made worse off in a state x as compared with state y, then x must be preferred to y even if the dictator is indifferent. In the two-person case above, point u_0 must be preferred to any point to its left by the strong Pareto principle. More generally, if there are more than two persons, one can always imagine there being a set of household preferences such that for two states x and y between which the dictator is indifferent, x will be preferred to y by at least one other household and not nonpreferred by any. If so, letting the dictator dictate social indifference would violate the strong Pareto principle (but not the weak). Thus, when the Pareto principle is strengthened from the PW to PS, the strong dictator is ruled out and we are left with the lexicographical dictatorship. The ordering of households is still done arbitrarily, so many different lexicographical dictatorships are possible.

It is fair to say that the Arrow theorem generated a lot of controversy. Statements such as 'Arrow's theorem implies that, in general, a non-dictatorial SWO is impossible' were not uncommon. Various ways of getting around the dictatorial result have since been sought. All of these necessarily relax Arrow's assumptions. One solution is to relax the invariance requirements and admit more information to the planner. Arrow's theorem can be interpreted as saying that the OS–NC invariance requirement, when combined with welfarism, is simply too restrictive to

[11] This possibility was noted by Gevers (1979).
[12] The strong dictatorship and the lexicographic dictatorship are not the only possible ways to rank points along the horizontal (or vertical) lines, and thus are not the only possible SWOs. Any way of arbitrarily ranking points along the horizontal line which is consistent with welfarism and PW is permissible (e.g. flipping a coin).

permit any meaningful SWO possibilities. An alternative procedure is to relax some of the requirements that the social ordering must satisfy. This is equivalent to relaxing the assumption of welfarism. The reader is referred to Sen (1970) for a discussion of this. We shall restrict our discussion to relaxing the informational restrictions on the planner which are really very strict in the Arrow framework.

We shall see that by relaxing the invariance requirements in certain ways, additional SWO possibilities will be available. Before proceeding, however, it is useful to point out that relaxing the measurability assumption, *ceteris paribus*, does not necessarily allow us to escape Arrow's dictatorship. In particular, the dictatorship (strong and lexicographic) results derived above hold with equal force if we assume cardinal non-comparability (CS–NC). That is, 'cardinalizing' household utility by permitting positive linear affine transformations $v^h = a^h + b^h u^h$ while maintaining non-comparability across households leaves the SWO possibilities unchanged. This result was proven by Sen (1970).

In terms of the diagrammatic framework, it is easily seen that the logic of the 'proof' is unchanged by allowing positive affine transformations (as in Blackorby, Donaldson and Weymark, 1983). All of the transformations utilized to prove dictatorship can be accomplished with CS measurability. This is shown for household h in figure 5.5 where the

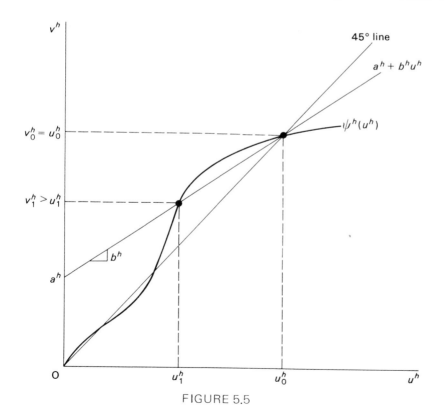

FIGURE 5.5

monotonic transformation that maps u_0^h back to itself and plots u_1^h to v_1^h is labelled $\psi^h(u^h)$. Exactly the same transformation can be accomplished by the positive affine transformation labelled $a^h + b^h u^h$. Thus, with NC, whether individual household utilities are cardinally or ordinally measurable is irrelevant to the question of SWO possibilities. Dictatorship (either of the strong sort or lexicographic) is the only possibility in either case.

Finally, note that more restrictive measurability assumptions cannot be combined with non-comparability; hence they cannot generate the Arrow result. RS measurability implies that proportional unit changes in utility must be comparable across households, since the household-specific transformation b^h cancels out when $\Delta v^h/v^h = \Delta u^h/u^h$ is calculated. Therefore, proportionate utility changes between two states are uniquely defined and comparisons of them can be made across households. As mentioned, AS measurability for every household implies full comparability across households.

5 SWO Possibilities with Full Comparability

Under FC the admissible transformations that can be applied to each household's utility function are the same. This means that the information available in making utility comparisons for the individual household is also available for utility comparisons across households. In contrast to the NC case, increasing the measurability of household utility significantly expands the SWO possibilities set under FC.

5.1 Ordinal scale measurability (SO)

Under this measurability assumption only utility levels can be compared by the individual household; that is, statements such as 'this *increment* in utility is larger (smaller) than that increment' have no meaning. Under FC, utility levels can also be compared across households whereas increments cannot be so compared. The combination of OS and FC means that any monotonic transformation can be applied to households' utility functions as long as the *same* transformation is applied to the utility function of every household; that is, $v^h = \psi(u^h)$ for all h. Formally, this means that $v^g(x) \gtrless v^h(y)$ as $u^g(x) \gtrless u^h(y)$ for any two households g and h and any two social states x and y. Thus Alice with x is better (worse) off than Bob with y both before and after the transformation, so such information on rankings is preserved and can be utilized by the social planner. Conversely, we can say that if the planner is only able to compare utility levels across and within households, the information available to the planner is OS–FC.

The fact that utility levels are comparable across households means that households can be ranked by utility position for any social state. This now permits SWO possibilities based on the utility positions of the households. Such possibilities were obviously excluded under the NC assumptions of Arrow and Sen.

If the requirements of welfarism and the weak Pareto principle are added to OS–FC, the ability to compare utility levels across households opens the SWO possibility of *positional dictatorships* in addition to the Arrow case of strong and lexicographic dictatorships. In this case, the SWO is dictated not by a particular household but by the preferences of the household occupying a particular utility position. A common example is the Rawlsian maximin case, where the SWO is dictated by the preferences of the household in the lowest utility position. If the worst-off household in state x is better off than the worst-off household in state y, then state x is preferred to state y in the SWO. Note that which household happens to be worst off can differ in the two states. Also note that the maximin case is an example of a positional dictatorship but not the only one possible under assumptions W, PW and OS–FC. For example, a maximax social welfare ordering would be possible, or a dictatorship by the nth well-off person. Only by adding an equity axiom of some type does one narrow the positional dictatorship to the maximin (Rawlsian) form.

Also possible under W, PW and OS–FC is the *positional lexicographic* SWO. In this case there is a hierarchy of households ranked according to utility level (first household, second household etc., not necessarily going from the worst-off to the best-off household or vice versa) such that the SWO is dictated by the first household in the hierarchy providing it has strict preference; if not, the strict preferences of the second household dictate the SWO etc. If one adopts the strong Pareto principle instead of the weak, the positional dictatorship is not possible. This is because allowing a household in a particular position in the ranking of utility levels to dictate indifference can violate PS, since it would be possible for the dictating household to be indifferent between states x and y whereas some other household prefers x and none prefers y. Thus, under PS, positional lexicographic SWOs (and lexicographic dictatorships) are possible but not positional (or strong) dictatorships.

The SWO possibilities are narrowed further by adding other restrictions. Adding anonymity rules out all of the dictatorship forms. If the further assumption of separability is made then the positional lexicographic forms are narrowed to the so-called leximin and leximax forms. The leximin is a positional lexicographic SWO where the positional hierarchy runs from this worst-off to the best-off position. For the leximax case the hierarchy runs in the opposite direction.

This result, which was proved by Hammond (1976) and Strasnick (1975), can be illustrated in figure 5.6 again adapted from Blackorby, Donaldson and Weymark (1983). By separability we can analyse the case of two households, g and h, independently of other households. We begin, as before, with an arbitrary reference point u_0. By the Pareto principle, points in the positive orthant (north-east of u_0) are ranked above u_0 whereas u_0 is ranked above points in the negative orthant (south-west

F

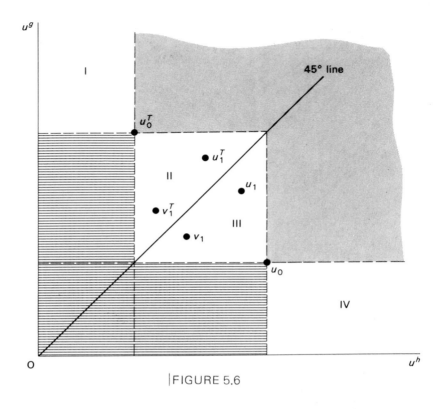

|FIGURE 5.6

of u_0). By anonymity, the transposed point u_0^T, where the utility levels of h and g are interchanged, must be ranked equivalently with u_0. The positive orthant of u_0^T must be preferred to u_0^T (and u_0), whereas u_0^T (and u_0) are preferred to the negative orthant. In figure 5.6 the combined preferred area is shaded and the combined non-preferred area is cross-hatched. This leaves four areas to consider, labelled I to IV.

Consider another point u_1 anywhere in region III which is to be ranked against u_0. By A, u_1^T must be ranked the same way. Since we can take any monotonic transformation of both households' utility we can map $v_0 = \psi(u_0)$ back to u_0 (and v_0^T to u_0^T) and $u_1(u_1^T)$ to any point $v_1(v_1^T)$ in region III (II). Note that the 45° line cannot be crossed because household h must remain better off than household g under OS–FC. Thus all points in II (and by anonymity, III) must be ranked the same way against u_0 and u_0^T.

By the logic followed in section 4, regions II and III must be strictly preferred or strictly not preferred to u_0 and points in areas I and IV must be ranked in the opposite way. This leaves two possibilities: II and III preferred and I and IV not preferred (figure 5.7(a)) or II and III not preferred and I and IV preferred (figure 5.7(b)). The former is a leximin result between the two households g and h, whereas the latter is the leximax. By SE, we can perform the same analysis for any two house-

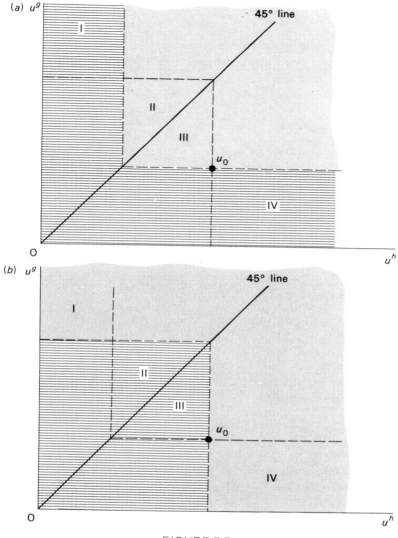

FIGURE 5.7

holds, so the two-household leximin–leximax results chain together to get
the H household result.

Finally we can narrow the possibilities to the leximin case along by
making the minimal equity assumption (EM). This rules out the leximax
case by excluding priority to the preferences of the best-off household.

5.2 *Cardinal scale measurability* (CS)

Under CS measurability levels of utility and increments in utility can both
be meaningfully compared for the individual household. By FC, such

comparisons can also be made across households. In addition to state-ments such as, 'Alice is better off (worse off) in x than Bob is in y', we can also make statements such as, 'The increment in Alice's utility is greater (smaller) than the increment in Bob's utility'. These sorts of com-parisons can be made because by CS measurability each household's utility function can be transformed by any positive affine transformation $v^h = a^h + b^h u^h$ and by FC, $a^h = a^g = a$ and $b^h = b^g = b$ for all h and g. It is then easily established that $v^g(x) \geqslant v^h(y)$ only as $u^g(x) \geqslant u^h(y)$ and $v^g(x) - v^g(y) \geqslant v^h(y) - v^h(z)$ only as $u^g(x) - u^g(y) \geqslant u^h(y) - u^h(z)$. In words, both levels and first differences in utility are comparable across households. The planner now has more information and this increases the range of SWOs possible.

Since levels of utility are still comparable, all of the positional forms of SWO obtained under OS are permissible as are the dictatorship forms of the non-comparable case. But since increments in (or 'units' of) utility are now meaningful for utility comparisons across households, additional SWO possibilities are admitted; specifically, those relying on cross-house-hold comparisons of changes in utility. The additional SWO possibilities include SWF of the utilitarian and generalized utilitarian forms. The former is a social welfare function (recall that an SWF is a continuous SWO) that ranks social states on the basis of the unweighted sum of household utilities. The latter SWF permits the household utilities to be 'weighted' with different but positive weights for each household.

Consider first the case where only welfarism and the weak Pareto principle are added to CS–FC. The simple and positional dictatorship and lexicographic possibilities are still open, of course, and in addition the generalized utilitarian SWF (of which utilitarianism is a special case) is possible. Also possible is some combination of the generalized utilitarian and the positional dictatorship SWF.

To see this geometrically, assume that the SWF is a differentiable function $W(u^1(\ ), \ldots, u^H(\ ))$ and that $u^h(\ )$ depends only on its own income m^h.[13] The social ordering can be depicted by a set of social indifference contours in income space. The absolute value of the slope of one of these contours at a given point m^g, m^h space is given by

$$\frac{\partial W/\partial m^g}{\partial W/\partial m^h} = \frac{\partial W/\partial u^g \ \partial u^g/\partial m^g}{\partial W/\partial u^h \ \partial u^h/\partial m^h} \tag{5.6}$$

These contours must be unchanged when the households' utility functions are submitted to allowable transforms, since the ordering of social states must be unchanged. Therefore, the left-hand side must be unchanged when the households' utility functions are transformed by identical

---

[13]   This 'selfishness' assumption involves no loss in generality. Specifically, one can let m^h be a money metric utility measure where actual utility is derived from the allocation vector in a manner which can include empathy, jealousy etc.

positive affine transformations. Suppose $v^h = a + bu^h$. Then

$$\frac{\partial v^g/\partial m^g}{\partial v^h/\partial m^h} = \frac{b\partial u^g/\partial m^g}{b\partial u^h/\partial m^h}$$

is unchanged by all such transformations. Therefore, for the left-hand side of (5.6) to be unchanged, we also require that $(\partial W/\partial u^g)/(\partial W/\partial u^h)$ be unchanged by the transformation.

The implication of all this is shown in figure 5.8, which depicts social welfare contours in utility space. At any arbitrary reference point u_0 the slope of the SWF indifference curve (i.e. $-(\partial W/\partial u^h)/(\partial W/\partial u^g)$) is given by the slope of the line segment through u_0. This slope must remain unchanged when we transform u^g and u^h by the same positive affine transformation. Such a transformation can relocate u_0 to any v_0 point below the $45°$ line by some combination of a movement along a ray through the origin (multiplying each household's utility by the same positive scalar) to bu_0 plus a movement along a $45°$ line through bu_0 (adding a common intercept term to each household's utility). By inspection it can be seen that v_0 can be placed anywhere below the $45°$ line by a positive affine transformation. Therefore, the SWF indifference curves must have the

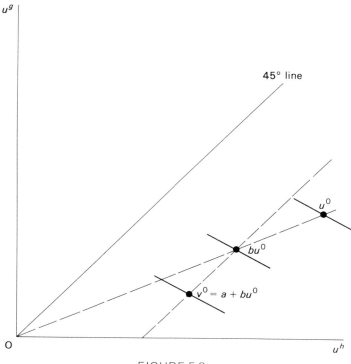

FIGURE 5.8

same slope as that at u^0 throughout that part of the quadrant. By the same logic the SWF indifference curves must also have a constant slope at all points above the 45° line (though not necessarily the same slope as below the line).

The types of SWF indifference curves admitted are shown in figure 5.9(a)–(c). In figure 5.9(b) the SWF indifference curves happen to have the same slope (not necessarily −1). This is the generalized utilitarian case (utilitarian if the slope is −1). In figure 5.9(a) the SWF is a linear combination of the (generalized) utilitarian and the maximax positional dictatorship. In figure 5.9(c), the utilitarian is combined with maximin. More generally we have

$$W = W^u + \alpha(W^d - W^u) \tag{5.7}$$

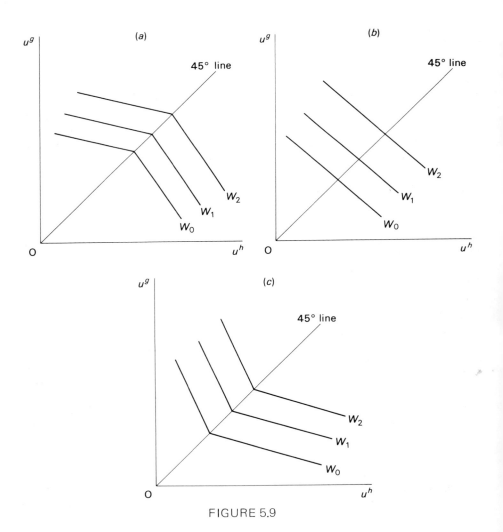

FIGURE 5.9

where W^u is the generalized utilitarian form, W^d is a positional dictator-ship form such as the maximin and α is a scalar between zero and one (for details see Roberts, 1980).

If the strong Pareto principle is invoked, the strong and positional dictatorship forms of the SWO are excluded but lexicographic forms remain possible. Adding anonymity precludes the lexicographic dictatorship and the generalized utilitarian forms, leaving the possibilities of the positional lexicographic and simple utilitarian forms. With the separability of indifferent individuals' requirements (SE), the lexicographic forms are narrowed to the leximin and leximax forms. Adding the minimal equity requirement (EM) leaves available the leximin and utilitarian forms (Deschamps and Gevers, 1978). Adding a continuity requirement leaves available only the utilitarian form (Maskin, 1978) while a strong equity requirement leaves only the leximin possibility.

5.3 Ratio scale measurability (RS)

When utility is measurable using a ratio scale, still further SWOs are admitted. With RS measurability, proportional changes in utility can be compared by the individual household and, under FC, can also be compared across households. Thus statements such as 'The proportional change in Alice's utility is greater (smaller) than that of Bob', are meaning-ful. Under RS, transformations of the type $v^h = b^h u^h$ are admitted, whereas FC implies that $b^h = b$ for all h. Then

$$\frac{v^g(y)}{v^g(x)} \gtrless \frac{v^h(y)}{v^h(z)} \qquad \text{as} \qquad \frac{u^g(y)}{u^g(x)} \gtrless \frac{u^h(y)}{u^h(x)}$$

Note that $v^g(y)/v^g(x)$ can also be written as $((v^g(y) - v^g(x))/v^g(x)) + 1$; thus proportional changes in utility are comparable. The reader can ascertain that such comparability is not possible with CS measurability. Levels and increments of utility still remain comparable across house-holds. Hence, the information available to the planner is again increased and further SWO possibilities are admitted.[14]

In figure 5.10 we have a reference point u^0 and a line segment the slope of which is equal to $-(\partial W/\partial u^h)/(\partial W/\partial u^g)$, the slope of the SWF in-difference curve through u_0. As before, this slope must be unchanged when utilities are transformed according to the linear transformation $v^h = bu^h$ for all h. This means that the slope of the SWF indifference curve must be the same along a ray from the origin through point u_0. As point u_0 is chosen arbitrarily, this condition must hold along any ray

---

[14] In the discussion of ratio scale measurability we restrict the range of individual utility functions to the positive real line. This is done in order that the addition of a positive proportion of the utility level to itself increases utility; that is, $(1+f)u \geqslant u$ if $f \geqslant 0$. This involves no loss of generality because we could have left the range of the utility functions as the entire real line and considered ratio scale measurability in terms of the ratio to the absolute value of utility.

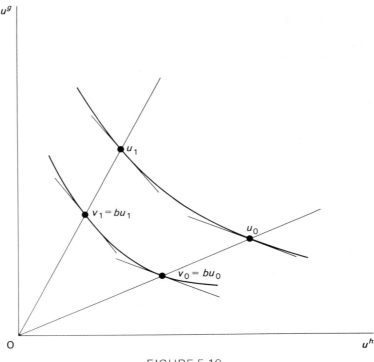

FIGURE 5.10

(e.g. the ray passing through u_1). Any homothetic SWF satisfies this property; but since the SWF indifference curves can be numbered in any increasing manner, we can restrict our attention to the linearly homogeneous SWF form. Thus the linearly homogeneous SWF possibility is added to the possibilities open under RS measurability. Adding A requires that the linearly homogeneous form be symmetric. Finally, if SE and A are assumed, the linearly homogeneous SWF must be of the constant elasticity of substitution form

$$W = \sum_{h=1}^{H} \frac{(u^h)^{1-\rho}}{1-\rho} \tag{5.5'}$$

where $1/\rho$ is the elasticity of substitution between any two households' utilities. As mentioned above, this SWF is very useful because ρ can be taken as an equity parameter. When $\rho = 0$, W is utilitarian. The limiting case as $\rho \to 1$ is the Bernoulli–Nash (Cobb–Douglas) case and the limiting case as $\rho \to \infty$ ($-\infty$) is the maximin (maximax) form. Note that the latter two are limiting cases since A precludes a positional dictatorship. In other words, as ρ increases, more weight is given to the equality of utilities *per se* and the SWF indifference curves become more convex.

5.4 *Absolute scale measurability* (AS)

When utility is measurable to an absolute scale and full comparability is assumed, the SWO possibilities are the widest possible. With AS, the only transformation permitted is the identity transform $v^h = u^h$ for all h. In this case the invariance requirement is trivial. In terms of figure 5.10, the only possible transformation of reference point u_0 is one which maps it back to itself; thus the slope of the SWF indifference curve can be different at every point in utility space. In other words, AS measurability of utility permits the general Bergson–Samuelson form of the SWF. The Pareto principle (strong) makes the SWF indifference curves negatively sloped, A makes the SWF symmetric, and SE makes the SWF additively separable, i.e. can be expressed in the form

$$W(x) = \sum_{h=1}^{H} g\,[u^h(x)]$$

An equity requirement is necessary to make the SWF indifference curves convex.

The results of sections 4 and 5 are summarized in table 5.1. It shows the sorts of SWOs that are possible under various informational assumptions. It shows that comparability is the *sine qua non* for non-dictatorial SWOs. With FC, the SWO possibilities are widened by greater measurability (less restrictive invariance requirements) of individual household utilities. The SWO possibilities are narrowed by the addition of requirements such as A, SE, EM or ES and CO.

6 SWO Possibilities with Partial Comparability

If some of the information implied by the measurability of the individual household's utility function is not available for comparisons across households, then comparability is said to be partial. In this case, certain utility comparisons can be made by the individual household which cannot be used for making comparisons across households.

6.1 *Cardinal scale measurability with unit comparability* (CS–UC)

In this case households can make comparisons both of levels and of increments in their own utility, but only increments can be compared across households. Formally, the utility functions of the households can be transformed by $v^h = a^h + b^h u^h$, where $b^h = b$ for all h but a^h can differ across households. Thus level comparisons across households are precluded by the transformation but increment comparisons are possible.

It is easily seen that CS–UC when combined with welfarism and the Pareto principle permits only the generalized utilitarian SWF (in addition to dictatorship). In figure 5.11, the reference utility point u_0 and a line

TABLE 5.1 SWF possibilities under non-comparability and full comparability*

Ethical requirement / Informational requirement	W + PW	W + PS	W + PS + A	W + PS + A + SE	W + PS + A + SE + EM	W + PS + A + SE + CO + ES
NC, OS or CS	DS, DL (Arrow (1951a), Sen (1970))	DL	none	none	none	none
FC (a) OS	above and DP, LP	above and LP	LP	LXN, LXX (Hammond (1976), Strasnick (1975))	LXN	none
(b) CS	above and UG UG-DP (Roberts (1980))	above and UG	above and U	above and U	above and U (Deschamps & Gevers (1978))	U (Maskin 1978))
(c) RS	above and H	above and H	above and HS	above and CE	above and CE	CEC
(d) AS	above and B	above and B	above and BS	above and BSS	above and BSS	above and BSSC

Note: * The above entries are not necessarily exclusive except where 'none' is indicated.

Abbreviations:

A	anonymity
AS	absolute scale measurability
B	Bergson–Samuelson SWF
BS	Bergson–Samuelson SWF (symmetric)
BSS	Bergson–Samuelson SWF (symmetric and separable)
BSSC	Bergson–Samuelson SWF (symmetric, separable and quasi-concave)
CE	constant elasticity SWF
CEC	constant elasticity SWF (concave, $\rho \geqslant 0$)
CO	continuity
CS	cardinal scale measurability
CSSB	quasi-concave separable symmetric Bergson–Samuelson SWF
DL	dictatorship (lexicographic)
DP	dictatorship (positional)
DS	dictatorship (strong)
EM	equity (minimal)
ES	equity (strong)
FC	full comparability
H	homogeneous SWF

HS	homogeneous (symmetric) SWF
LP	lexicographic by positions
LXN	leximin
LXX	leximax
NC	non-comparable
OS	ordinal scale measurability
PS	Pareto principle (strong)
PW	Pareto principle (weak)
RS	ratio scale measurability
SE	separability of indifferent households
U	utilitarian
UG	utilitarian (generalized)
UG–DP	linear combination of UG and DP

Permitted transformations

OS–NC	$v^h = \psi^h(u^h)$	$\psi^h(\ )$ any monotonic
CS–NC	$v^h = a^h + b^h u^h$	
OS–FC	$v^h = \psi(u^h)$	$\psi(\ )$ any monotonic
CS–FC	$v^h = a + bu^h$	
RS–FC	$v^h = bu^h$	
AS–FC	$v^h = u^h$	

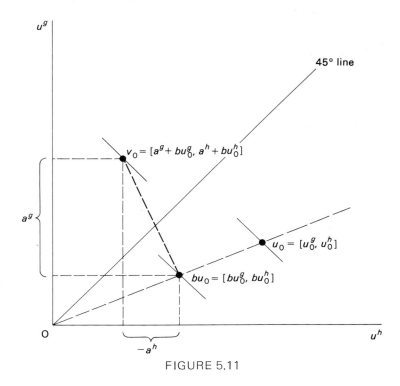

FIGURE 5.11

segment having a slope equal to the slope of the SWF indifference curve
are shown. As shown, the transform $a^h + bu^h$ permits u_0 to be mapped to
v_0 anywhere in the utility space, so the SWF indifference curves must have
the same slope everywhere in the utility space. The slope need not be
equal to -1, so the SWF is a generalized utilitarian form. Adding A
precludes the dictatorship possibility and leaves available the simple
(unweighted) utilitarian SWF (a version of this result was proved by
D'Aspremont and Gevers (1977)).

6.2 *Ratio scale measurability* (RS)

If utility is measurable by a ratio scale, then unit comparability implies
level comparability. However, it is possible for proportional comparisons
of utility (which are possible for the individual household under RS) to
be comparable across households even though units and levels are not. In
fact, this must be the case: non-comparability under RS measurability is
not possible.

Consider the case where the permissible transformations are $v^h = b^h u^h$
for all h and b^h can differ across households. Note that this transformation leaves $u^h(x)/u^h(y)$, and therefore $(u^h(x) - u^h(y))/u^h(y)$ unchanged

for every household. Thus

$$\frac{v^g(x) - v^g(y)}{v^g(y)} \gtreqless \frac{v^h(x) - v^h(y)}{\eta^h(y)}$$

as

$$\frac{u^g(x) - u^g(y)}{u^g(y)} \gtreqless \frac{u^h(x) - u^h(y)}{u^h(y)}$$

In other words, comparisons such as, 'Household Alice's increment in utility as a proportion of her utility level is greater (less) than that of Bob's', can still be made.

It can be shown that this admits the possibility that the SWF be of the Bernoulli–Nash (Cobb–Douglas) form. That is,

$$W = \prod_{h=1}^{H} (u^h)^{a_h} \tag{5.3'}$$

To see this, recall that we require

$$\frac{\partial W/\partial m^g}{\partial W/\partial m^h} = \frac{\partial W/\partial u^g}{\partial W/\partial u^h} \frac{\partial u^g/\partial m^g}{\partial u^h/\partial m^h} \tag{5.6}$$

to be unchanged when the permissible linear transformations of utility functions are undertaken. At first this seems impossible because $(\partial u^g/\partial m^g)/(\partial u^h/\partial m^h)$ will depend on the ratio b^g/b^h, which is arbitrary. However, multiplying and dividing the right-hand side of (5.6) by u^g/u^h we get

$$\frac{\partial W/\partial m^g}{\partial W/\partial m^h} = \frac{(\partial W/\partial u^g)u^g}{(\partial W/\partial u^h)u^h} \frac{(\partial u^g/\partial m^g)/u^g}{(\partial u^h/\partial m^h)/u^h} \tag{5.6'}$$

The last term is unchanged by the linear transformations even if $b^g = b^h$, since b^g cancels out of the numerator and b^h cancels out of the denominator. Thus $(\partial W/\partial m^g)/(\partial W/\partial m^h)$ will be unchanged for an SWF that satisfies

$$\frac{\partial W/\partial u^g}{\partial W/\partial u^h} = \beta \frac{u^g}{u^h} \qquad \text{for constant } \beta > 0 \tag{5.8}$$

In figure 5.12 we have reference point u_0 where the slope of the SWF indifference curve $(\partial W/\partial u^h)/(\partial W/\partial u^g)$ is equal to the (absolute) slope of the line segment through u_0. Expression (5.8) requires that the slope of the SWF indifference curve be inversely proportional to the slope of

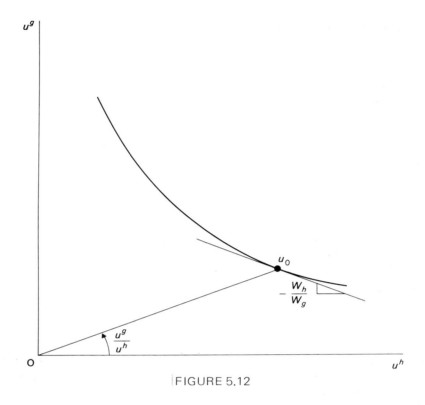

FIGURE 5.12

the ray from the origin through u_0. It immediately follows that all of the SWF indifference curves have the same slope along the ray, implying that the SWF is homothetic which, since we can number the social welfare indifference curves in any increasing way, is equivalent to a linearly homogeneous SWF form. However, (5.8) also implies that the slope of the SWF indifference curve must change in inverse proportion to the slope of the ray u^g/u^h. This requires that every SWF indifference curve must have an elasticity of substitution of unity at all points. The only SWF satisfying this property is the Bernoulli–Nash (Cobb–Douglas) form.

Adding anonymity makes the SWF symmetric; that is, $a^h = a$ for all h in (5.3'). It also precludes the dictatorship possibility leaving the symmetric Bernoulli–Nash as the only SWF possibility under RS–PC, W, P and A.

This exhausts the partial comparability cases since full comparability is implied by AS measurability whereas only FC or NC is possible under OS measurability. The results are summarized in Table 5.2.

7 Summary and interpretation

This chapter has presented what might be referred to as the *informational approach* to social welfare orderings. The informational approach builds

TABLE 5.2   SWF possibilities under partial comparability

Ethical restrictions / Informational restrictions	$W + PS$	$W + PS + A$
CS–UC	DS or DL UG	U (D'Aspremont and Gevers (1977))
RS–PC	DS or DL BN	BNS

Abbreviations

A	anonymity
BN	Bernoulli–Nash form
BNS	Bernoulli–Nash form (symmetric)
CS	cardinal scale
DL	dictatorship (lexicographic)
DS	dictatorship (strong)
PC	proportion comparability
PS	Pareto principle (strong)

PW	Pareto principle (weak)
U	utilitarian form
UG	utilitarian form (generalized)
W	welfarism

Permitted transformation

CS–UC	$v^h = a^h + bu^h$
RS–PC	$v^h = b^h u^h$

upon Arrow's (1951a) crucially important possibility theorem. According to that theorem, if we wish the social ordering to satisfy certain plausible axioms or value judgments (the Pareto principle, the independence of irrelevant alternatives, and unrestricted domain), and to be a complete and transitive ordering, and if we restrict the planner to knowing only the preference orderings of all households in the economy, then the only possible ordering is of a dictatorship form (either the dictatorship of a particular person or a lexicographical dictatorship of persons ordered in some particular way). The informational approach investigates how the set of possible SWOs expands as more 'information' is made available to the planner. This information can take the form of increasing degrees of measurability of household utilities and increasing degrees of interpersonal comparability of utilities. The latter is the *sine qua non* of meaningful SWOs. The more information that is available to the planner, the greater the range of possible SWO forms that are compatible with the value judgments being made. In the limit, full measurability of individual utilities and full comparability in conjunction with the axioms we have adopted permit the general Bergson–Samuelson form. On the other hand, the set of SWO possibilities is narrowed by allowing only partial comparability or measurability, or by imposing additional properties such as anonymity or separability.

It would, of course, have been possible to relax welfarism to obtain a different set of possible SWOs. We have chosen not to pursue that route here. (Interested readers may consult Sen, 1970 or Sen, 1977.) Instead, we have restricted ourselves to a similar set of axioms to those used by

Arrow. The only difference with Arrow's axioms is in our use of Pareto principle. Arrow required only the weak version of the Pareto principle, whereas we have also investigated the consequences of admitting Pareto indifference and the strong Pareto principle. As we have seen, the use of Pareto indifference together with the independence and unrestricted domain axioms implies that the SWO will be welfaristic; that is, the SWO depends only on utility outcomes of the social states. In addition to making the analysis more tractable, this seems to be a fairly reasonable requirement for choosing among alternative resource allocations.

The addition of measurability and comparability information, as in this chapter, complements the results of the preceding chapters. It will be recalled that if the Pareto and individualism are the only value judgments made and if household preference orderings are the only source of information, then social states cannot be completely ordered. Only those which are Pareto comparable can be ordered. This chapter has investigated the sorts of complete social orderings which are *possible* given the different kinds of information available to the planner. Except in a few special cases, the informational approach does not leave us with a unique SWO (or SWF if the ordering is continuous). To select a unique method of ordering social states from the various possible SWOs requires further ethical judgments. Ethical arguments for certain SWO forms which exist in the literature will be discussed in the next chapter.

Before considering these ethical arguments it is worth considering exactly how one might interpret the informational approach to social orderings. What does it mean to say that the planner has available information on the measurability and comparability of utilities? Is this to be taken as information obtained in a scientific or empirical fashion or is it information which represents some person's subjective evaluation of individual utility levels? It seems to us that there are at least two ways that one may interpret the informational approach, each of which leads to a slightly different view of the role of the planner.

First, one may take the view that the measurement of utility is, in principle, an objective matter. Once utility levels are empirically determined, they can then naturally be compared among individuals. This seems to have been the view taken by the classical utilitarians and their followers (e.g. Bentham, Mill, Edgeworth), but also appears to be held today by some (e.g. Ng, 1979). The planner then takes this information and chooses among the SWOs which the information permits. The choice itself involves an ethical judgment as to how to trade one person's utility off against another's, but the information used is treated as objective. Of course, as above, the information may involve only partial measurability or comparability, in which case the possible SWOs are restricted accordingly.

The theory developed in this chapter is perfectly compatible with this view; the objections to it may be both ethical and empirical. One may take the view that the measurement of utility and, even more, its comparability among persons involves a fundamental value judgment. Alternatively one may object that, even if one thought that utility were in principle measurable, there exists no agreed method for obtaining more than ordinal measurement or for comparing utility levels. This being the case, the objective information available to the planner as revealed by the behaviour of households is what we have called ordinal non-comparable utilities. If this is the only information allowed, we are back to the Arrow possibility theorem.

A second and more fruitful possibility is to view the information not as being given to the planner from an outside source but as reflecting the planner's own ethical judgment of the measurability and comparability of utility. Thus, OS–FC means the planner is ethically prepared to measure utility ordinally and to compare utility levels fully among persons but not utility increments. This is fundamentally different from the first view outlined above in that it is recognized that the information itself reflects an ethical judgment of the planner (or someone else) and does not comprise some objectively determined data. In a sense, the use of the term 'information' in the literature to convey the measurability and comparability of utilities is unfortunate, since it almost connotes empirical data.

If this is to be the interpretation placed on the information used by the planner, some further questions are raised. We have already seen that under most combinations of measurability and comparability, no unique SWO emerges. The planner has a set of possible SWOs from which one must be chosen. This choice requires a further ethical judgment involving how the measured utilities are to be traded off. It seems rather artificial to separate these two ethical judgments in the analysis. Furthermore, if the measurability and comparability assumptions reflect the planner's judgment, why should the planner restrict himself to partial rather than full measurability and comparability, especially since these restrict the set of SWOs from which he may choose? In other words, why not simply let him choose the Bergson–Samuelson SWO that represents his ethical preferences?

In any case, it is clear that the informational approach to SWOs does not generally leave the planner with a unique method of ordering social states, that is, with a unique SWF. What it does is provide the planner with a set of possible candidates for the SWF, a set which depends upon the information which is assumed to be available. The more information that is available, or the higher the degree of measurability and comparability the planner is faced with or is prepared to assume, the larger the set of SWOs there are to choose from. The choice of a specific form for the SWO then involves a further ethical judgment about how to aggregate the individual utilities.

CHAPTER 6

Fairness, Equity and Distributive Justice

1 Introduction

We have stressed that ethical premises or postulates must be made in welfare economics. The legitimacy of such assumptions cannot rest on appeals to the empirical validity of a theory but must be sought through introspection and the art of persuasion. When we go beyond the analysis of economic efficiency and the relatively innocuous Pareto principle to address the distributive question of choosing among social states in which some households are hurt while others gain (utility conflict), our ethical premises become more contestable. We have seen that a complete and non-dictatorial welfaristic social ordering will require interhousehold utility *level* comparisons at the very least. Even stronger utility comparisons must be made in order to obtain a richer menu of SWO possibilities. In any event, to go beyond the Pareto principle we must invoke additional and stronger ethical postulates.

In this chapter we survey the ethical foundations of choosing among social states that involve utility conflict. In section 2 we first consider ethical postulates that do not require interhousehold utility comparisons. For example, one possible definition of distributive 'fairness' is the absence of envy, where envy occurs when a household derives more utility from another household's consumption bundle than from its own. Such allocations are called 'fair' by Foley (1967). We also consider 'egalitarian equivalent allocations' introduced by Panzer and Schmeidler (1978).

These concepts of fairness do not utilize interhousehold utility comparisons so they cannot, in general, completely order social states. In addition, it is not clear that they capture the quality that many of us conceive as fairness despite the 'persuasive definition'. In section 3, we survey 'theories of justice' which attempt to derive equity concepts from an axiomatic foundation.

After distinguishing the 'end state' or social welfare philosophy (which is the basis for modern welfare economics) from absolute notions of right, we briefly survey the contributions of Fleming (1952), Harsanyi (1953, 1955, 1978) and Rawls (1971). All three authors have made forceful arguments in favour of particular forms for the social welfare function.

In section 4 we examine a (if not the) central question of welfare economics; how do we make interhousehold utility comparisons? This is then related to the problem of horizontal equity which, in one formulation at least, appears to represent an independent ethical postulate which may conflict with the social welfare philosophy underlying the bulk of welfare economics. We conclude with a brief summary of where this and preceding chapters leaves us in regard to our objective of a complete social ordering.

2 Fairness as Absence of Envy

One way of narrowing the set of Pareto optimal allocations, suggested by Foley (1967), that does not require interhousehold utility comparisons is to consider the set of 'fair' allocations. Foley's definition of 'fairness' in the distribution of utility is that no household should envy another. Household h is said not to envy household g if $u^h(x^g) \leqslant u^h(x^h)$, where $u^h( )$ is a utility function representation of the preferences of household h (with the usual properties), x^h is the consumption bundle of household h and x^g is that of household g. Similarly household g does not envy household h if $u^g(x^h) \leqslant u^g(x^g)$.

It is obvious that, without further restrictions, a fair allocation always exists. Let bundle $x^{e|} = \{x_1/H, \ldots, x_N/H\}$ denote the *equal division allocation* where x_i is the aggregate amount of good i consumed and H is the number of consumers. Since $x^h = x^{e|}$ for all h, there will be no envy with this allocation. Of course, it is very unlikely that the equal division allocation would be Pareto optimal.[1] Consequently, a more interesting (and less trivial) question concerns the existence of fair *and* efficient (Pareto optimal) allocations. These exist in a pure exchange economy at least.

The existence of a fair and efficient allocation in an exchange economy can be seen from figure 6.1. In any such economy we can consider the equal division allocation x^e and allow Alice and Bob to trade to any Pareto optimal allocation x lying between allocations y and z on the contract curve. It can now be seen that efficient allocation x must also be fair because both Alice and Bob find it at least as good as their endowment allocation x^e, which in turn is at least as good as allocation x^T formed by switching the consumption bundles received by the two parties at x. Thus, neither would prefer to have the other's bundle.

Unfortunately, this nice existence result does not extend to production economies, as shown by Panzer and Schmeidler (1974). Suppose Alice and Bob produce consumption good c by supplying labour (forgoing leisure l) but they differ in their ability to transform labour into goods (their real wages) and in their tastes. Both are endowed with a unit of leisure but Alice, the more able person, faces real wage w^a which exceeds w^b, the real wage of Bob. A Pareto optimal allocation is shown in figure

---

[1] A sufficient condition for it to be Pareto optimal is that all households have identical tastes.

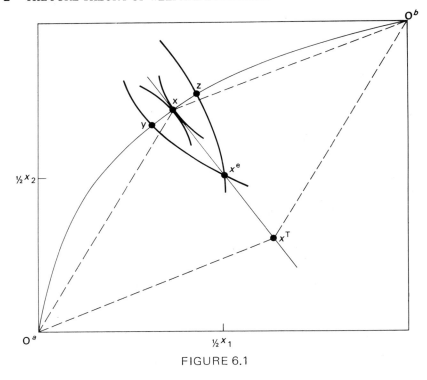

FIGURE 6.1

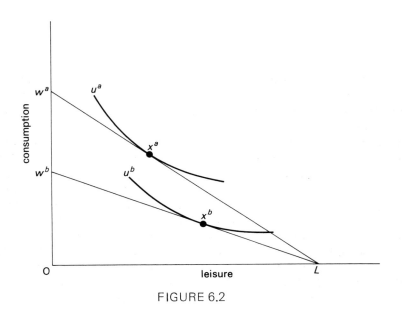

FIGURE 6.2

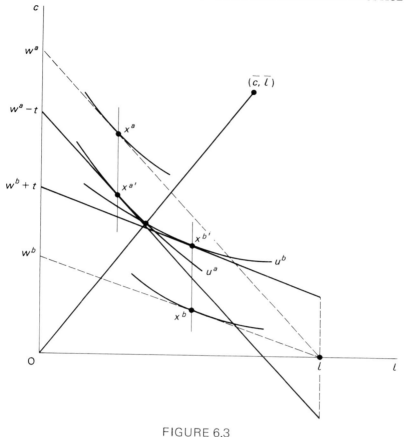

FIGURE 6.3

6.2, where Alice consumes bundle x^a and Bob consumes bundle x^b. Obviously, in this equilibrium, Bob envies Alice. But this is not the only Pareto optimal allocation because the consumption good (but *not* leisure) can be reallocated in a lump-sum transfer.

To simplify matters we assume the marginal propensity to spend on consumption goods is unity so that leisure has a zero income effect. In this case, the aggregate bundle does not change with lump-sum redistribution (t) and the income expansion paths are vertical as shown in figure 6.3. One might expect that by redistributing the consumption good from Alice to Bob, a fair (that is, envy-free) allocation must be reached. This is not the case, as Panzer and Schmeidler (1974) demonstrated with an algebraic counter-example. The intuitive reason why a fair allocation need not exist in the production economy can be seen with aid of figure 6.3. As consumption is reallocated from Alice to Bob by a transfer t it is possible that Alice will envy Bob before he ceases to envy her. This is shown in figure

6.3 where, after transfers, Alice consumes $x^{a'}$ and Bob consumes $x^{b'}$. In this equilibrium both households envy each other. Redistribution of consumption towards either household can eliminate the envy of one household but not both.

The upshot of this discussion is that the concept of fairness as represented by the absence of envy, although appealing on the basis of its symmetric treatment of households and because it does not require interhousehold utility comparisons, can conflict with the Pareto principle. Since that principle is too reasonable to abandon, this concept of fairness is seriously undermined. A weaker concept of fairness which has been advanced by Panzer and Schmeidler (1978) is that of *egalitarian equivalent allocations* (EEA). An allocation is an EEA if there is an aggregate bundle, not necessarily feasible, which can be equally divided to yield the same distribution of utility as the allocation in question. In other words, the distribution of utilities in an EEA could have, *in principle*, arisen from an equal division (and therefore envy-free) allocation.

All fair allocations are EEAs but not, generally, vice versa. However, if households have identical tastes it is obvious that an EEA is an equal division allocation and therefore is fair. But in this case we also know that the fair allocation is Pareto efficient. The desirable property of the EEA is that a Pareto optimal EEA always exists even if tastes and abilities differ among households.

A Pareto optimal EEA in an exchange economy is shown in figure 6.4. A Pareto optimal allocation of endowment $\bar{x}$ is (x^a, x^b). Although Alice envies Bob, the utility levels (u^a, u^b) could have been reached by an equal division (and envy-free) allocation of an endowment x^E. Similarly we see that in the production economy pictured in figure 6.3, the allocation (x^a, x^b), although not fair, is egalitarian equivalent since the associated utility distribution could have been reached by the equal division of $(\bar{c}, \bar{l})$.

One could weaken the equity criterion still further and consider fair equivalent allocations (FEA). An FEA is an allocation such that there exists an endowment, not necessarily feasible, for which a fair (envy-free) allocation yields the same distribution as the allocation in question. Since this includes equal division allocations it is obvious that all of the properties of the EEA are satisfied by the FEA.

Despite the appeal of these concepts, they are in fact of limited use in welfare economics since they cannot, even in conjunction with the Pareto principle, provide a complete social ordering. One can divide allocations into those which are fair or egalitarian equivalent (or fair equivalent) and those which are not. Then one can take the intersection of these 'equitable' allocations with the set of Pareto optimal allocations which, in general, will be a smaller set than both and, for EEAs at least, non-empty. There is still no way of choosing among two allocations that lie within (or without) the efficient and 'equitable' set.

At a more fundamental level, it is questionable whether the concept of lack of envy (or the equivalence concepts) adequately captures the notion of fairness. One can think of many cases where someone prefers the con-

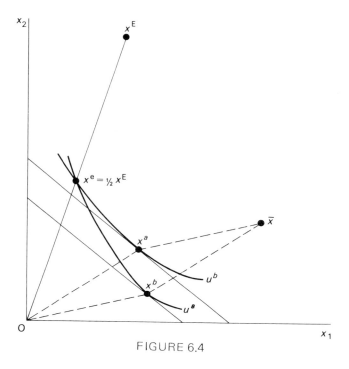

FIGURE 6.4

sumption bundle of someone else, yet everyone might agree that the economy is fair in the sense of being equitable. For example, I might envy a friend's 'lucky find' in an antique store yet perceive no 'unfairness' in the fact that he, not I, owns it.

In the next section, we shall delve into the metaphysics of fairness as developed in a joint philosophy and economics literature generally referred to as 'the theory of justice'. It is not a theory in the scientific sense, of course, but rather an attempt to uncover some axioms of fairness by means of thought experiments. We shall see that one can obtain very tractable social welfare functions out of an appealing framework of moral choice. Although one could support the concept of fairness as lack of envy on the basis of this framework, more attractive concepts are available at the cost of assuming interhousehold comparability of utility.

3 The Theory of Justice

The theory of justice is not a 'theory' in the scientific sense but, rather, is a logical structure erected around a set of ethical postulates. On the one hand, these postulates are supported by arguments which develop their innate appeal or 'reasonableness' and, on the other, the postulates are used to derive implications about the design of just institutions.

It is useful to identify two broad, competing concepts of justice. The first is the *social welfare* philosophy (or 'utilitarian' philosophy – defined broadly to include the social welfare functions of Bentham (1791), Bergson (1938), Samuelson (1947) and Rawls (1971)) – which defines the justice of a state in terms of its end state distributional results usually evaluated solely in terms of household utilities (welfarism). Actions are deemed just if they raise social welfare in some sense. A central postulate of the social welfare philosophy has been called *asset egalitarianism* by Arrow (1973). According to this postulate, all of the assets of a society including personal labour, skills and ability are, in some sense, the common wealth of humanity available for use in maximizing social welfare. In particular, redistributive policies which take (by threat of force) the product of some households and give it to others are just if they raise social welfare, appropriately defined. A typical implication of the social welfare approach is the principle of *ability to pay* in taxation.

The competing view is the Kantian philosophy of absolute (i.e. axiomatic) rights. Economic justice is variously defined under this approach depending on the absolute rights asserted. Kant proposed absolute rights to include subsistence, and others have proposed the absolute right of liberty as absence of compulsion (Peacock and Rowley, 1975). Still others might propose an absolute right of economic equality. One widespread concept of economic justice emanating from this philosophy is the *entitlement* or *desert* theory of justice. The basic postulate of this view is the so-called *productivity principle*, which asserts that each household has the right to consume that which it produces. The theory then stresses justice in terms of 'process' and the correspondence between actions and rewards. This approach has been used by conservative philosophers and economists to defend the existing distribution of wealth (Buchanan, 1954; Nozick, 1974). According to the entitlement theory, redistribution is unwarranted and unjust (violates various postulates of entitlement) except (perhaps) when it entails Pareto improving redistributions or retributions for past entitlement injustices. A particular implication of the entitlement theory is the *benefit principle* of taxation.[2]

The social welfare and the entitlement theories of economic justice are fundamentally irreconcilable, at least in terms of their postulates. The social welfare theory treats rights as justifiable only in terms of their contribution to social welfare and not as absolutes. More importantly, the existing distribution of the ownership of productive resources is (after accounting for differences in effort and accumulation) a historical and biological accident. There is no reason to postulate that a person who is born with sight and productive capacity is more entitled to consume than a person who is born blind and unproductive. Also, this postulate of asset egalitarianism is an implication of the popular *contractarian* view of justice considered below.

---

[2] Actually incentive effects may make the benefit principle desirable even if one accepts the social welfare philosophy.

A major criticism of the social welfare philosophy is that it is expedient and allows policy-makers excessive latitude in their endeavours. For example, social institutions that we intuitively believe to be sacrosanct, such as freedom of speech and the prohibition of slavery, could be violated or abolished if it were the case that social welfare, appropriately measured, would increase as a result. Indeed such arguments often motivate absolutist notions of ethics, and also were an important element in leading Rawls (1971) to his restatement of the theory of justice (discussed below). But in fact, when economic scarcity and economic incentives are introduced, social welfare arguments in favour of property rights, benefit taxation etc. are relatively easy to construct. More generally, entrenched human rights such as freedom of speech can be supported with social welfare arguments once political feasibility considerations are introduced. Although in many cases the violation of someone's freedom of speech may raise social welfare, freedom of speech as an entrenched right (not absolute; for example, US Justice Holmes drew the line at shouting 'fire' in a crowded theatre) may be appropriate if, in general, freedom of speech raises social welfare, and the costs of determining on a case-by-case basis when this is not the case are too high.

In other words, the social welfare philosophy is perfectly consistent with rules, obligations and entrenched rights. The value of such institutions lies not in their conformity with some pre-existing absolute ethics but because such institutions are essential to maximizing social welfare in a world of limited resources.[3, 4]

In summary, the dominant social welfare theory of justice underlies modern welfare economics. Its basic feature is to define the justice of various actions and institutions in terms of their contribution to social welfare rather than in terms of their compatibility with a postulated set of absolute rights and wrongs. If one begins with a postulate, 'Individuals have rights', as Nozick (1974, p. ix) does, and if one defines these rights to include whatever social institutions one seeks to defend (e.g. the distribution of income as determined by the existing system of property rights) then there is little left to say except that one's conclusions follow (trivially) from one's premises (or is it vice versa?).

With this said, we shall focus on theories of justice based on the social welfare philosophy. Having accepted this philosophy, one is faced with the ethical problem of defining social welfare. As mentioned in earlier chapters, modern welfare economics is largely based first on welfarism, which requires that social welfare depend on the utilities of the households and only on these utilities, and secondly on the Pareto principle, which requires social welfare to increase (or at least not decrease) when the utility of a household increases, *ceteris paribus*. Even with such restric-

---

[3] Similar arguments were made in regard to rule versus act utilitarianism by Harsanyi (1983).

[4] A related criticism of the social welfare philosophy is the apparent absence of supererogatory (beyond the call of duty) actions. Once it is recognized that certain obligations may arise on social welfare grounds, the compatibility of supererogatory actions and the social welfare philosophy is obvious.

tions, there are many different forms of the social welfare ordering representing different ethics and, as we saw in chapter 5, having different informational requirements in terms of the measurability and comparability of household utilities. We shall now consider some arguments in favour of certain forms of the social welfare ordering.

3.1 Separability of the social welfare ordering

If two households (call them a and b) *both* prefer state x to state y and all other households are indifferent between x and y, then any social welfare function that respects the Pareto principle must rank x above y, and does so independently of the level of utility of all households other than a and b provided that the others are indifferent between x and y. Fleming (1952) suggested that this *independence from indifferent households* notion should be extended to include all possible cases in which only households a and b have strict preferences and others are indifferent, whether or not a and b agree in their rankings of x and y. In other words, the social welfare ordering of any two states should always be independent of the utilities of all households that are indifferent between the two states being ranked. Let us refer to this property as Fleming's independence and denote it by E. It is similar to the notion of strong postulate separability. Not all social welfare functions that respect the Pareto principle do satisfy Fleming's independent postulate E.

As we know from demand theory (see chapter 2), if the social welfare function is strongly separable (i.e. satisfies E), then it can be written in the *additively separable* form:

$$W = \sum_{h=1}^{H} g^h(u^h) \qquad (6.1)$$

where $g^h(\ )$ is a monotonically increasing function of u^h, the utility indicator of household h. This function has the property that the marginal rate of social substitution between any two households' utility functions is independent of the level of utility of any other.

Another postulate which Fleming did not impose but which is ethically reasonable is *anonymity*. As mentioned in chapter 5, this requires that the social welfare ordering depends only on the utility numbers of the households and not on who gets what. In other words, all permutations among households of a given utility distribution must be ranked equivalently. In that case, $g^h(\ ) = g(\ )$ for all households and:

$$W = \sum_{h=1}^{H} g(u^h) \qquad (6.1')$$

Thus we obtain a utilitarian form of the SWF where the arguments are the function $g(\ )$ that the planner uses to attribute social utility to each person. On this interpretation, separability, anonymity and welfarism alone seem sufficient to generate a utilitarian SWF.

A few words should be said about the informational requirements of (6.1'). To begin with, notice that the *independence from indifferent households* postulate means that social institutions and policies are evaluated solely in terms of the households affected (that is, we can ignore indifferent households), which is, of course, a standard practice anyway.[5] Similarly, the *anonymity* postulate significantly economizes on informational needs. Households need only be identified by a measure of utility and households with the same utility levels need not be distinguished at all and can be grouped together.

The remaining informational requirements of a welfaristic, Pareto principle respecting, anonymous and separable SWF are found in tables 5.1 and 5.2. It is clear that a *continuous* SWF of the Fleming type is going to require at least that increments in utility be comparable across households, in which case the simple utilitarian form of sum of utilities is possible.

3.2 *Harsanyi's defence of the utilitarian SWF*

An important contribution by Harsanyi (1953, 1955, 1975) was to distinguish between a household's *personal* preferences and its impersonal or *moral* preferences. The moral preferences of a household are identified with its *unconditional* preferences – that is, unconditional on information deemed morally irrelevant – whereas its personal preferences (which economists usually think of as *the* preferences of the household) are *conditional*. For example, faced with choosing between two allocations, one equally divided among all households and the other not, a given household may express a personal preference for the unequal allocation conditional on the knowledge that it receives one of the largest shares, but may express a 'moral' preference for the equally divided allocation, unconditional on the knowledge of which share it is to receive. In other words, the moral preferences of a household are those that do not depend on its personal stake in the outcome and would be revealed in choices made by a reflective household that detaches itself from its vested interests.

Locating the source of morality in human decision-making is attractive from the social welfare philosophy point of view. However, we are left with the problem of analysing choices made by households who are ignorant of information that would normally be crucial to their decisions. Harsanyi postulated that households would retain their capacity of rational choice and, in particular, he attributed to them the postulates underlying the expected utility hypothesis of choice under uncertainty. Recall from chapter 3 that these postulates include not only the standard ones of consistency, completeness and continuity, but also *probabilistic*

---

[5] Of course, if there are interdependencies among household utility functions this would not be the case. However, for most purposes, the hypothesis of selfish households is relatively innocuous.

equivalence (that households do not care about the stochastic processes generating the same probabilities of a particular state of the world) and, importantly, *probabilistic independence* (or the 'sure thing'). The last states that if any two 'lotteries' (i.e. actions with uncertain outcomes) offer an outcome with the same probability, then the household's choice between the two lotteries is independent of this common outcome and depends only on the outcomes which differ between the lotteries. This means, by the expected utility hypothesis, that the household's preferences can be represented by the additively separable form:

$$u = \sum_{s=1}^{S} \pi_s v(x_s)$$

where x_s is the outcome in state s and π_s can be interpreted as the (subjective) probability associated with state s, $\Sigma_{s=1} \pi_s = 1$. The function $v(\ )$ is a subutility function which has cardinal numerical significance; that is, $v(\ )$ is unique up to a (i.e. as good as any other) cardinal transformation $v' = a + bv$ where $b > 0$. Note that whereas u is a representation of a household's preferences, so is $\phi(u)$ where $\phi(\ )$ is a positive monotonic transformation. Consequently, the $v(\ )$ function does not cardinalize the utility of income or 'happiness' in any absolute sense but, rather, cardinalizes the utility of income in one state of the world relative to another.

Harsanyi attributes ethical significance to the expected utility hypothesis by assuming that each household will, in making moral evaluations, treat the assignment of its particular identity as the uncertain event.[6] The household then evaluates an allocation *ex ante* by assigning a utility value $u^h(x)$ to being household h under allocation x. By the expected utility hypothesis, $u^h(x)$ is cardinally significant. Also, by the *principle of insufficient reason* the household assigns an equal probability to being any household. In this case, the household will rank x morally as good as y if

$$\sum_{h=1}^{H} u^h(x) \geqslant \sum_{h=1}^{H} u^h(y)$$

Thus the rational household's moral preferences can be represented by the sum of cardinal utilities (the Benthamite or utilitarian) form.[7]

The importance of the probabilistic axiom and its relation to Fleming's (1952) independence postulate E must be emphasized. Fleming introduced his independence postulate (and hence the separability of the social welfare ordering) as a 'basic ethical postulate'. In Harsanyi's framework, such separability emerges as a consequence of the probabilistic independ-

---

[6] Vickrey (1961) proposed a similar framework of moral choice.
[7] The household has linear SWF indifference curves with slope of minus unity in two-space. Of course $\psi(\Sigma_{h=1}^{H} u^h(x))$ is an equivalent ranking, so the SWF indifference curves of the household can be numbered in any increasing way.

ence posulate of rational choice under uncertainty. This postulate seems reasonable in the context of uncertain choice because the outcomes of an action are mutually exclusive; that is, the household's utility of consumption in state $s = 1$ is independent of the outcome in state $s = 2$ because only one state will be realized. Extending this to ethical choice, the moral household's evaluation of state x from the point of view of being any particular household h is independent (separable) from its evaluation of that state from the point of view of being any other household, because the household must in fact be one or the other. Although Diamond (1967b) and others have questioned the use of the probabilistic independence postulate in this context, the analogy is persuasive.

It also should be stressed that Harsanyi's propositions are constrained by the informational requirements discussed in chapter 5. Each household must, in one way or another, make interhousehold comparisons of utility (or utility increments at least). That is, each household must assign a utility value to being household h in allocation x for all h and x. Because each household may have different (but additively separable) moral preferences, a further assumption of interhousehold comparability among moral preferences is needed if a single and non-dictatorial SWF that aggregates the moral preferences of all households is to be obtained.

All this raises the informational issues of chapter 5 to the level of moral preferences. In this context, however, the Arrow dictator case (the only possibility if moral preferences are non-comparable) is less disturbing because it may be further assumed that the dictator is somehow restricted to acting only on its moral preferences (say, through the democratic process). Under Harsanyi's postulates, the moral dictator would dictate a utilitarian SWF.

Allowing for interpersonal comparability of moral preferences permits non-dictatorial forms of the SWF to be determined. For example, if household moral preferences are cardinally measurable and fully or partially (unit) comparable, the SWF possibility set includes the weighted sum of the household moral preferences which is, obviously, the generalized utilitarian (or simple utilitarian if anonymity is assumed) form.

The issue to be resolved in aggregating households' moral preferences concerns differences among households in making interhousehold utility comparisons. As we discuss below, there is no unique or natural way to define an equivalence between the indifference curves of households when their tastes differ. Obviously, if all households make interhousehold comparisons in the same way they will have identical moral preferences and aggregation of utilities is trivial. This possibility could be made plausible by arguing that all households are essentially identical when divested of personal interests.

3.3 Rawls and the maximin criterion

An important contribution to the theory of justice was made by Rawls (1971) who argued for a strongly egalitarian concept of economic justice.

He also accorded certain 'goods' distributed by the social order, such as liberty and opportunity, a degree of priority in the sense that there can be no amount of material goods that would compensate for their loss.

To support these concepts of justice, Rawls revived the old *contractarian* idea of Hobbes and Locke, who imagined an 'original position' in which self-centred households agree (unanimously) to a particular social order in preference to anarchy. He also extends Harsanyi's idea of identifying moral choice with the choice of households who are hypothetically ignorant of their personal wants and advantages. Rawls imagines that households are shielded from such morally irrelevant knowledge in the original position by a 'veil of ignorance'. He then argues that households in such circumstances would agree, solely on the basis of rational self-interest, to social insitutions that would share among all households the product and benefits made possible by the distribution of natural talents and abilities, whatever it may be (i.e. households agree to asset egalitarianism).

Rawls argues further that households in the veiled original position would agree to the 'difference principle'. This principle requires that all things of social value be distributed equally unless an inequality works to the advantage of (i.e. makes better off) the least-well-off household. Also, goods including liberty and (in agreement with Kant) subsistence consumption, which are deemed essential to the household's survival or self-respect, are assigned priority by postulating that the preferences of households in the original position lexicographically order primary and non-primary goods.[8] In other words there is no tradeoff between liberty (and other primary goods) and material (non-primary) goods.[9]

The household's adoption of the difference principle in the original state is a consequence of Rawls's assumption that the household follows the maximin decision rule. This decision rule leads the household to choose an action that yields the best outcome conditional on the worst eventuality occurring. In this context, every household presumes it will be the worst-off household in all circumstances and chooses social rules that *maxi*mize this *mini*mum utility. This decision rule is chosen by Rawls on the belief that all households would be very risk averse in the original position.

Rawls was led to this view of justice largely because he found the implications of the utilitarian cum social welfare philosophy unpalatable. The essence of the social welfare philosophy is that all desirable social rules and institutions derive their status by increasing the well-being of society's members, whereas utilitarianism (such as the Benthamite SWF) implies that a policy is socially good if the increase in the utility of those who gain more than offsets the decrease of those who lose. As mentioned above, this view is incompatible with the absolute primacy of certain

---

[8]   Recall that a lexicographic preference assigns priority to good x if a bundle with less of that good is non-preferred regardless of how much of the other goods it contains.

[9]   If there is more than one primary good then they may be lexicographically ordered or ordered in some other manner.

rights.[10] Rawls singled out a limiting case which eliminates all tradeoffs in ethical matters but preserves the end result principles of the social welfare philosophy.

The Rawlsian conception of economic justice has faced considerable criticism from economists. Perhaps the most damaging are those of Arrow (1973) and Harsanyi (1975). Arrow points out that Rawls's presumption that the utilitarian rule would only be agreed upon by households in the original position if they are risk neutral is wrong. In fact, the expected utility decision rule is a general one, and the maximin decision rule is just a special case of this rule that arises when risk aversion is infinite.

To see this, let a household's von Neumann–Morgenstern utility function $u^h(x)$ be equal to $[u^h(x)]^{1-\rho}$.[11] Then if households adopt the expected utility rule, $W = \Sigma_{h=1}^{H}(u^h)^{1-\rho}$. Since $W' = W/(1-\rho)$ is just a linear transformation of W, W and W' both order social states in the same way. Thus the expected utility hypothesis implies that a household's moral preferences take on the general form

$$W' = \frac{\sum\limits_{h=1}^{H}(u^h)^{1-\rho}}{1-\rho}$$

Harsanyi just took the special case where the admissible transformation, $\phi(\ )$, is the identity transformation (so $\rho = 0$). As discussed in chapter 5, W' approaches the Bernoulli–Nash (Cobb–Douglas) form as $\rho \to 1$ and the maximin (Rawlsian) form as $\rho \to \infty$.

The upshot of this is that the Rawlsian case can be viewed as a special case of the more generally expected utility hypothesis. The plausibility of this special case seems doubtful.[12] The maximin strategy has some plausibility in circumstances where a decision-maker is engaged in a 'zero-sum game' with a rational, selfish and utility maximizing opponent. But why should households in the original position believe that their social economic position is determined by a rational competitor rather than by some random process? Moreover, it is irrational for every household to believe it will be the worst-off household. If such a belief were to be consistent with the actual outcome, all households would have to receive the same level of utility, yet this outcome may not be desirable by Rawls's own difference principle.

---

[10] Entrenched rights and obligations are consistent with (indeed, may be required by) the social welfare philosophy once feasibility considerations are introduced. However, such rules are not absolute and can be revoked by society if a change in circumstances makes their costs too high; for example, wartime censorship.

[11] That is, $u^h(x) = \psi[u^h(x)]$ where $\psi(z) = z^{1/1-\rho}$, is the certain utility of being household h in allocation of x.

[12] Harsanyi (1975) has pointed out that households following a maximin rule would not cross a street (with the attendant small chance of being hit by a car) regardless of the reward for doing so. Since such behaviour seems so absurd in everyday affairs there is a reasonable doubt regarding its merit as a decision rule in the original position.

Although the maximin rule is implausible, it does have an advantage over the expected utility hypothesis on informational grounds. Moral households would only have to make level comparison of ordinal utility functions across households in order to determine the worst-off position. This may imply that unanimity in moral preferences is more likely under Rawls than under the expected utility hypothesis, which requires cardinal measurability and unit comparability.

The other contributions of Rawls's theory seem less fundamental. The idea of primary goods does accord certain principles a priority which cannot be traded off against mere material wealth; but Rawls's device, the lexicographic preference of moral households for primary goods, is independent of the difference principle and could easily be invoked in combination with the expected utility (utilitarian) hypothesis for the same purposes.

Rawls's other innovation, the rediscovery of the social contract, seems somewhat gratuitous. The justification of ethical behaviour in terms of a hypothetical contract is a circular argument. The moral authority of the contract – an ethic – is invoked to justify ethics. It is not obvious (to us, at least) that this contributes anything to the moral force of Rawls's arguments.

4 Interhousehold Utility Comparability and Moral Preferences

Perhaps the major difficulty with searching for distributive equity in the moral preferences of households behind the Harsanyi–Rawls 'veil of ignorance' lies in the problem of interhousehold (or interpersonal) utility level comparisons. This framework requires that each household put itself into another's shoes and evaluate a state of the world where it is any household with any allocation. For complete symmetry among households, every household would have to have perfect information about the utility function of every other household. Although this may seem surmountable in what is, after all, a totally hypothetical experiment, it does relate directly to a practical problem – how does the planner determine equivalence between the indifference curves of any two different households?

If households have identical ordinal preferences (i.e. the same indifference curve maps) the problem can be solved with a relatively natural ethical assumption; namely, that all households have the same capacity to generate utility. In this case, the same utility number is assigned to households consuming the same bundle of goods. Since the indifference curves of any two households are coincident (i.e. they intersect everywhere) the equivalence does not depend on which bundle of goods the two households consume.

If households have different ordinal preferences, there is an element of ambiguity in determining the equivalence between indifference curves. In figure 6.5, Alice has a preference for good x_2 relative to Bob, so their

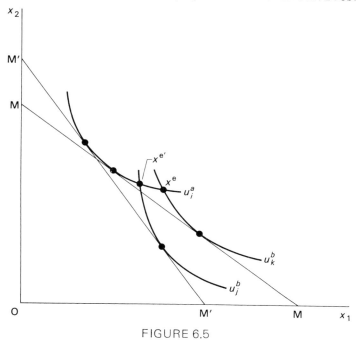

FIGURE 6.5

indifference curves are not coincident. If we assign equal utility levels to Alice and Bob when they both consume bundle x^e (so $u_i^a = u_k^b$) then their utility levels will not be equal when they both consume bundle $x^{e'}$.

An alternative (and standard) procedure is to assign the same utility level to individuals facing the same budget set. For example, in figure 6.5, if Alice and Bob both have budget set OMM then u_i^a is equated to u_j^b, since these indifference curves represent the maximum utility level possible for each respective household. Superficially, this procedure appears impartial because households with the same income are given the same utility level regardless of how they spend it. But the equivalence of u_i^a and u_k^b is determined for a particular set of relative prices. If, instead, the households are faced with the identical budget set OM'M' where the relative price of x^1 (Bob's preferred good) is higher, then u_i^a and u_j^b (which corresponds to a lower level of utility for Bob than u_k^b) are equivalent. In other words, this procedure of assigning equivalence among household utilities depends on the set of relative prices chosen. Only if Alice and Bob have identical preferences can two indifference curves be made unambiguously equivalent for all relative prices.

In summary, the assumption that households have the same capacity to generate utility yields an unambiguous equivalence relation between the utility levels of different households only if those households have identical ordinal preferences. If households have different ordinal preferences, we can assume that they generate the same utility level from a particular

G

bundle of goods or from the same income at a particular set of relative prices. However, this implies that the households would generate a different level of utility if they both consume some other bundle of goods or if they have the same income at some other set of relative prices. Consequently, when ordinal preferences differ among households no unambiguous meaning can be given to the assumption of 'equal capacity to enjoy' and interhousehold utility level comparisons necessarily involve an arbitrary assumption of some sort.

Consider again the problem faced by moral households behind the veil of ignorance. How can they assign a utility level to being household h with allocation x? We could accord them full knowledge, including that of every household's ability to generate utility, but this does not reveal to us what that knowledge (which every moral household supposedly knows) is. If, instead, we assume that the moral households do not have full knowledge, then they must make some arbitrary assumption (which may differ from household to household) on how to equate one household's indifference curve with that of another.[13] The veil of ignorance framework provides no guidance as to how this crucially important ethical decision is or should be made.

All this led Arrow (1973) to express a profound pessimism regarding the possibility of finding a 'theory of justice'. The recognition of human diversity is an essential element in the ethical resolution of conflicts of interest, yet 'theories of justice', in seeking universal ethical norms, universify them with constructs that require complete symmetry among households.

Another approach to interhousehold utility comparisons eschews utility *level* comparisons and makes interhousehold comparisons of utility increments or units instead. This approach was suggested by Edgeworth (1881) and, recently, by Ng (1975). The foundations of this approach lie in the finite sensibility of human perception. Psychologists have long known that human beings cannot discriminate among stimuli with infinite fineness. That is, there exists a quantum of human perception or just noticeable difference (JND). The unit approach to interhousehold comparisons equates the JNDs of different households as utility increments. That is, if $\nabla u^h = u^h(x) - u^h(y)$ is the JND of household h between two states and $\nabla u^g = u^g(x) - u^g(y)$ is the JND of household g between the same two states, then $\nabla u^h = \nabla u^g$.

The conclusion drawn from this approach (with the addition of some assumptions) is that the SWF is of the utilitarian sum of utilities form. (For a formal proof see Ng, 1975.) The reader can see why this result emerges by consulting table 5.2, where the SWF possibilities with unit comparability are listed.

This approach is far less important than it sounds. A household's JND may differ when judging two states under different circumstances. For

---

[13]   Also, since knowledge of their own preferences is morally irrelevant (knowing that I like wine relative to others would lead me to equate incomes and utilities at a low relative price of wine), households making moral decisions must be deprived of such knowledge.

example, its JND may depend on whether it compares two quantities simultaneously or sequentially. In this case, there is no such thing as *the* JND of income of a household. Even if this were not the case, the ethical content of the proposition is doubtul. Why should the JND (say 5 real dollars) to an insensitive household be equated to the JND (say 1 real dollar) of a sensitive household irrespective of their circumstances?

4.1 *A digression on horizontal equity*

A prevalent ethical norm is that of horizontal equity. It is often described as a requirement that 'equals should be treated equally'. The difficulty with this aphorism is that it does not offer an operational meaning of 'equals' or 'treated equally'. One suggested interpretation of 'equals' is 'having equal levels of utility', and horizontal equity is a requirement that some pre-existing| equality of utility levels among some subset of households must be preserved. In other words, households who have equal utility levels before a policy change must have equal utility levels afterwards. A slightly stronger definition requires that the ranking of households in terms of their utility levels must be unchanged by the policy (Feldstein, 1976).

It is now recognized that this definition of horizontal equity may (and, generally, will) be inconsistent with social welfare maximization (indeed with the social welfare principle itself). In fact, it conflicts with the Pareto principle, as can be seen from the following example. Consider an exchange economy with three goods: meat, vegetables and wine. Vegetarian Alice and carnivorous Bob have endowments of vegetables and meat, respectively, which they consume. Suppose that we assign them equal utility levels. Now introduce a carnivorous household Charlie who is an abstainer but has an endowment of wine. Clearly Pareto improving trades exist between Charlie and Bob (assuming the latter is not also an abstrainer) but Alice's utility level cannot be increased by any trades. Thus the horizontal equity requirement that Bob's utility level remain the same as that of Alice precludes a policy that permits Pareto improving trades between Bob and Charlie. Although this example only provides a conflict between horizontal equity (as defined above) and the strong Pareto principle, examples of conflict with the weak Pareto principle can also be constructed.

More generally, the horizontal equity requirement acts as a second-best type of constraint on the social welfare maximization problem. Suppose we wish to solve the following problem

$$\max W(u^1(x^1), \ldots, u^H(x^H))$$

subject to a production constraint

$$G\left(\sum_{h=1}^{H} x^h\right) = 0$$

Without a horizontal equity ethic we get the usual first-order conditions:

$$\frac{u_i^h}{u_j^h} = \frac{G_i}{G_j} \quad \text{for all } i \text{ and } j$$

$$\frac{w_h}{w_g} = \frac{u_i^g}{u_i^h} \quad \text{for all } i \text{ and } h$$

(6.2)

The requirement of horizontal equity adds the restriction:

$$u^g = u^h \quad \text{for all } g \text{ and } h \text{ belonging to } E$$

where E is some subset of households who are determined to have equal utility in the pre-existing state. Adding this constraint to the problem prevents the first-order conditions (6.2) from being satisfied if the households in the equality set differ in their tastes and/or their endowments. Thus, a horizontal equity requirement raises all of the difficult problems encountered in the theory of the second best.

Atkinson and Stiglitz (1976) have pointed out that this horizontal equity requirement may be violated when social welfare is maximized even if households are treated perfectly symmetrically in terms of preferences, endowments and within the SWF itself. They demonstrate that a violation of horizontal equity occurs in the event that a global convexity requirement is not satisfied. This point is illustrated in figure 6.6 (taken from Atkinson, 1980), where it is assumed that the utility possibility set is symmetric but non-concave in some range. With identical endowments and preferences the pre-existing equilibrium is at utility distribution C on the 45° line. Yet maximization of a symmetric social welfare function requires the reallocation of resources between households to reach distribution A or B where utilities differ between the households. Symmetry is preserved in the sense that it does not matter which household's utility is increased, but horizontal equity, in the sense of preserving a pre-existing utility equality, is clearly violated.

It is apparent from this discussion that the objective of horizontal equity, defined as the preservation of some pre-existing utility ranking of the households, cannot be supported with the end result principles of the social welfare philosophy but must be an independent ethical principle. Atkinson (1980) attempted a brief rationalization of this principle in terms of an original position where individuals are aware of the pre-existing state but uncertain about policy changes. At a practical level, Johnson and Mayer (1962) and others have actually constructed indexes of horizontal equity to complement the conventional indexes of inequality discussed in chapter 9.

An alternative interpretation of horizontal equity suggested by Musgrave (1959) seems to conform more closely with the social welfare (and welfarist) philosophy. In this view, horizontal equity is a requirement

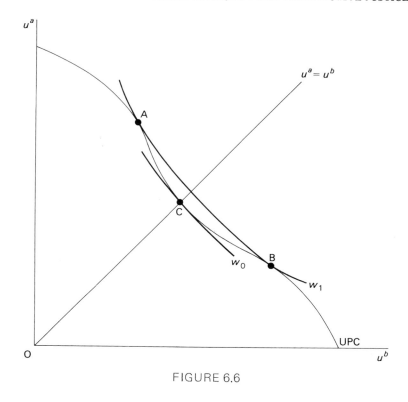

FIGURE 6.6

against 'capricious discrimination'. We all know that human beings, even identical twins, are not 'equals' in every attribute. But some inequalities (e.g. the colour of one's eyes or skin) are inappropriate criteria for unequal treatment. Consequently we can interpret horizontal equity as a requirement that households not be treated differently on the basis of irrelevant (non-utility) differences. In other words, only utilities, not identities, are important for social welfare purposes, so the SWF should be welfaristic and symmetric (i.e. satisfy anonymity). This criterion of horizontal equity is met in most formulations of any welfare economics problem.

5 Conclusions

In chapter 1 we described the theory of welfare economics as a framework for choosing among different social states. The ultimate goal was described as a complete and consistent ranking of all social states – that is, a social welfare ordering. In subsequent chapters we also introduced the concept of economic efficiency and its supporting ethical postulates, namely the Pareto principle and individualism.

In this chapter we have gone beyond the ethical foundations of mutual welfare concerns and have established the ethical foundations for choosing among social states involving utility conflict. This allows us to analyse distributive issues as well as efficiency issues. One distributive concept that does not require interhousehold utility comparisons is that of lack of envy. In particular we can select allocations in which no other household would prefer another household's consumption bundle. Such allocations are called 'fair'. Fair and efficient allocations always exist in exchange economies but do not necessarily exist in production economies. A more general concept is that of egalitarian equivalent allocations which include all fair allocations. An allocation is egalitarian equivalent if the associated utility distribution could have been attained by the equal division of some aggregate commodity bundle. Efficient and egalitarian equivalent allocations always exist.

The above concepts do not provide a complete social welfare ordering in general, nor do they necessarily provide the ethical sense of what many people regard as 'fairness'. In this chapter we have briefly surveyed theories of justice with special emphasis on those that are based on the end state social welfare concepts of justice rather than those based on absolute concepts of justice. A key idea is the Harsanyi–Rawls 'veil of ignorance', which shields households from knowledge of their actual socioeconomic position. Ethical or moral preference among social states is identified with the preferences of households over social states behind the veil of ignorance.

Two important, and competing, ethics are drawn from such a framework. The first is that the social welfare ordering is additively separable; that is, any two households' utilities can be aggregated independently of all others. Harsanyi finds this follows from the assumption that households will obey the expected utility postulates behind the veil of ignorance, whereas Fleming makes it a fundamental ethical postulate. In either case, many find it a reasonable assumption.

The second ethic is that certain goods, notably liberty and subsistence, have the status of inviolable rights, whereas distributive justice, as codified in the social welfare function, should concern only the welfare of the worst-off household. Rawls draws these conclusions from the assumptions that households have a lexicographic prior preference for particular goods and would choose among allocations of the remaining goods according to the maximin rule.

Both ethical conclusions would require households to make interhousehold utility comparisons behind the veil of ignorance. Rawls's households must be able to compare levels, whereas Harsanyi's must be able to compare units. We have stressed that when households have different preferences, there is no single and natural way to make interhousehold comparisons. This issue remains unresolved.

In various places in these first six chapters we have stressed that the end state principle of social justice (and the Pareto principle criterion, in particular) may be inconsistent with absolute ethical concepts. An example encountered in this chapter is horizontal equity. If horizontal equity is interpreted as preserving pre-existing equalities in the levels of utilities across households, then horizontal equity may conflict with the Pareto principle in particular and social welfare maximization in general. As such, horizontal equity must be invoked as a separate ethical principle.

Finally, we should briefly state what has been accomplished so far. We have laid out the ethical and informational postulates for a social welfare function that is additively separable, quasi-concave, welfaristic and respects the Pareto principle. Furthermore, postulates can be invoked to make the social welfare function symmetric and homothetic. In this case it can be represented by:

$$W = \sum_{h=1}^{H} \frac{(u^h)^{1-\rho}}{1-\rho}$$

where u^h is a utility indicator of household h and ρ is an equity parameter. We are now prepared to address the practical problems of applying the theory of welfare economics in the context of a market economy.

PART II

APPLIED WELFARE ECONOMICS:
THE THEORY OF WELFARE CHANGE
MEASUREMENT

CHAPTER 7

The Measurement of Welfare Change for an Individual

1 Introduction

Applied welfare economics is ultimately based upon measures of the change in the well-being for an individual household between two situations where, for simplicity, the two situations refer to different bundles of commodities consumed. From these measures we deduce measures of welfare change for entire economies which incorporate the production side of the economy and which are aggregated over several households. This chapter is concerned solely with measuring welfare change for a single household. The next two chapters investigate single-household economies and many-household economies, respectively. As we shall see, the adaptation of welfare change measures for a single household to welfare change measures for the economy as a whole requires both some approximations to make the measures empirically applicable, and some value judgments to enable one to go from single-household measures to many-household aggregates. We shall be careful to indicate what sorts of approximations and value judgments are typically made.

The principles of welfare measurement for the individual household are derived on the assumption that the only information available is the ordering of alternative situations by the household (i.e. its preference map). As was discussed in chapter 2, these preferences can be represented by an ordinal utility function under certain reasonable assumptions.[1] More specifically, a utility function $u(x)$ is a suitable representation of the household's preference ordering R if $u(x^1) \geqslant u(x^2)$ whenever $x^1 R x^2$ for all bundles x^1 and x^2. Any utility function that has this property is an adequate indicator of individual preference. It is readily apparent that once a particular utility function $u(x)$ is found to represent individual preferences R, any increasing function (i.e. monotonic transformation) is

---

[1] The assumptions are that preferences be complete, reflexive and transitive, increasing, and continuous everywhere.

also suitable;[2] that is, utility functions whose sole property is that they accurately reflect preference orderings are ordinal utility functions.

Observations of a household's choice among different alternatives can only reveal the household's ordinal ranking of those alternatives. This is the source of the difficulty in measuring welfare change. We seek a monetary measure or monetary equivalent of utility which yields a cardinal measure. The measure used will be the money metric developed in chapter 2. It is the purpose of this and the following chapters to analyse how the money metric can be applied to measure welfare change in a variety of circumstances. Two points should always be borne in mind throughout the following discussion. Firstly, until we are prepared to make more information available than just the preference orderings of the household, the monetary measures of welfare change derived here have only limited normative significance. They cannot be viewed as measures of utility change for an individual. Instead, they are derived from an arbitrary cardinalization of the individual's preference ordering. This will be particularly important if we wish to aggregate utility over households. Secondly, it is the case, as will be discussed below, that no unique monetary measure of welfare change is possible. There are an indefinite number of ways of obtaining monetary equivalents of alternative bundles of goods, so some arbitrary choice must be made as to which one to use.

2 The Problem Defined

To illustrate the problem geometrically, consider a household that consumes two goods x_1 and x_n according to the budget constraint $m = p_1 x_1 + p_n x_n$. Figure 7.1 illustrates the points on indifference curves attained in situations 1 and 2, where prices and income may have changed. The idea is to measure the 'distance' between indifference curves u_1 and u_2 in some way. It is obvious that there are a large number of ways to do that, and the purpose here will be to explore some appealing alternatives.

As a prelude to doing so, it is useful to clarify one problem of measurement that always arises. Each of the budget lines in figure 7.1 is compatible with a large number of combinations of prices and income. In particular, if all prices and income are changed in the same proportion, the budget line will remain unchanged and so will the chosen bundle of goods. This is a reflection of the property of homogeneity of degree zero of the household's demand function in prices and income. Since we do not wish proportionate changes to affect our measure of welfare change, a convention for pegging the price level must be adopted. The convention will be to use x_n as the *numéraire* good and set its price arbitrarily to unity. Thus we implicitly measure all other prices and income in units of that good. In figure 7.1, m^1 and m^2 are the incomes in the two situations

---

[2] Another utility function which adequately represents preferences will be a function $v(x)$ which has the property that $v(x^1) \geqslant v(x^2)$ whenever $x^1 R x^2$; that is, whenever $u(x^1) \geqslant u(x^2)$. Therefore, u and v will be increasing functions of one another.

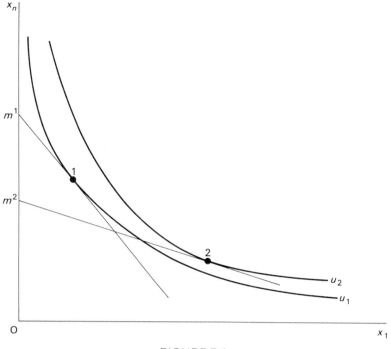

FIGURE 7.1

and the absolute values of the slopes of the budget lines are the prices of x_1, denoted p_1^1 and p_1^2. For some purposes, it will be useful to think of x_n as a composite of all goods other than x_1. As Hicks (1939) has shown, if the relative prices of all goods other than x_1 remain unchanged, they can be aggregated into a single composite commodity.

A possible candidate for measuring the change in welfare in going from state 1 to state 2 can be developed algebraically. Although it will turn out to be unsuitable, it is worth while going through the example because it illustrates the non-uniqueness of welfare change measures. Recall the formulation of the household's decision problem in the general case of n goods. It chooses $(x_1, \ldots, x_n)$ to maximize utility given a budget constraint, or

$$\max_x u(x_1, \ldots, x_n)$$

subject to

$$\Sigma p_i x_i = m$$

The solution to this problem gives a set of demand functions $x_i(p, m)$ and a value for the Lagrangian multiplier $\lambda(p, m)$, both of which depend upon the exogenous prices and income given in the problem. By substituting the demand functions back into the utility function we obtain the *indirect utility function v*:[3]

$$v(p, m) = u[x_1(p, m), \ldots, x_n(p, m)]$$

As we have seen, the indirect utility function satisfies Roy's theorem:

$$x_i(p, m) = - \frac{\partial v(p, m)/\partial p_i}{\partial v(p, m)/\partial m}$$

which yields the uncompensated or Marshallian demand functions by simple differentiation of the indirect utility function. This is extremely useful in empirical demand analysis. For our purposes, it is also useful for deriving a class of welfare change measures.

Consider an individual faced with differentially small changes in prices and income. Given a suitable ordinal indirect utility function, the change in utility can be derived by total differentiation and the application of Roy's theorem as:

$$dv = \Sigma (\partial v/\partial p_i)\, dp_i + (\partial v/\partial m)\, dm$$
$$= -\lambda \Sigma x_i(p, m)\, dp_i + \lambda\, dm$$

If we divide through by λ we obtain a perfectly adequate monetary measure of welfare change (appropriately measured in units of the *numéraire* good) for differential changes in the exogenous prices and income facing the consumer:

$$dW = dv/\lambda = - \Sigma x_i(p, m)\, dp_i + dm \qquad (7.1)$$

All terms on the right-hand side of dW are, in principle, measurable in an unambiguous way. This formulation is often used in deriving *shadow prices* for small projects in cost–benefit analysis, as will be discussed in chapter 10.

Unfortunately, once we attempt to extend the above measure to large or discrete changes we run into difficulties. Suppose prices and income change by discrete amounts between situations 1 and 2. To apply the above measure to discrete changes we would have to integrate the differential welfare changes between the initial and the final situations to obtain:

$$\Delta W = \int dW = - \Sigma \int_1^2 x_i(p, m)\, dp_i + \Delta m \qquad (7.2)$$

---

[3] The properties of the indirect utility function were discussed in chapter 2.

The right-hand side of (7.2) is what is known as a *line integral*. It is the sum of a series of integrals each one of which depends upon the values of variables which are variables of integration in the other integrals. For example, the value of $\int x_j(p, m) \, dp_j$ will depend upon the values of m and all other prices $p_i (i \neq j)$. If one considers evaluating (7.1) by allowing each of the prices and income to change from situation 1 to 2 consecutively, the value of the integral for any one price change (i.e. $-\int x_j \, dp_j$) will depend upon the order in which the prices and income are changed. Furthermore, the value of the sum of the integrals in (7.2) will, in general, depend upon the order in which the integration is done. The integral is said to be *path dependent*, and therefore the measure of welfare change is not unique. It is a theorem in mathematics that the value of a line integral is path independent only if the matrix of derivatives of the x_i functions is symmetric (e.g. $\partial x_i / \partial p_j = \partial x_j / \partial p_i$). There is no particular reason why this should be so in the case of uncompensated demand functions. Therefore, there is a fundamental ambiguity involved in obtaining monetary measures of welfare change which can only be resolved by arbitrarily selecting a particular path of prices and income in going from one situation to another.

Before turning to the selection of a particular path, it is worth pointing out that there are certain circumstances for which the path dependency problem does not arise in (7.2). When only a single price or income changes, a unique measure of ΔW is obtained from (7.2). If m changes by Δm with prices constant, ΔW is simply Δm. In terms of figure 7.1 this is simply the vertical distance between the budget lines tangent to the two indifference curves when Δm is measured in terms of x_n and relative prices do not change.

Suppose that p_1 changes while all other prices and income are held constant. The welfare change measure becomes:

$$\Delta W = -\int_{p_1^1}^{p_1^2} x_1(p, m) \, dp_1 \qquad (7.3)$$

This is illustrated in figure 7.2. In the upper diagram, all goods other than x_1 are aggregated into a composite commodity x_n in units of which prices and income are measured. The price of x_1 is assumed to fall from p_1^1 to p_1^2. The integral in (7.3) is evaluated by moving from 1 to 2 along the price consumption line denoted PC. Each point along PC corresponds to a point on the Marshallian demand curve for x_1 which is drawn in the lower diagram. From (7.3) it is apparent that the welfare change measure ΔW is given by the area $p_1^1 abp_1^2$ to the left of this demand curve. This area is usually referred to as the *Marshallian consumer surplus*, and we shall follow that convention.

Although (7.3) appears to avoid the path dependency problem and give a unique measure of welfare change, the uniqueness is really artificial. There are several ways of getting from point 1 to 2 by combinations of

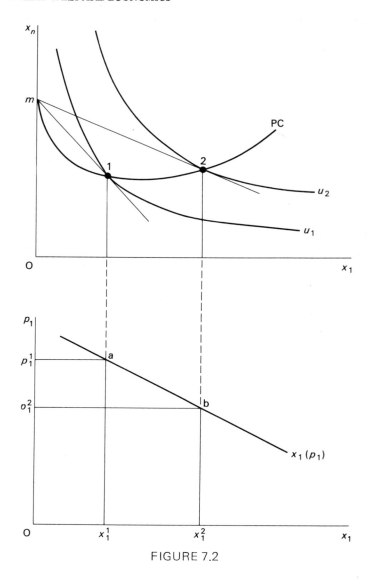

FIGURE 7.2

price and income changes, and each of them gives a different measure of welfare change. Two particular paths will be considered below.

In general, when more than one price and income change simultaneously even the apparent uniqueness obtained above is not achieved. An arbitrary method of selecting a path to measure the distance between indifference levels must be chosen. Two methods are conventionally used in applied welfare economics for reasons which will become apparent as we proceed. They are the *compensating variation* (CV) and the *equivalent variation* (EV), and each will be dealt with in turn. Both of them will be illustrated geometrically for the two-good case and then treated algebraically for the general case. They are basic concepts in applied welfare economics and cost–benefit analysis.

3 The Compensating Variation (CV)

The CV of a move from situation 1 to situation 2 is defined to be the amount of income that could be taken away from a household in the new situation in order to leave it as well off as in the old. Equivalently, it is the maximum amount of money the household would be willing to give up in order to have the change occur. If the household is better off in 2 than in 1, CV is positive; if worse off, it is negative.

Figure 7.3 illustrates CV for the two-good case. Relative prices and income have changed, so that the consumer is better off in going from 1 to 2. Assuming that all measurements have been made in terms of x_n, CV is given by the distance $m^2 e^1$. Notice that CV measures the vertical distance between budget lines tangent to u_1 and u_2 using the relative prices in situation 2. The amount of income that is required to attain utility level u_1 at the new set of prices is given by e^1.

The fact that the prices in situation 2 are used in calculating CV causes some ambiguities in its use. Suppose we want to know whether it is better to move from 1 to 2 or from 1 to 3. Comparing CVs from the two moves

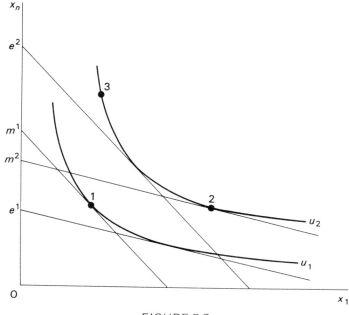

FIGURE 7.3

can give incorrect rankings of 2 versus 3 because different relative prices are used in evaluating the two moves.[4] For example, in figure 7.3, states 2 and 3 are on the same indifference curve yet CV associated with the move from 1 to 3 (not drawn) will generally differ from $m_2 e_1$. This ambiguity arises because of the manner in which CVs are constructed. The correct relative ranking of 2 and 3 can always be found by taking CV for a move from 2 to 3 directly rather than comparing them both with 1. This example illustrates that some care should be used in analytical applications of CV measure.

For the more general case of more than two goods, an algebraic expression for CV must be derived. Fortunately, this is a rather straight-forward matter using the *consumer expenditure function*. Recall that the expenditure function is derived from the dual to the utility maximization problem. Instead of maximizing utility subject to a given income con-straint, we imagine minimizing expenditures required to attain a given utility level. Formally, the expenditure minimization problem is as follows:

$$\min_x \Sigma p_i x_i$$

subject to

$$u(x_1, \ldots, x_n) = u$$

The first-order conditions to this problem can in principle be solved for the choice variables x_i in terms of the exogenous variables p and u, or

$$x_i = x_i(p, u) \qquad i = 1, \ldots, n \tag{7.4}$$

These are the *compensated demand functions* for the goods x_i since they indicate the demand for x_i at various sets of prices p for a given utility level u.

The expenditure function is derived by substituting (7.4) back into the objective function to yield:

$$e(p, u) = \Sigma p_i x_i(p, u) \tag{7.5}$$

The expenditure function $e(p, u)$ shows the income the individual would have to have to attain a utility level u at a set of prices p. Its properties were discussed in chapter 2. For the purposes of applied welfare economics the most important property is Hotelling's lemma, which states

$$\partial e(p, u)/\partial p_i = x_i(p, u) \qquad i = 1, \ldots, n \tag{7.6}$$

---

[4] This ambiguity was pointed out in Hause (1975); see also King (1981).

That is, the compensated demand functions are simply the derivatives of the expenditure function with respect to prices.

In figure 7.3 it is apparent that e^1 is simply the expenditure required to attain utility level u_1 at the prices p^2. Thus, CV may be written as:

$$CV = m^2 - e(p^2, u_1) \tag{7.7}$$

where p^2 is the vector of prices in the new situation. This expression is appropriate regardless of how many goods there are or how many prices change. Naturally, CV may be positive or negative depending upon whether the change has made the consumer better or worse off. This equation is perhaps the most important equation used in applied welfare economics. Much of our discussion in the next few chapters will be concerned with implementing it in various cases.

The CV may be written in another way which is useful for measurement purposes. Since $m^2 - m^1 = \Delta m$, (7.7) may be written:

$$CV = m^1 - e(p^2, u_1) + \Delta m$$
$$= e(p^1, u_1) - e(p^2, u_1) + \Delta m \tag{7.7'}$$

where $e(p^1, u_1)$ is the income required to reach u_1 at prices p^1 (i.e. m^1). Since e is continuous in p, this may be further rewritten:

$$CV = \int_{p^2}^{p^1} \Sigma \left(\partial e(p, u_1)/\partial p_i \right) dp_i + \Delta m$$

or, using Hotelling's lemma (7.6) and reversing the order of integration,

$$CV = - \int_{p^1}^{p^2} \Sigma x_i(p, u_1) dp_i + \Delta m \tag{7.8}$$

This equation is reminiscent of (7.2) for ΔW. This integral is a line integral involving the *compensated* demand functions $x_i(p, u_1)$ rather than the uncompensated demand functions. In this case the line integral is path independent because the cross-partial derivatives of $x_i(p, u_1)$ are symmetric.[5] Therefore, the mathematical conditions for uniqueness of the value of the line integral, or the so-called *integrability conditions*, are satisfied.

---

[5] This results from the fact that using Hotelling's lemma,

$$\partial x_i(p, u)/\partial p_j = \partial^2 e/\partial p_i\, \partial p_j = \partial^2 e/\partial p_j\, \partial p_i = \partial x_j(p, u)/\partial p_i$$

An interesting property of the CV measure in (7.8) is apparent if we imagine that only one price, say p_i, changes. Then CV becomes simply $-\int x_i(p, u_1) \, dp_i$. This expression can be given a straightforward geometric interpretation as in figure 7.4. In the upper diagram, CV is shown by me^1. As the above expression indicates, this CV is equal to the area in the lower diagram to the left of the compensated demand curve, labelled $x_i(p, \bar{u}_1)$, or $p_i^1 a c p_i^2$. As can be seen, if the good x_i is normal (so it has a positive income effect), the Marshallian demand curve $x_i(p, \bar{m})$ is flatter

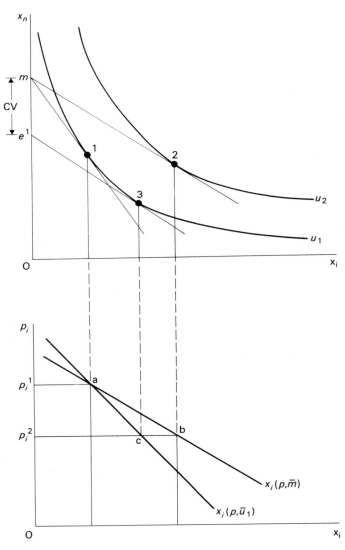

FIGURE 7.4

than the compensated demand curve, so CV $<$ ΔW. The difference can be attributed to the fact that the welfare measure CV is evaluated for a different 'path' in going from point 1 to point 2 than is ΔW.[6] Although the latter follows the price consumption line (see figure 7.2), CV from 1 to 3 is evaluated along a path that goes along u_1 (involving no welfare change) and then from 3 to 2 along an income expansion line (involving the welfare change me^1).

If several prices change, then one can sequentially add up areas like $p_i^1 ac p_i^2$ for each individual price change. The order in which the prices are changed has no influence on the value of CV obtained.

4 The Equivalent Variation (EV)

The EV is defined as the amount of income (positive or negative) that must be added to m^1 in the initial situation in order to give the household utility level u_2. Equivalently, it can be thought of as the minimum amount of income the consumer would be willing to accept in order to forgo the move from 1 to 2. The EV will always be positive if $u_2 > u_1$ and negative if $u_2 < u_1$.

The EV can be readily illustrated using figure 7.3. It is given by the distance $e^2 m^1$ along the vertical axis. Whereas CV was the vertical distance between budget lines tangent to u_1 and u_2 using the new set of prices, EV is the vertical distance using the old set. Notice that EV and CV are related in that the absolute value of CV for the move from 1 to 2 corresponds to the absolute value of EV for the move from 2 to 1, and vice versa. Since EV uses the original set of prices only, it is quite un-ambiguous as a method of comparing two or more alternative moves from an initial situation. For example, in figure 7.3, EV for the move from 1 to 2 is the same as EV from 1 to 3. Some authors have suggested that this makes EV a superior measure to CV (e.g. Hause, 1975). As we have shown earlier, if some care is used CV can give correct rankings over more than two alternatives.

As with CV, the expenditure function can be used to obtain an expression for EV in the general case. Using figure 7.3 again, EV is given by $e^2 - m^1$ or

$$EV = e(p^1, u_2) - m^1 \qquad (7.9)$$

This is the fundamental expression to be used to obtain EV when any number of goods or price changes are involved. As with CV, we can express (7.9) in an alternative, useful way. Since $\Delta m = m^2 - m^1$,

$$EV = e(p^1, u_2) - m^2 + \Delta m$$
$$= e(p^1, u_2) - e(p^2, u_2) + \Delta m \qquad (7.9')$$

---

[6]   A useful discussion of this point may be found in Burns (1973).

Also, since e is continuous in prices, the difference in expenditure in going from p^1 to p^2 but holding u_2 constant can be expressed in the integral form:

$$\text{EV} = \int_{p^2}^{p^1} \Sigma \, (\partial e(p, u_2)/\partial p_i) \, \mathrm{d}p_i + \Delta m$$

or, using Hotelling's lemma (7.6) and reversing the order of integration,

$$\text{EV} = -\int_{p^1}^{p^2} \Sigma \, x_i(p, u_2) \, \mathrm{d}p_i + \Delta m \tag{7.10}$$

This manner of expressing EV is analogous to that obtained for CV and ΔW earlier, but in this case it is the compensated demand functions at utility level u_2 that are used. Once again, the integral in (7.10) is a line integral, but one which is path independent. The integrability conditions are satisfied since $\partial x_i(p, u_2)/\partial p_j = \partial x_j(p, u_2)/\partial p_i$; that is, the substitution effects are symmetric. Therefore, EV is unambiguously defined.

As with CV, a simple geometric interpretation can be given to each term under the integral sign in (7.10). Consider a reduction in the price of x_i in isolation. The upper diagram in figure 7.5 shows EV as $e^2 - m$ in terms of the composite good x_n (expenditure on all other goods). In the lower diagram, the compensated demand curve along u_2 is drawn as $x_i(p, \bar{u}_2)$ and the Marshallian demand curve is $x_i(p, \bar{m})$. The EV is given by $-\int x_i(p, u_2) \, \mathrm{d}p_i$ or the area $p_i^1 \mathrm{d}bp_i^2$ in the lower diagram. Since the Marshallian consumer surplus is given by the area $p_i^1 abp_i^2$, we see that EV is greater than ΔW if x_i is normal. Combining this with our earlier result, we see that for normal goods $\text{EV} > \Delta W > \text{CV}$. This result, that ΔW lies between EV and CV, holds only for the case where a single price changes. If more than one price changes, the path dependency property of ΔW means that it can be greater or less than both EV and CV. We shall use CV and EV as our measures of welfare change in what follows. They are well defined, path independent, and can be interpreted using the expenditure function. They differ only in the set of reference prices they use – the initial or the final ones. In principle, any set of reference prices could be used to construct a welfare index.

5 An Example – The Deadweight Loss of Excise Taxation

As an introduction to the use of welfare change measures to evaluate resource allocation changes, let us consider the simple case of the imposition of an excise tax on a single good, say x_i. We shall look only at CV since it is the one conventionally used, although no new issues of principle

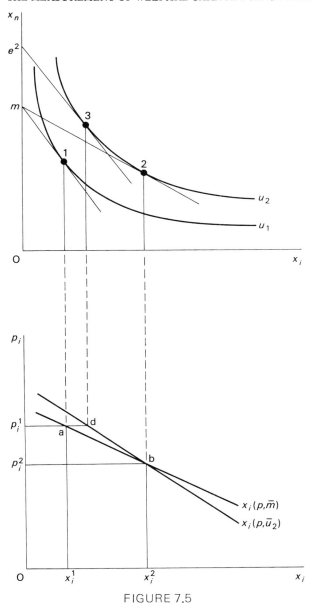

FIGURE 7.5

arise from using EV instead. Consider first the case in which an excise tax is imposed upon x_i in the absence of any other taxes. For simplicity, the revenue of the tax is assumed to be returned in a lump-sum manner to the household. The analysis is illustrated using figure 7.6.

In the upper part of the diagram, all goods other than x_i are aggregated together as a composite commodity, x_n, which can be considered as all

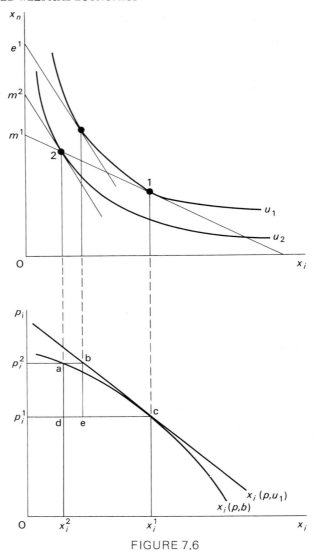

FIGURE 7.6

other expenditures in money terms. The consumer begins at point 1 in the absence of taxes. When the excise tax is imposed, the relative price of x_i rises and the consumer moves to point 2. Income at 2 has risen to m^2 where $m^2 - m^1 = T$, the excise tax revenues collected.[7] The CV for the change from 1 to 2 is obtained by applying (7.7) to this problem. In

---

[7] Excise tax revenues collected are $(p_i^2 - p_i^1)x_i^2$. Since p_i is the slope of the budget line, this equals $m^2 - m^1$.

the diagram it is $m^2 - e^1 (<0)$. Algebraically,

$$
\begin{aligned}
CV &= m^2 - e(p^2, u_1) \\
&= m^1| + T - e(p^2, u_1) \\
&= e(p^1, u_1) - e(p^2, u_1) + T \\
&= \int_{p_i^2}^{p_i^1} (\partial e(p, u_1)/\partial p_i) \, dp_i + T \\
&= - \int_{p_i^1}^{p_i^2} x_i(p, u_1) \, dp_i + T \quad\quad\quad (7.11)
\end{aligned}
$$

In arriving at (7.11) we have used Hotelling's lemma as before.

Expression (7.11) provides an exact measure of the distance $m^2 - e^1$ and can be given an alternative geometric interpretation in the lower part of figure 7.6. In that diagram we have drawn the compensated demand curve along u_1, $x_i(p, u_1)$, and another demand curve labelled $x_i(p, b)$. The latter is the demand curve obtained by finding x_i for various prices p_i but constraining the consumer to remain on the original budget line. Equivalently, it is the demand curve obtained by varying the excise tax on x_i and returning the tax revenue to the consumer. Note that this demand curve is tangential to the compensated demand curve at x_i^1. Points 1 and 2 correspond to points on that demand curve. In the diagram the area $\int x_i(p, u_1) \, dp_i$ is the area to the left of the compensated demand curve, and the tax revenue is the area $p_i^2 a d p_i^1$. Therefore, the exact value of CV is given by:

$$
\begin{aligned}
CV &= - p_i^2 b c p_i^1 + p_i^2 a d p_i^1 \\
&= - abcd
\end{aligned}
$$

This area abcd is the deadweight loss of the tax system. It is often approximated by the triangular area bce, the so-called 'Harberger triangle' (Harberger, 1964). The triangle bce will be an exact measure of deadweight loss if points a and b coincide; that is, if income effects are zero. Otherwise, the triangle is only an approximation to the true CV with the error of approximation being abed.

Notice that although the demand curve $x_i(p, b)$ is not identical to $x_i(p, u_1)$, it is a closer approximation to the latter than is the Marshallian demand curve $x_i(p, m)$ (not drawn). This is because the curve $x_i(p, b)$ involves partial compensation to the consumer, whereas the Marshallian demand curve involves no compensation at all. Specifically, the curve $x_i(p, b)$ compensates the consumer for the revenue effects of the tax system but not for the deadweight loss.

The path dependency property of the measure ΔW can easily be illustrated for this excise tax case. From (7.2) for ΔW we obtain directly that:

$$\Delta W = T - \int_{p_i^1}^{p_i^2} x_i(p, m) \, dp_i$$

where $T = \Delta m$ here. The evaluation of the integral term depends upon the value of m. If ΔW were valued as if the price changed first and the tax revenue returned later, then m_1 would appear under the integral sign and a particular value of ΔW would be obtained. If, however, the tax revenue were imagined to be returned before that, the evaluation of the integral would change and another value of ΔW would be obtained.

Let us now extend the above analysis slightly by assuming that a tax on x_i already exists and is to be increased. In figure 7.7 (which is labelled to correspond to figure 7.6) a further tax increase coupled with a return of the tax revenue takes the household from point 2 to point 3. The household's income rises from m^2 to $m^3 (= \Delta T)$. The CV from this change is given by $m^3 - e^2$ in the diagram. Naturally, this increase in the dead-weight loss is negative. Algebraically, it may be expressed as:

$$CV = m^3 - e(p^3, u_2)$$
$$= m^2 + \Delta T - e(p^3, u_2)$$
$$= e(p^2, u_2) - e(p^3, u_2) + \Delta T$$
$$= - \int_{p_i^2}^{p_i^3} x_i(p, u_2) \, dp_i + \Delta T$$

This is illustrated geometrically in the lower part of figure 7.7. The compensated demand curve along u_2 is labelled $x_i(p, u_2)$, and the demand curve obtained by moving along the original budget line is again shown as $x_i(p, b)$. Since the above integral is the area to the left of the demand curve, the CV measure can be given by:

$$CV = - p_i^3 \text{fa} p_i^2 + p_i^3 \text{gj} p_i^2 - \text{jadh}$$
$$= - \text{gfadh}$$

Once again, if income effects are zero, g and f will coincide and the increase in deadweight loss from the tax increase will be gadh. In applied work this area is often used as an approximation to the additional dead-weight loss associated with a tax increase (see for example Browning, 1978).

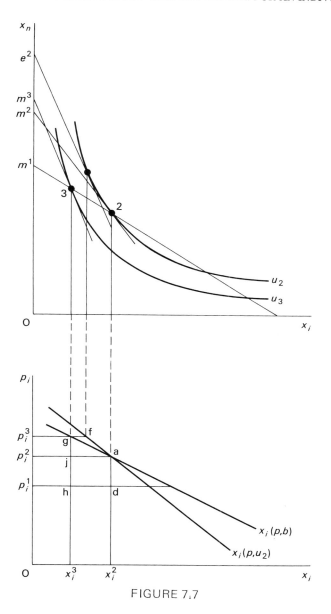

FIGURE 7.7

6 Approximate Measures of Welfare Change

The information required to obtain exact measures of welfare change, such as CV or EV, is very demanding; hence it is often necessary to resort to empirical approximations in applied work. This section will review some of the approximations that are often used and will discuss their relationship to the 'true measures' of welfare change. For this purpose, the 'true measures' are usually taken to be CV or EV although, as we have seen, measures using reference prices other than the initial or final prices are just as good as EV and CV in principle.

To begin with, suppose that the only data available are the prices and quantities consumed in the two situations. Two questions arise. The first is whether or not this is enough information to determine in which situation the household is better off. The second is whether or not an approximate measure of how much the household is better off or worse off can be established. We shall discuss both questions.

There are a variety of ways in which one may use the two sets of price and quantity observations. One common procedure is to construct quantity indices. Quantity indices are intended to indicate in one summary measure how much the quantities consumed have changed between the two situations. Since the change in quantities consumed will vary from one good to another, some method of aggregation is necessary. The two methods commonly used are the *Laspeyres quantity index* Q_L and the *Paasche quantity index* Q_P, defined as follows:

$$Q_L = \frac{\Sigma p_i^1 x_i^2}{\Sigma p_i^1 x_i^1} \quad \text{and} \quad Q_P = \frac{\Sigma p_i^2 x_i^2}{\Sigma p_i^2 x_i^1} \tag{7.12}$$

As can be seen from (7.12), the Laspeyres quantity index is the weighted ratio of quantities consumed in the two periods, where the weights are the initial prices. The Paasche quantity index uses the new prices.

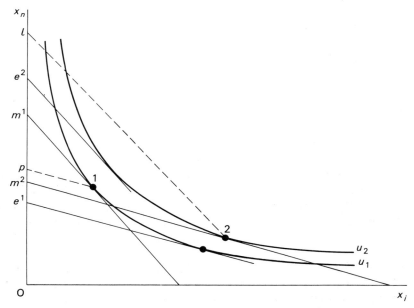

FIGURE 7.8

To illustrate these measures geometrically for the two-good case, consider figure 7.8. If we measure all prices in terms of good x_n, the Laspeyres quantity index will be given by $Q_L = \ell/m^1$. If we think of the true quantity index at the prices p^1 as being EV in ratio form, we obtain e^2/m^1. Since $Q_L > e^2/m^1$, the Laspeyres quantity index is an overestimate of the true quantity index. Similarly, the Paasche quantity index Q_P is given by m^2/p. The true quantity index using the new prices can be thought of as CV in ratio form, or m^2/e^1. It can be seen that the index Q_P is an underestimate of the true index. Indeed, here Q_P is actually < 1, whereas the true index is > 1.

An alternative way of looking at these indices is to write them in the level form. Using this method, the Laspeyres index is $\Sigma p_i^1 x_i^2 - \Sigma p_i^1 x_i^1 = \Sigma p_i^1 \Delta x_i$. In the two-good case, this would be $\ell - m^1$. The Paasche index would be $\Sigma p_i^2 \Delta x_i$, or $m^2 - p$ in the two-good case. In level form the indices are direct approximations of EV and CV. Indeed, they are *first-order approximations* in the following sense. Suppose we take a Taylor series expansion of the expenditure function around the final situation to express:

$$e(p^1, u_2) = e(p^2, u_2) - \Sigma x_i(p^2, u_2)\,\Delta p_i + R$$

where $\partial e/\partial p_i (p^2, u_2) = x_i(p^2, u_2)$, $\Delta p_i = p_i^2 - p_i^1$ and R is the sum of all terms higher than first order. Then we can substitute this Taylor series expansion into the definition of EV in (7.9′) to get

$$\text{EV} = -\Sigma x_i(p^2, u_2)\,\Delta p_i + \Delta m + R \tag{7.9″}$$

We can add and subtract $\Sigma p_i^1 x_i^2$ to Δm to get

$$\Delta m = \Sigma x_i^2(p_i^2 - p_i^1) + \Sigma p_i^1(x_i^2 - x_i^1)$$
$$= \Sigma x_i^2 \Delta p_i + \Sigma p_i^1 \Delta x_i$$

Substituting into (7.9″) we get

$$\text{EV} = \Sigma p_i^1 \Delta x_i + R$$

Neglecting R on the right-hand side yields the first-order approximation of EV as the Laspeyres quantity index in level form. Similarly, the Paasche quantity index is obtained if the expansion is carried out around the initial point. Notice that in order to evaluate higher order terms in R, more information than just initial and final prices and quantities is required.

As figure 7.8 indicates, the quantity indices sometimes give misleading indications of true welfare change in the sense that they can misrepresent the direction of welfare change. Before moving on to other approximate measures it is worth establishing conditions under which these quantity indices can indicate unambiguously the direction of change of welfare.[8] This can be done by applying the basic arguments of *revealed preference theory*. Suppose, for example, that $Q_P > 1$ so $\Sigma p_i^2 x_i^2 > \Sigma p_i^2 x_i^1$. This indicates that the income available in the new situation was more than enough to be able to purchase the old set of goods at the new prices. In other words, x^1 was inside the budget constraint in situation 2. Since x^2 was purchased when x^1 could have been, this implies that x^2 is preferred to x^1. By the same token, x^2 could not have been purchased when x^1 was (or else it would have been). Therefore, $\Sigma p_i^1 x_i^2 > \Sigma p_i^1 x_i^1$, or $Q_L > 1$.[9] Thus we have that $Q_P > 1$ implies that x^2 is preferred to x^1 and $Q_L > 1$.

A similar argument applies if $Q_L < 1$. Then, $\Sigma p_i^1 x_i^1 > \Sigma p_i^1 x_i^2$. In this case x^1 must be preferred to x^2 since the latter was a feasible choice in the original situation. Also, x^1 must not have been feasible in the new situation or else it would have been selected. Therefore, $\Sigma p_i^2 x_i^1 > \Sigma p_i^2 x_i^2$, or $Q_P < 1$.

In the above two cases the direction of welfare change is unambiguous; both quantity indices are either greater than unity or less than unity. Two other cases are possible. Suppose $Q_L > 1$ while $Q_P < 1$. This is the case illustrated in figure 7.8. It is easy to see that this case is compatible with the consumer being either better or worse off in one situation than in the other. In figure 7.8, 2 is preferred to 1; but the indifference curves could easily have been drawn so that 1 is preferred to 2. $Q_L > 1$ simply says that the bundle of goods in situation 2 could not have been purchased in the first situation ($\Sigma p_i^1 x_i^2 > \Sigma p_i^2 x_i^2$). From this information alone we cannot infer in which situation the consumer is better off.

The other possible case to consider is that in which $Q_L < 1$ and $Q_P > 1$. This case would be incompatible with rational consumer behaviour since revealed preference theory requires that $Q_L > 1$ if $Q_P > 1$. The reader can satisfy himself or herself that the combination $Q_L < 1$ and $Q_P > 1$ requires intersecting indifference curves which we can rule out as implying irrational behaviour.

These results on quantity indices are summarized in table 7.1, where P means 'preferred to'. It is apparent that the usefulness of these indices is

TABLE 7.1

	$Q_L > 1$	$Q_L < 1$
$Q_P > 1$	$x^2 P x^1$	inconsistent
$Q_P < 1$	ambiguous	$x^1 P x^2$

---

[8]   A full discussion of the properties of index numbers may be found in Usher (1980).
[9]   This result is known as the weak axiom of revealed preference; see a discussion in Varian (1978).

rather limited from the point of view of welfare measurement.[10] If we wish to obtain reliable approximations to welfare change measures we need more information than price and quantity observations in the two situations. We turn to this issue next.

Consider the CV and EV measures given by (7.7) and (7.9) and illustrated in figure 7.3. These can be considered as methods of 'cardinalizing' various utility levels. The EV 'measures' utility levels in monetary units by associating with each utility level an amount of income required to attain that utility level at prices p^1. The CV does the same thing at prices p^2. Any set of relative prices could have been used to obtain a cardinal measure of the utility level, or what is referred to as a *money metric* of utility. For the purpose of obtaining approximate measures of CV and EV, the measures of CV and EV given by (7.7) and (7.9) combine the effects of both price changes and income changes. It is useful for the purposes of approximation to separate the effects of price and income changes on CV and EV as we did earlier:

$$CV = e(p^1, u_1) - e(p^2, u_1) + \Delta m \qquad (7.13)$$
$$EV = e(p^1, u_2) - e(p^2, u_2) + \Delta m \qquad (7.14)$$

Since the term Δm involves no difficulty, let us concentrate on the first two terms on the right-hand side involving price changes.

For illustrative purposes consider the CV measure. We can apply a Taylor series expansion around the initial value of the expenditure function to give:

$$e(p^2, u_1) = e(p^1, u_1) + \sum_i \frac{\partial e(p^1, u_1)}{\partial p_i} \Delta p_i$$
$$+ \frac{1}{2} \sum_i \sum_j \frac{\partial^2 e(p^1, u_1)}{\partial p_i \partial p_j} \Delta p_i \Delta p_j + R$$

where R are the terms of higher than second order. From Hotelling's lemma we know that $\partial e(p, u_1)/\partial p_i = x_i(p, u_1)$ and $\partial^2 e(p, u_1)/\partial p_i \partial p_j = \partial x_i(p, u_1)/\partial p_j$. The latter is the compensated price derivative or substitution effect, and we shall denote it S_{ij}. Then, the Taylor expansion can be rewritten:

$$e(p^1, u_1) - e(p^2, u_1) = - \Sigma x_i(p^1, u_1) \Delta p_i - \tfrac{1}{2} \Sigma \Sigma S_{ij} \Delta p_i \Delta p_j - R \quad (7.15)$$

where S_{ij} is evaluated at u_1 and p^1.

[10] The same information used to construct quantity indices can be used to construct price indices. The Laspeyres price index is defined as $\Sigma p_i^2 x_i^1/\Sigma p_i^1 x_i^1$ whereas the Paasche is defined as $\Sigma p_i^2 x_i^2/\Sigma p_i^1 x_i^2$. Notice that if we divide the ratio of actual incomes in the two situations $(\Sigma p_i^2 x_i^2/\Sigma p_i^1 x_i^1)$ by the Laspeyres price index, we obtain the Paasche quantity index. This is the procedure often followed to obtain 'real income' measures.

By using higher order terms, a closer approximation to CV can be obtained. In an exactly analogous way, approximations to EV can be obtained by taking a Taylor expansion around $e(p^2, u_2)$.[11]

For applied purposes a second-order approximation to Δe is often used; that is, the term R is simply ignored in (7.15). In that case, the CV measure becomes:

$$CV = -\Sigma x_i^1 \Delta p_i - \tfrac{1}{2}\Sigma\Sigma S_{ij}\Delta p_i \Delta p_j + \Delta m \qquad (7.16)$$

where we have now allowed for both income and price changes. The only additional information required now to evaluate CV (other than that required for quantity indices) is the magnitude of the substitution effects S_{ij}.

Applying (7.16) to the example of the deadweight cost of taxation resulting from a change in a single excise tax rate CV becomes:

$$CV = -x_i^1 t_i - \tfrac{1}{2}S_{ii}t_i^2 + T \qquad (7.17)$$

where t_i is the rate of tax per unit of good i consumed. If we note that $x_i^1 t_i \approx T$, the CV measure reduces to $-S_{ii}t_i^2/2$, an approximate measure of the Harberger triangle.[12] An alternative way of writing this is in terms of elasticities. Define the compensated elasticity of demand ϵ_{ii} as $S_{ii}p_i/x_i$. Then the Harberger triangle becomes $-\epsilon_{ii}t_i^2 x_i/(2p_i) \approx -\epsilon_{ii}\tau_i T/2$, where $\tau_i = t_i/p_i$ is the *ad valorem* rate of tax.

To evaluate the above approximate measures of welfare change the magnitude of substitution effects must be known. Since these are not *directly* observable, even these approximations would seem to be beyond our reach. There have been two responses to this in the literature. One has been to use ordinary demand derivatives in place of substitution effects; in effect, to use Marshallian consumer surpluses as approximations to CVs. The other has been to recognize that, even though the compensated demand functions cannot be directly observed or estimated, their properties can be inferred from estimates of ordinary demand functions. This is because they are related through the well-known *Slutsky equations*. Let us consider each of these two procedures briefly in turn.

6.1 *The use of Marshallian consumer surpluses*

As we discussed earlier when taking the example of the welfare measure of a single price change, the Marshallian consumer surplus for a normal good is an overestimate of CV from a price change and an underestimate

---

[11] This procedure is equivalent to the method proposed by McKenzie and Pearce (1976) for measuring welfare change. They use an indirect utility function for their expansion but normalize it so as to make the result equivalent to that obtained by taking a Taylor expansion of an expenditure function.

[12] Note that the same approximation applied to the EV gives $EV = -x_i^2 t_i - \tfrac{1}{2}S_{ii}t_i^2 + T$, where now S_{ii} is evaluated at the new position. In this case $T = -x_i^2 t_i$ exactly so they cancel out.

of EV. If income effects are zero, the three measures have identical values. Similar approximations apply when other prices or income change as well, although there is the further ambiguity in that there exists no unique Marshallian consumer surplus measure of welfare change. None the less, the Marshallian surplus has some appeal as an approximate measure of welfare change. First, it is directly observable from the estimation of demand functions, whereas EV and CV measures are not. Secondly, because empirical estimation is an inexact science, errors of measurement are involved in any measure of welfare change, and the errors of measurement may well dwarf the theoretical differences among EV, CV and consumer's surplus. Finally, for the case of a single price change, the Marshallian consumer's surplus has as much claim to legitimacy as an exact measure of welfare change as do either CV or EV. Even when more than one price or income changes, either CV or EV can be used. Since the consumer's surplus is usually between these two, it would seem to be a useful approximation.

How good an approximation is essentially an empirical question revolving around the importance of the income effects. The greater are the income effects of a price change, the greater will be the deviation between ordinary and compensated demand curves and the greater will be the difference between CV, EV and consumer's surplus. Willig (1976), in an influential article, has argued that in most cases the Marshallian consumer's surplus from price changes will be a 'close' approximation to CV and EV which is well within the errors of empirical measurement. For example, for a single price change, he has established analytically the following result. Suppose we denote the Marshallian consumer's surplus by S and the income elasticity of demand by η.[13] Then, provided that the absolute value of $\eta S/2m$ is less than 0.05 and of $|S|/m$ is less than 0.9, the following inequalities hold:

$$\frac{S-CV}{|S|} < \frac{\eta|S|}{2m} < 0.05$$

$$\frac{EV-S}{|S|} < \frac{\eta|S|}{2m} < 0.05 \tag{7.18}$$

where m is income. Thus, the error involved in using the Marshallian measure as an estimate of CV or EV will be less than 5 per cent under the conditions postulated.

Although the above inequalities were derived rigorously by Willig, a simple intuitive interpretation of the terms in (7.18) can be given.[14] In figure 7.9 the compensated and Marshallian demand curves are drawn for a fall in the price of x_i from p_i^1 to p_i^2. The difference between the

[13] Since η is not typically constant, it ought to be interpreted as the largest value of the income elasticity of demand within the range being considered.
[14] A similar interpretation may be found in Just, Hueth and Schmitz (1982).

H

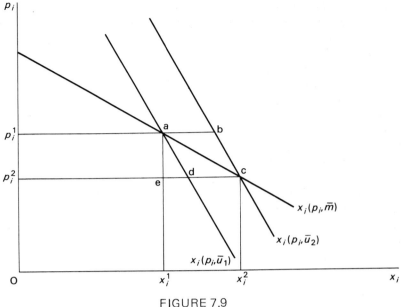

FIGURE 7.9

Marshallian consumer surplus $(p_i^1 a c p_i^2)$ and the CV $(p_i^1 a d p_i^2)$ is the triangular area adc where the base of the triangle dc is the income effect associated with an income change of CV at the new price p_i^2 (see figure 7.4). In calling these measures triangles we are, of course, assuming that the demand curves are approximately linear. The triangle adc is given by $\frac{1}{2} dc (p_i^1 - p_i^2)$. Since dc comes about solely from the income effect associated with CV, we can approximate it by:

$$dc \approx \eta S x_i / m$$

where η is the income elasticity of demand and S is (approximately) the income change giving rise to the income effect dc. Therefore, the difference between S and CV, the area adc, may be written:

$$S - CV \approx \frac{1}{2} \frac{\eta S}{m} x_i (p_i^1 - p_i^2)$$

Furthermore, since $x_i (p_i^1 - p_i^2)$ is approximately equal to S, this may be written:

$$S - CV \approx \frac{1}{2} \frac{\eta S^2}{m}$$

This corresponds to the inequality in (7.18).

The approximation formulae given in (7.18) are valid only if $|S|/m$ is less than 0.9. This is equivalent to saying that expenditure on the good, and the variations in question cannot be too large relative to the consumer's income. In the event that this is not the case, Willig also indicates how one might derive estimates of CV and EV from S. This might be necessary for deriving the welfare effects of, say, changes in broadly based taxes. In this case, the use of Marshallian surpluses may not be good approximations to CV and EV measures.

Another instance in which the approximation may not be too useful is where one wishes to measure the Harberger triangle of the deadweight loss associated with tax changes, as in section 5. In terms of figure 7.9 one may wish to measure the triangle ade (or, more precisely, the area abce if income effects are not zero; see section 5). As Hausman (1981) has shown, even if the Willig approximation is close for the entire area $p_i^1 a d p_i^2$, it may not be close if one is trying to isolate the deadweight loss of taxes under the assumption that the tax revenue is available for consumption purposes. Thus, one may want to obtain more exact measures of CV or EV if one chooses to use them as the preferred welfare measure.

6.2 *Inferring CV or EV indirectly*

Although one cannot observe CV or EV directly, it will often be possible to use observed demand relationships to infer the properties of the compensated demand functions or the expenditure function, and thus to obtain approximate or even exact measures of CV or EV. For example, suppose one accepts the second-order approximation of welfare change given by (7.16) above. In addition to observed prices and quantities in the two situations being compared, one needs to know S_{ij}, the substitution effect. If an empirical estimate of the consumer demand function is available, the substitution effect can be determined from the well-known Slutsky equation for consumer demand encountered in chapter 2:

$$S_{ij} = \partial x_i/\partial p_j + x_j \partial x_i/\partial m \tag{7.19}$$

Once S_{ij} is evaluated locally, the second-order approximation of CV or EV is easily calculated.

In principle, one may be able to do even better than that. As Hausman (1981) has pointed out, it is often possible to work back to the expenditure function that is consistent with the household's preferences from estimates of the household's demand functions. Naturally, it is necessary that the demand functions that are estimated satisfy the restrictions that make them consistent with utility maximization. As discussed in chapter 2, these include homogeneity of degree zero, the adding-up condition, symmetry of the substitution effect, and negative semi-definiteness of the matrix of substitution effects. When one price changes, the case Hausman considers, the steps in the procedure are as follows. Suppose the price of x_i changes. Roy's theorem applied to good i states:

$$x_i(p, m) = - \partial v / \partial p_i / (\partial v / \partial m)$$

If this partial differential equation is integrated, the indirect utility function can be recovered. The indirect utility function may be written as $u = v(p, m)$. Inverting this function for m yields $m = e(p, u)$, the expenditure function. Since CV and EV are constructed from the expenditure function, exact measures of the welfare change are obtained.

Hausman shows by example that one can often recover explicit functional forms for the expenditure function from commonly estimated demand functions using the above procedure. His analysis is restricted to the case in which only one price changes. In the more general case in which several prices change, the principle that indirect utility functions and expenditure functions ought to be recoverable from demand functions is still true. (See Bruce, 1981, for an analysis of the way in which this can be done.) However, in practice it is likely to be exceedingly difficult. Therefore, one is forced back to one or other of the approximations discussed above.

7 Producer's Surplus or Rent

So far we have considered the welfare change resulting from changes in the quantities of goods consumed by a household. Income has been taken as exogenously given. In practice, at least part of a household's income is obtained from the sale of factors of production. The household may get utility from retaining such factors for its own use (e.g. leisure) and makes the decision of how much factors to sell so as to maximize its utility. Such factors might include the supply of labour, risk, entrepreneurial effort, and savings (or forgone consumption). Increases or decreases in the supply of these factors will influence the utility level of the household, and it is useful to develop welfare change measures which account for them. In this section, the principles involved will be illustrated for the case of labour supplied, but the analysis can be generalized to any variable factors of production. The analogy to consumer's surplus or CV is producer's surplus or rent.

Once again, there will be a large number of ways of measuring welfare change when factor supplies are involved as well as goods. We begin by illustrating the derivation of CV both algebraically and geometrically. Suppose the household consumes n goods and supplies one variable factor labour, denoted L. Then, its utility function may be written $u(x_1, \ldots, x_n, L)$ where $\partial u / \partial L < 0$. The budget constraint may be written $\Sigma p_i x_i - wL = m$ where w is the wage rate. The household's expenditure function is derived as before from the solution to the problem:

$$\min_{x, L} \Sigma p_i x_i - wL \qquad (7.20)$$

subject to

$$u(x, L) = u$$

The exogenous variables to the problem are p, w and u. The solution to problem (7.20) for x_i and L, obtained by solving the first-order conditions, may be written as:

$$x_i = x_i(p,\!\backslash w, u) \qquad i = 1, \ldots, n$$

$$L = L(p, w, u) \tag{7.21}$$

These are, respectively, the compensated demand and supply functions for the household.

The expenditure function is defined as the value of the objective function in (7.20) when the choice variables x_i and L have been optimally chosen. Algebraically it is obtained by substituting the solutions for x_i and L from (7.21) into the objective function:

$$e(p, w, u) = \Sigma p_i x_i(p, w, u) - wL(p, w, u) \tag{7.22}$$

The properties of this expenditure function are similar to those obtained in section 3. The function $e(p, w, u)$ is continuous, increasing in p and u, decreasing in w, concave in p and w (so $\partial^2 e/\partial w^2 \leq 0$), and homogeneous of degree one in p and w. As before, Hotelling's lemma on p_i gives $\partial e/\partial p_i = x_i(p, w, u)$, the compensated demand function for x_i. In addition Hotelling's lemma on w gives:

$$\partial e(p, w, u)/\partial w = - L(p, w, u) \tag{7.23}$$

Thus, the compensated supply function for labour is the negative of the derivative of the expenditure function with respect to the wage rate.[15]

The CV measure of welfare change is defined as before by $m^2 - e(p^2, w^2, u_1)$, or equivalently $m^1 - e(p^2, w^2, u_1) + \Delta m$. Making use of Hotelling's lemma, this may be rewritten as follows:

$$CV = e(p^1, w^1, u_1) - e(p^2, w^2, u_1) + \Delta m$$

$$= - \int_1^2 [\Sigma \partial e/\partial p_i \, dp_i + \partial e/\partial w \, dw] + \Delta m$$

$$= - \int_1^2 [\Sigma x_i(p, w, u_1) \, dp_i - L(p, w, u_1) \, dw] + \Delta m \tag{7.24}$$

---

[15] The compensated supply curve of labour cannot slope downwards since $\partial L(p, w, u)/\partial w = -\partial^2 e(p, w, u)/\partial w^2 \geq 0$ by the concavity of the expenditure function.

The CV expression is the same as before except for the addition of the term in the wage change. This term can be illustrated geometrically as in figure 7.10. Only w is being allowed to change here, so all goods x are aggregated into a composite commodity x_n which is used as the *numéraire*. The diagram depicts an increase in the wage rate from w^1 to w^2, causing the individual to change labour supply from L^1 to L^2. If all other prices and income are held constant, the expression for CV may be written:

$$CV = m - e(p^2, w^2, u_1) \qquad (7.25)$$

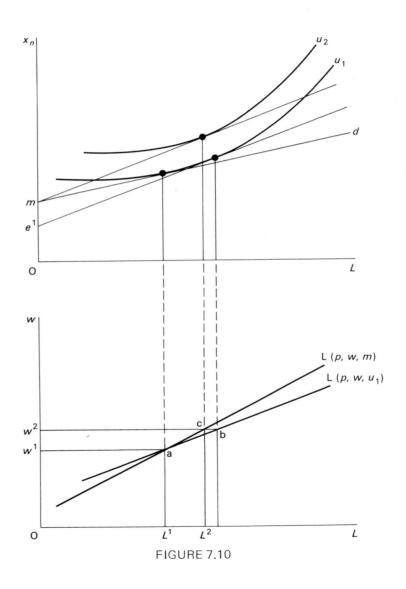

FIGURE 7.10

or, equivalently,

$$CV = \int_{w^1}^{w^2} L(p, w, u_1)\, dw \tag{7.26}$$

Equation (7.25) shows CV as the distance $m - e^1$ in the upper part of the figure. From (7.26) this will be identical to the area to the left of the compensated supply curve for labour. This is shown in the lower figure as w^2baw^1.

The diagram also shows the ordinary supply curve $L(p, w, m)$. The area to the left of this curve gives what may be referred to as the Marshallian producer surplus or rent. For the wage change in the diagram, the producer surplus is w^2caw^1. Notice that the producer surplus is less than CV. That will be the case whenever the labour supply has a negative income effect; or, to put it in other terms, whenever leisure is a normal good. The EV from a wage change could be depicted in a similar way using the compensated supply curve along u_2 rather than along u_1. The EV would be less than producer surplus for the case of figure 7.10. That demonstration is left to the reader.

To give an example of the use of CV from a wage change, consider the simple case of the imposition of a proportional tax on wage income with the proceeds returned to the household in a lump-sum manner. Since w is the only price which changes, CV from (7.24) is given by:

$$CV = \int_{w^1}^{w^2} L(p, w, u_1)\, dw + \Delta T \tag{7.27}$$

This is depicted in figure 7.11. The curve $L(p, w, u_1)$ is the compensated supply curve for labour, and $L(p, w, b)$ is the demand curve resulting from increasing the wage rate by taxes but returning the taxes in lump sum to the household. In other words, it is the demand for L obtained by changing the wage rate and constraining the household to stay on the original budget line md in figure 7.10. It is analogous to the demand curve $x_i(p, b)$ of figure 7.6. In terms of the diagram, the CV measure in (7.27) is given by:

$$CV = -w^1acw^2 + w^1dbw^2$$
$$\approx -abd \tag{7.28}$$

Thus, we obtain the triangular welfare cost of taxation as before.

8 Intertemporal Welfare Change Measures

So far our discussion has centred on welfare change in a single period. The introduction of time into the analysis can be readily done provided

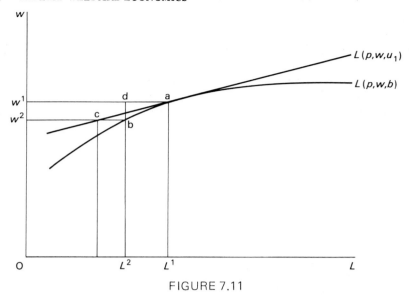

FIGURE 7.11

one ignores the difficulties of an uncertain future which inevitably plague intertemporal analysis. It will be assumed that the individual knows with certainty all prices and income in the future. It will suffice to extend the previous single-period analysis to two periods; generalizations to more periods are not difficult.

The household is assumed to choose a vector of first-period consumption $(x_1, \ldots, x_n)$ priced at $(p_1, \ldots, p_n)$ and a vector of second-period consumption $(y_1, \ldots, y_n)$ priced at $(q_1, \ldots, q_n)$. It has an exogenous stream of income in the two periods (m_1, m_2) which can be allocated to present and future consumption using perfect capital markets. The one-period interest rate is r and the household can allocate its income stream to consumption in the two periods so that the present value of the stream of consumption equals the present value of the stream of income.[16] Thus,

$$\Sigma p_i x_i + \Sigma q_i y_i/(1 + r) = m_1 + m_2/(1 + r) \tag{7.29}$$

The right-hand side of the equation is termed the household's wealth.

The household has a utility function of the form $u(x, y)$.[17] Its choice problem is:

$$\max_{x, y} u(x_1, \ldots, x_n, y_1, \ldots, y_n)$$

---

[16] This is derived as follows. Let S be the saving done in the first period (it could be positive or negative). Then, $\Sigma p_i x_i + S = m_1$. In the second period, $\Sigma q_i y_i = S(1 + r) + m_2$. Solving the latter for S and substituting in the former yields equation (7.29).

[17] This is often written in the additively separable form $u(x) + u(y)/(1 + \delta)$, where δ is the pure rate of time preference. Our analysis need not be restricted to that special case.

subject to

$$\Sigma p_i x_i + \Sigma q_i y_i / (1 + r) = m_1 + m_2 / (1 + r) \tag{7.30}$$

This yields a set of demand functions of the form $x_i(p, q, r, m_1, m_2)$ and $y_i(p, q, r, m_1, m_2)$ for all i. For our purposes it is more useful to write down the dual of the utility maximization problem, the expenditure minimization problem:

$$\min_{x, y} \Sigma p_i x_i + \Sigma q_i y_i / (1 + r)$$

subject to $\hspace{8cm}$ (7.31)

$$u(x_1, \ldots, x_n, y_1, \ldots, y_n) = u$$

The solution to the first-order conditions for this problem yields the compensated demand functions $x_i(p, q, r, u)$ and $y_i(p, q, r, u)$, where the arguments in these functions are the exogenous variables in the expenditure minimization problem.

From the solution to the expenditure minimization problem we can obtain the expenditure function. It is simply the value of the objective function with the optimal choices of x_i and y_i substituted, or

$$e(p, q, r, u) = \Sigma p_i x_i(p, q, r, u) + \Sigma q_i y_i(p, q, r, u)/(1 + r) \tag{7.32}$$

This gives the wealth required to attain utility level u at the given prices. The properties of this expenditure function are similar to before. Hotelling's lemma in this case yields:

$$\partial e / \partial p_i = x_i(p, q, r, u)$$
$$\partial e / \partial q_i = y_i(p, q, r, u)/(1 + r) \tag{7.33}$$

The measurement of welfare change proceeds in much the same manner as before. Let us ignore changes in r and delete it from all functions. The CV is now measured as $W^2 - e(p^2, q^2, u_1)$ where W^2 is the wealth in situation 2. Noting that $W^1 = e(p^1, q^1, u_1)$, CV can be rewritten as:

$$CV = e(p^1, q^1, u_1) - e(p^2, q^2, u_1) + \Delta W$$

$$= -\int_1^2 [\Sigma \partial e / \partial p_i \, dp_i + \Sigma \partial e / \partial q_i \, dq_i] + \Delta W$$

$$= -\int_1^2 \Sigma x_i(p, q, u_1) \, dp_i + \frac{\Sigma y_i(p, q, u_1)}{1 + r} dq_i + \Delta W \tag{7.34}$$

This measure of CV is very similar to before. The additional terms in dq_i integrate over the compensated demands for y_i and discount to the present by the rate of interest r. In other words, CV can be calculated by calculating a CV in each period and discounting future CVs to the present at the interest rate. Note, however, that the CVs in the two time periods are not independent. The CV in each period depends upon prices in the other.

Similar geometric interpretations can be given to these CV expressions. If only p_i changes, the CV expression is the area to the left of the compensated demand curve for x_i between the old and new prices. If q_i changes, CV is the area to the left of the compensated demand curve for y_i discounted by $(1 + r)$.[18]

9 Measurement of Welfare Change under Uncertainty

Suppose now that one or more of the exogenous variables (prices and income) facing the consumer are stochastic. There are certain circumstances in which we may be interested in obtaining a measure of welfare change from changes in these uncertain prices or income. A good example of this is the evaluation of the benefits of commodity price stabilization schemes or income stabilization schemes. In order to obtain a suitable measure of the benefits of such schemes, it is necessary to develop a theory of welfare cost measurement under uncertainty. That is accomplished in this section.

Following our discussion in earlier chapters it will be assumed that one of S mutually exclusive and exhaustive states of nature will occur in the future. The probability of each state occurring will be $\pi_s (s = 1, \ldots, S)$ so that $\Sigma \pi_s = 1$. From the point of view of our single household, each state of nature will have associated with it a set of prices and income (p^s, m^s). We shall assume that the individual's preferences defined over states of nature satisfy the Von Neumann–Morgenstern axioms, so that preferences over alternative courses of action can be represented by expected utility:

$$EU = \sum_{s=1}^{S} \pi_s v(p^s, m^s) \tag{7.34}$$

Recall from the discussion in chapter 2 that for EU to be a proper representation of the individual's preferences, the function $v(p^s, m^s)$ must

---

[18] Alternatively, we could have defined prices in period 2 as $q_i/(1 + r)$; that is, as present value prices. Then, CV would have been

$$CV = -\int [x_i(p, q/(1 + r), u)\, dp_i + y_i(p, q/(1 + r), u)\, dq_i] - \Delta W$$

The CV from a change in q_i would be $-\int y_i(p, q/(1 + r), u)\, d(q_i/(1 + r))$ and would be the appropriate area to the left of the compensated demand curve for y_i, treating $q_i/(1 + r)$ as the vertical axis.

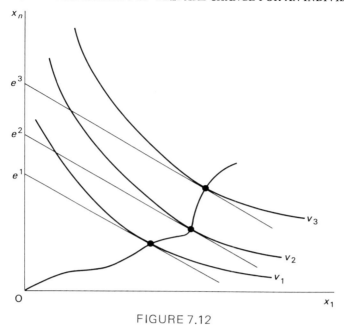

FIGURE 7.12

be cardinal; that is, it is unique up to a positive linear transform. This will
have implications for the sorts of money metrics that can be used to
represent the utility attained in each state of nature, $v(p^s, m^s)$. To see
this, consider the two-good case illustrated in figure 7.12. Three representative indifference curves are drawn. For a particular cardinalization of
utilities, the levels of utility obtained on these three indifference curves
are v_1, v_2, v_3. If this is a proper representation of the household's
preferences under risk, then so is any positive affine transform, such as
$a + bv$ where $b \geqslant 0$.[19]
    In measuring welfare change under certainty we showed that a legiti-
mate money metric is the value of the expenditure function in terms of
the *numéraire* good at a set of reference prices. This is shown in the
diagram as e^1, e^2 and e^3 at a particular set of prices given by the absolute
value of the slope of the budget line. If utility were ordinal this money
metric would be a perfectly legitimate way of 'measuring' the utility
attained on various indifference curves. That is, a monotonic transform
of the individual's utility function could always be found which would
associate with each indifference curve the utility levels e^1, e^2, e^3 etc. If
the utility function is cardinal, that is no longer possible. In general, it
will not be possible to convert v_1 by a positive affine transform into e^1.

---

[19] See the discussion in chapter 2 concerning the cardinality of v and the choice of an index as
revealed by behaviour under risk.

Therefore, the expenditure function e^1 will not be an appropriate money metric to use for welfare change measurement under uncertainty.

Instead we could proceed as follows. Suppose the utility function $v(p, m)$ as depicted in the diagram is a legitimate representation of the household's preferences. Then, given this particular utility numbering system, the relationship between the expenditure function money metric and utility will be given by:

$$v = f(e) \qquad (7.35)$$

This function $f(e)$ will be a legitimate measure of welfare change. Furthermore, any positive affine transformation $g(e) = a + bf(e)$ will also be a legitimate money metric for the consumer's utility. As mentioned, it will not generally be possible to transform $f(e)$ back to e using only positive affine transforms.

The importance of the restriction of legitimate transforms to positive affine ones is that such transforms preserve the sign of the second derivative of $f(e)$. That is, if $g(e) = a + bf(e)$, simple differentiation will show that $g'(e)$ has the same sign as $f'(e)$, and $g''(e)$ has the same sign as $f''(e)$. Thus, if $f''(e) < 0$, and so the person is a *risk-averter*, that property will be maintained regardless of the transform taken. Furthermore, the value of $-f''(e)/f'(e)$, called the coefficient of absolute risk aversion, and the value of $-f''(e)e/f'(e)$, called the coefficient of relative risk aversion, will be invariant to such transforms.

Armed with this money metric $f(e)$, let us now investigate its use in measuring welfare change. Consider the simple case of measuring the welfare change from an increase in the variability of income. In figure 7.12 suppose that we wish to compare a situation in which income e^2 is obtained with certainty to one in which e^1 is obtained with a probability π_1 and e^3 with a probability π_3 such that $\pi_1 + \pi_3 = 1$. Using expected utility as a measure of welfare, where utility is given by $f(e)$, the change in utility from an increase in variability is:

$$\Delta W = \pi_1 f(e^1) + \pi_3 f(e^3) - f(e^2) \qquad (7.35)$$

Assuming that $f(e)$ is continuous and differentiable, this may be rewritten:

$$\Delta W = \pi_1 \int_{e^2}^{e^1} f'(e)\, de + \pi_3 \int_{e^2}^{e^3} f'(e)\, de \qquad (7.36)$$

That is, the welfare change in each state of nature is the weighted sum of change in the money metric, where the weights are the marginal utilities of real income.

The first term in (7.36) will be negative (assuming $e^2 > e^1$) and the second term positive (assuming $e^2 < e^3$). However, the overall magnitude of the change will depend upon the exact values of e^1, e^2 and e^3 and the form of $f(e)$. For example, suppose e^2 is the expected value of e^1 and e^3 so that $e^2 = \pi_1 e^1 + \pi_3 e^3$. Then the variability in income will be a mean-preserving spread, to use the terminology of Rothschild and Stiglitz (1970). Next, suppose the person is risk neutral, so $f''(e) = 0$. In this case, the weights $f'(e)$ are constant, so that the measure of utility change becomes:

$$\Delta W = f'(e)[\pi_1(e^1 - e^2) + \pi_3(e^3 - e^2)]$$
$$= f'(e)[\pi_1 e^1 + \pi_3 e^3 - e^2] = 0 \qquad\qquad (7.36')$$

Thus the individual is no worse off from a mean-preserving spread.

On the other hand, it should be obvious that if $f''(e) < 0$, and so the household is a risk-averter, the weights $f'(e)$ associated with the first term in (7.36) will be higher than those associated with the second term since the value of e is lower between e^1 and e^2 than between e^2 and e^3. Thus, the overall value of ΔW will be negative. Hence, for a risk-averter, welfare will decrease if income is subject to a mean-preserving spread. The opposite will obviously hold for a risk-lover, for whom $f''(e) > 0$.

A useful approximation of ΔW can be obtained by applying a Taylor series expansion to $f(e)$. Expanding $f(e)$ around e^2 one obtains:

$$f(e^i) \approx f(e^2) + f'(e^2)(e^i - e^2) + \tfrac{1}{2}f''(e^2)(e^i - e^2)^2 + R_i \qquad i = 1, 3$$

where R_i is the sum of terms higher than second order. Substituting this into (7.35), one obtains:

$$\Delta W = \pi_1[f'(e^2)(e^1 - e^2) + \tfrac{1}{2}f''(e^2)(e^1 - e^2)^2 + R_1]$$
$$+ \pi_3[f'(e^2)(e^3 - e^2) + \tfrac{1}{2}f''(e^2)(e^3 - e^2)^2 + R_3] \qquad (7.37)$$

Consider the special case in which e^2 is the mean of e^1 and e^3, and higher order terms R_1 and R_3 are ignored. In this case, ΔW reduces to:

$$\Delta W = \tfrac{1}{2}f''(e^2)\,\mathrm{var}(e)$$
$$= f'(e)\,k \qquad\qquad (7.38)$$

where $k = \tfrac{1}{2}f''(e^2)\,\mathrm{var}(e)/f'(e)$ is usually referred to as the *cost of risk-taking* and $\mathrm{var}(e)$ is the variance of e^1 and e^3 about e^2.

Next consider the example of price variability. To use geometric techniques we restrict ourselves to the case of variability in the price of a single good x_1. Figure 7.13 illustrates this case. Suppose the household faces a change from an income of e^2 and a certain price of p^2 to the same income but a variable price of p^1 with a probability π_1 and p^3 with probability π_3. The problem is to obtain a measure of welfare change corresponding to this introduction of variability in the price of x_1.

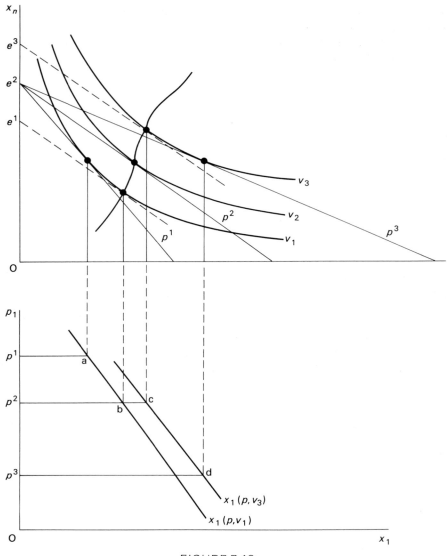

FIGURE 7.13

As before, a money metric is constructed using the value of the expenditure function at a set of reference prices, in this case p^2. The values of this money metric for the prices p^1, p^2 and p^3 are shown as e^1, e^2 and e^3 in figure 7.13. As above, the utility function v can be written as a function of the money metric $v = f(e)$. Since the utility function v is cardinal, it is only unique up to a positive affine transformation. Thus, $f(e)$ is also only unique up to a positive affine transform. Let us suppose we have selected a particular cardinalization of utility and thus a particular function $f(e)$ as our measure of utility.

Using expected utility as a measure of welfare, the welfare change in going from the fixed price to the variable price situation is given by:

$$\Delta W = \pi_1 f(e^1) + \pi_3 f(e^3) - f(e^2)$$
$$= \pi_1(f(e^1) - f(e^2)) + \pi_3(f(e^3) - f(e^2)) \tag{7.39}$$

Equivalently, if $f(e)$ is a continuous and differentiable function, (7.39) may be written as:

$$\Delta W = \pi_1 \int_{e^2}^{e^1} f'(e)\, de + \pi_3 \int_{e^2}^{e^3} f'(e)\, de \tag{7.40}$$

In words, the welfare change is the expected value of the weighted sum of changes in the money metric e where the weights are $f'(e)$, the marginal utility of real income. For the case of an increase in price variability, the first term is negative (corresponding to the case where p_1 is higher than p_2) and the second term is positive (since p_2 exceeds p_3). Whether or not ΔW will rise or fall with price variability depends upon the relationship among the prices as well as the functional form of $f(e)$.

To illustrate, consider the special case in which $f'(e)$ is constant so the person has constant marginal utility of real income and is thus risk neutral. The welfare change measure then becomes:

$$\Delta W = f'(e)[\pi_1(e^1 - e^2) + \pi_3(e^3 - e^2)] \tag{7.41}$$

That is, welfare change is proportional to the expected change in the value of the expenditure function.[20] This expected value of the change in e can be given a geometric interpretation using the lower diagram of figure 7.13. Equation (7.41) can be rewritten as follows:

$$\frac{\Delta W}{f'(e)} = \pi_1[e(p^2, u_1) - e(p^2, u_2)] + \pi_3[e(p^2, u_3) - e(p^2, u_2)]$$
$$= \pi_1[e(p^2, u_1) - e(p^1, u_1)] + \pi_3[e(p^2, u_3) - e(p^3, u_3)]$$
$$= \pi_1 \int_{p^1}^{p^2} x_1(p, u_1)\, dp_1 + \pi_3 \int_{p^3}^{p^2} x_1(p, u_3)\, dp_1$$
$$= -\pi_1(p^1 ab p^2) + \pi_3(p^2 cd p^3) \tag{7.42}$$

---

[20] The factor of proportionality $f'(e)$ could be eliminated by an appropriate cardinal transform of $f(e)$.

In deriving (7.42) we have used the fact that $e(p^2, u_2) = e(p^3, u_3) = e(p^1, u_1) =$ the income of the consumer. The welfare change can therefore be represented as the expected value of the compensating variations from the rise and fall in the price of x_1. Notice that the compensating variations are evaluated as areas under different compensated demand curves.

A celebrated result pointed out by Samuelson (1972) can be obtained as a special case of (7.42). Suppose that the certain price p^2 is the expected value of the uncertain prices, so $p^2 = \pi_1 p^1 + \pi_3 p^3$. Then the welfare change measure (7.42) is the change obtained from a mean-preserving increase in the variability of prices. In that case, it is clear from (7.42) and figure 7.13 that the expected gain to the consumer from the price fall, $\pi_3(p^2 cd p^3)$ will exceed the expected loss from the price rise, $\pi_1(p^1 ab p^2)$.[21] This is the Samuelson result that an individual can be better off under price uncertainty than under price fixity.

Once the person is made risk averse this Samuelson result will no longer necessarily hold. Under risk aversion, the welfare change measure will no longer be the expected value of the compensating variation. Instead, as in (7.40), it will be given by the weighted change in the compensating variation. Since $f''(e) < 0$, the weight attached to the gain in welfare from a possible price fall will exceed the weight attached to the loss in welfare from a possible price rise. With a sufficiently strong degree of risk aversion, ΔW in (7.40) could be negative for a mean-preserving spread in prices.

This can be seen by taking a Taylor expansion of $f(e)$ around e^2 as before. If we take (7.37) and ignore the higher order terms and R_i, the welfare change measure becomes:

$$\frac{\Delta W}{f'(e^2)} = \pi_1(e^1 - e^2) + \pi_3(e^3 - e^2) - \frac{r}{2} \text{var}(e) \qquad (7.43)$$

where r is the coefficient of absolute risk aversion. Thus, the welfare change measure is the expected value of the compensating variation (as given by (7.42)) amended by a term involving the variability of returns e and the coefficient of absolute risk aversion.[22] The sign of (7.43) is ambiguous, being more likely to be negative the greater is the variance of outcomes e and the more risk averse the person is.

The above examples all involve moves from a certain price (or income) to a mean-preserving spread in prices (or income). Indeed, they are usually designed to show the benefits to an individual from a price (or income) stabilization scheme. It would, however, be a very special type of price stabilization scheme which stabilized prices at the expected value of the uncertain price. In addition, by concentrating on a single individual, the costs of financing such a scheme are ignored. Since price stabilization

---

[21] Note that this result would not necessarily hold if x_1 is inferior so $x_1(p, v_1)$ is to the right of $x_1(p, v_3)$.

[22] This is a similar expression to that derived in Dahlby (1981).

involves some uncertainty in the financing required, the financing would have to be done by a risk-neutral source in order that its variability be ignored. This might be the case if the price uncertainty facing the individual were diversifiable, in which case no financing risk would be involved. This would require that the price uncertainty facing each individual be uncorrelated with the price uncertainty facing all others. Furthermore, if this were the case, private insurance markets might well be set up to remove the price uncertainty.

Suppose that the price uncertainty is not diversifiable. To take the extreme case, suppose every household in the economy is faced with the same price fluctuations. It is easy to show that in this case, once we take account of the risk involved in financing, no price stabilization scheme can improve social welfare. This can be illustrated by imagining the economy to consist of several households identical in taste and income to the one depicted in figure 7.13. In this case we can treat the economy as if it consisted of a single representative household. To simplify matters further, suppose that the production possibility curve is linear so that the budget lines drawn in figure 7.13 are also society's production possibility curves.

Figure 7.14 illustrates the effect of a price stabilization scheme which is financed by a set of lump-sum income transfers. The production possibility curves depict uncertainty in the producer cost of good x_1.

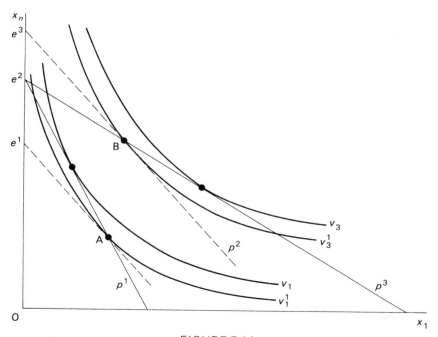

FIGURE 7.14

In the poor state the price of x_1 is p_1^1 and in the good state it is p_1^3 as before. In the absence of price stabilization the representative household attains utility levels v_1 and v_3 with probabilities π_1 and π_3. Consider now an attempt to stabilize the price of x_1. Unlike the case of the single individual the relative price of x_1 cannot be stabilized along a budget line with income e^2 and price p^2 as shown in figure 7.13. Such a scheme would violate society's resource constraint. In particular, in the bad state society is constrained to produce somewhere along the production possibility curve with income e^1 and price p_1^1.

Consider a scheme which stabilized prices at some price p_1^2 betweer p_1^1 and p_1^3 (not necessarily the mean). In the bad state an income tax would have to be levied such that when the price is p_1^2, the household selects a point along its budget line which is also a point on society's production possibility curve. Such a point is shown as A in figure 7.14. Clearly, this will yield a utility level *lower* than that attained in the bad state in the absence of price stabilization.

Similarly, in the good state an income transfer must be made to the household to allow it to purchase a bundle of goods on the production possibility curve corresponding to the good state. The point B is chosen. Here too the household is worse off than it otherwise would be if the price had been allowed to fall in the good state.

The price stabilization scheme financed by income tax unambiguously makes the household worse off in this case, because a lower level of utility is attained in both the good and the bad states of the world. Since the risk is undiversifiable, the price uncertainty has merely been transformed into income uncertainty and a price distortion has been introduced. In order for a price stabilization scheme to improve the lot of a household, it must be the case that the risk facing it is diversifiable to some extent. In the above example, with perfect diversification, no net financing of the scheme is necessary since the good and bad states for various households are offsetting. Thus, no income transfers are needed.

CHAPTER 8

Welfare Change Measurement in Single-Consumer Economies

1 The Interpretation of Single-Consumer Economies

Actual economies consist of millions of consumers, many of whom could be affected by any given change in the allocation of resources. Yet it is conventional in welfare economics to proceed as if the consumers could be aggregated into a single composite or representative consumer. The advantage of this procedure is that it allows us to use aggregate market data in evaluating welfare change. It also allows us to eschew the thorny distributional or ethical issues involved in aggregating welfare change measures over individuals. Instead, we can appear to be concentrating on 'efficiency' effects of welfare changes. From a pedagogical point of view, the single-consumer economy is a useful construct since it is a simple extension of the analysis of the last chapter pertaining to a single individual. We shall therefore analyse a single-consumer economy as a prelude to considering the many-person economy in the next chapter.

Before proceeding, it is worth being very clear about what assumptions are involved in analysing a single-person economy. In other words, we shall discuss the circumstances under which a single-person economy is a sensible surrogate for a multi-person economy. This question was carefully addressed by Samuelson (1956) and we do little more here than summarize his views.

Treating a many-person economy as if it were a single-person economy implies first of all that aggregate demand functions, which give the aggregate demand for each commodity as a function of prices and aggregate income,[1] have the same properties as individual demand functions. That is, just as individual demand functions reflect the preference orderings of an individual, the aggregate demand function represents an aggregate preference ordering, or set of social indifference curves. Thus, not only can

---

[1] Equivalently, we could represent the demand function of the representative individual as the per caput aggregate demand, this being a function of prices and average per caput income. The following discussion would apply to that case as well.

demand functions be derived uniquely as a function of prices and aggregate income; so also can aggregate CVs and other welfare change measures. Secondly, the aggregate welfare change measures must have normative significance in the sense that if, say, aggregate CV rises, society must be better off, and vice versa.

It is well known that, in general, aggregate demand in the economy cannot be written as a unique function of prices and aggregate income; income distribution will influence aggregate demand as well. Samuelson pointed out two circumstances in which this non-uniqueness could be avoided and a single-person economy could legitimately be used to represent a many-person economy for normative purposes. The first occurs when it is assumed that the government is continually distributing income optimally by a set of lump-sum transfers. The second occurs when preferences are restricted to be identical and homothetic for all persons. We consider these in turn.

1.1 *Income distributed optimally*

Here it is assumed that the government ensures that income is optimally distributed at all resource allocations using lump-sum taxes and transfers. This implies that, given the social welfare function used by the government, the marginal social utility of income is identical for all individuals. A unique distribution of income will be associated with each resource allocation or set of prices and aggregate income, so that a unique aggregate demand function as a function of prices and aggregate income will exist. If one goes from these aggregate demand functions back to a preference ordering which would generate them, one obtains a set of indifference curves which ranks alternate bundles of aggregate output. These indifference curves are referred to as social indifference curves by Samuelson.

Since these social indifference curves are constructed on the assumption that income has been optimally distributed at all points on the diagram according to the prevailing social welfare function, it can be readily demonstrated that they provide a proper social ordering of all aggregate commodity bundles for the economy. Samuelson (1956) showed this to be the case. This in turn implies that if we apply a money metric such as the expenditure function to this social indifference map, the money metric will be a proper representation of the social ordering of commodities. Thus, the aggregate CV or EV will be a consistent way of measuring welfare change.

Unfortunately, the conditions required to interpret aggregate demands as being generated by Samuelson social indifference curves are very stringent. It must be assumed that the government is continually redistributing income optimally. If not, observed aggregate demands and the aggregate CV obtained from them will not be those corresponding to the social indifference curves, and this justification for treating the economy as if it were a single-person economy breaks down.

1.2 Identical homothetic preferences

It is a well-known result that if all persons have identical and homothetic preferences, this is a sufficient condition for aggregate demand functions to be uniquely defined.[2] A unique indifference map in aggregate commodities exists from which aggregate demand functions in prices and aggregate income can be derived. This indifference map is independent of the distribution of income. Consequently, a unique measure of the aggregate CV or EV for aggregate commodity bundles can readily be defined and, in principle, measured on the basis of observable data.

The ability to measure an aggregate CV which is independent of the distribution of income does not ensure that the measure has any normative significance. It turns out that if one subscribes to certain welfare criteria, the aggregate CV thus measured does have some normative significance. In particular, if one uses the Kaldor compensation criterion, and if preferences are identical and homothetic, the aggregate CV will provide a ranking of resource allocations identical to that of the Kaldor compensation criterion.

Since the applicability of the Kaldor compensation test is described in the next chapter, we leave the demonstration of the proposition until then. The essential point is that identical homothetic preferences give rise to a unique map of non-intersecting community indifference curves (not to be confused with Samuelson's social indifference curves). As will be shown in the next chapter, if preferences are not identical and homothetic, this one-to-one relation between the aggregate CV and the Kaldor compensation criterion no longer holds, and this justification for using a single-person economy is lost.

Note finally that with identical and homothetic preferences, the aggregate CV (as with the Kaldor test) only gives a partial ranking of resource allocations. It does not change for pure redistributions of income from one person to another which, by the nature of preferences, does not affect aggregate demands. Thus it cannot provide the same ranking as would be obtained by a social welfare function.

These issues will be returned to in the next chapter. For now, we concentrate on the measurement of welfare change in single-person economies.

2 The Welfare Cost of Taxation in a Single-Consumer Economy

Ultimately, a measure of welfare change in single-person economies involves evaluating CV or EV given by (7.7) or (7.9). No new matters of principle are involved. The only additional issue to be taken account of

---

[2] It is not a necessary condition, however. As long as all individuals have identical marginal propensities to consume for any given good (though not necessarily identical across goods), individual demands can be aggregated to aggregate demand functions uniquely. For a more complete discussion of this, see Deaton and Muellbauer (1980).

is the general equilibrium nature of the problem arising from society's production possibilities. The production possibility frontier of society takes the place of the budget constraint of the individual. Since the application of welfare cost measurement to single-consumer economies involves no new problems of analysis, we shall proceed by considering a series of specific examples. In these examples, we shall use CV as the measure of welfare change for expositional purposes. Similar sorts of analyses would apply to the use of EV or any other appropriate measure.

The simplest case to consider is the imposition of an excise tax on one commodity in an otherwise undistorted economy. If the production possibilities constraint of the economy is linear, so all relative prices on the supply side are fixed, the analysis of chapter 7, section 5 applies exactly with minor reinterpretation. In figure 7.6 the initial budget constraint facing the consumer with income m^1 is now the production possibility curve of society in the two-good case.[3] The slope of this budget line is society's marginal rate of transformation between goods x_i and x_n. Equivalently it can be viewed as the ratio of marginal costs of producing the two goods, or the relative supply prices. With a linear transformation curve, relative supply prices are fixed at all output combinations.

In the lower part of figure 7.6, the demand curve $x_i(p, b)$ is the demand curve obtained by facing the household with different relative prices in consumption, but constraining it to remain on society's production possibilities curve. That is, it is constructed by taking the slope of the consumer's indifference curve (p_i) at all points along the transformation curve (x_i). The resulting curve is known as the *general equilibrium demand curve*, or the *Bailey demand curve*.[4] The CV measures here are exactly the same as they were for the single-consumer case in the absence of general equilibrium considerations. We maintain the assumption that the tax revenues are returned to the consumer in lump-sum form.

General equilibrium considerations only become important once we allow relative supply prices to change. This case is illustrated for the two-good economy in figure 8.1. In this economy, factor supplies are assumed fixed, so utility changes arise solely out of changes in consumption. The imposition of an excise tax on x_i with the proceeds returned to the consumer causes the state of the economy to change from the undistorted equilibrium 1 to the distorted equilibrium 2 with the associated utility levels u_1 and u_2. At 1, the value of output of the economy and the consumer's income measured in terms of x_n is m^1. At 2, output measured in supply prices (factor cost) is Y^2, and the consumer's income is m^2. The difference $m^2 - Y^2$ is the tax revenue collected, $(p_i^2 - q_i^2) x_i^2$, where q_i^2 is the supply price in situation 2, and so $p_i^2 - q_i^2$ is the tax per unit of

---

[3] This would also be the production possibility curve between x_i and all other goods in the case in which producer's prices are fixed so that all other goods can be aggregated into a single commodity. A linear production possibility curve would arise in the two-good case, for example, if both goods were produced with constant returns to scale and using identical factor proportions.

[4] See Bailey (1954).

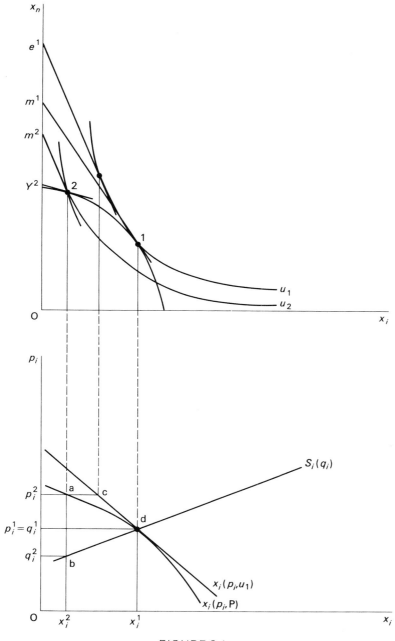

FIGURE 8.1

output.[5] The CV associated with the excise tax is, as before, $m^2 - e^1$, which is negative here.

In the lower diagram of figure 8.1, $x_i(p_i, u_1)$ is the compensated demand curve along the utility level u_1, and $x_i(p_i, P)$ is the general equilibrium demand curve when demands are constrained to lie along the production possibility curve. The curve $S_i(q_i)$ is the general equilibrium supply curve showing the supplies that would be forthcoming at various values of q_i, the relative supply price of x_i (i.e. the slope of the production possibility curve).

The geometric interpretation of CV in terms of demand and supply curves is derived as follows:

$$\begin{aligned} CV &= m^2 - e(p^2, u_1) \\ &= m^1 - (m^1 - Y^2) + (m^2 - Y^2) - e(p^2, u_1) \\ &= e(p^1, u_1) - e(p^2, u_1) - (m^1 - Y^2) + (m^2 - Y^2) \end{aligned}$$

where we have used the fact that $m_1 = e(p^1, u_1)$. As mentioned above, $m^2 - Y^2$ equals T, the tax revenue generated. Furthermore, $m^1 - Y^2$ can be shown to equal

$$\int_{q_i^2}^{q_i^1} S_i(q_i)\, dq_i.[6]$$

Therefore, CV becomes:

$$\begin{aligned} CV &= -\int_{p_i^1}^{p_i^2} x_i(p, u_1)\, dp_i + \int_{q_i^1}^{q_i^2} S_i(q_i)\, dq_i + T \\ &= -p_i^2 \mathrm{cd} p_i^1 - p_i^1 \mathrm{db} q_i^2 + p_i^2 \mathrm{ab} q_i^2 \\ &= -\text{acdb} \end{aligned}$$

Notice that if income effects are negligible, point c will coincide with point a and this deadweight loss measure will be the triangle adb. Other-

---

[5] Geometrically, $p_i^2 - q_i^2$ is the angle formed by the lines of slope p_i^2 and q_i^2 through point 2 and tangential to the indifference curve and production possibility curve, respectively.

[6] This can be derived as follows. m^1 can be seen to be the value of output of the economy at factor cost when relative producer prices are those of situation 1; denote that by $F(q^1)$. Similarly, Y^2 is $F(q^2)$. In moving from situation 2 to situation 1, only q_i changes; therefore

$$m^1 - Y^2 = \int_{q_i^2}^{q_i^1} (\partial F/\partial q_i)\, dq_i$$

It can be shown using the theory of duality that $\partial F/\partial q_i = S_i$ (see Diewert, 1974). Therefore we obtain the result in the text.

wise, the triangular measure of deadweight loss is only an approximation. As mentioned earlier, the general equilibrium demand curve $x_i(p_i, P)$ is likely to be much closer to the compensated demand curve $x_i(p_i, u_1)$ than is the Marshallian demand curve. That is because the general equilibrium demand curve incorporates some compensation in it; namely, an amount equal to tax revenues. Of course, for empirical applications the general equilibrium demand curve may be no easier to observe than the compensated demand curve. One may end up using parameters of the Marshallian demand curve as approximate measures for estimating the CV, as discussed in the last chapter.

3 Welfare Change Measures in a Distorted Economy

An interesting case to consider is that in which a policy change is made in an economy in which pre-existing distortions already exist. This is an example of the principle of second best and is applicable in a wide variety of situations.[7] In order to facilitate geometric interpretation, consider the special case of a three-good economy with fixed supply prices. The three goods will consist of x_n, x_1 and x_2. Good x_n will be used as the *numéraire*; its market price is undistorted, so that the consumer's price and the producer's price both equal unity. The good x_2 has a fixed distortion per unit of output of t_2. This implies that when the consumer price is p_2, the supply price is $p_2 - t_2$. Since supply prices are fixed, so will be the consumer's price p_2. The remaining good x_1 initially has a consumer's price of p_1^1, which is equal to the supply price. The exercise whose welfare change is to be evaluated is to impose a tax on good x_1 of t_1 per unit of output. The tax revenues generated both on the market for x_1 and on x_2 are assumed to be returned as lump-sum payments to the consumer.

Using CV as a measure of welfare change, we have again that CV $= m^2 - e(p^2, u_1)$. Since consumer income includes tax revenues raised, and since supply prices are constant, $m^2 - m^1 = \Delta T_2 + T_1$, where T_i is the tax revenue on market i. Therefore CV becomes:

$$
\begin{aligned}
\text{CV} &= m^1 + \Delta T_2 + T_1 - e(p^2, u_1) \\
&= e(p^1, u_1) - e(p^2, u_1) + \Delta T_2 + T_1 \\
&= - \int_{p_1^1}^{p_1^2} x_1(p, u_1)\, dp_1 + \Delta T_2 + T_1
\end{aligned}
\tag{8.1}
$$

In deriving (8.1) we have made use of the fact that with fixed supply prices, only the price of x_1 will change if a tax is imposed on it. If pro-

---

[7] The literature on the theory of second best has become immense since the concept was first introduced into the literature by Meade (1955) and Lipsey and Lancaster (1956). A survey of the literature may be found in Harris (1981).

ducer prices were variable, all prices would change and the analysis would become correspondingly more complicated.

It is useful to depict the welfare change (8.1) geometrically. In figure 8.2 the demand and supply curves for x_1 and x_2 are drawn. The ordinary demand curves for x_2 corresponding to the initial and final situations are shown. These curves have been drawn as shifting to the right when p_1^1 is increased or when m rises from m^1 to m^2. This would be consistent with x_1 and x_2 being gross substitutes and x_2 being a normal good. On the market for x_1, two demand curves are drawn. One is the compensated demand curve $x_1(p_1, u_1)$ and the other is the general equilibrium (or Bailey) demand curve $x_1(p_1, b)$. These have exactly the same interpretation as before. In particular, the general equilibrium demand curve is that obtained by moving along the society's linear production possibility surface, holding all prices other than p_1 constant.

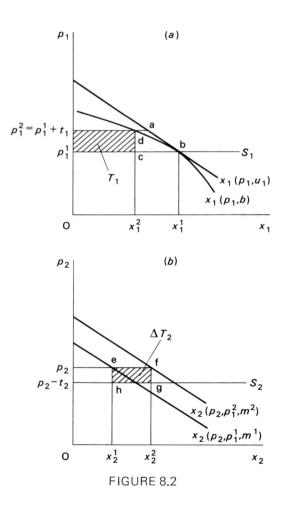

FIGURE 8.2

The terms in (8.1) correspond to areas in figure 8.2. The integral expression is simply the negative of the area $p_1^2 abp_1^1$ as before. The tax revenue terms are given by the shaded areas. Adding these up we obtain CV $= -abcd + efgh$, which could be positive or negative. If the income effects on market x_1 were zero, the term abcd would collapse to a triangle.

The above result is similar to that derived by Harberger (1964), who implicitly assumed income effects to be negligible. As he pointed out there, and developed more fully in Harberger (1971a), the welfare measure can readily be extended to the more general case in which several distortions exist on other markets in the economy. In this case, the CV measure of welfare change would become:

$$CV = - \int_{p_1^1}^{p_1^2} x_1(p, u_1) \, dp_1 + \Sigma \Delta T_i + T_1 \tag{8.2}$$

where ΔT_i is the change in tax revenues on the market for x_i. Notice that this expression also applies to the general case in which some goods are taxed and some are not. For those goods which are not taxed, the term ΔT_i is obviously zero.

Expression (8.2) becomes somewhat more difficult to evaluate if supply prices are not fixed, since in this case all prices, including factor prices, change in response to a change in one of the tax rates. Following the same procedure as before, the welfare change measure becomes

$$CV = e(p^1, u_1) - e(p^2, u_1) + \Sigma \Delta T_i + T_1 + \text{change in factor income}$$

$$= - \int_1^2 \Sigma x_i(p, u_1) \, dp_i + \Sigma \Delta T_i + T_1 + \int_1^2 \Sigma S_i(q_i) \, dq_i \tag{8.3}$$

In order to evaluate this expression one has to know how all prices respond to an exogenous change in the tax on good 1 through the general equilibrium workings of the system.

4 Project Evaluation Criteria

Another interesting application of welfare cost measurement concerns the evaluation of discrete or large projects; that is, projects which influence the price of the commodity being produced. We shall first consider the case of an investment financed with tax revenue obtained in a lump-sum manner. This parallels the case presented in Diamond and McFadden (1974). Next, we shall inquire into how the decision rule must be amended if distortionary taxation is required to finance the investment.

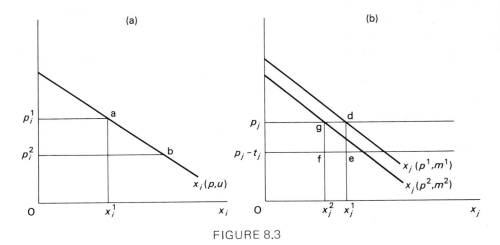

FIGURE 8.3

Consider an investment project which expands the capacity to produce good x_i.[8] In general, we might expect this project to change all prices and incomes in the economy. To simplify matters let us suppose that only the price p_i changes, all other prices being fixed by, say, fixed producer prices. There are no distortions in the economy. We can, therefore, aggregate all other goods into a composite good x_n which is also the *numéraire*. The usual CV measure, $m^2 - e(p^2, u_1)$ applies here, where now m^2 differs from m^1 by the cost of the project, denoted C. This is the amount of lump-sum income taken from the household to finance the project. The CV resulting from the project is thus:

$$
\begin{aligned}
CV &= m^1 - e(p^2, u_1) - C \\
&= e(p^1, u_1) - e(p^2, u_1) - C \\
&= -\int_{p_i^1}^{p_i^2} x_i(p, u_1)\, dp_i - C
\end{aligned}
\tag{8.4}
$$

In figure 8.3, the CV is given by the area $p_i^1 ab p_i^2$ less the cost of the project C (not shown). If the compensating variation from the price fall, $p_i^1 ab p_i^2$, exceeds the cost of the project, it should be undertaken.

Suppose next that there is another commodity, say x_j, which has a pre-existing tax distortion t_j on its price. Ordinary demand curves are drawn for x_j in the initial and the final situations. The curves are drawn such that when p_i falls from p_i^1 to p_i^2 and m falls from m^1 to m^2 to finance the project, the demand curve for x_j shifts left. Obviously, the opposite could

---

[8] We could equally think of a project which produces a public intermediate good which lowers the marginal costs of production of all firms producing x_i.

have happened as well. If the tax revenue is returned lump sum to the consumer, then $m^2 - m^1 = -C + \Delta T_j$, where ΔT_j ($= -$ gdef) is negative here. The CV from the project is now $p_i^1 a b p_i^2 - C -$ gdef.

Finally, suppose that instead of financing the project using lump-sum income transfers, the project must be financed by increasing the tax rate on good x_j. The tax rate increase is such that the change in tax revenue generated by the tax increase and the project expenditure is just sufficient to finance the cost of the project; that is, the consumer's income does not change. We retain the assumption of fixed producers' prices so that the project cum tax increase results in a fall in the price of x_i (due to the investment) and a rise in the price of x_j (due to the tax increase).

The change in consumer welfare resulting from these price changes can be obtained by applying our usual CV measure:

$$CV = m^2 - e(p^2, u_1)$$
$$= m^1 - e(p^2, u_1)$$
$$= e(p^1, u_1) - e(p^2, u_1)$$
$$= -\int_1^2 \sum_{i,j} x_k(p, u_1)\, dp_k \tag{8.5}$$

That is, the change in consumer welfare is the sum of the compensating variations resulting from the two price changes, that for p_i and that for p_j. Since the integral in (8.5) is path independent, its value does not depend on the order in which the price changes are taken. The same CV measure will always be obtained.

It is useful to illustrate this geometrically. In figure 8.4 the appropriate demand curves for x_i and x_j have been drawn. In the right-hand diagram,

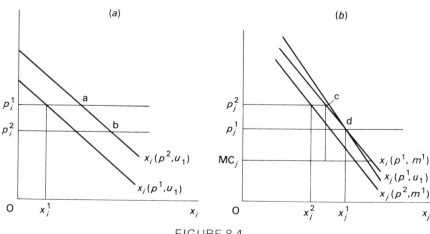

FIGURE 8.4

the ordinary demand curve for the initial situation is labelled $x_j(p^1, m^1)$. At the price p_j^1 it yields an output of x_j^1. The compensated demand curve corresponding to the initial allocation is drawn as $x_j(p^1, u_1)$. In the left-hand diagram the compensated demand curve corresponding to the initial allocation is $x_i(p^1, u_1)$. As mentioned above, the move to the new situation involves a rise in the price p_j and a fall in p_i. The CV will be evaluated by imagining the price changes to have occurred in the order p_j then p_i. The CV corresponding to the rise in p_j is the negative of the area $p_j^2 c d p_j^1$. This rise in p_j will cause the compensated demand curve for x_i to shift. In the diagram it has been assumed that the curve will shift to the right, implying that x_i and x_j are net substitutes (the cross-substitution effect $S_{ij} > 0$). The investment then causes the price of x_i to fall to p_i^2. The CV of this price fall is the area $p_i^1 a b p_i^2$. Therefore, the welfare change for this tax-financed investment is simply $p_i^1 a b p_i^2 - p_j^2 c d p_j^1$. Note that the fall in price of x_i will generally induce a shift in demand for x_j and cause a change in tax revenue. The initial change in tax rate t_j has been assumed to be sufficient for the overall increase in tax revenues just to cover the cost of the project, and consumer income does not change.

5 The Social Cost of Public Funds

This analysis of investment projects in distorted economies can be used to illustrate what is referred to as the social cost of public funds.[9] Consider as an example a project which purchases labour and uses it to produce a project output which has as its effect a lowering of the price of x_i. This project is similar to that considered in the previous section except now the cost is specified as a purchase of labour rather than as a transfer of resources valued at C. The purchase of labour at a cost C is financed by an increase in the proportional rate of tax levied on labour income. Once again it is assumed that the production possibility curve for the economy is linear so that all prices are fixed except that of the good x_i. The good x_n is treated as the *numéraire*.

From the point of view of the single consumer, the effect of the project is to reduce the price p_i and reduce the after-tax wage received for labour supplied. All other prices are fixed by the assumption of fixed supply prices, and the consumer's non-labour income is fixed since the project is financed entirely out of the change in the wage tax. Since only two prices change, the CV for the consumer from the project can be written as follows:

$$CV = -\int_{p_i^1}^{p_i^2} x_i(p, w, u_1) \, dp_i + \int_{w^1}^{w^2} L(p, w, u_1) \, dw \qquad (8.6)$$

[9] This notion is implicit in much of cost–benefit analysis. The particular application considered here is similar to that discussed in Browning (1978) and Usher (1982).

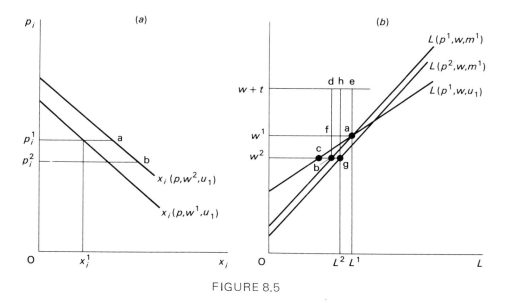

FIGURE 8.5

where $x_i(p, w, u_1)$ and $L(p, w, u_1)$ are the compensated demand and supply curves for x_i and L, respectively. This equation is a straight application of (7.24) derived in the previous chapter.

The evaluation of this expression can readily be depicted geometrically. In order to do so, a particular path of change for p_i and w must be chosen arbitrarily.[10] Figure 8.5 illustrates the case in which w changes first followed by p_i. The wage rate w here refers to the net-of-tax wage received by the consumer. It corresponds to a gross wage of $(w + t)$, where t is the rate of tax expressed in per unit terms. By the fixed supply price assumption the gross price $w + t$ is fixed, so increases in t lead to equivalent reductions in w.

The first step is to evaluate the CV from the wage reduction resulting from the increase in the tax on labour (the second integral on the right-hand side of (8.6)). In terms of figure 8.5 it is given by the negative of the area to the left of the compensated supply curve for labour, $-w^1acw^2$. This fall in w in turn causes the compensated demand curve for x_i to shift. The diagram shows it shifting to the right.[11] Notice that the change in tax revenue resulting from this fall in w is the area $w^1fbw^2 - $ deaf.

The next step is to evaluate CV from the reduction in p_i induced by the project. This is the first integral on the right-hand side of (8.6) evaluated with the wage rate at w^2. In figure 8.5 it is given by the area $p_i^1abp_i^2$. This change in p_i generally causes the supply curve for L to shift. The diagram

[10] Recall that the CV of (8.6) is path independent, so it does not matter in which order the price changes are assumed to be made.
[11] This is equivalent to assuming that leisure and x_i are net complements.

shows it shifting to the right to $L(p^2, w, m^1)$. This generates the additional tax revenue dbgh.

The overall CV from the change is given by:

$$CV = p_i^1 abp_i^2 - w^1 acw^2 \qquad (8.7)$$

This can be interpreted loosely as the difference between the benefits of the project measured as a change in the consumer's surplus and the costs of the project measured as a change in the producer's surplus.

There is an alternative way to express these costs which can be used as a basis for determining the likely magnitude of rates of return required on public projects. The method involves making some approximations. If the tax increase required for the project is relatively small, the cost of the project can be approximated by the producer's surplus area to the left of the uncompensated labour supply curve. That is,

$$w^1 acw^2 \approx w^1 abw^2$$

In turn, for a small tax increase, the triangular area abf will be negligible, so

$$w^1 acw^2 \approx w^1 fbw^2 \qquad (8.8)$$

To obtain another interpretation of $w^1 fbw^2$, note that the total cost of the project C, which is the total cost of labour hired by the project at the market price $w + t$, must equal the net tax revenues generated:

$$C = w^1 fbw^2 - \text{deaf} + \text{dbgh} \qquad (8.9)$$

Thus, the net benefit of the project given by (8.7) can be approximated using (8.8) and (8.9) by:

$$CV = p_i^1 abp_i^2 - w^1 fbw^2$$
$$= p_i^1 abp_i^2 - C - \text{deaf} + \text{dbgh} \qquad (8.10)$$

In words, an additional cost premium of deaf $-$ dbgh must be added to the labour costs of the project. These additional items represent the extra deadweight loss incurred from the financing of the project. This is similar to the procedure used by Browning (1978), though he ignores the area dbgh in his calculation. Recall that although this area is a positive addition to the cost as drawn here, it could have been negative depending upon the relationship between x_i and L. Browning argues that the area deaf represents about 7–16 per cent of the project costs, given what he assumes to be realistic values for the supply elasticities of labour and for the marginal tax rate on labour in the US.

There is another useful way to interpret the net beneficial expression (8.10), this time by obtaining another approximation to the cost $w^1 fbw^2$.

Consider the expression for the resource cost C given by (8.9). It can be rewritten:

$$C - dbgh = w^1 fbw^2 - deaf$$

$$= w^1 fbw^2 \left(1 - \frac{deaf}{w^1 fbw^2}\right)$$

Since $deaf \approx -t\Delta L$ and $w^1 fbw^2 \approx L\Delta t$, where ΔL and Δt are the changes in labour supply and the tax rate induced by the project, the above can be approximated by:

$$C - dbgh \approx w^1 fbw^2 \left(1 + \frac{t\Delta L}{L\Delta t}\right)$$

$$\approx w^1 fbw^2 (1 - \tau\epsilon) \tag{8.11}$$

where τ is the proportional tax rate t/w and ϵ is the uncompensated elasticity of supply of labour. Rearranging (8.11) we obtain:

$$w^1 fbw^2 = \frac{C - dbgh}{1 - \tau\epsilon} \tag{8.12}$$

This expression for the cost of the project $w^1 fbw^2$ has the following interpretation. The numerator is the net financing requirements of the project; that is, the project cost C net of the tax revenue generated indirectly from the shift in the supply curve for L induced by the price-reducing effect of the project (this may be positive or negative and is often ignored). This project net cost is then grossed up by the factor $1/(1 - \tau\epsilon)$, a term which has been referred to as the *private cost of public funds*.[12]

To provide a rough estimate of the likely magnitude of this term, suppose the uncompensated supply elasticity for labour ϵ is taken to be 0.2 (it could be positive or negative in principle). Let the marginal income tax applied to gross labour income be 50 per cent; that is, $t/(w + t) = 0.5$. Therefore τ, defined as t/w, will be 1.0. Then, the private cost of public funds would be $1/(1 - 0.2) = 1.25$. Therefore, the net benefit rule from (8.10) would be:

$$CV = p_i^1 abp_i^2 - 1.25(C - dbgh)$$

If we ignore the induced tax revenue dbgh, then the net benefit rule suggests that benefits must be 25 per cent higher than costs to justify undertaking the project.

---

[12] This term is similar to that derived by Usher (1982), who uses the phrase 'private cost of public funds'. The expression may also be found in Atkinson and Stern (1974). Both those papers derive it in an optimizing framework, but it is obvious from the text that it applies more generally to the evaluation of any project whether optimally chosen or not.

J

This result depends critically on the value assumed for the elasticity of labour supply. For example, if labour supply were inelastic and so $\epsilon = 0$, the private cost of public funds would be unity and no premium would be required. This is because with a fixed labour supply no deadweight loss is incurred with the increase in taxes needed to finance the project.

6 An Alternative Way to Express Welfare Change Measures

There is another way to express the welfare changes accruing to an individual from changes in prices and income. The method involves converting CV or consumer's surplus measures into equivalent 'total benefit' changes, where a total benefit is attributed to the consumption of each good. This method turns out to be particularly useful in the exposition of the techniques of cost–benefit analysis. The method will only be applicable to situations in which we can view the economy as consisting of a single individual. If distributional weights need to be attached to CV of each consumer type, the method of measuring welfare change using total benefits will be difficult to apply.[13] Also, in all that follows, income effects must be ignored, so compensated and uncompensated demand curves can be thought of as approximately the same. We proceed by developing the method for a single individual first; then we extend it to single-person economies.

6.1 *Single individual*

Consider our individual of the preceding chapter who has a utility function $u(x_1, \ldots, x_n)$ defined over the n commodities $x_i (i = 1, \ldots, n)$. To begin with, consider the welfare change resulting from a *ceteris paribus* change in a single price. We have already seen that the welfare change (CV) can be depicted geometrically by the consumer surplus area to the left of the compensated demand curve, approximated here by the area to the left of the ordinary demand curve. The principles involved can be readily illustrated by assuming the consumer consumes only two goods. Figure 8.6 illustrates the case in which the price of x_1 falls from p_1^1 to p_1^2. The ordinary demand curves for the initial situation show the quantities x_1^1 and x_2^1 being consumed. When p_1 falls, the demand for x_1 rises to x_1^2. On the assumption that x_1 and x_2 are gross substitutes, the demand curve for x_2 shifts left and x_2^2 is now consumed.

The welfare change can be measured by the Marshallian consumer surplus area $p_1^1 a b p_1^2$. Since income m is held constant, the sum of the changes in spending on x_1 and x_2 must be zero. In terms of figure 8.6,

$$x_1^1 \mathrm{cb} x_1^2 - p_1^1 \mathrm{ac} p_1^2 - x_2^2 \mathrm{de} x_2^1 = 0$$

---

[13] This is discussed in Harberger (1978). The use of distributive weights is taken up again in the next chapter.

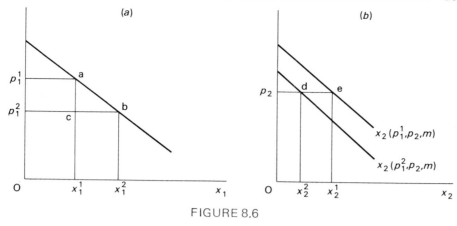

FIGURE 8.6

Therefore, the welfare change measure from the price fall, denoted ΔW, can be written:

$$\Delta W = p_1^1 ab p_1^2 = p_1^1 ac p_1^2 + abc = x_1^1 abx_1^2 - x_2^2 dex_2^1 \qquad (8.13)$$

We refer to the area $x_1^1 abx_1^2$ as the change in total benefit from consuming x_1 and $-x_2^2 dex_2^1$ as the change in total benefit from consuming x_2.

Consider the change in total benefit $x_1^1 abx_1^2$. It is given algebraically by the expression $\int p_1^1 dx_1$ and can be thought of as the sum of the changes in x_1 evaluated at the marginal benefit associated with each unit of x_1. Equivalently, it can be thought of as the maximum amount of the *numéraire* good that the household would be willing to pay to increase its consumption of x_1 from x_1^1 to x_1^2.[14] Equivalently, the change in total benefit to x_2, $-x_2^2 dex_2^1$, is given by $p_2 \Delta x_2$. It is the change in x_2 evaluated at the fixed price p_2 (which is also the marginal benefit x_2 to the consumer). In the general case of n goods, when one price changes the welfare change can be written as:

$$\Delta W = \int_{x_1^1}^{x_1^2} p_1 dx_1 + \sum_{i=2}^{n} p_i \Delta x_i \qquad (8.14)$$

Next, consider a *ceteris paribus* change in income. In this case the welfare change is given trivially by Δm, or equivalently $\Sigma p_i \Delta x_i$. There is no need to distinguish between the CV and the total benefit methods in this case. For both, the welfare change is given as the sum of areas such as $x_2^2 dex_2^1$ in figure 8.6.

---

[14] In terms of figure 7.4, $x_1^1 abx_1^2$ would be given by the vertical distance between points 1 and 3.

From these two special cases, we can construct welfare change measures resulting from more than one price change or price and income change. The changes are treated as if they occurred in some sequence and the total benefits associated with each price or income change in the sequence are simply summed. In principle, because of the path dependency problem discussed in chapter 7, the welfare change measure obtained would depend upon the order in which the price and income changes were taken to occur. However, if income effects really were relatively small on the goods whose prices have changed, one would expect the differences along different paths to be small, and probably of smaller magnitude than the measurement errors themselves.

6.2 Single-individual economies

Examples of the use of the total benefit method in single-consumer economies can best be illustrated by assuming the economy has a linear production possibilities constraint. This implies that supply prices (marginal costs) are fixed, and enables us to illustrate the principles geometrically. Let us take the special case considered in section 3 of a three-good economy consisting of a *numéraire* good x_n, a tax-distorted good x_2 and a good x_1 upon which a tax is to be imposed. All tax revenues gathered are returned in a lump-sum manner to the consumer. In figure 8.7 the relevant demand curves are drawn for all three goods, where we are simply ignoring the differences between ordinary and compensated demand curves. These diagrams assume x_2 and x_n are both gross substitutes for x_1.

Earlier we saw that CV from this sort of change was the appropriate area to the left of the compensated demand curve plus the change in tax revenue. The approximate equivalent in figure 8.7 is as follows:

$$\Delta W = -p_1^2 abp_1^1 + T_1 + \Delta T_2 = -\text{abc} + \text{fged} \qquad (8.15)$$

An alternative way to derive this measure, one which can be interpreted in terms of total benefits, is as follows.

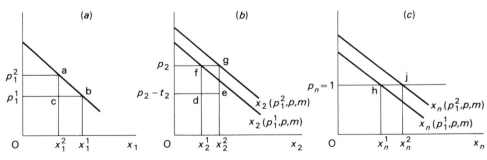

FIGURE 8.7

The general formula for CV for a single price and income change, as we have seen earlier, is $CV = -\int x_1(p, u_1)\,dp_1 + \Delta m$. Using figure 8.7, we can approximate this measure as follows:

$$\Delta W = -p_1^2 \mathrm{ab} p_1^1 + \Delta m$$
$$= -p_1^2 \mathrm{ab} p_1^1 + p_1^2 \mathrm{ac} p_1^1 - x_1^2 \mathrm{cb} x_1^1 + x_2^1 \mathrm{fg} x_2^2 + x_n^1 \mathrm{hj} x_n^2$$
$$= -x_1^2 \mathrm{ab} x_1^1 + x_2^1 \mathrm{fg} x_2^2 + x_n^1 \mathrm{hj} x_n^2 \tag{8.16}$$

Expression (8.16) gives the change in welfare in terms of total benefits. The three terms correspond to the change in total benefit from consuming x_1, x_2 and x_n, respectively, exactly as outlined earlier in this section for the single-individual case. That is, ΔW can be thought of as

$$\int_{x_1^1}^{x_1^2} p_1\,dx_1 + \sum_{i \neq 1} p_i \Delta x_i$$

Next, consider the production side of the economy. Since the production possibility constraint for the economy is linear, we can write it as follows:

$$\sum_{i=1}^{n} MC_i x_i = R \tag{8.17}$$

where R is a constant (the value of resources of the economy in terms of x_n). Since MC_i, the marginal social cost of producing x_i, is constant, from (8.17) we obtain

$$\sum MC_i \Delta x_i = 0 \tag{8.18}$$

Any changes in resource allocation in the economy must satisfy (8.18). In terms of figure 8.7, this equation may be written:

$$-x_1^2 \mathrm{cb} x_1^1 + x_2^1 \mathrm{dex}_2^2 + x_n^1 \mathrm{hj} x_n^2 = 0 \tag{8.19}$$

Subtracting (8.19) from (8.16) we obtain:

$$\Delta W = (-x_1^2 \mathrm{ab} x_1^1 + x_1^2 \mathrm{cb} x_1^1) + (x_2^1 \mathrm{fg} x_2^2 - x_2^1 \mathrm{dex}_2^2)$$
$$+ (x_n^1 \mathrm{hj} x_n^2 - x_n^1 \mathrm{hj} x_n^2)$$
$$= -\mathrm{abc} + \mathrm{fged}$$

which is exactly the same expression as in (8.15).

The interpretation of this last expression is instructive. The terms $-x_1^2 \mathrm{cb} x_1^1$, $x_2^1 \mathrm{dex}_2^2$ and $x_n^1 \mathrm{hj} x_n^2$ can be interpreted as the change in total costs of production of x_1, x_2 and x_n. Therefore, to obtain the welfare change, one calculates the difference in total benefit and total cost on each market, and then aggregates the differences over markets.

One important implication of the above analysis is the following. In evaluating welfare changes for economies as a whole, one must take account of output changes in all markets for which price differs from marginal cost. On the other hand, if price equals marginal cost on a market, changes in total benefits will equal changes in total cost and no account need be taken of output changes in the market for x_n. This implication is easily seen if we write the general formula for the welfare change resulting from the change in one price in a distorted economy with fixed producer prices as:

$$\Delta W = -\,\text{abc} + \sum_{i=2}^{n} (p_i - \text{MC}_i)\,\Delta x_i \tag{8.20}$$

This equation is a simple extension of the above analysis to more than three goods.[15] Naturally, it applies to cases in which $p_i < \text{MC}_i$ for some i as well as to cases in which $\Delta x_i < 0$. If supply prices are variable, the derivation of the expression requires an algebraic treatment as is presented in the next section. None the less, the same principle is involved: changes in resource allocation in undistorted markets can be ignored. Before turning to that case, it is useful to examine an important and interesting application of the above methodology to the theory of second best.

A natural extension of the above analysis is to assume that the tax to be imposed on x_1 is a choice variable. An example of the problem of second best is to select the optimal tax distortion to impose on x_1 given the existing and unchangeable tax on x_2. The solution to this problem is to select t_1 so as to maximize the value of ΔW given by (8.15).

For the case of figure 8.7, where the price exceeds marginal cost in the distorted market and where x_1 and x_2 are gross substitutes, it is clear that at the second-best optimum, price should exceed marginal cost for x_1 as well (i.e. $t_1 > 0$). That is so since, starting at $t_1 = 0$, the loss from a small increase in t_1 will be a very small triangular area like abc whereas the gain will be a larger rectangular area like fged. As t_1 is increased the triangular loss will become larger relative to the rectangular gain, so that eventually the increment to each will be the same. At this point the optimal second-best distortion will have been reached. Any further increases in t_1 will reduce welfare, and if t_1 is large enough, welfare could actually be lower than if t_1 were zero; that is, ΔW would be negative.

The requirement that t_1 be positive is specific to the circumstances under consideration. It should be obvious that if x_1 and x_2 are gross complements, the optimal second-best distortion would be negative (i.e. a subsidy). That is because a subsidy on x_1 would be required to shift the demand curve for x_2 to the right so that the rectangular area fged is positive. Equivalently, if the pre-existing distortion on x_2 is a subsidy so price

---

[15] Equation (8.20) corresponds to what Harberger (1971a) has advocated as the fundamental measure of welfare change in a distorted economy.

TABLE 8.1   Second-best pricing policy

		Sign of distortion in x_2	
		$t_2 > 0$	$t_2 < 0$
Relation between x_1 and x_2	Gross substitutes	$t_1 > 0$	$t_1 < 0$
	Gross complements	$t_1 < 0$	$t_1 > 0$

is always less than marginal cost, all of the results are reversed. In this case, a shift in the demand curve to the right would cause a loss rather than a gain. Table 8.1 summarizes these results.

Note finally that this analysis has been carried out under the simplification of fixed producer's prices and approximate measures of welfare change. None the less, the qualitative nature of the second-best optimum is not changed if we take these complications into account.

7 An Algebraic Demonstration

It is useful to complete this discussion of welfare change measures by deriving algebraically an expression corresponding to (8.20) for an economy in which the supply prices are not fixed. Suppose the single consumer has a utility function $u(x_1, \ldots, x_n)$ where x_i is the consumption of commodity i. Commodities can be thought of as including both goods and factors. Next, let $(y_1, \ldots, y_n)$ be the vector of private sector outputs and inputs in the economy produced according to the production possibilities constraint $F(y_1, \ldots, y_n) = 0$. We are assuming that the production efficiency conditions are satisfied so that production is on the frontier of the production possibilities set. Suppose that there is also some net output produced in the public sector, denoted by $(z_1, \ldots, z_n)$. Some of these may, of course, be zero. Market clearing requires

$$x_i = y_i + z_i \qquad i = 1, \ldots, n \tag{8.21}$$

Suppose that the consumer prices are $(p_1, \ldots, p_n)$ and that the distortions per unit of output are $(t_1, \ldots, t_n)$, some of which may be zero or negative.

We begin by deriving an expression for the welfare change of the consumer for a differential change in resource allocation. Totally differentiating the utility function yields:

$$du = \Sigma (\partial u / \partial x_i) \, dx_i$$

Suppose good n is chosen to be the *numéraire*. Dividing both sides of this expression by $\partial u / \partial x_n$ yields:

$$dW = \Sigma p_i \, dx_i \tag{8.22}$$

where $dW (= du/(\partial u/\partial x_n))$ is the welfare change measured in units of the *numéraire*. The prices $p_i (= (\partial u/\partial x_i)/(\partial u/\partial x_n))$, the marginal rate of substitution of x_i for x_n) are positive for goods and negative for factors. From the market clearing conditions (8.21) this welfare change can be rewritten as:

$$dW = \Sigma p_i (dy_i + dz_i) \qquad (8.23)$$

The production possibilities constraint indicates what combinations of private sector outputs are permitted. Totally differentiating it yields:

$$\Sigma(\partial F/\partial y_i) \, dy_i = 0$$

The ratio $(\partial F/\partial y_i)/(\partial F/\partial y_n)$ gives the producer's price of y_i in terms of the *numéraire* good or $p_i - t_i$. Therefore, dividing the above expression by $\partial F/\partial y_n$ yields:

$$\Sigma(p_i - t_i) \, dy_i = 0 \qquad (8.24)$$

where we shall assume that $t_n = 0.$[16]
By substituting (8.24) into (8.23), the welfare change measure becomes:

$$dW = \Sigma t_i \, dx_i + \Sigma(p_i - t_i) \, dz_i \qquad (8.25)$$

For differential changes this gives a unique measure of welfare change. Any differential exogenous change in the economy can be evaluated using (8.25) if one knows the responsiveness of x_i and z_i to the change. For discrete changes, the welfare change measure becomes:

$$\Delta W = \int \Sigma t_i \, dx_i + \int \Sigma (p_i - t_i) \, dz_i \qquad (8.26)$$

The first of these integrals will not, in general, be path dependent but we shall simply ignore that. Equation (8.26) is the same as Harberger's (1971a) general rule for welfare change measurement.

It might be useful to illustrate the use of (8.26) with two simple applications. Consider first the case in which all t_i are fixed. Then ΔW simplifies to:

$$\Delta W = \Sigma t_i \Delta x_i + \int \Sigma (p_i - t_i) \, dz_i \qquad (8.27)$$

If a public project is being undertaken, the changes in the z_i could be evaluated at producer's prices, the second term in (8.27). In addition, the

---

[16] Technically, this is simply a normalization that can be carried out with no consequences for the result. As discussed in Diamond and Mirrless (1971), the general equilibrium system is homogeneous of degree zero in consumer's prices and in producer's prices. The setting of $t_n = 0$ merely serves to specify the relation between the producer price level and the consumer's price level.

effects of changes in outputs on distorted markets (including those directly involving the project) are captured by the first term. We shall return to a further discussion of this in chapter 10 when we apply it in cost–benefit analysis.

Next, consider the case of imposing a tax on good x_i of t_i, holding all other taxes fixed. In this case, (8.26) becomes:

$$\Delta W = \sum_{j \neq i} t_j \Delta x_j \Big| + \int_0^{\bar{t}_i} t_i \, dx_i \qquad (8.28)$$

The second term is the triangular deadweight loss area under the demand curve for x_i, whereas the first term is again the indirect effect on other markets.

8 The Theory of Optimal Economic Policy

So far we have been concerned with obtaining a measure of welfare change from any discrete change in exogenous parameters, such as taxes. A natural extension to this which has been hinted at in the discussion of the theory of second best is to inquire as to what is the best value that the exogenous parameters should take. For example, in the theory of second-best analysis of section 6, what is the optimal value for the tax distortion imposed on x_1, given that an uncontrollable distortion exists on x_2? In this section we consider the methodology that is used in single-person economies to answer that question.

There are some sorts of problems for which this would be a trivial exercise. In the second-best problem, if the planner could remove the distortion on x_2 itself, that would obviously be the 'first-best' policy since then the economy could be moved to a Pareto optimum allocation of resources, or a first-best allocation. The problem only becomes interesting if there is something to preclude the planner from eliminating all distortions from the economy. The two most common sets of circumstances in which this has arisen in the literature are as follows.

Second-best problems   As mentioned, these are problems in which the planner is faced with exogenously given distortions between consumer prices and marginal costs in some sectors and has control over the prices in other sectors. Examples of this might include the existence of monopoly firms in the economy or tariff distortions which have been negotiated internationally. Or, the planner in question may be a project evaluator who has direct control only over the inputs and outputs of the project that is being considered. Policy rules for the project evaluator are deferred to chapter 10.

Optimal tax problems   The other sort of problem is that which arises when the planner must raise tax revenues to pay for, say, public goods expenditures or income redistribution, but is precluded from raising them in a non-distorting way. It may simply be infeasible to levy lump-sum taxes. In this case, the problem is to find the least distorting way to raise such taxes.

Our purpose is not to present a detailed survey of either of these two problems. Instead, we shall outline the basic method of analysis which is used, and illustrate its application with a simple problem in optimal taxation. The use of the tools of duality theory have contributed to significant advances in this area in recent years, and we shall use these tools here.

The optimal economic policy problem is usually posed as a two-stage maximization problem, or as what is referred to as a *principal agent problem*. At the first stage are the households and firms in the economy. Each of these acts independently so as to maximize utility or profits as the case may be, and the result of these independent actions will be a general equilibrium allocation of resources with an associated set of utility levels for the household. This allocation will typically depend upon some variables, exogenous to the agent, that the planner has control of, such as taxes or government expenditure. At the second stage of the problem the planner sets the values of the exogenous variables, knowing how the decision-makers will respond and how the general equilibrium system will adjust, so as to maximize the welfare of the households in the economy. The planner is said to be the principal, who takes the behaviour of the actors in the decentralized economy as given, and the firms and households the agents who respond to the exogenous variables set by the planner. Such a methodology makes it possible to model the workings of the decentralized economy. In the example we turn to now, the economy is assumed to be perfectly competitive with no distortions other than those imposed by the planner.

The simplest example to consider is that of a single-consumer competitive economy with a linear production possibility surface. The latter simplifies matters because producers' prices are fixed. The government is assumed to require a certain amount of tax revenue and can only raise it by imposing distortionary commodity taxes.[17] The economy will be similar to the one presented in the last section, but we shall ignore public sector output. The single consumer (i.e. the agent) consumes a bundle of commodities $(x_1, \ldots, x_n)$, some of which could be factors supplied. Consumer prices are $(p_1, \ldots, p_n)$, positive for goods and negative for factors. All of the consumer's income is assumed to be earned from the sale of variable factors, so the budget constraint is $\Sigma p_i x_i = 0$. The problem for the consumer is to choose the commodity bundle so as to maximize $u(x_1, \ldots, x_n)$ subject to the budget constraint. The solution to this problem is a set of commodity demand functions $x_i(p_1, \ldots, p_n, m)$ where m refers to his lump-sum income, which is zero here and will simply be

---

[17] This example may be found in several places in the tax literature, such as Ramsey (1927), Harberger (1964), Diamond and Mirrlees (1971), Atkinson and Stiglitz (1972) and Sandmo (1976). For a broad survey of optimal taxation theory, see Atkinson and Stiglitz 1980).

dropped unless needed. These commodity demand functions are homogeneous of degree zero in prices, so we can arbitrarily normalize prices by
selecting a *numéraire* good. For this purpose good x_1 is chosen, so p_1 is
set to unity. This is equivalent to measuring all consumer demands in
terms of good x_1.

The utility level that the consumer attains is found by substituting the
demand functions into the utility function to obtain the indirect utility
function:

$$v(p_1, \ldots, p_n) = u[x_1(p_1, \ldots, p_n), \ldots, x_n(p_1, \ldots, p_n)] \qquad (8.29)$$

As we discussed in chapter 7, this indirect utility function satisfies Roy's
theorem:

$$-x_i(p_1, \ldots, p_n) = \frac{\partial v/\partial p_i}{\partial v/\partial m} \qquad (8.30)$$

Since consumer's prices equal producer's prices plus taxes, the indirect
utility function of the consumer can be written as $v(q_1 + t_1, \ldots, q_n + t_n)$
where q_i is the producer price of good i and t_i is its tax.

On the supply side, society's production possibility constraint is linear
and can be written as $\Sigma q_i x_i = -G$, where G is the value of resources
required in the public sector. Once again, q_i is positive for goods and
negative for factors. Since the supply side of the economy is also homogeneous of degree zero in its prices, supply prices can be arbitrarily
normalized by choosing x_1 as *numéraire* and setting $q_1 = 1$. This is equivalent to setting $t_1 = 0$. Notice that combining the consumer's budget
constraint with the production possibility constraint yields $\Sigma t_i x_i = G$; that
is, the tax revenues of the government just equals G, the resources
required. Note that for goods a positive t_i implies a tax, but for factors a
positive t_i implies a subsidy.[18] It can readily be shown that the 'level' of
tax rates is in a sense irrelevant. This is so because the general equilibrium
system is homogeneous of degree zero in both the consumer's and producer's prices. A proportionate increase in the consumer's prices leaves the
consumer demands unchanged and does not affect revenue allocation.
Similarly, a proportionate increase in the producer's prices leaves supplies
unchanged. Since the level of consumer's prices and the level of producer's
prices can be varied independently, this is equivalent to varying the level
of taxes since taxes are the differences between the consumer's and producer's prices. This implies that we can arbitrarily tie down the consumer
price level to the producer level by normalizing prices so that $t_1 = 0$.

---

[18] This is the reason why a first best is not feasible. If the same set of *ad valorem* tax rates could
be imposed on all goods, marginal rates of substitution (p_i/p_j) would equal marginal rates of
transformation (q_i/q_j) and a first best would be achieved. Unfortunately, no tax revenues would
be raised since the revenues from taxes on goods would just equal the disbursement on subsidies
to factors.

The problem of the government can now be stated. It is to choose the tax rates $(t_2, \ldots, t_n)$ so as to maximize the consumer's utility subject to the requirement to raise tax revenues equal to G, or

$$\max v(q_1 + t_1, \ldots, q_n + t_n)$$

subject to   (8.31)

$$\Sigma \, t_i x_i (q_1 + t_1, \ldots, q_n + t_n) = G$$

If it is recalled that producer prices q_i are fixed and so is G, this is a straightforward constrained maximization problem. The first-order conditions with respect to t_i may be written:

$$\frac{\partial v}{\partial p_i} - \lambda \left(x_i + \Sigma_j t_j \frac{\partial x_j}{\partial p_i} \right) = 0 \qquad i = 2, \ldots, n \qquad (8.32)$$

where λ is the Lagrangian multiplier and can be interpreted as the marginal social value of an additional pound of tax revenue. Together with the budget constraint, these equations can in principle be solved for the tax rates $(t_2, \ldots, t_n)$ and λ.

Equations (8.32) do not have a straightforward intuitive interpretation as they stand. There are several alternative ways of characterizing the solution to these equations in the literature, and it is beyond the scope of this study to go into them. The interested reader is referred to Sandmo (1976). One example is as follows. Substituting Roy's theorem (8.30) for $\partial v / \partial p_i$ and rearranging, (8.32) becomes:

$$\Sigma_j t_j \frac{\partial x_j}{\partial p_i} = - \left(\frac{\lambda + \gamma}{\lambda} \right) x_i \qquad i = 2, \ldots, n$$

where γ is the marginal utility of income, $\partial v / \partial m$. Next, substituting Slutsky's equation (7.19) for $\partial x_j / \partial p_i$, we obtain:

$$\Sigma_j t_j \, S_{ji} - x_i \frac{\partial x_j}{\partial m} = - \left(\frac{\lambda + \gamma}{\lambda} \right) x_i \qquad i = 2, \ldots, n$$

where S_{ji} is the substitution effect. Using the symmetry of the substitution effect ($S_{ij} = S_{ji}$) and rearranging we obtain:

$$\Sigma_j t_j \, S_{ij}/x_i = - \left(\frac{\lambda + \gamma}{\lambda} \right) + \Sigma t_j \frac{\partial x_j}{\partial m} \qquad i = 2, \ldots, n \qquad (8.33)$$

Since the right-hand side of (8.33) is the same for all goods x_i, it must be the case that $\Sigma_j t_j S_{ij}/x_i$ is identical for all goods x_i. This is sometimes referred to as Ramsey's proportionate reduction rule. The left-hand side can be interpreted roughly as the proportionate reduction in demand for x_i as a result of the tax change if it is assumed that the consumer is compensated so as to stay on the same indifference curve. In fact, for infinitesimally small taxes, the left-hand side is exactly the proportionate reduction in demand for good i. It must be the same for all goods if taxes are levied optimally. Other interpretations may be found in Sandmo (1976).

As mentioned, this discussion was intended merely to give a simple example of the use of the two-stage maximization methodology. The methodology has been widely used both in the theory of optimal taxation and in the theory of second best. The interested reader can find surveys of the optimal tax applications in Atkinson and Stiglitz (1980) and of applications in the theory of second best in Harris (1981).

CHAPTER 9

Measuring Welfare Changes in a Many-Consumer Economy

1 Introduction

The welfare change measures developed in the previous chapter were constructed on the assumption that we could aggregate all consumers into a single representative consumer for welfare measurement purposes. The conditions under which this can be done are very stringent, as discussed earlier. Basically, it is necessary that the marginal social utility of income be identical for all persons, whether that be due to a clever government that continually redistributes income so as to maintain the equality of marginal social utilities, or whether it be because one is prepared simply to assume that the marginal utility of income is the same for all households. As discussed in chapter 6, section 4, the latter is straightforward only in the case where household indifference curve maps coincide. Failing either of these, we cannot aggregate the entire demand side of the economy into a single individual from a social welfare point of view.[1]

None the less, most practitioners of applied welfare economics proceed to measure welfare change by simply aggregating CVs or consumer's surpluses over individuals.[2] The question naturally arises as to what interpretation can be given to the results of such exercises. The usual argument is that the use of aggregated CVs to measure welfare change should not be interpreted as measuring social welfare in any direct sense but, rather, it should be interpreted as indicating whether or not there has been a *potential Pareto improvement in social welfare*. A potential Pareto improvement means that the gainers from the change could hypothetically compensate the losers from the change.

In the first section of this chapter we investigate the relationship between the aggregate CV and the satisfaction of hypothetical compensation tests. We show that even if we accept the principle of hypothetical

---

[1] From a purely positive point of view, we may be able to aggregate individual demand functions into an aggregate demand function which depends on prices and aggregate income alone. However, welfare change measures based on this aggregate demand function will not generally have normative significance.

[2] A strong case for this procedure may be found in Harberger (1971a).

compensation, the aggregated CV may not indicate when a compensation test is passed. As a result, in many cases the welfare economist has no alternative but to attach distributional weights to the individual CVs before aggregating them. This procedure is discussed in the later sections of the chapter.

2 What Does the Aggregate CV Actually Measure?

In order to be able to present our analysis geometrically, we assume the economy consists of two persons and two goods. This is a simplifying assumption only and the results derived here are applicable in more general models. The aggregate CV, denoted from here on by ΣCV, can be given a precise interpretation in terms of the compensation tests by using the construct of Scitovsky or community indifference curves (CICs). We begin by reviewing compensation tests and the concept of a CIC.

Recall from section 6 of chapter 3 that a compensation test is passed if the redistribution of goods from one group to another can result in the unanimous opinion that a policy change is desirable. The Kaldor test is passed if those who gain from the change can hypothetically compensate those who lose yet remain better off. The Hicks test is passed if the potential losers are unable to compensate the potential gainers and remain better off than they would be if the change occurs. We also identified the strong version of the compensation test which restricts the hypothetical redistribution of goods to the actual aggregate commodity bundle realized after (Kaldor) or before (Hicks) the change. The weak test permits the aggregate production bundle to vary in a manner consistent with the production possibilities set existing after (Kaldor) or before (Hicks) the change. This is equivalent to the redistribution of generalized purchasing power (income).

We saw in chapter 3, section 6, that the weak compensation test is passed if and only if a policy change makes possible a potential Pareto improvement. This is not true of the strong test, thus the weak test is the most interesting of the two. We also saw that both the strong and weak tests are subject to serious shortcomings even if one accepts the premise of hypothetical and lump-sum redistribution. In particular, neither test can provide a complete social ordering of states and even the partial orderings obtained are subject to 'reversal' and 'intransitivity' paradoxes.

A CIC is the locus of aggregate output combinations which just allow the two persons to maintain given levels of utility. The construction of a CIC is illustrated in figure 9.1, where x_n and x_1 are the two goods, and A and B are the two individuals. The diagram illustrates a particular allocation of resources, labelled 1. The economy produces x_1 and x_n of the two goods and allocates them in an exchange efficient manner so that utility levels u_1^a and u_1^b are attained by the two persons. A's indifference curves are drawn from the origin labelled O_a, and B's are drawn southwest from O_b.

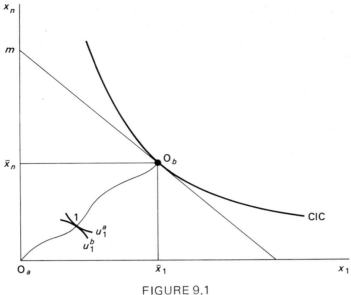

FIGURE 9.1

The CIC corresponding to these two utility levels is drawn. It is the locus of all combinations of x_1 and x_n which will leave the individuals on indifference curves u_1^a and u_1^b, and is constructed by rotating the origin O_b around while keeping u_1^a and u_1^b tangential.

The reader should recall from chapter 3 several properties of the CIC which are relevant here:

(1) A CIC is strictly convex and has a slope at each point equal to the common marginal rate of substitution of the indifferent curves. Thus, the slope at O_b equals the slope at 1 and both are equal, in absolute terms, to the relative price of x_1 in terms of x_n.

(2) All points along a CIC are points of exchange efficiency by construction.

(3) All points northeast of a CIC (i.e. on the opposite side of a CIC from the origin), are interior points of the *Scitovsky set* and can be distributed in a way that makes everyone better off than along the CIC. Conversely, for a point southwest of the CIC (i.e. on the same side of CIC as the origin), there are not enough goods to make everyone as well off as along the CIC.

(4) There are a large number of CICs passing through O_b, each of which represents a higher level of utility for one person and a lower one for the other, and each of which has a different slope at O_b. In general, there is a different CIC corresponding to each point along the contract curve joining O_a and O_b.

(5) In general, two CICs representing utility levels for the two persons which are not Pareto comparable will intersect. The exception to this is the case in which all individuals have identical homothetic preferences. In this case, contract curves are linear and have a common marginal rate of substitution at all points on a given curve. In this case only, there is a unique set of non-intersecting community indifference curves for society.

(6) The income level m (in terms of x_n) in figure 9.1 is the aggregate amount of income required at the relative price given by the slope at O_b in order to allow the two individuals to reach utility levels u_1^a and u_1^b. In other words, m is the sum of the value of the two individuals' expenditure functions:

$$m = e(p^1, u_1^a) + e(p^1, u_1^b)$$

We can now address two questions. First, if a compensation test is passed, is it the case that $\Sigma CV > 0$? Secondly, if $\Sigma CV > 0$, can we infer that a compensation test is passed? If the first question is answered affirmatively, a positive value of ΣCV is *necessary* for a compensation test to be passed or a negative value of ΣCV is *sufficient* for it to be failed. If the second question is answered affirmatively, a positive value of ΣCV is sufficient for a compensation test to be passed or a negative value of ΣCV is necessary for it to be failed. It would be most desirable for $\Sigma CV > 0$ to be both necessary and sufficient for a compensation test to be passed. Recall that $CV > 0$ is both necessary and sufficient for a single household's utility to have increased. Basically we would like to know whether a similar relationship holds between ΣCV and (potential) increases in every household's utility.

3 The Aggregate CV and the Strong Test

We will restrict our analysis to the Kaldor version of the test and ignore the problem of reversals. In figure 9.2a, the posterior (post change) aggregate production bundle is labelled point 2. We also assume this aggregate bundle of goods is distributed efficiently so that it lies on the posterior CIC (labelled CIC_2). The tangent line at 2 has a slope of absolute value equal to the relative price and the common MRS of the two goods. It intersects the vertical (*numéraire* good) axis at a posterior aggregate income level m^2. The tangent line to CIC_1 at posterior prices intersects the vertical axis at $e^1 = e(p^2, u_1^a) + e(p^2, u_1^b)$ which is the aggregate expenditure needed for every consumer to reach its initial utility when faced with posterior prices. Then $\Sigma CV = m^2 - e^1$, which is assumed to be positive in figure 9.2a.

The Kaldor strong test is passed if and only if the posterior production point 2 lies in the interior of the initial (pre-change) Scitovsky set (that is, northeast of CIC_1). If CIC_2 lies northeast of CIC_1 in its entirety as shown

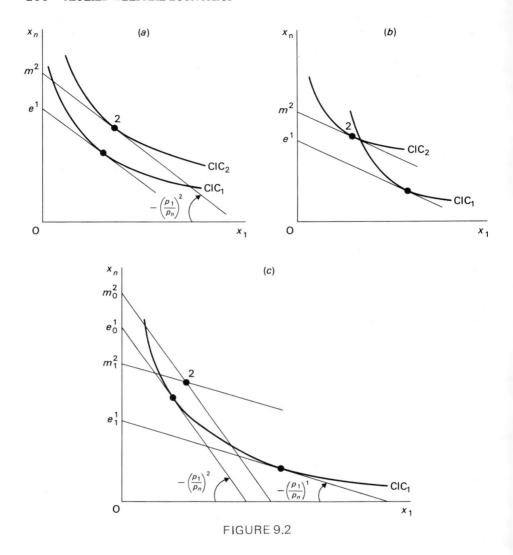

FIGURE 9.2

in figure 9.2a then the Kaldor strong test must be satisfied. Geometric reasoning will convince the reader that, in this case, ΣCV must always be positive as shown and ΣCV will always be negative if CIC_1 lies northeast of CIC_2 in its entirety. Thus if community indifference curves, like household indifference curves, do not intersect then $\Sigma CV > 0$ is both necessary and sufficient for the satisfaction of the Kaldor strong test.

Unfortunately, as mentioned earlier, community indifference curves may intersect unless very stringent conditions (parallel and linear Engel's curves for all households) are met. Once the possibility that CIC_1 and CIC_2 can intersect is allowed for, $\Sigma CV > 0$ is no longer sufficient for the strong test to be passed as shown in figure 9.2b. In this figure, a case is drawn where $\Sigma CV = m^2 - e^1 > 0$ but the posterior production bundle does not lie in the interior of the initial Scitovsky set and, therefore, cannot be distributed so that utility is higher than it was initially for everyone.

It remains true, however, that whenever the strong test is passed (point 2 lies northeast of CIC_1), $\Sigma CV > 0$. This is shown in figure 9.2c. The reader can ascertain that regardless of the price line passing through point 2 (the different price lines are drawn), $m^2 - e^1$ is positive. Thus $\Sigma CV > 0$, is necessary for the Kaldor strong test to be passed (or $\Sigma CV < 0$ is sufficient for it to be failed).

Unfortunately, this result is of limited use because, as we saw in chapter 3, satisfying the strong test is sufficient but not necessary for a policy change to yield potential Pareto improvements. That is, potential Pareto improvements may be possible even if the strong test is failed. This is because the strong test allows only a particular production point to be redistributed.

We summarize this section in the following proposition.[3]

Proposition 9.1   A positive (non-positive) value of the aggregated CV is necessary (sufficient) for the Kaldor strong test to be passed (failed) but is not, in general, sufficient (necessary) for the Kaldor strong test to be passed (failed) except in the case of non-intersecting CICs.

This leads us to the weak compensation test which, if it is passed, is necessary and sufficient for potential Pareto improvements.

4 The Aggregate CV and the Weak Test

As in the previous section we will consider only the Kaldor version of the test and ignore reversals and intransitivities. We will also assume that producers and consumers face the same set of relative prices, an assumption which was unnecessary in the discussion of the strong test.

The Kaldor weak test is passed if the posterior production possibilities set (bounded by the posterior production possibilities curve labelled PPC_2) intersects the interior of the initial Scitovsky set as shown in figure 9.3. In this case, by reallocating production and redistributing goods it is possible for every household to enjoy a level of utility after the change which is higher than the household's initial utility level.

As in the case of the strong test, $\Sigma CV > 0$ is both necessary and sufficient for the weak test to be passed if the CICs do not intersect. Indeed, in this case the two tests are equivalent because the strong test must be passed (failed) if the weak test is passed (failed).

When intersecting CICs are allowed for, the equivalence between the weak and strong test is broken. In figure 9.3, the weak test is passed even though the strong test is failed because the posterior production point

---

[3] This result may be found in Boadway (1974). See also Smith and Stephen (1975), Foster (1976) and Bruce and Harris (1982) for extensions.

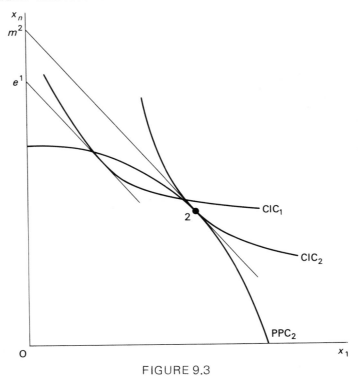

FIGURE 9.3

(labelled 2) lies outside the initial Scitovsky set. Of course, whenever the strong test is passed, the weak test must also be passed.

Figure 9.3 illustrates that, providing producers and consumers face the same prices, $\Sigma CV > 0$ is necessary for the Kaldor weak test to be passed. The line tangent to PPC_2 has a slope of absolute value equal to posterior relative producers' prices and intersects the vertical axis at aggregate income m^2. The line tangent to CIC_1 at posterior prices intersects the vertical axis at e^1 and, as shown, $m^2 - e^1 = \Sigma CV > 0$. It should be clear from the geometry of figure 9.3 that $\Sigma CV > 0$ whenever the weak test is passed, thus $\Sigma CV > 0$ is necessary ($\Sigma CV < 0$ is sufficient) for the weak test to be passed (failed). Moreover, since passing the weak test is both necessary and sufficient for a policy change to yield a potential Pareto improvement with lump-sum redistribution, $\Sigma CV > 0$ is necessary ($\Sigma CV < 0$ is sufficient) for a policy change to yield (fail to yield) potential Pareto improvements. Unfortunately, it is not the case that $\Sigma CV > 0$ is, in general, sufficient for the weak test to be passed or, equivalently, $\Sigma CV \leqslant 0$ is not necessary for the weak test to be failed. This is illustrated in figure 9.4 where $\Sigma CV = m^2 - e^1 > 0$ but the posterior production possibilities set does not intersect the interior of the initial Scitovsky set.

It is interesting to note, however, that the non-sufficiency example in figure 9.4 depends on our drawing the posterior production possibilities

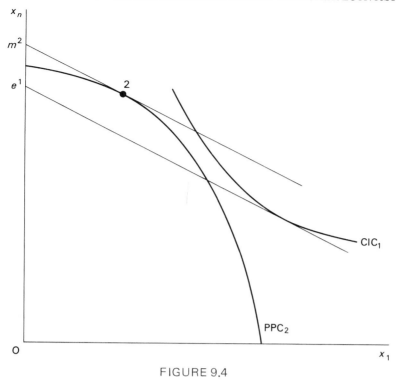

FIGURE 9.4

set strictly convex. If in fact the production possibilities set is linear (constant costs) then PPC_2 will coincide with the tangent line and the weak test must be passed. Thus $\Sigma CV > 0$ is both necessary and sufficient for the weak test to be passed (and for policy changes to make possible potential Pareto improvements) in the case of linear production possibilities sets when producers and consumers face the same prices.

We summarize the results of this section in the following proposition.

Proposition 9.2 A positive (non-positive) aggregated CV is necessary (sufficient) for the Kaldor weak test to be passed (failed) but is not, in general, sufficient (necessary) for it to be passed (failed) except in the case of non-intersecting CICs or linear production possibilities curves. Again, this holds only when producers and consumers face the same prices.

5 Other Tests and Other Measures

Thus far we have considered only the Kaldor version of the compensation tests and the aggregate CV as a welfare change measure. The reader might reasonably wonder if stronger results can be obtained with other compensation tests (e.g. the Hicks version) and/or other welfare change measures (e.g. the aggregate equivalent variation (EV) denoted ΣEV).

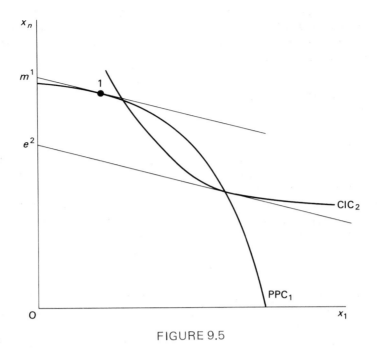

FIGURE 9.5

In figure 9.5 we illustrate the case where the Hicks weak compensation test is failed. It is failed if the initial production possibilities set (bounded by PPC_1) intersects the interior of the posterior Scitovsky set (bounded by CIC_2). In this case, lump-sum redistribution of income from the potential losers to the potential gainers after the change makes possible a utility distribution in which all households get higher utility than at the posterior utility distribution.

Also shown in figure 9.5 is the aggregate equivalent variation (ΣEV). The line tangent to PPC_1 at initial prices intersects the vertical axis at aggregate initial income m^1. The line tangent to CIC_2 at initial prices intersects the vertical axis at $e^2 = e(p^1, u_2^a) + e(p^1, u_2^b)$ which is the minimum aggregate expenditure needed for all households to retain their posterior utilities at initial prices. Then $\Sigma EV = e^2 - m^1$ is negative as shown in figure 9.5.

The reader should recognize that the relationship between the Hicks weak compensation test and the ΣEV is exactly the negative of the relationship between the Kaldor weak compensation test and ΣCV. The Hicks test is passed if the Kaldor test, which we get by treating the posterior state 2 as the initial state, is failed; and the aggregate equivalent variation is the negative of the aggregate compensating variation we would get if we treated state 2 as the initial state. Thus we can state the following proposition which holds when producers and consumers face the same prices:

Proposition 9.3   A non-positive aggregate equivalent variation is necessary for the Hicks weak test to be failed but is not, in general, sufficient for it to be failed except in the case of non-intersecting CICs or linear production possibilities curves.

We leave it to the reader to ascertain that, when CICs intersect, $\Sigma CV > 0$ ($\Sigma EV > 0$) is neither necessary nor sufficient for the Hicks (Kaldor) test to be passed.

The upshot of propositions 9.2 and 9.3 is that we have a necessary condition ($\Sigma CV > 0$) for the Kaldor weak compensation test to be passed and a sufficient condition ($\Sigma EV > 0$) for the Hicks weak compensation test to be passed. The crucial importance of Scitovsky reversals is now obvious. If the Kaldor and Hicks tests were both passed whenever one of them was passed, we could obtain necessary and sufficient conditions for a Pareto improvement by calculating both the ΣCV and ΣEV. Unfortunately, the possibility of reversals prevents us from finding necessary and sufficient conditions for Pareto improvements using the aggregate compensating and equivalent variations.

Further complications arise if we assume the economy is distorted in a way that prevents the producers and consumers from facing the same set of prices. Boadway (1974) showed that the aggregate compensating variation is neither necessary nor sufficient for the Kaldor weak test to be passed under such circumstances. Bruce and Harris (1982) found that, at least for small projects, a necessary and sufficient welfare change measure for the weak test could be obtained using a weighted average of producers' and consumers' prices.

We conclude this section with a general *caveat*. The use of the unweighted sum of household compensating or equivalent variations as a necessary and sufficient indicator of potential Pareto improvement is rife with difficulties. At best such measures can be used as a preliminary attempt to rank social states.

6 Measuring Welfare Change Using a Social Welfare Function

The preceding section illustrated the difficulties with applying the compensation principle as a method for ordering social states. More generally, the use of the compensation test as a welfare criterion is fraught with several difficulties. First, as discussed in chapter 3, the use of a compensation test involves the implicit acceptance of a value judgment that many would reject. The economy must be said to be better off in one state rather than another if it is hypothetically possible to make everyone better off with a particular set of transfers of purchasing power or goods among persons. This must be the case despite the fact that the actual transfers do not take place, and some persons can, in fact, be much worse off in the 'preferred' state. Even if one accepts the compensation test, it is clear from the foregoing discussion that the applicability of the test is severely limited. In general, one cannot rely upon measurements of compensating variations among persons as an indicator of whether or not the test is satisfied. This problem is exacerbated by the fact that there are many different notions of compensation test, depending upon one's view of the method by which compensation is hypothetically paid. In the previous section we discussed two versions of the compensation test – a strong one involving reallocating a given bundle of goods and a weak one involving redistribution through lump-sum transfers. Alternatively, one could imagine compensation involving redistribution through distortionary transfers. Each of these would yield differing rankings of resource allocations. Finally, even if one adhered to a compensation test and found a means of implementing it, one is still left with only a partial ordering of alternative resource allocations.

To obtain a measure of welfare change in many-consumer economies which serves to rank all alternatives, there appears to be no alternative but to employ a social welfare function. This, of course, was precisely what the compensation test literature was trying to avoid. As we have seen in the first part of this book, the ranking of social states according to an SWF involves making value judgments regarding measurability and comparability which are not required when using the Pareto criterion or the compensation test. We shall sidestep that issue here as well by assuming that the appropriate form of the SWF has already been decided. The purpose of this section is to discuss how an SWF may be applied in particular circumstances to measure welfare change. In the general case, the measurement problems are rather cumbersome even for a well-defined SWF. However, if one is prepared to make certain simplifying assumptions, the problem becomes much more tractable.

Suppose the SWF is a reasonably general one, restricted only to be of the Bergson–Samuelson type. In the terminology of the first part of this book, it is assumed to satisfy the property of welfarism so that social welfare depends simply on the utility levels of the members of society. Individual utilities are assumed to be fully measurable and comparable, thus affording the planner the richest of information and, therefore as discussed earlier, putting no restrictions on the form of the SWF. The SWF itself is an ordinal function of the well-defined utilities of individuals, so any monotonic transformation of the SWF will serve equally well to order social states. It is assumed that a particular functional representation has been chosen. The 'measurement' of welfare change in going from one resource allocation to another then involves calculating the utility of each type of individual in each state and aggregating the utilities according to the SWF.

This is likely to be a rather complex procedure since the utility level of each and every type of person must be computed for each state, even for those persons whose utility level has not changed. The measurement problem can be made tractable only by imposing further restrictions on the SWF, for example by reducing the information available to the planner.

Before turning to appropriate restrictions it is worth investigating the role that a money metric of utility such as the expenditure function can

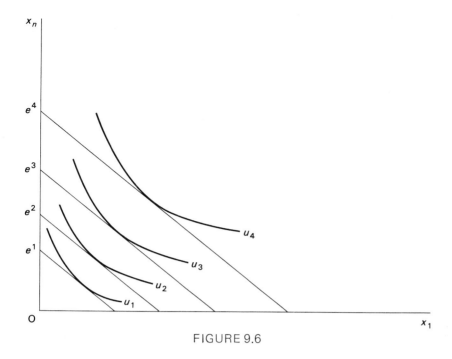

FIGURE 9.6

play in measuring social welfare. Recall first that the utility of an individual may be written as a function of a money metric representing the
expenditure function. Figure 9.6 illustrates this for a representative individual in the two-good case. A sample of indifference curves is shown,
with a uniquely defined utility associated with each one. Taking good x_n
as the *numéraire* and selecting an arbitrary relative price, the expenditure
associated with utility level u_i is labelled e^i. Analytically e^i is defined by
the expenditure function

$$e^i = e(p, u_i)$$

where p is the reference price vector chosen. Inverting the function $e(p, u_i)$
we see that utility can be written as a function of expenditure e given the
reference price vector. We shall use the following notation to represent
this functional relation

$$u = f(e) \tag{9.1}$$

where it is understood that p is also an argument in f. This demonstrates
that utility can always be depicted as some function of expenditures, or of
the money metric.[4] Equation (9.1) can, of course, be interpreted as the

---

[4] This will also be true if there are externalities in consumption so that an individual's utility
depends not only on his own consumption vector but on that of others as well.

value of the indirect utility function of the consumer at the reference prices, given that utility is fully measurable.

The function f which relates utility to the value of the expenditure function will generally vary from one person to the next, so $u^i = f^i(e_i)$. That being the case, the SWF may be written as follows:

$$W(u^1, \ldots, u^H) = W[f^1(e_1), f^2(e_2), \ldots, f^H(e_H)] \qquad (9.2)$$

That is, social welfare may be written as a function of the individual expenditure functions at a given set of reference prices. The measurement of social welfare can then proceed by using an appropriate aggregation of the money metric measures of utilities rather than of the utilities themselves.

Suppose now it is assumed that the SWF is anonymous so that each person's utility enters the SWF in the same way. This implies that the SWF will be symmetric in *utilities*. However, it will not necessarily be symmetric in the e_i. This is because different individuals obtain different levels of utility from the same e_i. One way to obtain a symmetric form is to amend the e_i in such a way as to reflect systematic differences in the ability of individuals to convert expenditure into utility. This can be done conceptually by the use of equivalence scales as follows.[5]

Suppose that one can attribute all differences in individual utility functions to some measurable attribute or characteristic, denoted c^h for individual h. Then, one might write an augmented utility function for individual h as $u^h = u(x^h, c^h)$, where the same utility function applies to all persons once both the vector of consumption x^h and the characteristic c^h are included as arguments. The expenditure function now indicates the level of expenditures required by a person of type h to attain a given utility level at the reference prices. It will depend upon the characteristic of the person in question and may be written $e(p, u^h, c^h)$.

According to this formulation, persons of different characteristics will require different levels of income to achieve the same utility level. For a given set of reference prices, the relation between utility and expenditures, previously given by (9.1), now becomes $u^h = f(e_h, c^h)$ and the arguments of the SWF are all of this form. The SWF will clearly not be symmetric in e_h. In order to make it so, we choose a reference characteristic level c^0 and define our money metric utility measure for the individual having this characteristic. Thus, the measure of real income adopted as a measure of utility is the expenditure required to attain a given utility level by a person of type 0, or

$$e(p, u, c^0)$$

A person of type h with an expenditure function valued at $e(p, u^h, c^h)$ can be made comparable to the reference person by defining his or her

[5] The concept of equivalence scales is discussed fully in Deaton and Muellbauer (1980). See also the discussion of horizontal equity in chapter 6.

equivalent real income to be the income that would be required to attain utility level u^h if prices were p and if the person had characteristic c^0. Equivalent real income e_h^* is written:

$$e_h^* = e(p, u^h, c^0) \tag{9.3}$$

where u^h is the utility function actually achieved by person h. The relationship between the observed real income $e(p, u^h, c^h)$ for individual h and the equivalent real income can be obtained by rewriting e_h^* as follows:

$$e_h^* = e(p, u^h, c^0) \frac{e(p, u^h, c^h)}{e(p, u^h, c^h)}$$

$$= \frac{e(p, u^h, c^h)}{s^h} \tag{9.4}$$

where s^h is known as an *equivalence scale* for the set of reference prices chosen. It can be interpreted as the number of households of type h that are equivalent to one reference household in terms of utility-generating ability at the given set of reference prices. Equivalent real income is simply observed real income deflated by this equivalence scale. That is, equivalent real income is a suitable money metric for utility. Deaton and Muellbauer (1980) have discussed how this equivalence scale can be empirically estimated.

Assuming that all differences in utility can be attributed to the characteristic c^h, a SWF which is symmetric in utilities will also be symmetric in equivalent real incomes. To see this, note that the inversion of (9.3) yields

$$u^h = f(e_h^*, c^0)$$

for a given set of reference prices. The SWF may then be written

$$W[f(e_1^*, c^0), f(e_2^*, c^0), \ldots, f(e_H^*, c^0)]$$

Since this function is symmetric in the utility levels, and since the same function $f(\ )$ applies to all persons, $W(\ )$ will be symmetric in e_h^*.

Alternatively, if all persons have identical utility functions, the SWF would also be symmetric in e_h if it were symmetric in u_h. This symmetry property is often assumed in empirical work either by assuming identical utility functions or by using equivalent real income measures as defined above. In what follows we assume SWF to be symmetric in e_h; however, the same analysis would apply for symmetry in e_h^*.

If the SWF is well defined in terms of e_h, welfare change can be measured by calculating the value of the e_h before and after the change. This procedure could be simplified if *changes* in social welfare could be expressed as a function of *changes* in e_h for all members of society. To see how this might be done, consider first a differentially small change in resource allocation. Total differentiation of the SWF yields:

$$dW = \sum_{h=1}^{H} \frac{\partial W}{\partial u^h} \frac{\partial f^h}{\partial e_h} de_h \qquad (9.5)$$

The social welfare change is thus a weighted sum of changes in individual expenditures, where the weights can be called *marginal social utilities of income*. Since W is a function of all expenditure levels, so too will the marginal social utility be a function of all individual e_h. Let us denote it by $\beta^h(e)$ where e is the vector of e_h.

For a discrete change, the expression for dW must be integrated over the change to give:

$$\Delta W = \int \Sigma \, \beta^h(e) \, de_h \qquad (9.6)$$

It will be possible to define an 'intermediate' marginal social utility of income for individual h as $\bar{\beta}^h$ such that $\bar{\beta}_h \Delta e_h = \int \beta^h(e) \, de_h$. Then, the welfare change measure may be written:

$$\Delta W = \Sigma \, \bar{\beta}^h \Delta e_h \qquad (9.7)$$

However, the weights $\bar{\beta}^h$ will in general depend upon the expenditure levels of all persons in the economy in a fairly complicated way.

The situation is considerably simplified if we assume the SWF to be strongly separable in utilities. Recall the definition of strong separability. In the context of an SWF, $W(u)$ is strongly separable if and only if the ratio $(\partial W/\partial u_i)/(\partial W/\partial u_j)$ is independent of the level of utility of any other person, $h \neq i, j$. That is, the tradeoff between utilities of any two persons does not depend upon the level of anyone else's utility. This means that a unique diagram of social welfare contours or indifference curves can be drawn in u_i–u_j space. These contours remain unchanged for changes in other persons' utility levels.

From demand theory we know that a function will be strongly separable if and only if it can be written in the strongly additive form.[6] Therefore, there will be a transform of the SWF which allows it to be written:

$$W = w^1(u_1) + w^2(u_2) + \ldots + w^H(u_H) \qquad (9.8)$$

We are assuming the u_i to be fully measurable. As above we can write u_i as a function of a well-defined money metric such as the value of the expenditure function in terms of a *numéraire* using a set of representative prices. Now in considering differential changes in e_i, the marginal social utilities of income β^i become simply:

$$\beta^i = \frac{\partial w^i}{\partial u_i} \frac{\partial f^i}{\partial e_i} = \beta^i(e_i)$$

---

[6] This result is proved in Goldman and Uzawa (1964).

The value of β^i depends only on e_i and not on the level of real income of others in the population. This adds considerable simplification to the computational problem. For discrete changes, the welfare change measure becomes:

$$\Delta W = \Sigma \, \bar{\beta}^i \Delta e_i \qquad (9.9)$$

where $\bar{\beta}^i$ is defined implicitly by

$$\bar{\beta}^i \Delta e_i = \int \beta^i(e_i) \, de_i \quad \text{or} \quad \bar{\beta}^i = \frac{\int \beta^i(e_i) \, de_i}{\Delta e_i}$$

Thus, $\bar{\beta}^i$ is a weighted average of the β^i over the range of e_i changes being considered. It depends only on e_i and not upon the value of the money metric for any other person. Thus, only the real income of those persons affected by a change need be known to measure the resulting welfare change.

A commonly used example of a social welfare function which is separable is the anonymous homothetic separable form:[7]

$$W = \Sigma \, \frac{(u_i)^{1-\rho}}{1 - \rho} \qquad (9.10)$$

We saw in chapter 5 that this general form arises when individual utilities are comparable by ratio scale and the SWF is separable. This form has the following properties:

(1) The parameter ρ reflects the degree of aversion to inequality in utilities. If $\rho = 0$, the SWF is the simple utilitarian form, Σu_i. As ρ increases, the SWF exhibits a more egalitarian ethic in the sense that social indifference curves in utility space become more convex. In the extreme, $\rho = \infty$ and the SWF becomes Leontief.[8] Figure 9.7 illustrates this for two persons.

(2) The SWF has a constant elasticity of marginal social utility. Thus

$$\frac{\partial W}{\partial u_i} \frac{u_i}{W} = 1 - \rho$$

(3) The marginal social utility itself may be written:

$$\frac{\partial W}{\partial u_i} = (u_i)^{-\rho}$$

[7] This form is discussed in the context of income distribution theory by Atkinson (1970) and has been used in applied welfare economics by Little and Mirrlees (1968) and their followers (e.g. Stern, 1972). It is analogous to the homothetic separable individual utility function analysed by Hicks (1965) and Arrow (1965).

[8] Note that when $\rho = 1$, W takes on the form $\Sigma \ln u_i$.

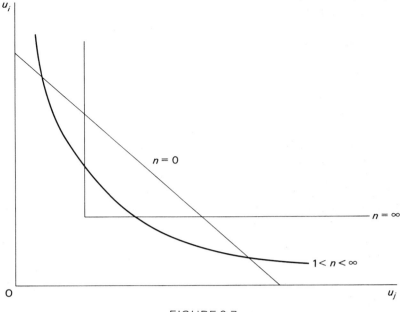

FIGURE 9.7

Thus for $\rho = 0$ this expression is unity, whereas for $\rho > 0$ it declines in u_i as expected. Note that it depends only upon u_i and not upon any other utility levels.

Now suppose that individual utility functions are all identical and that they are also isoelastic in terms of e_i:

$$u_i = f(e_i) = \frac{e_i^{1-\epsilon}}{1-\epsilon}$$

Here $1-\epsilon$ is the elasticity of the marginal utility of real income at the relative prices chosen.[9] Then $\partial f/\partial e_i = e_i^{-\epsilon}$. This is the individual's marginal utility of real income, and it declines in e_i provided $\epsilon > 0$.

Combining these two isoelastic functional forms, the marginal social utility of real income β^i may be derived as follows:

$$\beta^i = \frac{\partial W}{\partial u_i} \frac{\partial f}{\partial e_i} = u_i^{-\rho} e_i^{-\epsilon}$$

$$= \left(\frac{e_i^{1-\epsilon}}{1-\epsilon}\right)^{-\rho} e_i^{-\epsilon}$$

$$= K e_i^{-\sigma} \tag{9.11}$$

[9] If individual utility functions are homothetic, the value of $f(e_i)$ will be identical for all reference price vectors.

where K is a constant over all persons and $\sigma = \rho + \epsilon - \rho\epsilon \approx \rho + \epsilon$ is the elasticity of marginal social utility of income. Since K is the same for all persons, the SWF could be transformed to eliminate it. Then, welfare change in a many-person economy can be written:

$$\Delta W = \int \Sigma \beta^i \, de_i = \int \Sigma e_i^{-\sigma} \, de_i \qquad (9.12)$$

where σ is a parameter. This is a form which is often used in applied welfare economics.

The above techniques for calculating welfare change require that for each change one must measure real incomes for all those who are affected by the change. The assumption of separability implies that one can simply ignore those persons not affected. Even so, in some actual applications the computational difficulties can be immense. Welfare changes for all types of individuals affected must be calculated. It would be much simpler to treat applied welfare economics in many-person economies if aggregate market data could be used rather than data on individuals. There is a method for converting the above marginal social weights β^i into a set of weights applying to market transactions so that given these weights they can be applied to the market data by the practitioner. This makes the job of the applied welfare economics practitioner much simpler, given that the weights have been appropriately computed for the practitioner by, say, a central body.

The technique is as follows.[10] Consider a differential change in resource allocation. From (9.5) the change in welfare may be written:

$$dW = \sum_i \beta^i \, de_i \qquad (9.13)$$

where β^i is the marginal social utility of real income. The expenditure function can be defined for any set of prices, so let us suppose we use the prices in the new situation as the reference set. In that case de_i is just the CV of individual i from the change. If we suppose the change comes about purely from price changes, with income constant, then using the results from chapter 7, de_i may be written:

$$de_i = - \sum_j x_j^i(p, u^i) \, dp_j \qquad (9.14)$$

where $x_j^i(p, u^i)$ is the compensated demand for good j.
Substituting this expression for de_i into (9.13), we obtain:

$$dW = - \sum_i \sum_j \beta^i x_j^i \, dp_j$$

---

[10] This technique was introduced in the context of public utility pricing by Feldstein (1972a) and extended to cost–benefit analysis by Boadway (1976).

or

$$dW = - \sum_j R_j x_j \, dp_j \tag{9.15}$$

where x_j is the aggregate demand for commodity j and R_j is the *distribution characteristic* of good j defined as:

$$R_j = \frac{\sum\limits_i \beta^i x_j^i}{x_j}$$

The distribution characteristic is a weighted average of the β^i, where the weights reflect the proportion of aggregate demand for x_j consumed by household of type i. If β^i diminishes with real income, R_j would be higher for necessities than for luxuries. This is because for luxuries a low β^i would be associated with a high x_j^i/x_j and vice versa.

Notice that the welfare change measure advocated here involves weighting the aggregate CVs for each good whose price has changed by the appropriate distribution characteristic. If discrete changes are being evaluated, the R_j used would have to be some sort of average since it would generally change with changes in resource allocation.

The application of this sort of technique in a partial equilibrium setting has been developed by Harberger (1978). His approach can be illustrated

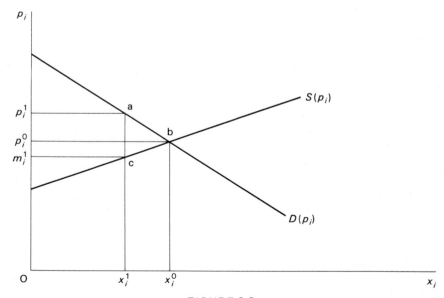

FIGURE 9.8

for the simple case of an excise tax applied to a market for commodity x_i.[11] Figure 9.8 illustrates. The curves $D(p_i)$ and $S(p_i)$ are the partial equilibrium demand and supply curves for x_i. Imagine introducing a tax on x_i when none existed before. The consumer price rises from p_i^0 to p_i^1, and the supply price falls to m_i^1. Consumer's surplus falls by $p_i^1 \mathrm{ab} p_i^0$; producer's surplus falls by $p_i^0 \mathrm{bc} m_i^1$; and the government obtains tax revenues of $p_i^1 \mathrm{ac} m_i^1$. In the absence of distributive weights, the net change in aggregate CV is (approximately) the negative of the triangular area abc.

When distributive weights are incorporated, these surplus losses and tax revenue gains cannot be simply added. There will be a distributive weight R_d associated with the consumers of x_i. This will be of the sort derived earlier. There will also be a distributive weight associated with the suppliers of x_i, denoted R_s. Finally, the tax revenue will have a distributive weight R_t. Applying these distributive weights, the change in social welfare becomes,

$$\Delta W = - R_d (p_i^1 \mathrm{ab} p_i^0) - R_s (p_i^0 \mathrm{bc} m_i^1) + R_t (p_i^1 \mathrm{ac} m_i^1)$$

This could clearly be positive or negative depending upon the relative magnitudes of R_d, R_s and R_t. For example, if high income persons tend to consume x_i while 'average' persons supply it and benefit from the tax revenues, R_d would be smaller than R_s and R_t and the welfare change could well be positive.

Harberger then goes on to consider the evaluation of changes in tax rates and the determination of the optimal tax rate incorporating both equity and efficiency considerations. However, since no new methodological insights are gained, we do not pursue the analysis further.

7 The Use of Aggregate Income Distribution Statistics

There are a number of conventional ways of characterizing income distributions. These are often used as summary statistics for evaluating inequality in the distribution of income or for evaluating the distributive impact of, say, tax policy changes. They include the Gini coefficient, or its graphical counterpart the Lorenz curve, the variance of incomes, the relative mean deviation, the standard deviation of logarithms of incomes and the like.[12] The question to be investigated in this section is the extent to which these summary measures correspond to orderings of alternative social states according to a social welfare function.

There are two approaches found in the literature. One is to identify the general properties that a social welfare function would have to possess

[11] This simple illustration does less than full justice to the contribution in Harberger's paper. He also discusses the use of distributive weights in the contexts of optimal taxation, cost–benefit analysis and progressive income taxation, as well as discussing the broader issues surrounding the use of distributive weights in the first place.

[12] A convenient summary of these measures may be found in Sen (1973).

K

in order, for example, to say that an income distribution whose Lorenz curve lies everywhere inside that of another is socially preferred. The following discussion will consider some examples of this approach. Typically, this analysis is concerned with income distribution comparisons which yield partial orderings of social states. In the above example, only those income distributions with Lorenz curves that do not cross are comparable.

The alternative approach is to derive the form of the social welfare function which would correspond exactly to the ranking of income distributions according to one of these summary statistics, assuming these statistics are measures of inequality in some sense. One common way to proceed is to use a measure of inequality defined by Atkinson (1970). Examples of this will be discussed at the end of this section.

In order to use income distribution statistics as welfare change measures, it is necessary to view individual income as an appropriate measure of individual welfare. We shall assume that to be the case. It is well known that if relative prices change, income will not be a satisfactory money metric for utility unless severe restrictions are placed on the utility function.[13] This difficulty can be circumvented by using the value of the expenditure function at a set of reference prices, and one may view the following analysis in that context. Yet another problem arises from the fact that most income distribution statistics are calculated for the flow of income measured over a specific period of time, say a year. In principle, a measure of lifetime income might be a more appropriate measure for utility. There are, of course, the additional problems of evaluating imputed consumption from leisure and other intangibles, which are simply ignored here.

In addition to requiring that the income measure used in income distribution statistics be an appropriate measuring rod of each individual's utility, it is necessary to assume that these income measures are comparable between persons. As pointed out in the previous section, one way of ensuring that this is the case is to assume that all persons have identical utility functions, and that is what is normally assumed in the literature. Alternatively, it is possible to amend the measure of income by systematic differences in individual or household characteristics which give rise to different required expenditures to reach a given utility level. Thus, equivalent income m^* could be given by actual income deflated by an *equivalence scale* where, as defined earlier, the latter gives the ratio of the costs required by a household to attain a given utility level to those required by the representative household.

In what follows we shall simply assume that the income measure accurately accounts for the above difficulties. We shall therefore assume that the social welfare function which is symmetric in utilities itself can be written as a symmetric function of incomes appropriately measured:

$$W = W(m_1, \ldots, m_H)$$

[13] This has been carefully established in Roberts (1980).

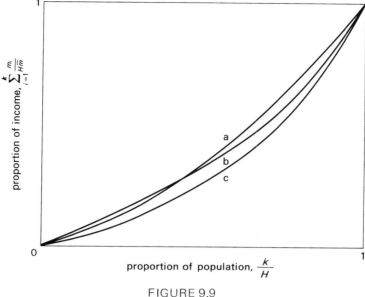

proportion of income, $\sum_{i=1}^{k} \frac{m_i}{H\bar{m}}$

proportion of population, $\dfrac{k}{H}$

FIGURE 9.9

A common way to depict an income distribution is by the Lorenz curve shown in figure 9.9. A Lorenz curve is obtained by ordering the population by income from lowest to highest and plotting a curve of the proportion of income earned to the proportion of population covered as one moves up the income scale. Algebraically, if the population is ranked by income so that $m_1 \leqslant m_2 \ldots \leqslant m_H$, then the Lorenz curve is a plot of

$$\sum_{i=1}^{k} \frac{m_i}{H\bar{m}} \quad \text{against} \quad \frac{k}{H}$$

as k goes from 1 to H, where $\bar{m}$ is average income and H is population size. According to the Lorenz curve ranking, one distribution is unambiguously preferred to another if its Lorenz curve lies everywhere northwest of the other. Thus, in figure 9.9, both distributions a and b are preferred to c. On the other hand, the ordering of distributions is partial since if the Lorenz curves intersect, neither can be said to be preferred. We cannot rank a and b by this criterion.

The question to be investigated is: What, if any, general sorts of social welfare functions provide the same partial ranking as the Lorenz curve rankings? It turns out that a number of interesting equivalences have been derived in the literature, all emanating from the original work of Atkinson (1970). The simplest results arise when comparisons are restricted to alternative income distributions with the same mean income and a given population size. The original result is due to Atkinson:

Atkinson's theorem   Suppose the social welfare function is utilitarian, so $W(m) = \Sigma u_i(m_i)$, and individual utility functions are strictly concave. Then, given $\bar{m}$, if the Lorenz curve of distribution 1 lies everywhere inside the Lorenz curve for distribution 2, social welfare will be higher under distribution 1 than 2.

Notice that the theorem does not state that the SWF must be utilitarian for this to be so. As we shall see shortly, it is only one of a more general class for which the property holds.

The proof of the Atkinson theorem will not be repeated here, but the intuition behind it is fairly straightforward. It can be shown that in moving from an income distribution such as c to one such as a in figure 9.9, it is always possible to break the move down into a sequence of changes involving the reallocation of income from a higher income person to a lower income person.[14] Each of these moves increases social welfare since, with diminishing marginal utility of income, the gain to the lower income person exceeds the loss to the higher. Thus, aggregating all these changes together, the sum of utilities must have increased.

As mentioned, the utilitarian SWF is not the only one which has this property. It can be shown that any SWF which is strictly quasi-concave in income will partially rank income distributions in the same manner as the Lorenz curve.[15] Recall that strict quasi-concavity implies that the social indifference curves in income space are strictly convex; that is, they put a premium on equality. This class of SWFs includes the utilitarian form as a special case, but is much more general than it. Indeed, it turns out that the class of SWFs which partially rank income distributions in the same way as the Lorenz curve is even more general than those which are strictly quasi-concave. It includes all those which are *Schur concave* where Schur concavity is defined as follows. Let B represent a square matrix $(H \times H)$ in which all entries are non-negative and all rows and columns sum to unity. This is called a bistochastic matrix. If a vector of incomes m is pre-multiplied by B, the result will be a vector of incomes which has the same sum as m, but which is distributed differently (assuming B is not the identity matrix). More particularly, imagine that the initial distribution $(m_1, \ldots, m_H)$ is permuted among alternative persons. Since the SWF is symmetric, this will not affect the level of social welfare. It can be shown that the vector Bm is a linear combination of the various possible permutations of m. A *Schur concave* SWF is defined to be one which has the property

$$W(Bm) > W(m)$$

---

[14]   For the details of this, see Atkinson (1970). Analytically, Lorenz dominance can be shown to be equivalent to a mean-preserving reduction in the spread of the outcomes of a statistical distribution, as discussed in Rothschild and Stiglitz (1970). The proof of these results is originally due to Hardy, Littlewood and Polya (1934).

[15]   Strict quasi-concavity in demand theory is the property which makes indifference curves strictly convex to the origin. It is unaffected by monotonic transforms, and so can be applied to ordinal functions. Similarly, the SWF is an ordinal function, so strict quasi-concavity is an unambiguous concept.

for any bistochastic matrix B which is not a permutation matrix. It can be shown that strict quasi-concavity is a special case of Schur concavity. One can think of a Schur-concave SWF as one which is 'equality preferring'. A further discussion of the Schur concavity concept may be found in Sen (1973).

The following theorem is attributable to Dasgupta, Sen and Starrett (1973):

Dasgupta–Sen–Starrett's theorem   One income distribution m^1 has a Lorenz curve everywhere northwest of that of another distribution m^2 with the same mean $\bar{m}$ if, and only if, social welfare is higher under m^1 than m^2. $(W(m^1) > (W(m^2))$ for all Schur concave SWFs.

The proof may be found in Dasgupta, Sen and Starrett (1973). It uses some results from the mathematics literature which imply that if the Lorenz curve for m^1 is northwest of that for m^2 (so the distribution is unambiguously preferred) then m^1 can be obtained by premultiplying m^2 by some bistochastic matrix.[16]

Remarkable though this result may seem, its applicability is still rather limited. For one thing, we still only obtain a partial ordering from the Lorenz criterion. For another, the above results are applicable only for income distribution comparisons having the same mean income and population. Ideally, we would like a more general statistic than that. Let us deal with the latter point first, the extension to variable means and populations.

In most circumstances in which we make income distribution comparisons, mean income is likely to vary from one distribution to another. This is certainly true of cross-country comparisons, and also of comparisons before and after policy changes. It would seem reasonable to assume that if one income distribution was unambiguously more equally distributed than another according to the Lorenz criterion, and if mean income were also higher, then social welfare ought to be higher. Shorrocks (1983) has argued that this will be true wherever the SWF is Schur concave and increasing in incomes. However, the ranking obtained over social states is still quite limited since the dual criteria of Lorenz dominance and higher mean income must be satisfied. It would not, for example, allow one to judge redistributive changes in which efficiency losses occurred in the process of redistribution.

Fortunately, the ability of Lorenz curves to provide social rankings when mean income is allowed to change can be improved somewhat once we extend the concept of Lorenz curves to incorporate mean income changes. Following Shorrocks (1983), the *generalized Lorenz curve* can be defined as the product of the mean of the distribution $\bar{m}$ and the value of the ordinate of the ordinary Lorenz curve. Thus, the generalized Lorenz curve is a plot of

$$\bar{m} \sum_{i=1}^{k} \frac{m_i}{H\bar{m}} \quad \text{against} \quad \frac{k}{H}$$

---

[16]   A simple three-person geometric illustration of the theorem may be found in Sen (1973).

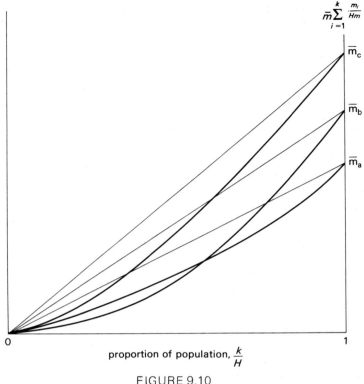

$$\bar{m}\sum_{i=1}^{k}\frac{m_i}{Hm}$$

$\bar{m}_c$

$\bar{m}_b$

$\bar{m}_a$

0   1

proportion of population, $\frac{k}{H}$

FIGURE 9.10

Figure 9.10 illustrates the notion of a generalized Lorenz curve for three alternative cases of a, b and c. According to the generalized Lorenz criterion, one social state is preferred to another if its generalized Lorenz curve lies everywhere to the northwest of the other. Thus, c is preferred to both a and b. Its larger mean income is more than enough to compensate for whatever differences in income distribution may exist. The ordering remains partial, however, since the generalized Lorenz curves for a and b intersect and hence cannot be ordered. The larger mean at b, $\bar{m}_b$, is not enough to overcome the fact that the distribution at b is not necessarily preferred to that at a.

Shorrocks (1983) has proved a rather interesting result which extends the Dasgupta–Sen–Starrett theorem to variable mean comparisons. It is:

Shorrocks' theorem   One income distribution m^1 will have a generalized Lorenz curve everywhere northwest of that of another distribution m^2 (possibly with a different mean) if and only if social welfare is higher under m^1 than m^2 for all Schur concave increasing SWFs.

The use of generalized Lorenz curves thus increases the ability to order income distributions to allow those with varying means. We are still, however, left with a partial ordering.

The results obtained so far are also restricted to given populations. One may wish to compare welfare levels in economies with differing populations. This, of course, raises issues of fundamental philosophical importance which we are unlikely to resolve here. We shall simply point out a result obtained in the context of the literature being discussed. Suppose that the ordering of social states depends upon per caput welfare in some sense rather than aggregate welfare. The distinction, of course, is only relevant if population varies. Sen (1973) has used the notion of a symmetry axiom for population which states, essentially, that social welfare will not change if the existing population is replicated. Formally, $W^{rH}(m, m, m, \ldots, m) = W^H(m)$ for all r, where rH is the population obtained when H persons (with a vector of income m) are replicated r times. As Sen (1973) and Shorrocks (1983) have proved, all the above theorems apply to the case of variable populations when the SWF has this property.

We are still left with a partial ordering when using the criterion of Lorenz curve dominance or generalized Lorenz curve dominance. It remains to consider how we can use income distribution statistics so as to obtain complete orderings and what SWFs these orderings would be consistent with.

We begin, following Atkinson (1970), by defining a particular measure of inequality or equality, the one being the obverse of the other. Consider the social indifference curves in income space in figure 9.11 illustrating the two-person case. Suppose that income is distributed as at x with $m_1 > m_2$. The mean income associated with x is shown as $\bar{m}$ along the 45° line. Atkinson has suggested measuring inequality in the following way. Define the equally distributed equivalent income m_e as that amount of income which, if given equally to all persons, would provide the same level of social welfare as at x. Thus, m_e is defined implicitly by:

$$W(m_e, m_e, \ldots, m_e) = W(m_1, m_2, \ldots, m_H)$$

Then the measure of inequality is defined by Atkinson as:

$$I(m) = 1 - \frac{m_e}{\bar{m}} \tag{9.16}$$

As is apparent, $I(m)$ will be greater the greater is the curvature of the social indifference curve. It will be bounded by 0 (when $m_e = \bar{m}$) and 1. Since most inequality measures that are conventionally used are mean independent, suppose we restrict our analysis to cases in which the Atkinson inequality measure is mean independent. This may be interpreted as requiring that if all incomes increase proportionately (so that the mean does as well), the inequality measure must remain unchanged. In the diagram, as x changes to x^1, we require that $m_e^1/\bar{m}^1 = m_e/\bar{m}$. It is apparent that this will occur only if the SWF is homothetic in incomes. Also, it is usually assumed that the SWF is anonymous. This implies that it is sym-

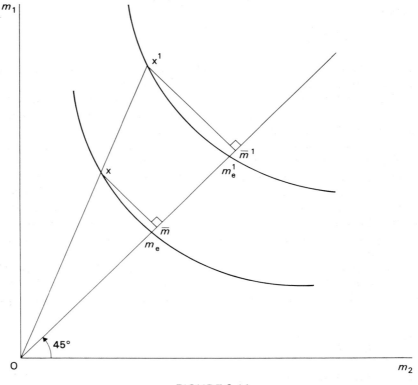

FIGURE 9.11

metric in income space if, as we assume, all persons have identical utility functions. We shall restrict our analysis to the case of symmetric homothetic SWFs.

The Atkinson inequality index $I(m)$ thus defined can then be shown to be consistent with a specific SWF as follows.[17] From the inequality index (9.16),

$$m_e = \bar{m}(1 - I(m))$$

Therefore, from the definition of m_e:

$$W(m_1, \ldots, m_H) = W(m_e, \ldots, m_e)$$
$$= W(\bar{m}(1 - I(m)), \ \bar{m}(1 - I(m)), \ldots, \bar{m}(1 - I(m)))$$

[17] The original discussion of the relationship between inequality measures and the SWF was due to Atkinson (1970). The technical analysis for deducing SWF forms from specific inequality measures was developed by Blackorby and Donaldson (1978) and applied to several cases. See also Shorrocks (1981).

Since the SWF is simply an ordering, the value of W can clearly be transformed so that

$$W(m_1, \ldots, m_n) = \bar{m}(1 - I(m)) \tag{9.17}$$

Thus, we have derived a fairly simple form for the SWF which will be consistent with an inequality measure $I(m)$. Given a specific form for $I(m)$, the SWF giving the same ordering of income distributions can be derived from (9.17). We have to be very careful about exactly what is implied by this derivation. The statistical inequality measures we shall talk about are ones which will give a complete ranking of income distributions of a given mean. Obviously, $\bar{m}(1 - I(m))$ will give the same ranking as $(1 - I(m))$ whenever $\bar{m}$ is held constant. In that sense, we are moving beyond the Lorenz curve type of comparisons which only gave a partial ordering of distributions of equal mean. We shall return to the question of variable mean distributions shortly. First, it is useful to consider the SWFs that would be generated by the above measure for specific forms of $I(m)$. The following analysis is due to Blackorby and Donaldson (1978).

Consider first the Gini coefficient, a well-known index of inequality which measures the area between the diagonal in figure 9.10 and the Lorenz curve. The formula for the Gini coefficient can be shown to equal[18]

$$G = 1 + \frac{1}{H} - \frac{2}{H^2 \bar{m}} (m_1 + 2m_2 + \ldots + .Hm_H)$$

where individuals are ordered so $m_1 \geqslant m_2 \geqslant m_3 \ldots \geqslant m_H$. The Gini coefficient has the property that it is bounded by 0 and (approximately) 1. If G is substituted for $I(m)$ in (9.17), the SWF which would rank equal income distributions the same as the Gini coefficient is:

$$W(m) = (m_1 + 3m_2 + 5m_3 + \ldots + (2H - 1) m_H)/H^2 \tag{9.18}$$

It has the unfortunate property that it is linear in income changes which do not affect the ranking of persons. In the two-person case this gives rise to social indifference curves as shown in figure 9.12.

Another inequality measure might be the coefficient of variation, which is defined as:

$$V = \frac{\left(\sum_{i=1}^{H} (m_i - \bar{m})^2 \right)^{1/2} \Big/ H}{\bar{m}} = \frac{\sigma}{\bar{m}} \tag{9.19}$$

where σ^2 is the variance of the distribution. To ensure that it falls between the limits 0 and 1, it must be divided by $\sqrt{H}$.[19] From the definition of

[18] The derivation of this formula is discussed in Sen (1973).
[19] This case is also discussed by Deaton and Muellbauer (1980).

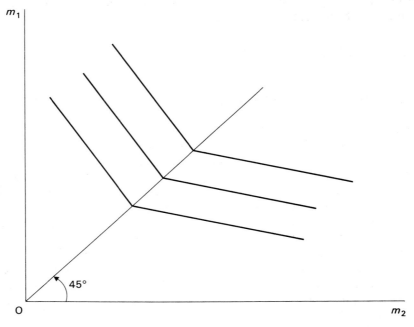

FIGURE 9.12

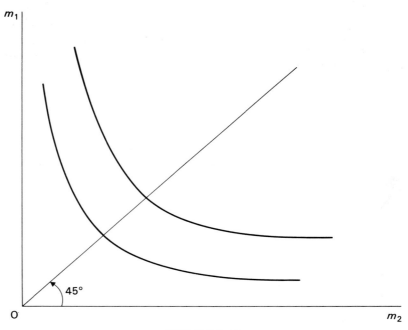

FIGURE 9.13

the SWF in (9.17), an SWF which will give equivalent rankings of income distributions of identical means is as follows:

$$W(m) = \bar{m} - \frac{\sqrt{(\Sigma(m_i - \bar{m})^2)}}{H} \qquad (9.20)$$

These give rise to the social indifference contours of figure 9.13, which are symmetric parabolas around the 45° line.

Other properties of inequality measures are discussed in Atkinson (1970) and Sen (1973). It is, however, worth noting that the above discussion remains incomplete for two reasons. First, the inequality measures themselves give only partial rankings since they will completely rank only those distributions having equal means. Secondly, as Shorrocks (1981) has pointed out, the above simple form of the SWF given by the mean income multiplied by the measure of equality $(1 - I(m))$ is not the only form which will rank equal mean distributions in the same way as particular indexes of inequality. It just happens to be the SWF that is derived when one uses Atkinson's definition of the inequality measure. There are certainly other ways of defining an index of inequality so that it has the properties required of it. As Shorrocks points out, we could define $I(m)$ by a function $\phi(\bar{m}, m_e)$ with $\partial\phi/\partial\bar{m} < 0$, $\partial\phi/\partial m_e > 0$ and which will be independent of the mean of the distribution for proportionate increases in all incomes (i.e. homothetic of degree zero in $\bar{m}$ and m_e). If we do so, the SWF that will be recovered by following the above procedure will differ from those obtained above.[20] Therefore, it is incorrect to say that income distribution statistics of a particular sort imply a particular social welfare function. Income distribution statistics do not go beyond equal mean comparisons. For a complete ranking of social states, there is no alternative but to specify a full SWF.

---

[20] For example, starting with $I(m) = \phi(\bar{m}, m_e)$, we obtain by inversion $m_e = \phi^{-1}(\bar{m}, I(m))$. From the definition of m_e,

$$W(m_1, \ldots, m_H) = W[\phi^{-1}(\bar{m}, I(m)), \phi^{-1}(\bar{m}, I(m)), \ldots)$$
$$= \phi^{-1}(\bar{m}, I(m)) \text{ by normalization of } W$$

CHAPTER 10

Cost-Benefit Analysis

1 Introduction

In its broadest sense, the term 'cost–benefit analysis' can refer to the measurement of the economic costs and benefits from any change in resource allocation in the economy. As such it is the application of the tools of applied welfare economics already developed in the preceding three chapters. The interpretation of cost–benefit analysis which we are adopting in this chapter is the narrower, more conventional one of evaluating the net benefits to society from a specific investment project. In fact, our focus will be narrower still since we shall deal primarily with 'small' projects; that is, projects which have no perceptible effects on the market prices for goods and factors of production in the economy.

It might be thought that a project's private profitability is an accurate measure of its effect on social welfare. If so, the cost–benefit analyst would only be required to measure the private profits of a project. There are several reasons why private profitability may not coincide with 'social profitability', and we begin by listing those reasons. Essentially these are reasons why market prices at which projects buy and sell their inputs and outputs do not coincide with marginal social costs and benefits.

(1) In a many-consumer economy, market prices will not reflect marginal social values if income is not optimally distributed. In principle this can be accounted for by using a system of distributive weights as discussed in chapter 9. Such a procedure has been advocated in a number of cost–benefit manuals (e.g. Little and Mirrlees, 1968) and requires prior agreement on the social welfare function. Much of the literature on cost–benefit analysis, and most of the issues we wish to deal with here, are involved with using 'efficiency' criteria for project evaluation. Consequently, we shall assume for the purposes of this chapter that the economy can be treated as if all persons are identical, so that no distributive weights are needed.

(2) Project prices will not coincide with marginal social values when the commodities are transacted in distorted markets. For example, if an input is purchased in a market which is distorted due to taxes or the presence of monopoly power, the purchase price will not reflect the true opportunity cost of drawing the input out of the private sector. It

is therefore appropriate to evaluate such inputs at a price different from their market price. The appropriate price is the marginal opportunity cost of the input and is referred to as the *shadow price*. Shadow pricing techniques are discussed in section 3.

(3) The project may also cause changes in output in markets other than those in which it directly transacts. The existence of distortions elsewhere, as the analysis of the theory of second best discussed in chapter 8 shows, gives rise to indirect welfare effects which must be included in the cost–benefit calculation.

(4) Some inputs and outputs of a project may not be transacted in markets and therefore no corresponding market prices exist for them. This may be true if the project output is of the nature of a public good or if it produces external benefits or costs which are not captured in the price mechanism. Benefits and costs of such 'intangibles' cannot be observed directly from market prices, but must then be inferred from other information, market or otherwise.

(5) If a project's output is produced with increasing returns to scale then, as a consequence of *Euler's theorem*, operating the project at marginal cost pricing would imply operating at a loss.[1] Nevertheless, it may be socially beneficial to introduce the project.

(6) There may be distortions in capital markets which affect the efficiency with which resources are allocated intertemporally. For one thing, the market interest rate may not reflect the rate at which society discounts future versus present consumption, the so-called *social discount rate*, if there are capital market distortions. These distortions may take the form of taxes on capital income or imperfections in the ability of individuals to borrow against future income. In addition, there may be externalities involved in the act of saving arising out of interdependent utility functions between generations. Also, if risk is not allocated efficiently in the economy, resources will not be efficiently allocated intertemporally. We shall discuss the implications of these distortions below.

In the space available we cannot provide an exhaustive treatment of all these issues. Instead, we shall discuss representative types of analysis in order to illustrate the sorts of problems which might arise and to indicate how these problems might be handled on the basis of the principles of welfare economics that have been developed in preceding chapters. We begin in the next section with a discussion of the *decision rule* that project evaluators should use. This is followed by a discussion of the problems inherent in measuring benefits and costs as they accrue. Finally, the

---

[1] Euler's theorem says that if a function $y = f(x_1, \ldots, x_n)$ is homogeneous of degree r so that for any positive constant λ, $\lambda^r y = f(\lambda x_1, \ldots, \lambda x_n)$, then $ry = \Sigma x_i \, \partial f/\partial x_i$. If y is output and x_i are inputs, and if we multiply through by the output price, we obtain $rpy = \Sigma w_i x_i$, where w_i is the factor price of x_i (assumed to equal $p \, \partial f/\partial x_i$ for the marginal cost pricing firm). In other words, total cost equals r times total revenues. If there are increasing returns to scale, $r > 1$ and total cost exceeds total revenue.

intertemporal problems concerning the choice of a discount rate and the treatment of risk are considered.

2 The Appropriate Decision Rule

When a project is undertaken, it causes a reallocation of resources in the economy. The project itself draws inputs from the rest of the economy which are used to produce output. In addition to the outputs and inputs directly associated with the project, there will typically be a rearrangement of demands and supplies in other markets through the interconnections of the general equilibrium system. Both the direct effects of project and the indirect effects may occur over several periods of time. The role of the project evaluator is to obtain an aggregate measure that indicates by how much society is better off or worse off with the project in place. This aggregate measure is obtained by evaluating each and every direct and indirect effect of the project in terms of some *numéraire*.

The conventional way to proceed is in two steps. First, the direct and indirect effects are evaluated in each period at current values or prices. In the case of direct resource allocation effects, inputs used in the project are evaluated at their social opportunity cost; that is, at the true cost to society incurred by drawing the resources from alternative uses. Similarly, the value of outputs is the benefit to society from having the additional outputs. The value of the indirect effects is the welfare change to society from the resource reallocations induced elsewhere by the project. These evaluations are done for every relevant time period and yield a stream of net benefits, denoted NB_t, in current values for each period $t = 0, \ldots, T$, where T is the last period that the project affects benefits and costs (which could be infinity).

Secondly, this stream of net benefits must be aggregated in some common unit. This is done by expressing all values in the units of a common *numéraire*. For the purposes of this chapter, the *numéraire* is assumed to be present (time period zero) consumption, but there is no reason in principle why one cannot use consumption in any period as the *numéraire*. The conversion of future consumption values to present consumption values is done using the discount rate at which society is willing to transform present into future consumption. If capital markets were perfect and free of distortions and externalities, that discount rate would simply be the market interest rate. If not, the appropriate discount rate (the social discount rate) would have to be imputed according to the principles discussed in section 4. The aggregation of current values to present values using the social discount rate yields the *net present value* of the project, denoted NPV. Algebraically:

$$NPV = \sum_{t=0}^{T} \frac{NB_t}{(1 + r)^t} \tag{10.1}$$

where r is the (one-period) social discount rate. For simplicity we assume that r is constant over time, although there is no particular reason why it should be.

The sign of the NPV indicates whether or not society would be better off with the project in place. However, it does more than that. The magnitude of the NPV indicates by how much society is better off, in terms of present consumption. The project evaluator can therefore compare projects and rank them in terms of their contribution to social welfare. This is important from a practical point of view, since it means that a positive NPV is not a sufficient criterion for a project to be undertaken. If there are a number of mutually exclusive projects, the one with the highest NPV should be undertaken in order to maximize social welfare.

The existence of mutually exclusive alternatives is more common than one might first suspect. For one thing, if the project can be undertaken at various scales, these themselves constitute mutually exclusive alternatives. Likewise, if the project can be undertaken at different times it should be introduced at the time at which its NPV is a maximum. More generally, indivisible projects such as transportation facilities often involve mutually exclusive alternatives.

The relationship between the NPV and the social discount rate r can be depicted geometrically. A typical project might incur a capital cost early on and yield a stream of benefits throughout its life. If so, NB is negative in early periods and positive thereafter. In this case, the NPV curve for a project will intersect the horizontal axis once, as shown in figure 10.1 for projects A and B.[2] The ranking of projects A and B would depend upon the discount rate. At $r < r_e$, project A would be preferred to project B, and vice versa for $r > r_e$.

Sometimes project returns are summarized by an *internal rate of return*. This is defined as the discount rate which would make the NPV equal to zero. It is given by the value of λ which satisfies the following equation:

$$\sum_{t=0}^{T} \frac{NB_t}{(1 + \lambda)^t} = 0 \tag{10.2}$$

In figure 10.1, λ_a and λ_b indicate the internal rates of return of projects A and B. The internal rate of return criterion for project selection suggests that if $\lambda > r$ a project should be undertaken, whereas if there is more than one mutually exclusive project, the one with the highest λ should be chosen.

Ranking projects by the relative sizes of λ is unreliable, as the example of figure 10.1 indicates. Since $\lambda_b > \lambda_a$, the internal rate of return criterion would always select project B over project A, whereas in present value terms A would be preferable at discount rates below r_e. The difficulty

---

[2] This is a well known mathematical theorem on polynomial equations.

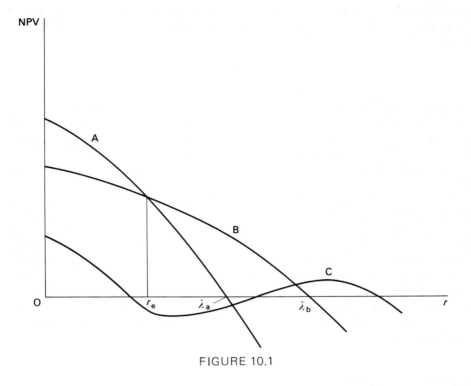

FIGURE 10.1

stems from the fact that the internal rate of return criterion makes no
direct use of the social discount rate. An equivalent way to see this point
is to note that if project A is preferred to project B on the basis of the
NPV criterion and if the social discount rate is the market interest rate, it
would always be possible to undertake a series of capital market transactions at the discount rate r so as to obtain a stream of consumption
from A's stream of net benefits which *dominates* B's stream of net
benefits.

A simple numerical example illustrates this point. Consider two projects
A and B which have the following streams of net benefits:

	Year 0	Year 1	Year 2
Project A	− 1000	550	634
Project B	− 1000	1150	0

The internal rate of return λ for A is 12 per cent and for B 15 per cent;
thus this criterion would rank B above A. However, if the discount rate r
is 5 per cent, then the NPV of project A (100) will exceed that of project
B (95). If funds can be borrowed and lent at a rate of interest of 5 per
cent, the stream of net benefits of project A can be converted into a
stream of consumption benefits through capital market transactions which

dominate the stream of net benefits from B. For example, if 600 is borrowed in year 1 at 5 per cent and paid back in year 2, A's stream is converted to

Year 0	Year 1	Year 2
-1000	1150	4

Obviously, this benefit stream dominates that of B. In general, it will always be possible to use capital market transactions to convert the stream of benefits from a project with a higher NPV into a stream which dominates the stream of net benefits of a project with a lower NPV. In this sense, the internal rate of return criterion can be said to ignore the social costs of finance.

Figure 10.1 illustrates yet another difficulty with the internal rate of return criterion. For Project C, the NPV does not monotonically decline as r rises. In fact, there are three discount rates at which NPV $= 0$, and therefore three internal rates of return. The possibility of multiple solutions to (10.2) exists because that equation is a polynomial of degree T. As our previous discussion makes clear, these multiple solutions occur only if the sign of the net benefit stream changes more than once. If so, the internal rate of return criterion is ambiguous if one solution is above r and the other below. For most practical applications this is unlikely to be a difficulty.

3 Evaluating the Net Benefits of a Project

For the purposes of this section we shall ignore intertemporal considerations and discuss how, in principle, one evaluates the welfare effects in a given period of introducing a project. When a project is introduced into the economy, it will alter the entire equilibrium allocation of resources. Our purpose is to evaluate the costs and benefits of that change. We have already discussed in chapter 8 the methodology for evaluating a welfare change in a single-person economy. Project evaluation is just an application of that methodology.

Consider the general expression for welfare change derived in chapter 8, section 7 and referred to as Harberger's measure of welfare change (e.g. (8.25)). For differentially small changes it may be written:

$$dW = \Sigma (p_i - t_i) \, dz_i + \Sigma t_i \, dx_i \qquad (10.3)$$

where x_i is the consumption of commodity i, z_i is the project production (the rest of x_i being produced, say, in the private sector), p_i is the consumer price of x_i and t_i is the distortion that exists in the market for good i. This distortion could be a tax, or it could be anything else which causes the consumer price p_i to differ from the producer price or marginal cost $p_i - t_i$. Of course, t_i could be negative, as in the case of a subsidy. The project quantities dz_i will be positive for outputs supplied and negative for inputs demanded. Note that this expression implicitly assumes that all inputs and outputs of the project are traded in markets and have observable market prices. If not, then $p_i - t_i$ could be thought of as the shadow (or imputed) cost of the good to society.

Generally, it is the case that the project operates directly in only a small number of the many markets in the economy. For all others, $dz_j = 0$. It is useful to rewrite (10.3) so as to differentiate between those markets that the project affects directly and those that it affects only indirectly. Suppose we use subscript i to index the former and subscript j the latter. Then (10.3) can be written:

$$dW = \sum (p_i - t_i)\, dz_i + \sum t_i\, dx_i + \sum_{j \neq i} t_j\, dx_j \qquad (10.4)$$

The first two terms on the right-hand side of (10.4) represent the direct effects of the project on the markets in which it operates and form the basis for shadow pricing rules. The last term represents the indirect effects. We shall discuss each of these in turn in the following subsections. This discussion will be followed by a brief discussion of the special problems that arise when no market prices exist for project inputs and/or outputs.

Notice first of all that if no distortions exist in the economy, the welfare change expression (10.3) would reduce to simply $dW = \sum p_i\, dz_i$; that is, the welfare change of the project is evaluated using market prices p_i as shadow prices. Private profitability would coincide with social profitability. It is precisely because of existing distortions that project evaluators cannot rely on private profit changes as an indication of social welfare.

3.1 Shadow pricing of purchases on distorted markets

Consider the effect on social welfare of a project using an input z_k which is traded in a distorted market. We shall derive an expression for the shadow price of z_k which corresponds to the shadow pricing rule advocated by Harberger (1972). From (10.4), the social welfare effect of a change in z_k will be given by:

$$\frac{\partial W}{\partial z_k} = p_k - t_k + t_k \frac{\partial x_k}{\partial z_k} + \sum_{j \neq k} t_j \frac{\partial x_j}{\partial z_k} \qquad (10.5)$$

In the case in which z_k is an input purchased, this will be the opportunity cost to society of the project removing an increment of z_k from the market. (Note that since z_k is measured negatively for an input, $\partial W/\partial z_k$ actually represents a small *reduction* in the use of z_k by the project.) The first three terms on the right-hand side constitute the direct effect of a change in z_k and will be referred to as the *shadow price* of z_k. The last term involving the summation is the indirect effect in other markets and will be dealt with in the next section.

Denoting the shadow price of z_k by s_k, we can express it as:

$$s_k = p_k - t_k + t_k\, \partial x_k / \partial z_k \qquad (10.6)$$

The shadow price could be used in this form provided one can observe the prices p_k and t_k and the response of the market for x_k to an exogenous change in the demand for commodity k by the project. It is useful to alter this expression slightly by writing $\partial x_k / \partial z_k$ in another form. Suppose we take a partial equilibrium point of view and think of the demand for x_k as depending primarily upon its own price p_k. Similarly, the non-project supply y_k depends upon the supply price $p_k - t_k$. Market equilibrium for commodity k is given by:

$$x_k(p_k) = y_k(p_k - t_k) + z_k \qquad (10.7)$$

This equation determines p_k in terms of t_k and z_k. Differentiating (10.7) with respect to z_k holding t_k constant, we obtain:

$$\frac{\partial p_k}{\partial z_k} = \frac{1}{x_k' - y_k'} \qquad (10.8)$$

where x_k' and y_k' are the price derivatives of demand and supply. The term $\partial x_k / \partial z_k$ in (10.6) can be rewritten as $(\partial x_k / \partial p_k)(\partial p_k / \partial z_k)$. Using (10.8) and this decomposition of $\partial x_k / \partial z_k$, (10.6) becomes:

$$
\begin{aligned}
s_k &= p_k - t_k + t_k x_k' / (y_k' - x_k') \\
&= \frac{(p_k - t_k)\, y_k' - p_k x_k'}{y_k' - x_k'}
\end{aligned}
\qquad (10.9)
$$

Equation (10.9) is known as Harberger's (1969) weighted average shadow pricing formula. It expresses the shadow price s_k as a weighted average of the supply price $(p_k - t_k)$ and the demand price p_k, where the weights are the proportions in which a change in net output of k by the project results in a reduced supply on the one hand and an increased demand on the other.[3] Or, if k is an input used by the project, the weights are the proportions in which the project use comes from an increased supply in the market on the one hand and a reduced demand on the other. Denoting the elasticity of demand by $\eta_k (= x'p/x)$ and the elasticity of supply by $\epsilon_k (= y'(p-t)/y)$, (10.9) may be written in the following form:

$$s_k = \frac{\epsilon_k - \eta_k}{\epsilon_k / (p_k - t_k) - \eta_k / p_k} \qquad (10.10)$$

---

[3] To see this, note that $\partial x_k / \partial z_k = (\partial x_k / \partial p_k)(\partial p_k / \partial z_k) = x_k' / (x_k' - y_k')$ using (10.8). This is just the weight on p_k. A similar derivation holds for $\partial y_k / \partial z_k$.

As the expression indicates, if supplies are perfectly elastic ($\epsilon_k \to \infty$) or demands are completely inelastic ($\eta_k = 0$), the shadow price is the supply price $p_k - t_k$. If demands are perfectly elastic ($\eta_k \to \infty$) or supplies are completely inelastic ($\epsilon_k = 0$), the shadow price is the demand price p_k.

The intuition behind this shadow pricing rule can be illustrated geometrically in terms of the simple supply and demand diagrams of figure 10.2 for the case in which z_k is an input purchased by the project. They show the market for x_k with an initial equilibrium with consumer price p_k^0 and demand x_k^0. When the project uses Δz_k of the input, the demand curve shifts to the right generating a new equilibrium price p_k^e with a non-project demand of x_k^e and a supply of y_k^e. The opportunity cost of the forgone demand is the area $x_k^e a b x_k^0$, the shaded area beneath the demand curve. The cost of the additional supply is $x_k^0 c d y_k^e$, the shaded area beneath the supply curve. The sum of these opportunity costs can be approximated by:

$$x_k^e \text{ab} x_k^0 + x_k^0 \text{cd} y_k^e \approx - p_k \Delta x_k + (p_k - t_k) \Delta y_k$$

The opportunity cost per unit of input (the shadow price) is thus

$$s_k = (p_k - t_k)\, \Delta y_k / \Delta z_k - p_k \Delta x_k / \Delta z_k \qquad (10.11)$$

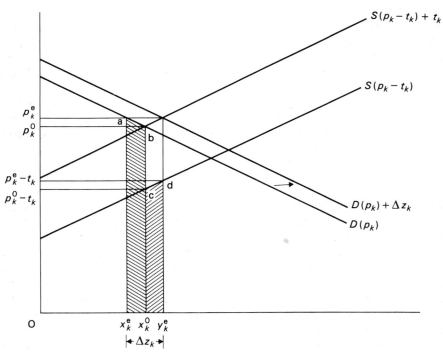

FIGURE 10.2

This is the Harberger weighted average formula. An analogous argument could be constructed to obtain the shadow benefit of additional output contributed to a distorted market. In this case, it is the supply curve which is shifted right rather than the demand curve.

Before considering the indirect effects of the project (the last term in (10.4)), it is worth briefly considering some applications of the weighted average shadow pricing rule. Three cases will be considered – the shadow price of foreign exchange. the shadow wage rate and the social cost of public funds.

Shadow price of foreign exchange   The analysis of figure 10.2 can readily be adapted to the case in which the input being purchased is a tradeable commodity in a tariff-distorted economy. Let us construct an example which allows us to treat traded goods as a composite commodity called *foreign exchange*, so that x_k can be interpreted as the quantity of foreign exchange demanded and p_k can be interpreted as the price of foreign exchange or the exchange rate.

Assume that the economy is small and open so that the world prices of exports and imports are fixed in units of foreign exchange. Suppose also that there is a common *ad valorem* tariff rate of τ on all imported goods. We denote by e the market price of foreign exchange. Since the world price of all exports is fixed, we can aggregate all types of exports into a composite commodity and think of e as being the domestic price of that composite commodity. Thus, the quantity of exports is defined as the amount that can be sold for one unit of foreign currency. The supply curve for exports can then be represented by a supply curve for foreign exchange at various exchange rate values, $S(e)$. Similarly, the domestic demand for imports can be represented by a demand curve $D(e(1 + \tau))$ showing the imports that would be purchased (in units of foreign exchange) at domestic price, $e(1 + \tau)$.

Now consider a project that requires an amount of foreign exchange ΔG, say, by using a traded commodity as an input. Applying Harberger's weighted average shadow pricing rule (10.11), we obtain the opportunity cost per unit of foreign exchange as:

$$s = e\Delta S/\Delta G - e(1 + \tau)\, \Delta D/\Delta G \qquad (10.12)$$

where ΔS is the additional foreign exchange generated by an induced increase in exports and ΔD is the use of foreign exchange forgone by others in the economy. This is the so-called shadow price of foreign exchange. Notice that in general $s > e$ since $\Delta D < 0$ and $\Delta S > 0$; there-fore, the shadow price of foreign exchange exceeds the market exchange rate due to the tariff distortion. That being the case, the use of a shadow exchange rate, relative to the use of a market exchange rate, will dis-courage the use of tradeable commodities as inputs, and encourage the production of tradeable outputs.

The above analysis can be readily extended to more general cases. For example, if the tariff rate varies by commodity, the shadow price formula would be:

$$s = e\Delta S/\Delta G - \Sigma e(1 + \tau_i) \, \Delta D_i/\Delta G$$

where D_i is the demand for the ith import.

The shadow wage rate   Labour market distortions can arise for a variety of reasons, some of which cause the shadow wage to differ from the market wage and some of which do not. The presence of income and payroll taxes will cause the wage rate paid by firms (the *gross wage*) to exceed that received by households (the *net wage*). Costs of moving from one location to another can introduce a wage differential for the same type of labour in different industries and in different regions. The existence of involuntary unemployment implies that the wage rate at which workers would be willing to work (the *supply price of labour*) is different from the market wage rate. Finally, the simple lack of a properly functioning labour market in developing countries allegedly gives rise to dual (or segmented) labour markets, one in the urban sector and one in the rural sector, each of which has a different wage rate.

Each of these phenomena can be properly accounted for by a careful application of the weighted average shadow pricing formula. The general principle is straightforward. Consider a project that hires workers at the going wage rate. To attribute the proper social cost to the workers hired, one must identify the alternative use to which the workers would have been put. Leaving aside the question of moving costs for the time being, the workers could be drawn from three sources. Some may have been employed elsewhere. The opportunity cost of this forgone demand elsewhere is the gross wage paid there, since that is presumed to be the value of their marginal product in other uses. Some may be drawn from the voluntarily unemployed. This represents an increase in the supply of labour and should be valued at the net wage since that was the amount actually required to induce the workers into the labour force. The remainder will be drawn from the involuntarily unemployed. The opportunity cost of employing each of these persons is their supply price of labour.

The shadow wage can thus be viewed as a weighted average of the gross wage, the net wage and the supply price of labour, the weights being the proportions in which labour is drawn from employment elsewhere, the voluntarily unemployed and the involuntarily unemployed, respectively. One of the difficulties with estimating the shadow wage (over and above having to estimate the proportions drawn from various sources) is that the supply price of labour is not observed in the market. The best we can do is to provide some bounds for it. We know that it must be below the net wage, for otherwise there could be no involuntary unemployment. On the other hand, it is presumably above zero assuming that leisure time has some value. Since the exact supply price cannot be observed, the project evaluator would probably end up having to choose an arbitrary number between the above bounds, and doing some sensitivity analysis with alternative values.

There are two potential complications that may arise in the application of the weighted average shadow pricing rule to labour markets. Both result from induced migration from one area to another. The first concerns the existence of wage differentials for the same type of labour in different locations, and the second concerns the potential complications that arise from alternative migration mechanisms. We consider each of these in turn.

The existence of wage differentials may be attributed to the costs of migration in moving from one location or industry to another, or, as is often alleged in developing countries,[4] may be due to improperly functioning labour markets. Costs of migration can take two forms – pecuniary and non-pecuniary. The former involves actual resource costs incurred from moving, and the latter involves the psychic or utility costs. In either case, ignoring unemployment, the wage rate paid on a project must exceed the wage rate in the location from which the labour is drawn by the cost of migration of the marginal worker. Thus, in equilibrium there will be a wage differential $w_a - w_b = m$ where w_a is the project wage, w_b is the wage rate elsewhere and m is the migration cost. In this case, the opportunity cost of hiring a worker from the alternative location is the forgone output w_b plus the cost of moving m; that is, the shadow wage rate is simply the wage rate paid on the project, w_a.

If, on the other hand, the wage differential arises from segmentation (dualism) in the labour market for, say, institutional reasons, a different result is obtained. In this case, w_a would exceed w_b but the differential would not reflect a cost of migration because wage rates do not act as equilibrating devices. In this case, if a project worker hired at the wage w_a is drawn from the other industry, the forgone output would be w_b and that would be the shadow wage rate. In other words, the shadow wage rate could be significantly below the wage paid by the project. This is the procedure advocated in some influential project evaluation manuals for developing countries (e.g. Little and Mirrlees, 1968, and Dasgupta, Marglin and Sen, 1972).

In the dual labour market example, the wage differential is more or less arbitrarily imposed on the economy and does not reflect equilibrium in the labour market. Economists have not been content with this rather arbitrary view of the workings of labour markets, because if such wage differentials did exist and did not reflect migration costs, self-interested workers would be induced to migrate from the low wage to the high wage location. The wage differential would be eliminated in equilibrium. This has led some authors to construct labour migration mechanisms which would yield an equilibrium with wage differentials. One such model has been proposed by Harris and Todaro (1970) and by Harberger (1971b). It is worth considering the implications of this model for the shadow pricing of labour in an economy with wage differentials.

---

[4] The classic argument to this effect may be found in Hagen (1958). This is the assumption that has been adopted in some well-known project evaluation manuals for developing countries, as discussed later.

The basic idea of the Harris–Todaro–Harberger model is quite simple. Suppose that the wage rate in A is artificially high for institutional reasons such as unions etc., but that the wage rate in B clears the labour market in B. There will be unemployment in A. If workers are free to migrate and care only about their expected wage rate (i.e. are risk neutral), labour market equilibrium will occur when the expected wage in A equals the actual and certain wage in B, so

$$\pi w_a = w_b \tag{10.13}$$

where π is the probability of obtaining employment for the marginal migrant. In simple models it is often assumed that employment is allocated randomly, in which case π is simply the ratio of total employment in A to the labour force in A. Given full employment in B, workers will migrate until (10.13) is satisfied. Since $w_a > w_b$ by the rigidity of wages in A, $\pi < 1$ at equilibrium. That is, an unemployment rate of $1 - \pi$ will exist in equilibrium.

Consider now the implications of this labour market mechanism for the shadow wage rate. Suppose a project creates a job in location A and that job is filled from the pool of unemployed. If the job is filled by random selection, then for each job created, $1/\pi$ workers will migrate from B to A in order to restore the equilibrium; that is, in order to keep the ratio of total jobs to total work force at π. The opportunity cost of drawing these $1/\pi$ workers from B is w_b each, for a total of w_b/π. By equation (10.13) this is just w_a, the wage paid by the project. In other words, by introducing this equilibrating migration mechanism, the shadow wage is just the market wage.

This approach can be applied in somewhat more complicated situations and different shadow pricing rules can result. Let us adopt the slightly more formal Harris–Todaro framework to the problem of obtaining shadow wage rates. Suppose the production functions in sectors A and B can be written as:

$$X_a = f_a(N_a) \tag{10.14}$$
$$X_b = f_b(N_b) \tag{10.15}$$

where we have suppressed all inputs other than labour for simplicity. Suppose further that output prices are taken as fixed and quantities of output are measured such that all prices are unity. For example, the economy may be small and open with prices determined in world markets. Wage rates in the two sectors are set equal to the values of the marginal product of labour so that:

$$w_a = f_a'(N_a) \tag{10.16}$$
$$w_b = f_b'(N_b) \tag{10.17}$$

Suppose w_a is fixed above the market clearing wage so that unemployment exists in sector A. Suppose also that jobs are filled randomly in that sector so that the probability of obtaining a job in A is $N_a/(N - N_b)$, where N is the total nationwide labour force. Suppose, finally, that the value that unemployed workers place on the leisure they obtain is given, in monetary units, by h and that there is a cost of migration from B to A equal to m, both of which are assumed constant for simplicity.[5]

Given these assumptions, migration equilibrium will occur when the wage rate for the fully employed workers in B equals the expected income, including the value of leisure, in A less the migration costs. This equilibrium condition may be written:

$$f_b'(N_b) = \frac{w_a N_a}{N - N_b} + \left(1 - \frac{N_a}{N - N_b}\right)h - m \tag{10.18}$$

Since w_a is fixed, N_a will be predetermined by (10.16). Therefore, the equilibrium condition (10.18) can be solved for N_b, the number of workers remaining in B.

Suppose now an extra job is created in A over and above the exogenous number of jobs N_a already existing. We can determine the migration response to this event by differentiating (10.18) with respect to N_a while holding all other exogenous variables fixed (N, w_a, h, m) and treating N_b as a function of N_a:

$$\frac{\partial N_b}{\partial N_a} = \frac{(w_a - h)}{(N - N_b) f_b''(N_b) - (w_a - h)\pi} \tag{10.19}$$

where π is the probability of employment in A, or $N_a/(N - N_b)$. Notice that if $f_b'' = 0$, $\partial N_b/\partial N_a = - 1/\pi$; that is, an additional job would attract $1/\pi$ migrants from B to A as in the simple example above. If $f_b'' < 0$, fewer than $1/\pi$ would be attracted.

The opportunity cost of creating the job in A can now be totalled up. It consists of the forgone output in B, $-w_b \partial N_b/\partial N_a$, the migration costs, $-m \partial N_b/\partial N_a$, less the additional value of leisure created, $-h(\partial N_b/\partial N_a + 1)$. Adding these up gives the shadow wage rate:

$$s = - (w_b + m - h) \partial N_b/\partial N_a + h \tag{10.20}$$

Suppose that $f_b'' = 0$ so that $1/\pi$ workers are attracted to A. Using the labour market equilibrium condition (10.18) together with the definitions of w_b and π, this expression for s reduces to w_a; that is, the shadow wage

5 A more realistic assumption might be that the cost of migration to the marginal worker rises with migration, reflecting the fact that the less attached migrants move first whereas others are induced to migrate by an increasing advantage from so doing. In terms of the model, m could be made a function of N_a with $\partial m/\partial N_a > 0$. This would complicate the analysis unduly, so we ignore it for simplicity.

is equal to the market wage and no adjustment is needed. Of course, if $f_b'' < 0$ so the migration response is less than $1/\pi$, the shadow wage rate s would be less than the market wage rate w_a.[6]

These examples illustrate the use of the weighted average shadow pricing rule applied to labour used in a project. It is obviously important to specify exactly how the labour market is assumed to operate; in particular, it is important whether or not wage differentials can be viewed as reflecting equilibrium in the labour market.

The opportunity cost of public funds   The final example of shadow pricing we consider is the opportunity cost of financing a project. If financing could be obtained in a lump-sum manner in an economy with no distortions, one pound of financing would have an opportunity cost of one pound. However, if distortions exist, or if the method of financing itself introduces distortions, a pound of financing has an opportunity cost exceeding one pound, the excess being the deadweight loss due to the financing. This deadweight loss should be included as one of the costs of introducing the project. In chapter 8 we considered the deadweight loss associated with the financing of a project using distortionary taxes. In this section, we consider another case which has been prominent in the cost–benefit analysis literature. It is the evaluation of the opportunity cost of financing a project with debt when capital markets are distorted. This example is interesting because it introduces the additional complication of intertemporal inefficiency of resource allocation into cost–benefit analysis.

Suppose that the rate of return on investment in the private sector exceeds the net return to savers r because a tax is levied on capital income. If capital markets are perfect so households can borrow and lend freely against their lifetime wealth, and if there are no externalities arising out of savings decisions, $1 + r$ will be the rate at which society discounts future versus present consumption. We refer to r as the social discount rate. This distorted capital market is depicted in figure 10.3. In the initial equilibrium, investment is I^0 with a rate of return ρ, and the return to savings after tax is shown as r. The difference between ρ and r is the tax rate t.

Consider a project requiring financing of B. If the project is financed by bonds, the demand for funds curve shifts right by the amount B causing the gross return to rise to ρ' and the return to savers to rise to r'. The bond financing partly crowds out investment by an amount $I^0 - I'$ and partly induces extra savings of $S' - I^0$. The question is: What is the opportunity cost per pound of financing?

Since increased saving is equivalent to reduced consumption, the opportunity cost of each pound of induced saving is just one pound in terms of forgone current consumption. (Equivalently, the present value of

---

[6]   It turns out also to be the case that if m were made an increasing function of N_a, this would tend to reduce the migration response and thereby reduce the shadow wage below the market wage in A.

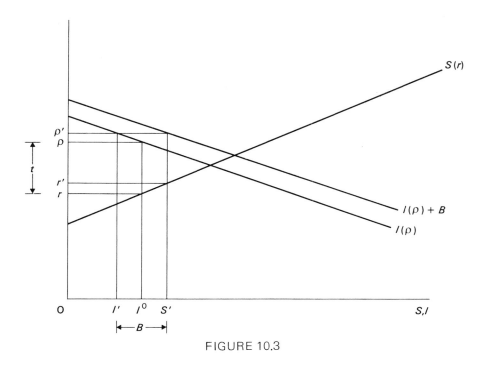

FIGURE 10.3

the stream of consumption the saving would have yielded to the consumer is just one pound.) The opportunity cost of forgone investment is a bit more complicated. The forgone investment would have yielded a stream of future consumption. The task is to identify and evaluate that stream.

Consider the simplest case analysed by Marglin (1963a) in which the return to investment in the private sector is entirely consumed. In this case, since the return to investment is ρ and is assumed to be constant, one pound of investment will yield a perpetual stream of consumption of ρ pounds per year. It is important to note that ρ is the rate of return after depreciation, and that returns covering depreciation are continually reinvested to maintain the initial capital investment intact. This perpetual stream of consumption must now be converted to an equivalent present value to make it comparable with current consumption. This is done by discounting it at the social discount rate r which is the rate at which society discounts future consumption. Since the present value of a perpetual stream of consumption ρ discounted at r is just ρ/r, this is the opportunity cost of one pound of forgone investment.[7]

---

[7] The present value of a perpetual stream of consumption is $\int_0^\infty e^{-rt}\rho \, dt$ which is just equal to ρ/r. A similar result is obtained in a discrete time framework, where

$$\sum_{t=1}^{\infty} \frac{\rho}{(1+r)^t} = \rho/r$$

The opportunity cost of one pound of financing will be a weighted average of the costs of forgone investment and forgone consumption, where the weights correspond to the proportions of financing coming from each source. The weights will depend upon the elasticities of the investment demand and savings supply curves, as is obvious from our discussion of the weighted average shadow pricing rule. Suppose we denote by θ the proportion of financing (whether by debt or taxes) coming at the expense of reduced investment elsewhere. Then, the opportunity cost of one pound of public funds, denoted a, is:

$$a = \theta\rho/r + (1 - \theta) \tag{10.21}$$

If it is assumed that $\theta > 0$ and $\rho > r$, a exceeds unity. We can think of $a - 1$ as the deadweight loss per pound of financing which must be included as a cost of the project.

The simplicity of this expression is partly a result of the simplifying assumptions we have made, especially those regarding the treatment of depreciation and the use of the net proceeds of the project. The stream of forgone consumption that results from reduced private sector investment would be more complicated if these assumptions were changed. For example, suppose that a proportion σ of the return to the project after depreciation is reinvested at the return ρ rather than consumed. Then one pound of initial investment will give rise to a growing stream of future consumption as the reinvestment augments the capital stock exponentially over time. In particular, the initial pound of capital stock will grow at the rate $\sigma\rho$ per period since a proportion σ of the return ρ is reinvested. Thus, at time t, the capital stock would be $e^{\sigma\rho t}$, assuming continuous time for simplicity.[8] The return to this capital at time t is $\rho\, e^{\sigma\rho t}$, of which $1 - \sigma$ will be consumed. Thus forgone future consumption at time t is $(1 - \sigma)\rho\, e^{\sigma\rho t}$ which, when discounted at the social discount rate r, gives a present value of $(1 - \sigma)\rho/(r - \sigma\rho)$. In this case the opportunity cost of public funds is:

$$a = \frac{\theta(1 - \sigma)\,\rho}{r - \sigma\rho} + (1 - \theta) \tag{10.22}$$

In a similar way we could determine the stream of consumption that results if private sector investments were allowed to depreciate rather than being maintained; that is, if that part of the return covering some of the depreciation were consumed. We shall return to this below.

We have already mentioned how the cost of financing should be incorporated into cost–benefit analysis. The deadweight loss of the financing should be treated as a cost of the project. Thus, following the

---

[8] Under discrete time analysis, the capital stock at time t would be $(1 + \sigma\rho)^t$. The same qualitative results for the cost of public funds can be derived as in the continuous case.

analysis of Feldstein (1972b), the following present value rule could be used:

$$\text{NPV} = \sum_{t=0}^{T} \frac{\text{NB}_t - (a-1) D_t}{(1+r)^t} \qquad (10.23)$$

where NB_t is the benefits of the project net of resource costs, r is the social discount rate, D_t is the financing requirements of the project and $a-1$ is the deadweight loss per pound of financing. In principle, D_t could be positive or negative in a given year, and this formula implicitly assumes that revenues earned on a project are returned to the economy with a symmetrical reduction in deadweight loss of $a-1$.

The general present value rule (10.23) reduces to some well-known special cases when particular assumptions are made. We present a simple example based on the work of Bradford (1975) to illustrate some of these special cases. Consider the case of a project which lasts for only one period into the future. If one pound of financing is raised and invested in the project, investment is reduced by θ and consumption by $1 - \theta$. Let v be the present value of the stream of forgone consumption resulting from one pound of forgone investment. Then the opportunity cost of the project in the initial period is $\theta v + (1 - \theta)$. In the next period, the project yields a return of $1 + \delta$, where δ is the rate of return and 1 represents the compensation for depreciation. A fraction α of this total yield is re-invested in the private sector and is valued at αv, and the rest is consumed. Thus, the present value of the consumption stream arising out of the project output next period is

$$\frac{1 + \delta}{1 + r} (1 - \alpha + \alpha v)$$

The project will have a positive present value if $(1 + \delta)(1 - \alpha + \alpha v)/(1 + r)$ exceeds the initial cost $\theta v + (1 - \theta)$; that is, if

$$\frac{1 + \delta}{1 + r} > \frac{1 + \theta(v - 1)}{1 + \alpha(v - 1)} \qquad (10.24)$$

From this criterion we can obtain two special cases. The first is the Arrow and Kurz (1970) case where the rate of return on public projects should equal the social discount rate.[9] If the reinvestment rates on both the financing of the project and the proceeds of the project are the same ($\theta = \alpha$), then (10.24) reduces to the requirement that $\delta > r$; that is, the deadweight loss terms drop out altogether. This case can easily be generalized to public investments of more than one year's duration.

---

[9] This result is also derived in Kay (1972). A synthesis of this and other results may be found in Boadway (1978).

At the other extreme we have the Baumol (1968) case which suggests that the rate of return on public projects should be at least as great as the rate of return in the private sector. If $\theta = 1$ and $\alpha = 0$, (10.24) reduces to $(1 + \delta)/(1 + r) > v$. If we now assume that none of the proceeds of investment is reinvested in the private sector, then $v = (1 + \rho)/(1 + r)$. In that case, the criterion reduces to $\delta > \rho$. By assuming that the project completely crowds out investment and that public project proceeds are consumed, we obtain the result that the gross returns to public projects must be at least as great as the return on private projects, a far more stringent requirement than the preceding case.

We could go on to consider other assumptions and obtain different rules of thumb. The reader will recognize that the rules of thumb obtained depend critically on the assumptions that are made about reinvestment from the project as well as from private sector returns, and the treatment of depreciation. Let us complete this discussion by considering one further well-known rule of thumb – the *Harberger weighted average discounting procedure* – and by investigating the assumptions required to generate it.

Harberger (1969) has suggested applying the weighted average shadow pricing rule in the following way. Let d be a weighted average of the gross return to investment and the net return to savings such that the weights are the proportions in which a pound of financing comes from forgone investment and forgone consumption. Then

$$d = \theta\rho + (1 - \theta)r \tag{10.25}$$

Harberger suggests that the rate of return on public projects δ should be at least as great as d in order for the project to be socially worth while. In other words, the appropriate present value rule should be

$$NPV = \Sigma \frac{NB_t}{(1 + d)^t} \tag{10.26}$$

This differs from (10.23) in that the capital market distortion is incorporated into the discount rate rather than as a current cost. Recall that (10.23) represents the present value of all displaced and generated consumption resulting from undertaking the project. The question is: Under what circumstances will the Harberger shadow pricing rule be equivalent to (10.23)?

As Feldstein (1972b) has argued, it is easy to find several circumstances in which it will *not* be equivalent to (10.23). For example, two projects which have the same stream of financing requirements D_t are ranked differently by (10.23) and (10.26). Using (10.23), the NB_t streams are compared when discounted at r, whereas in (10.26) the same streams are compared when discounted at d. Similarly, self-financing projects $(D_t = 0)$ would have different present values under the two methods. Also, projects which produce only current benefits from current costs may be ranked differently under the two criteria.

None the less there is an intuitive appeal to the notion that if a proportion of the project financing would have earned ρ in the private sector and the rest r, the funds ought to yield an equivalent amount in the public sector. This suggests an example for which the two methods ought to be equivalent. Suppose there is no reinvestment of the proceeds of private investment so ρ actually represents the stream of consumption that would be generated by one pound of investment in the private sector. Suppose also that the net proceeds of the public project δ are sustained in perpetuity by maintaining the value of the capital stock intact through replacement investment (equal to depreciation), and that the net returns δ are all consumed and generate no new finance. In this case the present value of the stream of consumption benefits of one pound of investment in the project is δ/r and the cost of the project – that is, the present value of the forgone consumption from financing a one pound project – is a, where $a = \theta\rho/r + (1 - \theta)$ by (10.21).[10] Thus, the NPV formula (10.23) yields:

$$\text{NPV} = \frac{\delta}{r} - \frac{\theta\rho}{r} - (1 - \theta) \qquad (10.27)$$

The project would be worth undertaking if $\text{NPV} > 0$.

An equivalent project ranking criterion can be obtained by dividing both sides of (10.27) by $a = \theta\rho/r + (1 - \theta)$ to yield:

$$\frac{\text{NPV}}{a} = \frac{\delta}{\theta\rho + (1 - \theta)r} - 1 = \frac{\delta}{d} - 1 \qquad (10.28)$$

using definition (10.25). This is simply the Harberger weighted average discount rule because the right-hand side is the stream of project returns δ discounted at the weighted average discount rate d less the initial capital cost of the project. Thus, the Harberger weighted average rule works perfectly well if there is no reinvestment of public or private investment returns and if the capital investment in the project is maintained in perpetuity.

Suppose we relax the assumption that the public project's capital is maintained in perpetuity by taking the other extreme of a one-period investment. Sjaastad and Wisecarver (1977) have derived the conditions under which the Harberger weighted average rule would be equivalent to the present value rule (10.23) for this case. One pound of financing invested in a public project will yield $1 + \delta$ as a return next period. Suppose the net return δ is consumed but the 'depreciation' component, unity, is returned to the private sector. If the return of funds to the private sector is symmetric to funds being removed, θ of the pound will be invested and the remainder consumed. The private sector capital will be restored to

---

[10] To be more precise it is $1 + (a - 1)$, representing the one pound capital cost plus the $a - 1$ pounds of deadweight loss from financing it.

what it otherwise would have been, since θ pounds of investment had been forgone the previous period. Thus, the economy has to do without θ pounds of capital or $\rho\theta$ pounds of consumption for one period, owing to the temporary diversion of funds to the public sector. Summing up the changes in consumption benefits resulting from the project, we obtain:

$$\text{NPV} = \frac{\delta}{1+r} + \frac{1-\theta}{1+r} - (1-\theta) - \frac{\theta\rho}{1+r} \tag{10.29}$$

The first term is the one-period consumption benefit of the project, the second is the consumption generated by returning the depreciation to the private sector, the third is the initial forgone consumption and the last is the forgone consumption from the one-period reduction in private sector capital. Equation (10.29) can be rewritten as:

$$\frac{(1+r)\,\text{NPV}}{d} = \frac{\delta}{\theta\rho + (1-\theta)\,r} - 1 = \frac{\delta}{d} - 1$$

Once again, the Harberger weighted average discount rule will give the same ranking of projects as the NPV in this case.

This equivalence breaks down when the assumptions of the above simple model no longer hold; for example, when there is some reinvestment out of public or private sector net returns. The details of some of these other cases are worked out in Sjaastad and Wisecarver (1977) and in Boadway (1978). As shown there, the Harberger weighted average discounting rule does not generally give the same ranking of projects as the present value rule adjusted for the deadweight loss of financing.

3.2 Indirect effects of a project

So far we have included as benefits and costs of a project those changes arising in the markets in which the project is directly involved as demander or supplier. However, as (10.4) and (10.5) indicate, these are not the only welfare changes associated with the project. If the project induces changes in output in distorted markets elsewhere in the economy, there are additional welfare changes which in principle ought to be attributed to the project. These are referred to as the indirect effects of the project and are given by the last term in (10.4), $\Sigma t_j\, dx_j$, where the x_j are the commodity demands in markets elsewhere in the economy and t_j is the distortion in that market. For those markets which are not distorted (i.e. for which the consumer price is the marginal cost), this term is zero, so only changes in the distorted market are relevant.

The importance of these indirect effects depends upon the project under consideration. In some cases they may be negligible; in others they may be significant. One example of a case in which they turned out to be relatively important is the well-known cost–benefit analysis of the Victoria line extension to the London Underground System, as reported in Foster and Beesley (1963). In this case, the transportation services to be provided by the Victoria line were a substitute for travel by road and could be expected to divert traffic from the road. Since the effective consumer 'price' for using the road (i.e. time and operating costs) was less than the social cost of using the road (the consumer's price plus the external costs of congestion from road use), an indirect welfare effect would occur to the extent that road use was changed. Since price was less than marginal social cost and traffic use on the roads was predicted to fall, there would be an indirect *benefit* attributable to the Victoria line from the induced reduction in road use. In fact, this indirect benefit was the major benefit predicted to occur from the project's introduction.

3.3 *Intangibles*

So far we have assumed that all project benefits and costs consist of changes in commodity inputs and outputs which have a market price attached to them. However, it is often the case, and indeed often the rationale for the cost–benefit analysis itself, that some of the benefits or costs consist of non-marketed items. These are referred to in the literature as *intangibles*. Some common examples of these include time saved travelling, health improvement including reductions in lives lost, costs of pollution of various sorts, and the benefits of education.

Since these intangible costs or benefits have no market price directly associated with them, marginal benefits and costs must be inferred by other means. Two methods are used in practice. One is to estimate the *hedonic price indices* based on the observed behaviour of individuals when faced with choices which might reveal the value that they implicitly place on intangibles. The other is to use survey techniques and elicit evaluations by the means of a questionnaire. We briefly discuss these in turn.

To use the hedonic price index technique one has to identify choice situations from which an imputed evaluation can be made. Consider two examples. The value of travelling time saved can be determined by observing circumstances in which consumers actually choose between modes of transport or routes which differ in various characteristics including time per trip. Alternative ways of taking the same trip will vary in the resource costs incurred on the one hand, and in the utility affecting characteristics of the trip on the other. The latter may include not only time required per trip, but also comfort, safety, privacy etc. If one has a sample of observations on trips taken, a statistical regression analysis can be performed by regressing costs or cost differences against the characteristics obtained from the alternative means of taking the trip. The regression coefficient associated with each characteristic will represent the hedonic or implicit price representing the marginal value the market places on that characteristic. This technique has been used on transportation projects to estimate the value of travelling time saved (see Harrison and Quarmby, 1972, for a survey) and the value of comfort and convenience (e.g. Foster and Beesley, 1963), and on recreational projects to

L

evaluate the benefits of trips to recreational facilities (e.g. Mansfield, 1971).

Another example concerns the evaluation of the risk of loss of life. As Mishan (1971) has emphasized, the application of the notion of the compensating variation to projects involving the risk of death involves estimating the amount of money that would be just sufficient to compensate all those persons in a society for whom the risk of death has increased.[11] In some cases, if the risk is voluntarily undertaken, as with the risk of death on highways, the cost of the risk has already implicitly been accounted for in estimating the demand curve for use of the project's output. In this case, no additional estimation of the costs of risk need be undertaken. However, if the risk of death is imposed involuntarily on individuals in the population, a separate estimate of this cost must be made.

The hedonic price technique involves finding circumstances in which persons actually do implicitly trade off additional risk of death for, say, monetary reward. The customary example given is the case of choice among occupations of varying degrees of risk. Given observations of differential wage rates among occupations as well as differing characteristics associated with the occupations including risk of death, regression techniques can be used to attribute the wage differential to the various differences in occupational characteristics. In principle, this ought to yield estimates of the amount of money that the marginal worker would just be willing to accept to incur an increase in the risk of death. One such estimate based on US data was done by Thaler and Rosen (1975). More extended discussions of this problem may be found in Usher (1973) and Jones-Lee (1976).

The other method for estimating intangible benefits and costs is to do a sample survey asking persons directly how much they would be willing to pay to obtain certain intangible benefits, or how much they would have to be compensated to accept certain costs. An example of the use of this technique may be found in the estimation of the costs of noise pollution associated with the construction of the third London airport (Commission on the Third London Airport, 1970). The approach used there is summarized in Flowerdew (1972) and criticized in Mishan (1970), and the reader is referred to them for further details.

4 Choice of a Social Discount Rate

To this point we have discussed the analysis involved in arriving at suitable measures for costs and benefits in terms of current period consumption. To aggregate these measures into a single cost–benefit measure, it is necessary to know the relative value society places on consumption

[11] For a survey of the literature on the value of life, see Jones-Lee (1976). A contrary view to the conventional methodology has been expressed by Broome (1978).

occurring at different times. Since everything is to be measured in terms of present consumption, we need the relative value of future versus present consumption, or the social discount rate. We shall think of the social discount rate r as being the premium society places on consumption in period t relative to $t + 1$; that is, it is a one-period discount rate. For simplicity, we assume that the social discount rate does not change over time. The discount factor applicable over several periods is, therefore, $1 + r$ appropriately compounded.

At first sight, it might seem that the net-of-tax return to savings ought to be the social discount rate. It is, after all, the rate at which households in the economy can apparently transform present into future consumption. There are, however, a number of potential difficulties with using this net return as the social discount rate. Here we outline what those difficulties are. For the policy analyst, it will be a matter of judgment which of these are important and which are not.

4.1 Capital market imperfections

The after-tax return to savings would be the rate at which households trade off present versus future consumption only if there exist perfect capital markets. By perfect capital markets we mean that all households are able to borrow fully against their lifetime wealth no matter what form it takes. It is often alleged that early in the life cycle when one's consumption exceeds income, institutional borrowing constraints prevent the household from borrowing the desired amount against future earned income. To the extent that this is the case, households are not able to arrange their lifetime consumption streams such that, at the margin, the rate of substitution between consumption in adjacent periods is $1 + r$.

The situation is exactly like that of a quantity rationed household as discussed in chapter 2. The observed interest rate cannot be taken as the household's consumption discount rate. The latter cannot be observed in the market, but presumably it is higher than the market rate; that is, the household would be willing to pay more than the going rate to borrow but is constrained from doing so. For this reason, the social discount rate may exceed the interest rate.

An additional difficulty here is that, presumably, the rate at which households discount future consumption will differ over households if there are borrowing constraints. Some will be constrained while others (e.g. lenders) will not be, and those constraints will be affected to different degrees. If different households have differing consumption discount rates, then there is no single social discount rate that applies to all households. The same problem arises with unconstrained capital markets if different households face different taxes on capital income. This makes the after-tax returns to savings different from household to household. In principle, in order to do cost–benefit analysis perfectly, one must identify the stream of benefits and costs to each individual and discount it appropriately. This is obviously impractical, so the assumption of a single social discount rate is always made. In the following discussion we shall ignore this problem by assuming that all households face perfect capital markets and have the same after-tax return to savings.

4.2 *Capital market inefficiencies of the Samuelson–Malinvaud consumption-loan model type*

As discussed in chapter 3, capital markets may not be efficient at allocating resources over time in an economy with overlapping generations. In particular, there may be an excess of capital accumulation. Suppose all households in the economy save only for their own future consumption. Thus, they save enough in their working years to support their desired consumption in retirement and plan to leave no bequests. In such an economy, the savings will fund capital accumulation whose ownership changes hands as generations pass on. Perfectly functioning capital markets will yield a common equilibrium rate of return to investment and savings, which we shall denote ρ. In this type of economy, capital is created partly as a vehicle for each generation to postpone consumption. A typical generation acquires capital assets in its working years by saving and sells those assets in retirement to finance consumption. Thus there is a continuous series of transactions between generations, with the existing working generations purchasing assets from existing retired generations. This is the manner in which society as a whole facilitates the postponement of consumption until retirement.

As Samuelson (1958) pointed out, this is not the only way in which consumption streams may be smoothed in models of overlapping generations, and it may not be the most efficient way. An alternative way is through the institution of a contract between overlapping generations whereby the current working generation agrees to fund the consumption of the currently retired in return for a commitment that the next generation does the same for it when it reaches retirement. Provided this process goes on indefinitely, all generations can be made better off. The enforcement of such a contract among generations is a difficult matter; each generation has to be satisfied that the next will not renege. Samuelson argued in the context of an economy without capital that fiat money provided one type of asset which could fulfil this function implicitly. Interest-bearing government debt would be required in an economy with capital in order to make the holding of the debt attractive. Alternatively, explicit intergenerational income transfers through an unfunded social security system could fulfil the same function.[12] The point about these alternative ways of facilitating life cycle smoothing through intergenerational transfers is that they do not involve the accumulation and exchange of a stock of physical capital; instead they involve a simple pact

---

[12] An unfunded social security system is one in which the benefits paid to the retired are totally financed from current tax revenues, rather than from a fund accumulated in the past. There is a vast literature on this topic emanating from the original contribution by Feldstein (1974). For a recent survey and critique see Aaron (1982).

or social contract among generations, possibly involving a paper asset such as fiat money or government bonds.

In certain circumstances it may be more efficient for society to save at the margin through one of these alternative means rather than through capital accumulation. This will be the case if the rate of return on capital ρ is less than the rate at which society's income can be expected to grow indefinitely, say n. The latter rate is the rate of return that could potentially be earned by each generation in a 'Ponzi game' with all future generations. Each generation would be made better off if their savings were reallocated from real capital asset holdings to the alternative asset holdings (e.g. government debt) until the capital stock fell and the rate of return rose to $\rho = n$.

Considerations of this sort would call for using a social discount rate above the market interest rate so as to encourage current consumption and discourage more capital formation. This is only a second-best policy alternative; the first-best is to facilitate the alternative means of inducing current consumption directly such as through the creation of government debt.

This inefficiency occurs only if the growth of national income exceeds the rate of return on capital in the economy. Feldstein (1977) has argued convincingly that the rate of return on capital exceeds the rate of growth of gross national product by a good margin, at least in the USA. The reason lies in the fact that capital taxes have imposed large enough distortions in the capital market to make ρ quite large. If that is the case, the problem addressed in this section does not arise; that is, capital over-accumulation is not a problem.

The conceptual difficulties raised in sections 4.1 and 4.2, to the extent that they exist, both suggest that the social discount rate should be higher than the after-tax return to savings in the economy. The next two sections suggest just the opposite.

4.3 *Inefficiency of capital markets in an economy with bequests*

Section 4.2 was concerned with economies that comprise overlapping generations of persons and in which market failure results because certain transactions or contracts between generations do not exist. In this section we consider economies in which transfers of resources between generations are voluntarily undertaken, say, through bequests or *inter vivos* transfers. This would occur if utility functions are interdependent in the sense that the members of one generation obtain utility from the well-being of the members of another generation. As with the analogous phenomenon of interdependent utilities in static models (e.g. Hochman and Rodgers, 1969), the existence of interdependent utilities may give rise to gifts between generations. The special case we consider here is one in which the members of each generation obtain utility from the utility level achieved by their own heirs. Obviously, the interdependency could have been reciprocal or could have been between non-adjacent generations.

However, this special case is the one dealt within the literature and provides some justification for the use of the fictitious individual of infinite lifespan often found in dynamic analysis.

Suppose that the utility of the representative person of generation zero is denoted u_0, and that this utility is given by:

$$u_0 = u_0(x_0, u_1)$$

where x_0 is the vector of goods consumed by this person over his or her life cycle and u_1 is the utility level of the next generation's representative person. Similarly, u_1 depends on the utility level of its heir, u_2, and so on. This holds for every generation, so we can write for generation t:

$$u_t = u_t(x_t, u_{t+1}) \qquad t = 0, \ldots, \infty \tag{10.30}$$

The representative person of each generation is also presumed to be endowed with a certain amount of wealth, if only in the form of a stream of labour earnings. The existing generation also presumably 'owns' the existing stock of capital, including non-renewable resources.

In the absence of intergenerational transfers, each generation would choose a lifetime consumption stream so as to maximize its own utility and use up all its wealth. In the presence of interdependent utility functions, the running down of wealth may not lead to an efficient allocation of resources. It may be the case that the present generation is much better off than succeeding generations since, without this interdependency, it would be consuming the total stock of physical capital of the economy. If it has a strong enough sense of altruism, the marginal utility it would get from having more wealth in the hands of its heirs would exceed the marginal loss from having less wealth itself. In that case, it could make itself better off with a transfer of wealth, say, through a bequest, to the next generation. The bequest size would be such that, at the margin, an additional unit of wealth in its own hands is worth the same to the present generation if they consume it themselves than if they leave it to their heirs. This, of course, need not imply equal wealth for the two generations since the present generation might be expected to get more utility from its own consumption than from an equivalent amount in the hands of its heirs.

The next generation, generation one, makes the same calculation as the present generation. It takes its own wealth plus that inherited as a bequest, and uses it for its own consumption and for a bequest to its heirs, generation two. Then generation two does the same, and so on into the indefinite future. The upshot is that the wealth of the present generation is spread over all future generations by a series of bequests.

Intuitively, it is easy to see that the end result of these transactions is an efficient allocation of resource through time. It also represents an allocation of resources over time which would correspond to that chosen by the present generation if it had the choice. The present generation leaves to generation one a bequest which is efficient in the Pareto optimal sense that it would not be possible to make both generations better off by further reallocations. Generation one then uses its wealth plus its bequests in an efficient way and chooses its own consumption stream plus bequests so as to maximize u_1. Since u_1 enters the present generation's own utility function, this is exactly the way in which the present generation would have used it. Similarly, generation two uses its wealth plus bequest to maximize its utility u_2, and this is efficient since it corresponds to what generation one would have done and consequently what the present generation prefers. The same holds for all generations.

The result is that resources are allocated efficiently through time. Furthermore, the particular Pareto optimum which is achieved is the one which maximizes the present generation's utility, taking account of its altruism, direct and indirect, for succeeding generations. We can thus view the allocation of resources as being determined by a representative individual of infinite lifespan. The market interest rate (after personal taxes) would represent the rate at which this individual would trade off future versus present consumption, and therefore would be an appropriate social discount rate.

There are two reasons why one may not wish to use the after-tax return to savings as the social discount rate in an economy like the one above. One has to do with the possibility of a type of market failure in giving bequests. The other, discussed in the next subsection, has to do with equity. The market failure argument, due to Sen (1961) and Marglin (1963b),[13] arises from the fact that bequests might have a public goods element to them which gives rise to the so-called free rider problem. Suppose that there exist a large number of persons in each generation and that each household's utility function contains as arguments the utility levels of both its own heirs and the heirs of its contemporaries; that is, it includes the utility level of all members of the next generation. Under these circumstances each household's bequest will benefit not only itself but also all its contemporaries, since they will benefit from the higher level of utility of the recipient of the bequest.

This is a classic externality problem whereby the actions of a household A (the bequestor) benefit other households (i.e. its contemporaries). In deciding on the amount of bequest, household A trades off the private cost (the loss of its own purchasing power) with the private benefit (the higher utility level of its own heirs). However, it neglects the benefit conferred upon contemporaries who also get utility from improvements in the well-being of A's heirs. As a result there is an incentive to bequeath too little from an efficiency point of view. Since all members of the present generation face the same incentives to save, there will be undersaving in the aggregate. Society would be better off if each person agreed

---

[13] The argument is analytically similar to the argument that income redistribution has a public goods characteristic which requires that it be done collectively. This may be found in Thurow (1971).

to save more, but it is not in the private interest of any one person to do so.

This undersaving result provides an argument for interfering with the market mechanism collectively to induce more saving. In the absence of intervention, the market interest rate which guides individual savings decisions does not reflect the rate at which society trades off future versus present consumption. For this reason Sen and Marglin have suggested that the social discount rate should lie below the market interest rate. This would provide an artificial incentive for projects to provide more future consumption benefits relative to that provided by discounting at the market rate of interest.[14]

4.4 *Inequity of capital markets in an economy with or without bequests*

One other reason appearing in the literature as to why one might wish not to use the market interest rate as the social discount rate has to do with the intergenerational inequities which may result from the market mechanism. Even in an economy with optimal bequests, the intergenerational income distribution may be very uneven since it depends upon the utility that the present generation obtains from the well-being of future generations. That being the case, one might expect the present generation to take a rather large share of the capital resources of the economy. On the other hand, if earned incomes per caput were expected to grow over time due to technical progress, there would be no incentive for positive bequests and equity considerations might well dictate policies which redistribute from future generations to the present one.

Under these circumstances the interest rate at which the market allows individuals to transform present into future consumption and vice versa would not be the rate at which an intergenerational social welfare function would trade off present versus future consumption. The latter would, of course, depend upon the social welfare function one adopts. Begging the question of how this social welfare function is determined, we can illustrate how the social rate of discount could be deduced for particular cases. The general method of proceedings is as follows. Suppose the intergenerational social welfare function is written in the following form:

$$W = W(C_0, C_1, C_2, \ldots, C_n, \ldots) \tag{10.31}$$

where C_n represents the consumption level of generation n. Totally differentiating (10.31) and using the present generation's consumption as the *numéraire* we obtain:

$$\frac{dW}{W_0} = dC_0 + \frac{W_1}{W_0} dC_1 + \frac{W_2}{W_0} dC_2 + \ldots \frac{W_n}{W_0} dC_n + \ldots \tag{10.32}$$

[14] The exact relationship between the market interest rate and the social discount rate is developed in detail in Sen (1967). It depends critically upon the assumptions made concerning tastes.

where $W_i = \partial W/\partial C_i$. This expression gives the change in welfare in terms of present consumption of any small change in consumption over generations. The coefficient W_n/W_0 is the discount factor applied to consumption of generation n.

In order to determine the qualitative properties of this discount factor, it is necessary to be more specific about the functional form of W. A commonly used example is the following:

$$W = \sum_{n=0}^{T} \frac{u(C_n)}{(1 + \lambda)^n} \qquad (10.33)$$

Thus, social welfare is an additively separable weighted sum of the utility of each generation, where the same utility function is applied to each generation and in addition there is some pure discount rate λ.[15] In this case, (10.32) becomes:

$$\frac{dW}{W_0} = dC_0 + (1 + \lambda)^{-1} \frac{u_1}{u_0} dC_1 + (1 + \lambda)^{-2} \frac{u_2}{u_0} dC_2 \dots$$

$$+ (1 + \lambda)^{-n} \frac{u_n}{u_0} dC_n \dots \qquad (10.34)$$

where $u_n = \partial u/\partial C_n$.

Next, assume that the marginal utility function itself takes the form

$$u_n = AC_n^{-\epsilon} \qquad (10.35)$$

where ϵ and A are parameters. This functional form has the property that the elasticity of the marginal utility of consumption, $-\epsilon$, is a constant. Note that $\epsilon > 0$ if there is diminishing marginal utility of consumption. Consider now the discount factor applied to period n. It is

$$(1 + \lambda)^{-n} \frac{u_n}{u_0} = (1 + \lambda)^{-n} \left(\frac{C_n}{C_0}\right)^{-\epsilon}$$

$$= (1 + \lambda)^{-n}(1 + g)^{-\epsilon n}$$

$$\approx (1 + \lambda + g\epsilon)^{-n} \qquad (10.36)$$

where g is the proportionate growth in consumption each period (assumed here to be constant).

According to (10.36), the social discount rate to be used to trade off future versus present consumption should be $\lambda + g\epsilon$. The first term λ represents the discount factor applicable to utility. The second term $g\epsilon$ represents the effect of changes in the level of consumption. If consump-

[15] In a classic contribution to the literature, Ramsey (1928) argued that there was no good reason for λ to be other than zero. He argued that for λ to exceed zero would reflect pure myopia.

tion per caput is growing so $g > 0$, future consumption will be worth less because of the assumption of diminishing marginal utility. There is, of course, no particular reason why the social discount rate $\lambda + g\epsilon$ should bear any resemblance to the market rate of interest.

The analysis of this section has shown that there are a number of reasons why the market interest rate may not be the appropriate social discount rate. Some reflect efficiency considerations and others reflect equity considerations. In the end, the appropriate discount rate to use will reflect individual judgment.

5 The Treatment of Risk

Most public projects involve a stream of benefits and costs which will occur into the future, and also involve a displacement of private sector benefits and costs which would have occurred in the future. Since the future is uncertain, the social evaluation of a project ought to reflect the imputed cost of the risks involved in the changes in resource alloca-tion induced by the project. In principle, this should include both the direct risks arising on the project itself as well as the indirect risk changes elsewhere in the economy, such as any reduction in risk as a result of forgone investment in private sector projects. We begin this section with a general discussion of the concept and measurement of the cost of risk-taking. Then the use of this concept in the context of project evaluation is discussed. Throughout the discussion, it is assumed that the representa-tive household in the economy behaves according to the expected utility hypothesis as outlined in chapter 2. It knows the outcomes that will occur in various future states of the world and attaches probabilities to those states of the world occurring.[16]

To develop the notion of the cost of risk, consider an individual faced with the possibility of various outcomes Y_i, where i refers to the state of nature. These outcomes can be thought of as the real income in state i as measured by, say, the value of the expenditure function at a given set of reference prices (what we have referred to as our money metric measure of utility). Thus Y_i can incorporate the effects of both price and income differences between states. The probability of state i occurring is denoted π_i and there are assumed to be S possible states of nature. The individual expected utility is defined to be:

$$Eu(Y) = \sum_{i=1}^{S} \pi_i u(Y_i) \qquad (10.37)$$

where $u(Y_i)$ is a cardinal index of utility as discussed in chapter 2. We assume that the individual is risk averse, so $u''(Y_i) < 0$.

---

[16]   There is a literature on project evaluation decision rules when probabilities cannot be attached to states of the world; only outcomes themselves are known. For a survey of this literature see Dorfman (1962).

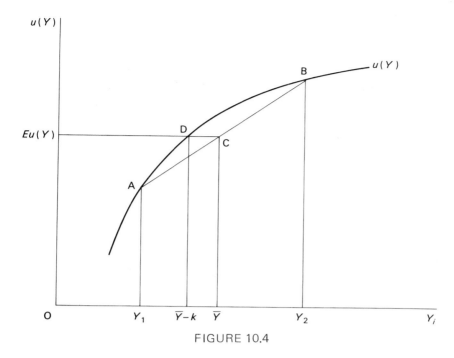

FIGURE 10.4

The cost of risk is defined to be the amount of expected income the household would be willing to pay in order to avoid the risk. It is thus analogous to the compensating variation of removing the risk. Suppose the expected income in the presence of the risk is denoted $\bar{Y}$; thus, $\bar{Y} = \Sigma \pi_i Y_i$. Then the cost of risk k is defined implicitly by the following:

$$u(\bar{Y} - k) = \Sigma \pi_i u(Y_i) \tag{10.38}$$

In the case in which there are two states of the world, the cost of risk can be depicted geometrically as in figure 10.4. In this diagram, Y_1 and Y_2 represent the outcomes in states 1 and 2. Since, by (10.37), expected utility is a weighted average of $u(Y_1)$ and $u(Y_2)$, the straight line AB represents the expected utility curve, showing the value of $Eu(Y)$ for various values of π_1 and π_2. For example, the risky situation which yields an expected income of $\bar{Y}$ has an expected utility given by the distance $\bar{Y}C$.[17] Applying the definition of the cost of risk from (10.38), the latter is given by the distance CD. As can be seen from the construction of the diagram, the cost of risk k will be greater the more concave is the utility function (i.e. the more risk averse the household is) and the wider is the spread (or variance) of the outcomes.

An alternative geometric way of depicting this is in the state preference diagram of figure 10.5. In this diagram the indifference curve labelled

[17] It can be readily shown from (10.37) and the definition of $\bar{Y}$ that $\bar{Y}Y_2/Y_1Y_2 = BC/AC = \pi_1/\pi_2$.

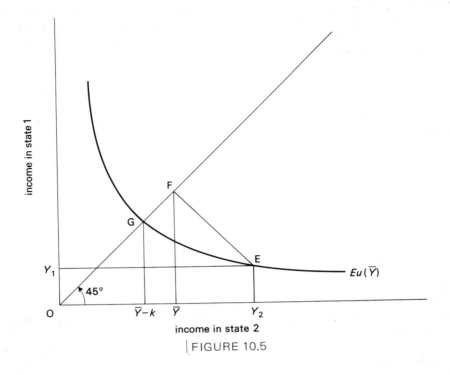

| FIGURE 10.5

$Eu(\bar{Y})$ shows the various combinations of incomes in the two states which would yield the same level of expected utility as the risky outcome Y_1 and Y_2, given the probabilities π_1 and π_2. The point E on this curve shows the outcome of the risky situation currently facing the individual. The line EF represents the locus of combinations of Y_1 and Y_2 yielding the same expected outcome $\bar{Y}$ as at E. It is referred to as the *fair bet* line and is simply a depiction of $\bar{Y} = \pi_1 Y_1 + \pi_2 Y_2$. The slope of the fair bet line is $-\pi_2/\pi_1$. The 45° line is the *certainty line* since along it the outcomes are the same in both states. The income at G is referred to as the *certainty equivalent income* and corresponds to $\bar{Y} - k$ in figure 10.5. The cost of risk is the difference in income measured on the horizontal axis between F and G along the certainty line. Once again it should be obvious that the distance FG will be greater the greater is the difference between Y_1 and Y_2 and the more convex is the expected utility indifference curve (i.e. the more concave is the utility function).

Since the cost of risk is defined only implicitly by (10.38), we cannot immediately deduce its properties. However, we can derive an approximate expression for k by applying a Taylor series approximation to (10.38) around the mean outcome $\bar{Y}$. The value of $u(Y_i)$ can be obtained to any desired degree of approximation by the following Taylor series expansion:

$$u(Y_i) = u(\bar{Y}) + u'(\bar{Y})(Y_i - \bar{Y}) + \tfrac{1}{2}u''(\bar{Y})(Y_i - \bar{Y})^2 + R \qquad (10.39)$$

where R represents the higher order terms. Suppose we approximate $u(Y_i)$ by ignoring these higher order terms.[18] Also, since k is presumably relatively small compared with $\bar{Y}$ for most applications, we can approximate $u(\bar{Y} - k)$ to the first order as follows:

$$u(\bar{Y} - k) \approx u(\bar{Y}) - ku'(\bar{Y}) \tag{10.40}$$

Using (10.40) for the left-hand side of (10.38) and inserting (10.39) into the right-hand side, we obtain

$$u(\bar{Y}) - ku'(\bar{Y}) \approx \Sigma \pi_i [u(\bar{Y}) + u'(\bar{Y})(Y_i - \bar{Y}) + \tfrac{1}{2}u''(\bar{Y})(Y_i - \bar{Y})^2]$$

Using the fact that $\Sigma \pi_i = 1$ and the definition of the mean $\Sigma \pi_i Y_i = \bar{Y}$, this expression simplifies to the following:

$$k \approx -\frac{u''(\bar{Y})}{2u'(\bar{Y})} \text{ var } (Y_i) \tag{10.41}$$

where var (Y_i) is the variance of Y_i defined as $\Sigma \pi_i (Y_i - \bar{Y})^2$.

This expression for the cost of risk generalizes the result that we obtained from the geometric analysis. The cost of risk is approximately proportional to the variance of the outcomes, and also to the ratio $-u''(\bar{Y})/u'(\bar{Y})$. The latter is a measure of the concavity or curvature of the utility function and is known as the *degree of absolute risk aversion*, following Arrow (1965) and Pratt (1964). These results are to be expected intuitively. The greater the spread of possible outcomes, the greater the cost of risk; and the more strongly that marginal utility diminishes, the greater is the cost of risk.

The final question to be considered is how the cost of risk enters into the evaluation of projects. As mentioned earlier, changes in risk can occur both directly from the future flow of net benefits of the project itself and indirectly from changes in the stream of risky outputs elsewhere. In principle, both should be taken into account, though in practice this may be somewhat difficult. Consider the indirect changes in risk first. One source of this is the forgone risk as a result of the fact that the financing of the project crowds out investment elsewhere in the economy. Consider the simple example discussed earlier, in which a proportion of project financing θ comes from forgone investment and $1 - \theta$ comes from forgone consumption (increased savings). Suppose all the returns to private sector investment are consumed so that in the absence of risk the opportunity cost of one pound of financing is just $(1 - \theta) + \theta \rho/r$, where ρ is the rate of return on private sector investment and r is the social discount rate. If, however, private sector projects are risky, the gross return to investment ρ will include a risk premium to compensate investors for the cost of bearing the risk. When the investment is crowded

[18] The approximation will be exact if the utility function is quadratic. In this case R will be zero since all higher order derivatives will be zero.

out, that risk is no longer borne, so that the opportunity cost of displaced private investment should be the net-of-risk return on investment discounted at the social discount rate. If the risk premium is β per pound of investment, then the opportunity cost of public funds would be $(1 - \theta) + \theta(\rho - \beta)/r$. This opportunity cost of financing should enter the project evaluation just as the variable a did before. Of course, since β is not readily observable in the market, one may not be able to measure $(\rho - \beta)$ with much precision.

In addition to these indirect effects, the net output stream of the project itself may be uncertain and the project evaluator, acting on behalf of the representative citizen, should take account of the cost associated with the direct change of risk. There are two procedures that could be undertaken. One would be for the project evaluator to evaluate the expected utility of the project explicitly by measuring the stream of real incomes obtained in alternative states of nature and calculating the expected utility using (10.37). The alternative, and perhaps more practical way, is to evaluate the project in terms of expected *value* and to evaluate separately the cost of the risk of the project. Thus, one would have to subtract the cost of risk k from the expected net benefit stream of the project. Once again, the latter procedure involves informational problems since k is not a variable which is readily observable in markets. However, it has been suggested in the literature that the cost of risk on a public project may be negligible because of risk-pooling and risk-spreading. We conclude this section with a resumé of these arguments.

5.1 Risk-pooling

Risk-pooling refers to the phenomenon by which the variance of a portfolio of outcomes is reduced as the portfolio is diversified, provided that the elements of the portfolio are to some extent independently distributed. To be more specific, consider a portfolio consisting of n assets such that the share of the portfolio taken up by asset i is a_i and the return per pound is x_i. For a portfolio consisting of one pound's worth of assets, the return on the portfolio is $\Sigma a_i x_i$, which is random since each x_i is a random rate of return. The mean of the portfolio $\bar{x}$ is just its expected value, $E(\Sigma a_i x_i)$ or $\Sigma a_i \bar{x}_i$ where $\bar{x}_i$ is the mean return of asset i. Thus, the mean of the portfolio is simply the weighted sum of the means of the component assets.

The variance and the covariance between assets i and j are defined as follows:

$$\text{var}(x_i) = E[(x_i - \bar{x}_i)^2]$$
$$\text{cov}(x_i x_j) = E[(x_i - \bar{x}_i)(x_j - \bar{x}_j)]$$

Similarly, the variance of the entire portfolio of assets is defined as:

$$\text{var}(x) = E[(\Sigma a_i x_i - \Sigma a_i \bar{x}_i)^2]$$

That is, it is the squared value of the difference between the portfolio outcomes and the mean outcome of the portfolio. As Markowitz (1959) showed, the variance of the portfolio is related to the variance and co-variance of the assets as follows:

$$\text{var}(x) = \Sigma a_i^2 \, \text{var}(x_i) + 2\Sigma\Sigma a_i a_j \, \text{cov}(x_i x_j) \tag{10.42}$$

Notice that when the assets of the portfolio are independently distributed, so $\text{cov}(x_i x_j) = 0$, the portfolio variance is $\Sigma a_i^2 \, \text{var}(x_i)$, which is less than the sum of the variances of the assets $\Sigma a_i \, \text{var}(x_i)$ since $a_i < 1$.

As more independently distributed assets are added to a portfolio, the variance of the portfolio falls, reaching zero in the limit. To see this, consider the simple example of a portfolio consisting of equal amounts of identically but independently distributed assets so that $\text{var}(x_i)$ is the same for all i and $\text{cov}(x_i x_j) = 0$. Let n be the number of assets in the portfolio, so $a_i = 1/n$. Then, by applying (10.42), the variance of the portfolio is given by

$$\text{var}(x) = \Sigma \, \text{var}(x_i)/n^2 = \text{var}(x_i)/n$$

From this it can be seen that as n increases the portfolio variance falls. Furthermore, the limiting value of $\text{var}(x)$ as n approaches infinity is zero. This is known in the statistics literature as the *law of large numbers*.

The implication of this for project evaluation is as follows. Consider the entire group of public projects as a portfolio. If the number of such projects is sufficiently large for each to be a small part of the portfolio, and if the projects are independently distributed, then the variance of all projects in the public sector taken together would be close to zero; hence the direct cost of risk k could be close to zero. In this case the risk of any one project can be ignored. Whether or not the returns to public projects are independently distributed is, of course, an empirical question.

5.2 Risk-spreading

A related phenomenon is that of risk-spreading, whereby the risk of a project is made negligible if it is shared by a large number of persons. Arrow and Lind (1970) showed that if the returns of a project are shared among n persons and if the returns of the project are small relative to GNP, the risk of the project will fall to zero as n becomes indefinitely large.

An intuitive demonstration of this result, drawn from Layard and Walters (1978), is as follows. Using the same notation as above, consider a project with a random return of x which is shared among n persons so each person obtains x/n. The variance of this return is $\text{var}(x/n) = E(x/n - \bar{x}/n)^2 = \text{var}(x)/n^2$. Using our expression for k given by (10.41), the cost of risk to an individual is

$$k = -\frac{u''(\bar{x})}{2u'(\bar{x})} \frac{\text{var } x}{n^2}$$

Notice that as n increases, k decreases, so that in the limit k approaches zero as n approaches infinity. More importantly, the total risk of the project is the sum of the risks to all individuals, or

$$nk = -\frac{u''}{2u'}\frac{\text{var } x}{n}$$

As n increases, the total risk to society nk also falls, falling to zero in the limit. Thus we have the Arrow–Lind result that if the risk is shared by a large enough number of persons, total risk will be negligible and can be ignored.

How large is 'large' is, of course, an empirical question. Thus whether or not the Arrow–Lind results hold depends on the specifics of the situation. It also depends on the assumption that project returns are small and independent of GNP. And, it depends upon the assumption that as the number of persons in the economy rises, the returns per person will accordingly fall. This, of course, would not happen if the output of the project were a public good so that additional users could be admitted without affecting the benefits received by existing users. None the less, the power of the Arrow–Lind argument for ignoring risk on small public projects is strong.

References

Aaron, H. J. (1982), *Economic Effects of Social Security*, Washington DC: Brookings Institution.

Akerlof, G. (1970), 'The Market for Lemons', *Quarterly Journal of Economics*, 84, pp. 488-500.

Archibald, G. C. and Donaldson, D. (1976), 'Non-Paternalism and the Basic Theorems of Welfare Economics', *Canadian Journal of Economics*, 9, pp. 492-507.

Arnott, R. J. and Stiglitz, J. E. (1983), 'Moral Hazard and Optimal Commodity Taxation', Discussion Paper #500, Queen's University, Kingston, Ontario, Canada.

Arrow, K. J. (1951a), *Social Choice and Individual Values*, New Haven and London: Yale University Press.

— (1951b), 'An Extension of the Basic Theorems of Classical Welfare Economics', *Proceedings of the Second Berkeley Symposium*, Berkeley: University of California Press, pp. 507-32.

— (1963), *Social Choice and Individual Values*, 2nd edn, New York: Wiley.

— (1965), *Aspects of the Theory of Risk-Bearing*, Helsinki: Academic Book Store.

— (1973), 'Some Ordinalist-Utilitarian Notes on Rawls's Theory of Justice', *Journal of Philosophy*, 70, pp. 245-63.

Arrow, K. J. and Kurz, M. (1970), *Public Investment, The Rate of Return and Optimal Fiscal Policy*, Baltimore, Md: Johns Hopkins Press.

Arrow, K. J. and Lind, R. C. (1970), 'Uncertainty and the Evaluation of Public Investment Decisions', *American Economic Review*, 60, pp. 364-78.

Atkinson, A. B. (1970), 'On the Measurement of Inequality', *Journal of Economic Theory*, 2, pp. 244-63.

— (1980), 'Horizontal Equity and the Distribution of the Tax Burden', in Aaron, H. J. and Boskin, M. J. (eds), *The Economics of Taxation*, Washington DC: Brookings Institution.

Atkinson, A. B. and Stern, N. H. (1974), 'Pigou, Taxation and Public Goods', *Review of Economic Studies*, 41, pp. 119-28.

Atkinson, A. B. and Stiglitz, J. E. (1972), 'The Structure of Indirect Taxation and Economic Efficiency', *Journal of Public Economics*, 1, pp. 97-119.

— (1976), 'The Design of Tax Structure: Direct versus Indirect Taxation', *Journal of Public Economics*, 6, pp. 55-76.

— (1980), *Lectures on Public Economics*, New York and Maidenhead, England: McGraw-Hill.

Bailey, M. J. (1954), 'The Marshallian Demand Curve', *Journal of Political Economy*, 62, pp. 255-61.

Baumol, W. J. (1968), 'On the Social Rate of Discount', *American Economic Review*, 57, pp. 788-802.

Bentham, J. (1791), *Principles of Morals and Legislation*, London: Doubleday.

Berglas, E. (1976), 'Distribution of Tastes and Skills and the Provision of Local Public Goods', *Journal of Public Economics*, 6, pp. 409-23.

—— (1981), 'The Market Provision of Club Goods Once Again', *Journal of Public Economics*, 15, pp. 389-93.

Bergson, A. (1938), 'A Reformulation of Certain Aspects of Welfare Economics', *Quarterly Journal of Economics*, LII, pp. 310-34.

Blackorby, C. and Donaldson, D. (1978), 'Measures of Inequality and their Meaning in Terms of Social Welfare', *Journal of Economic Theory*, 18, pp. 59-80.

Blackorby, C., Donaldson, D. and Weymark, J. (1983), 'Social Choice with Interpersonal Utility Comparisons: A Diagrammatic Introduction', forthcoming, *International Economic Review*.

Boadway, R. W. (1974), 'The Welfare Foundations of Cost-Benefit Analysis', *Economic Journal*, 84, pp. 426-39.

—— (1976), 'Integrating Equity and Efficiency in Applied Welfare Economics', *Quarterly Journal of Economics*, 90, pp. 541-56.

—— (1978), 'Public Investment Decision Rules in a Neo-classical Growing Economy', *International Economic Review*, 19, pp. 265-87.

—— (1979), *Public Sector Economics*, Cambridge, Massachusetts: Winthrop Publishers.

Boadway, R. W. and Harris, R. G. (1977), 'A Characterization of Piecemeal Second Best Policy', *Journal of Public Economics*, 8, pp. 169-90.

Bradford, D. F. (1975), 'Constraints on Government Investment Opportunities and the Choice of Discount Rate', *American Economic Review*, 65, pp. 887-99.

Broome, J. (1978), 'Trying to Value a Life', *Journal of Public Economics*, 9, pp. 91-100.

Browning, E. K. (1978), 'The Burden of Taxation', *Journal of Political Economy*, 86, pp. 649-71.

Bruce, N. (1981), 'Approximate and Exact Consumer's Surplus', Discussion Paper #455, Queen's University, Kingston, Canada.

Bruce, N. and Harris, R. G. (1981), 'The Compensation Principle and Cost Benefit Analysis: Consistency, Application and Decision Rule Error', Discussion Paper #422, Queen's University, Kingston, Canada.

—— (1982), 'Cost-Benefit Criteria and the Compensation Principle in Evaluating Small Projects', *Journal of Political Economy*, 90, pp. 755-75.

Buchanan, J. M. (1954), 'Individual Choice in Voting and the Market', *Journal of Political Economy*, 62, pp. 334-43.

—— (1965), 'An Economic Theory of Clubs', *Economica*, 32, pp. 1-14.

Buchanan, J. M. and Stubblebine, W. C. (1962), 'Externality', *Economica*, 29, pp. 371-84.

Burmeister, E. (1980), *Capital Theory and Dynamics*, Cambridge: Cambridge University Press.

Burns, M. E. (1973). 'A Note on the Concept and Measure of Consumer's Surplus', *American Economic Review*, 53, pp. 335-44.

Cheung, S. N. S. (1973), 'The Fable of the Bees: An Economic Investigation', *Journal of Law and Economics*, 16, pp. 11-34.

Coase, R. H. (1960), 'The Problem of Social Cost', *Journal of Law and Economics*, 3, pp. 1-44.

Commission on the Third London Airport (1970), *Papers and Proceedings: Stage III Research and Investigation – Assessment of Short-Listed Sites*, 7, Parts 1 and 2, HMSO.

Corlett, W. J. and Hague, D. C. (1953), 'Complementarity and the Excess Burden of Taxation', *Review of Economic Studies*, 21, pp. 21-30.

Dahlby, B. G. (1981), 'Measuring the Effect on a Consumer of Stabilizing the Price of a Commodity', *Canadian Journal of Economics*, XIV, pp. 440-49.

Dasgupta, P. S., Marglin, S. A. and Sen, A. K. (1972), *Guidelines for Project Evaluation*, New York: United Nations.

Dasgupta, P. S., Sen, A. K. and Starrett, D. (1973), 'Notes on the Measurement of Inequality', *Journal of Economic Theory*, 6, pp. 180-87.

D'Aspremont, C. and Gevers, L. (1977), 'Equity and the Informational Basis of Social Choice', *Review of Economic Studies*, 46, pp. 199-210.

Davis, O. A. and Whinston, A. B. (1965), 'Welfare Economics and the Theory of the Second Best', *Review of Economic Studies*, 32, pp. 1-14.

Deaton, A. and Muellbauer, J. (1980), *Economics and Consumer Behavior*, Cambridge University Press.

Deschamps, R. and Gevers, L. (1978), 'Leximin and Utilitarian Rules: A Joint Characterisation', *Journal of Economic Theory*, 17, pp. 143-63.

Diamond, P. A. (1967a), 'The Role of a Stock Market in a General Equilibrium Model with Technological Uncertainty', *American Economic Review*, 57, pp. 759-76.

— (1967b), 'Cardinal Welfare, Individualistic Ethics, and Interpersonal Comparisons of Utility: Comment', *Journal of Political Economy*, 75, pp. 765-6.

Diamond, P. A. and McFadden, D. L. (1974), 'Some Uses of the Expenditure Function in Public Finance', *Journal of Public Economics*, 3, pp. 3-21.

Diamond, P. A. and Mirrlees, J. A. (1971), 'Optimal Taxation and Public Production. I: Production Efficiency. II: Tax Rules', *American Economic Review*, 61, pp. 8-27 and 261-78.

Diewert, W. E. (1974), 'Applications of Duality Theory', chapter 3 in Intriligator, M. D. and Kendrick, D. A. (eds), *Frontiers of Quantitative Economics*, vol. II, Amsterdam: North Holland/American Elsevier.

Dorfman, R. (1962), 'Basic Economic and Technological Concepts: A General Statement', in Maass, A. et al. (eds), *Design of Water Resource Systems*, Cambridge, Mass.: Harvard University Press, pp. 129-58.

Edgeworth, F. Y. (1881), *Mathematical Psychics*, Routledge and Kegan Paul, London.

Feldstein, M. S. (1972a), 'Distributional Equity and the Optimal Structure of Public Sector Prices', *American Economic Review*, 62, 32-6.

— (1972b), 'The Inadequacy of Weighted Discount Rates', in Layard, R. (ed.), *Cost-Benefit Analysis*, Harmondsworth: Penguin, pp. 311-32.

— (1974), 'Social Security, Induced Retirement and Aggregate Capital Accumulation', *Journal of Political Economy*, 82, pp. 905-26.

— (1976), 'On the Theory of Tax Reform', *Journal of Public Economics*, 6, pp. 77-104.

— (1977), 'Does the United States Save Too Little?', *American Economic Review, Papers and Proceedings*, 67, no. 1, pp. 116-21.

Fleming, M. (1952), 'A Cardinal Concept of Welfare', *Quarterly Journal of Economics*, 66, pp. 366-84.

Flowerdew, A. D. J. (1972), 'Choosing a Site for the Third London Airport: The Roskill Commission's Approach', in Layard, R. (ed.), *Cost-Benefit Analysis*, Harmondsworth: Penguin.

Foley, D. K. (1967), 'Resource Allocation and the Public Sector', *Yale Economic Essays*, 7, pp. 45-98.

Foster, C. D. and Beesley, M. E. (1963), 'Estimating the Social Benefit of Constructing an Underground Railway in London', *Journal of the Royal Statistical Society*, series A126, pp. 46-92.

Foster, E. (1976), 'The Welfare Foundations of Cost-Benefit Analysis - A Comment', *Economic Journal*, 86, pp. 353-8.

Foster, E. and Sonnenschein, H. (1970), 'Price Distortions and Economic Welfare', *Econometrica*, 38, pp. 281-97.

Galbraith, J. K. (1953), *American Capitalism*, Cambridge, Massachusetts: Riverside Press.

Gevers, L. (1979), 'On Interpersonal Comparability and Social Welfare Orderings', *Econometrica*, 47, pp. 75-89.

Goldman, S. M. and Uzawa, H. (1964), 'A Note on Separability in Demand Analysis', *Econometrica*, 32, pp. 387-98.

Gordon, H. S. (1954), 'The Economic Theory of a Common-Property Resource: The Fishery', *Journal of Political Economy*, 62, pp. 124-42.

Gorman, W. M. (1955), 'The Intransitivity of Certain Criteria Used in Welfare Economics', *Oxford Economic Papers*, NS 7, pp. 25-35.

— (1961), 'On a Class of Preference Fields', *Metroeconomica*, 13, pp. 53-6.

Green, H. A. J. (1976), *Consumer Theory*, 2nd edn, New York: Macmillan.

Green, J. and Laffont, J. J. (1979), *Individual Incentives in Public Decision-Making*, Amsterdam: North-Holland.

Hagen, E. E. (1958), 'An Economic Justification of Protectionism', *Quarterly Journal of Economics*, 72, pp. 496-514.

Hammond, P. J. (1976), 'Equity, Arrow's Conditions and Rawls's Difference Principle', *Econometrica*, 44, pp. 793-804.

Harberger, A. C. (1964), 'Taxation, Resource Allocation and Welfare', in *The Role of Direct and Indirect Taxes in the Federal Reserve System*, Princeton: Princeton University Press, for the National Bureau of Economic Research.

— (1969), 'Professor Arrow on the Social Discount Rate', in Somers, G. G. and Wood, W. D. (eds), *Cost–Benefit Analysis of Manpower Policies*, Proceedings of a North American Conference, Kingston, Ontario: Industrial Relations Centre, Queen's University.

— (1971a), 'Three Basic Postulates for Applied Welfare Economics: An Interpretive Essay', *Journal of Economic Literature*, IX, pp. 785-97.

— (1971b), 'On Measuring the Social Opportunity Cost of Labour', *International Labour Review*, 103, pp. 559-79.

— (1972), *Project Evaluation*, University of Chicago Press.

— (1978), 'On the Use of Distributional Weights in Social Cost–Benefit Analysis', *Journal of Political Economy*, 86, pp. S87-S120.

Hardy, G. M., Littlewood, J. E. and Polya, G. (1934), *Inequalities*, London: Cambridge University Press.

Harris, J. R. and Todaro, M. P. (1970), 'Migration, Unemployment and Development: A Two-sector Analysis', *American Economic Review*, 60, pp. 136-42.

Harris, R. G. (1976), 'A Note on Convex-Concave Demand Systems with an Application to the Theory of Optimal Taxation', discussion paper no. 197, Queen's University, Kingston, Canada.

Harris, R. G. (1981), 'The General Theory of the Second Best after Twenty-Five Years', Queen's University, Kingston, Ontario, Canada.

Harrison, A. J. and Quarmby, D. S. (1972), 'The Value of Time', in Layard, R. (ed.), *Cost Benefit Analysis*, Harmondsworth: Penguin, chapter 6, pp. 173-208.

Harsanyi, J. C. (1953), 'Cardinal Utility in Welfare Economics and in the Theory of Risk-Taking', *Journal of Political Economy*, 61, pp. 434-5.

— (1955), 'Cardinal Welfare, Individualistic Ethics and Interpersonal Comparisons of Utility', *Journal of Political Economy*, 73, pp. 309-21.

— (1975), 'Can the Maximin Principle Serve as a Basis for Morality? A Critique of John Rawls's Theory', *The American Political Science Review*, 69, pp. 594-606.

— (1978), 'Bayesian Decision Theory and Utilitarian Ethics', *American Economic Review Papers and Proceedings*, 68, pp. 223-8.

— (1983), 'Rule Utilitarianism, Equality and Justice', a paper for the Conference on Philosophy, Economics and Justice at the University of Waterloo, Canada, May 20-22.

Hause, J. C. (1975), 'The Theory of Welfare Measurement', *Journal of Political Economy*, 83, pp. 1145-82.

Hausman, J. A. (1981), 'Exact Consumer's Surplus and Deadweight Loss', *American Economic Review*, 71, pp. 662-76.

Hicks, J. R. (1939), *Value and Capital*, London: Oxford University Press.

— (1940), 'The Valuation of Social Income', *Economica*, NS 7, pp. 105-24.

— (1965), *Capital and Growth*, Oxford: Oxford University Press.

Hirshleifer, J. and Riley, J. G. (1979), 'The Analytics of Uncertainty and Information: An Expository Survey', *Journal of Economic Literature*, XVII, pp. 1375-421.

Hochman, H. M. and Rodgers, J. D. (1969), 'Pareto Optimal Redistributions', *American Economic Review*, 59, pp. 542-57.

Johnson, S. B. and Mayer, T. (1962), 'An Extension of Sidgwick's Equity Principle', *Quarterly Journal of Economics*, 76, pp. 454-63.

Jones-Lee, M. W. (1976), *The Value of Life: An Economic Analysis*, University of Chicago Press.

Just, R. E., Hueth, D. L. and Schmitz, A. (1982), *Applied Welfare Economics and Public Policy*, Englewood Cliffs, NJ: Prentice-Hall.

Kaldor, N. (1939), 'Welfare Propositions and Interpersonal Comparisons of Utility', *Economic Journal*, XLIX, pp. 549-52.

Kay, J. A. (1972), 'Social Discount Rates', *Journal of Public Economics*, 1, pp. 359-78.

King, M. A. (1981), *Welfare Analysis of Tax Reforms Using Household Data*, discussion paper, University of Birmingham, series A, June 1981, Birmingham.

Knight, F. H. (1924), 'Some Fallacies in the Interpretation of Social Cost', *Quarterly Journal of Economics*, 37, pp. 582-606.

Lange, O. (1938), *On the Economic Theory of Socialism*, Minneapolis: University of Minnesota Press.

Layard, P. R. G. and Walters, A. A. (1978), *Microeconomic Theory*, New York and London: McGraw-Hill.

Lerner, A. P. (1944), *The Economics of Control*, New York: Macmillan.

Lipsey, R. G. and Lancaster, K. J. (1956), 'The General Theory of Second Best', *Review of Economic Studies*, 24, pp. 11-32.

Little, I. M. D. (1957), *A Critique of Welfare Economics*, 2nd edn., Oxford: Clarendon Press.

Little, I. M. D. and Mirrlees, J. A. (1968), *Manual of Industrial Project Analysis for Developing Countries*, II, Paris: OECD.

Malinvaud, E. (1953), 'Capital Accumulation and Efficient Allocation of Resources', *Econometrica*, XXI, pp. 233-68.

Mansfield, N. W. (1971), 'The Estimation of Benefits from Recreation Sites and the Provision of a New Recreation Facility', *Regional Studies*, 5, pp. 56-9.

Marglin, S. A. (1963a), 'The Opportunity Costs of Public Investment', *Quarterly Journal of Economics*, 77, pp. 274-89.

— (1963b), 'The Social Rate of Discount and the Optimal Rate of Investment', *Quarterly Journal of Economics*, 77, pp. 95-112.

Markowitz, H. (1959), *Portfolio Selection: Efficient Diversification of Investment*, New York: Wiley.

Marshall, J. M. (1976), 'Moral Hazard', *American Economic Review*, 66, pp. 880-90.

Maskin, E. (1978), 'A Theorem on Utilitarianism', *Review of Economic Studies*, 45, pp. 93-6.

McFadden, D. L. (1969), 'A Simple Remark on the Second Best Pareto Optimality of Market Equilibria', *Journal of Economic Theory*, 1, pp. 26-38.

McKenzie, G. and Pearce, I. (1976), 'Exact Measures of Welfare and the Cost of Living', *Review of Economic Studies*, 43, pp. 465-8.

McManus, M. (1958), Comments on 'The General Theory of Second Best', in Farrell, M. J. (ed.), *Readings in Welfare Economics*, London and Basingstoke: Macmillan Press.

Meade, J. E. (1952), 'External Economies and Diseconomies in a Competitive Situation', *Economic Journal*, 62, pp. 54-67.

— (1955), *Trade and Welfare: Mathematical Supplement*, Oxford: Oxford University Press.

— (1976), *The Just Economy*, London: Allen and Unwin.

Mishan, E. J. (1970), 'What is Wrong with Roskill?', *Journal of Transport Economics and Policy*, 4, pp. 221-34.

— (1971), 'Evaluation of Life and Limb: a Theoretical Approach', *Journal of Political Economy*, 79, pp. 687-705.

Mohring, H. (1971), 'Alternative Welfare Gain and Loss Measures', *Western Economic Journal*, 9, pp. 349-68.

Musgrave, R. A. (1959), *The Theory of Public Finance*, New York: McGraw-Hill.

Musgrave, R. A. and Musgrave, P. B. (1976), *Public Finance in Theory and Practice*, 2nd edn, New York: McGraw-Hill.

Neary, J. P. and Roberts, K. W. S. (1980), 'The Theory of Household Behaviour under Rationing', *European Economic Review*, 13, pp. 25-42.

Neumann, J. von and Morgenstern, O. (1947), *Theory of Games and Economic Behavior*, Princeton: Princeton University Press.

Ng, Y. K. (1975), 'Bentham or Bergson? Finite Sensibility, Utility Functions and Social Welfare Functions', *Review of Economic Studies*, XLII, pp. 545-69.

— (1979), *Welfare Economics: Introduction and Development of Basic Concepts*, London: Macmillan.

Nozick, R. (1974), *Anarchy, State, and Utopia*, New York: Basic Books.

Panzer, E. A. and Schmeidler, D. (1974), 'A Difficulty in the Concept of Fairness', *Review of Economic Studies*, XLI (3), pp. 441-3.

— (1978), 'Egalitarian Equivalent Allocations: A New Concept of Economic Equity', *Quarterly Journal of Economics*, 92, pp. 671-87.

Peacock, A. T. and Rowley, C. K. (1975), *Welfare Economics: A Liberal Restatement*, New York: Wiley.

Phlips, L. (1974), *Applied Consumption Analysis*, Amsterdam and Oxford: North-Holland.

Pratt, J. W. (1964), 'Risk Aversion in the Small and the Large', *Econometrica*, 32, pp. 122-36.

Ramsey, F. P. (1927), 'A Contribution to the Theory of Taxation', *Economic Journal*, 37, pp. 47-61.

— (1928), 'A Mathematical Theory of Savings', *Economic Journal*, 38, pp. 543-59.

Rawls, J. (1971), *A Theory of Justice*, Cambridge, Mass.: Harvard University Press; and Oxford: Clarendon Press.

Reder, M. W. (1982), 'Chicago Economics: Permanence and Change', *Journal of Economic Literature*, XX, pp. 1-38.

Roberts, K. W. S. (1980), 'Possibility Theorems with Interpersonally Comparable Welfare Levels', *Review of Economic Studies*, 47, pp. 409-20.

Rothschild, M. and Stiglitz, J. E. (1970), 'Increasing Risk. I: A Definition', *Journal of Economic Theory*, 2, pp. 225-43.

— (1976), 'Equilibrium in Competitive Insurance Markets', *Quarterly Journal of Economics*, 90, pp. 629-50.

Samuelson, P. A. (1947), *Foundations of Economic Analysis*, Cambridge, Mass.: Harvard University Press.

— (1950), 'Evaluation of Real National Income', *Oxford Economic Papers*, NS 2, pp. 1-29.

— (1954), 'Pure Theory of Public Expenditure', *Review of Economics and Statistics*, 36, pp. 387-89.

— (1956), 'Social Indifference Curves', *Quarterly Journal of Economics*, 70, pp. 1-22.

— (1958), 'An Exact Consumption-Loan Model of Interest With or Without the Social Contrivance of Money', *Journal of Political Economy*, LXVI, pp. 467-82.

— (1972), 'The Consumer Does Benefit from Feasible Price Stability', *Quarterly Journal of Economics*, 86, pp. 476-93.

— (1974), 'Complementarity – An Essay on the 40th Anniversary of the Hicks–Allen Revolution in Demand Theory', *Journal of Economic Literature*, 4, pp. 1255-89.

Sandmo, A. (1976), 'Optimal Taxation – An Introduction to the Literature', *Journal of Public Economics*, 6, pp. 37-54.

Schall, L. D. (1972), 'Interdependent Utility Functions and Pareto Optimality', *Quarterly Journal of Economics*, 86, pp. 19-24.

Scitovsky, T. (1941), 'A Note on Welfare Propositions in Economics', *Review of Economic Studies*, 9, pp. 77-88.

Sen, A. K. (1961), 'On Optimizing the Rate of Saving', *Economic Journal*, 71, pp. 479-96.

— (1967), 'Isolation, Assurance and the Social Rate of Discount', *Quarterly Journal of Economics*, 81, pp. 112-24.

— (1970), *Collective Choice and Social Welfare*, San Francisco: Holden Day; and Edinburgh: Oliver and Boyd.

— (1973), *On Economic Inequality*, Oxford: Clarendon Press; and New York: Norton.

— (1975), 'The Concept of Economic Efficiency', in Parkin, M. and Nobay, R. (eds), *Contemporary Issues in Economics: The Proceedings of the Annual Meeting of the Association of University Teachers of Economics, 1973*, Cambridge University Press.

— (1977), 'Social Choice Theory: A Re-examination', *Econometrica*, 45, pp. 53-89.

— (1979), 'The Welfare Basis of Real Income Comparisons. A Survey', *Journal of Economic Literature*, 17, pp. 1-45.

Shorrocks, A. F. (1983), 'Ranking Income Distributions', *Economica*, 50, pp. 3-17.

— (1981), 'Ranking Income Distributions', Discussion Paper No. 438, Queen's University, Kingston, Canada.

Sjaastad, L. A. and Wisecarver, D. L. (1977), 'The Social Cost of Public Finance', *Journal of Political Economy*, 85, pp. 513-47.

Smith, A. (1776), *An Inquiry into the Nature and Causes of the Wealth of Nations*, (ed. E. Cannon), 1904, London: Methuen.

Smith, B. and Stephen, F. (1975), 'The Welfare Foundations of Cost-Benefit Analysis: Comment', *Economic Journal*, 85, pp. 902-5.

Spence, M. and Zeckhauser, R. (1971), 'Insurance, Information, and Individual Action', *American Economic Review. Papers and Proceedings*, 61, pp. 380-7.

Stern, N. H. (1972), *An Appraisal of Tea Production on Small Holdings in Kenya*, Development Centre of the OECD.

Strasnick, S. L. (1975), 'Preference Priority and the Maximization of Social Welfare', doctoral dissertation, Harvard University, 1975.

Thaler, R. and Rosen, S. (1975), 'The Value of Saving a Life', in *Conference on Income and Wealth, Household Production and Consumption*, New York: NBER.

Thurow, L. C. (1971), 'The Income Distribution as a Pure Public Good', *Quarterly Journal of Economics*, 85, pp. 327–36.

Tiebout, C. M. (1956), 'A Pure Theory of Local Expenditures', *Journal of Political Economy*, 64, pp. 416-24.

Usher, D. (1973), 'An Imputation to the Measure of Economic Growth for Changes in Life Expectancy', in Milton R. (ed.), *The Measurement of Economic and Social Performance*, New York: NBER.

— (1980), *Measurement of Economic Growth*, Oxford: Basil Blackwell.

— (1982), 'The Private Cost of Public Funds: Variation on Themes by Browning, Atkinson and Stern', Discussion Paper 481, Queen's University, Kingston, Canada.

Varian, H. R. (1978), *Microeconomic Analysis*, New York: Norton.

Vickrey, W. S. (1961), 'Risk, Utility and Social Policy', *Social Research*, 28, pp. 205–17. pp. 205-17.

Viner, J. (1950), *The Customs Union Issue*, New York: Carnegie Endowment for International Peace.

Walters, A. A. (1961), 'The Theory and Measurement of Private and Social Costs of Highway Congestion', *Econometrica*. 29, pp. 676-99.

Willig, R. (1976), 'Consumer's Surplus Without Apology', *American Economic Review*, 66, pp. 589-97.

Author Index

Subject Index